Ordnance Survey
London
and beyond
Landranger Guidebook

Historical consultant – Felix Barker
Series editor – Peter Titchmarsh

JARROLD

How to use this guide

We have endeavoured to include all Places of Special Interest in the Inner or Outer London sections of this guide. Inner London (on pages 18-93) may be regarded as that area covered by the Atlas section on pages 181-191, although a few places in this section lie just beyond the limits of the Atlas. Outer London as described in this guide (on pages 94-133) is chiefly the area covered by Landranger Map Sheets 176 and 177, the extent of which is indicated on page 4. However, we have also included certain places of exceptional interest which can be easily reached by using the M25 London Orbital Motorway, and these are shown on the special map on pages 134-135.

Places of exceptional interest have been highlighted by being printed in blue, and any place which has a separate entry in either of the 'Places of Special Interest' sections is identified in the text by the symbol ★.

Each entry in the **Inner London Section** is identified first with the atlas page number, and this is followed by a letter and number providing a simple cross reference on the atlas page.

Each entry in the **Outer London Section** is identified first with the number of the Landranger map or maps on which it appears (e.g. 176, 177, etc.). This is followed by two letters (e.g. TQ) and by a four-figure reference number (e.g. 07-37). The first two figures of this number are those which appear in blue along the north and south edges of all Landranger maps; the other two appear in blue along the east and west edges. Therefore, to locate any place or feature referred to in this section of the book on the relevant Landranger map, first read the two figures along the north or south edges of the map, then the two figures along the east or west edges. Trace the lines adjacent to each of the two sets of figures across the map face and the point where they intersect will be the south-west corner of the grid square in which the place or feature lies. Thus Aldenham Country Park falls in the grid square 16-95 on Landranger map 176.

The special map on pages 136-137 identifies the suggested starting points of the 12 Inner London walks and the Key Maps on pages 5-7 identify the suggested starting points of the eight Outer London walks; in the 'Walks' sections, all places which also have a separate entry in the 'Places of Special Interest' sections are in bold type.

Acknowledgements

We would like to thank Denise Silvester-Carr for her work on the twelve Inner London Walks, and Gerald Colton for his work on the eight Outer London Walks. This included walking over the routes concerned, and provision of the detailed directions for walkers which will be found in the guide. Thanks are also due to Reg Jones for his article on Natural History, and to the following for providing illustrations: London Planetarium (p. 51); Madame Tussaud's, London (p. 52); The Museum of London (p. 56); The National Portrait Gallery, London (p. 57); Sotheby's (p. 80); The Guinness World of Records (p. 87); The Trustees of The Wallace Collection (p. 89); The Geffrye Museum (p. 107); The Horniman Museum, London (p. 115); The Royal Air Force Museum, Hendon (p. 125), and Wembley Stadium Ltd (p. 130).

First published 1988 by Ordnance Survey and Jarrold Colour Publications

Ordnance Survey
Romsey Road
Maybush
Southampton SO9 4DH

Jarrold Colour
Publications
Barrack Street
Norwich NR3 1TR

Contents

KEY MAP INDEX

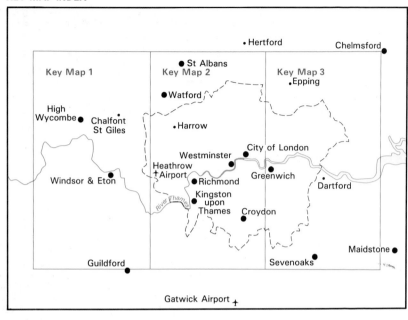

Outer London Walk start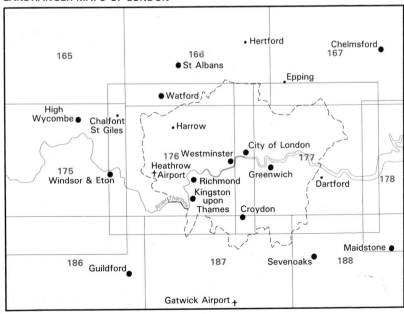

Greater London County Boundary _ _ _ _ _

NOTE: For Walks 1 to 12 see Inner London Walks Key Map.

LANDRANGER MAPS OF LONDON

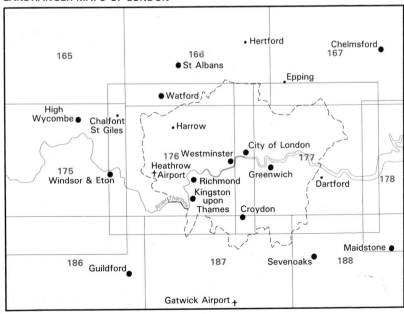

4

Key Map 1

SCALE 1:250 000 or 4 MILES to 1 INCH

0 1 km = 0·6214 mile 5   10   Kilometres 15

0 1 mile = 1·61 kms   5   Miles   10

London — The Expanding City

by Felix Barker

Since the Second World War more than a million people have moved out of the crowded centre of London and deserted the inner suburbs. Now honorary Londoners, they have found new homes far beyond the limits of what we are accustomed to think of as our capital city. In this modern population explosion they are living in towns and villages and on new estates as far as 50 miles from Charing Cross. It is increasingly difficult to comprehend London's size and define its limits.

If you turn to the map on page 134, which shows London's Orbital Motorway — the M25, completed in 1986 — you will see that it is like some encircling corridor with 31 exits which has the effect of giving London a new, even greater perimeter. It has become a city unimagined by our ancestors. As this guide looks prophetically as far as Windsor, Hatfield and Westerham, we can envisage London as it may well become for our great-grandchildren.

The infant London was born and took shape just under 2,000 years ago. The genesis of this, one of the earliest cities of modern Europe, occurred at the first point up the Thames where the river could be forded. It was the crossing point for 40,000 Romans who landed in Kent in AD 43 and whose successors were to settle on the river's north bank. Stand on the London Bridge and you are as near as needs be to that point.

Within ten years 'Londinium' was a flourishing trading town and before they left some 400 years later the Romans had built a city with a forum, basilica, governor's palace, temples and merchants' houses covering 330 acres encircled by a defensive wall. Ruins of that wall are still to be seen, and the names of such gateways as Ludgate, Aldgate and Bishopsgate survived in the mediaeval city and have lived on to lose their old meaning in their modern context. The area was to extend a little into what became 'the Square Mile' and, if you ignore the quite separate royal suburb of Westminster, this was London until the time of the Tudors.

Following the line of the river eastwards, in the 16th century the Strand linked the City with Westminster, and prepared the way for the first great expansion. When Queen Elizabeth I came to the throne London's population was 120,000 and what we know today as the West End was still meadowland with a few scattered farmhouses and rutted lanes between hawthorn hedges; by the end of the next century the population had doubled and roughly one person in ten in Britain was living in London. Shortage of houses after the Great Fire of 1666 had caused an exodus westwards into the newly built streets and a formal square near St James's. Fine terraced houses around private gardens — Georgian squares which are London's particular glory — developed in the next half-century.

Expansion now became remorseless. The City's power as a financial and trading capital saw to that, and helped by the particular magic of its 18th-century beauty London also

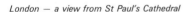

London — a view from St Paul's Cathedral

became Europe's largest capital. The statistics are startling. In the 19th century the population doubled twice: from one million to two million by 1851, and then to four million by the end of Queen Victoria's reign. A once leafy semi-rural city had turned into a metropolis of rooftops blackened by factory smoke; grand houses and overcrowded tenements were the diverse dividends of Victorian commercial prosperity.

It was a century in which the City's dominating population was outstripped by sixteen other districts, of which St Pancras was the largest with buildings stretching from Bloomsbury to Camden Town. The Regency gave us John Nash's 'Improvements', among them the monumental thoroughfare from Carlton House, up Regent Street to Regent's Park — the last building development of consequence in the West End. Nash inspired the stuccoed elegance of Belgravia and the more stolid Italianate houses of Bayswater. Pushing tentacles further out into the suburbs, roads of artisans' houses stretched to Highgate and Brixton. Gentlemen exchanged homes in London squares for the airy suburbs and put on their top hats to drive into the City from Primrose Hill and Denmark Hill. They travelled in spanking carriages and first-class compartments on the increasing network of railways.

Edwardian London continued to break out of old confines with the first trams swaying from Hammersmith to Kew, the District Line linking Ealing to Whitechapel and a fleet of 200 motorbuses frightening a diminishing number of horses. The Underground tunnelled through the heights of Hampstead to join central London with what had once been Middlesex. The ravenous metropolis chewed off pieces of Kent, Essex and Surrey. Buckinghamshire and Hertfordshire were next on the menu. It was already past the time when local authorities could cope, and in 1889 the London County Council came into existence to govern 28 boroughs over an area of 117 square miles.

By the turn of the century London had reached far beyond the Inner London confines of this gazetteer and was moving into what we are describing as Outer London. Another explosion occurred in 1965, when many of these old boroughs disappeared or expanded, extending the metropolis to a total of 616 square miles. This is today's Greater London, with a population of eight million: instead of alleys, rents and passages we are talking of places with names like Enfield Chase, Petts Wood, Hainault Forest, Carshalton Beeches, Bushey Heath and Ruislip Lido. By contrast the old Square Mile's population has shrunk to a few hundred, mostly office caretakers, boosted by 6,000 at the Barbican but drawing its lifeblood from the 360,000 City workers who come in and leave daily.

Our Outer London gazetteer ventures out even further to include Windsor, which is trespassing on Berkshire but comes within the Metropolitan Green Belt area and is on the fringe of Professor Abercrombie's 1944 Greater London Plan. And we have suggested some places to visit which are a little further out still.

At the present rate of expansion these may be regarded as part of London by the middle of the next century and will have probably come within the web of numbered postal districts.

The inclusion of these amenities may, we hope, tempt expeditions in search of the astonishing variety of places offered by the Green Belt, that imprecise but enlightened conservation concept that captured people's imaginations between the wars. The largest and most spectacular is the Lee Valley Leisure Park, 23 miles of sport and leisure facilities developed on unwanted ground along the inconsistently spelt River Lea, no longer a commercial waterway. The park offers visitors hides for birdwatching, reservoirs for sailing, a lido (with artificial waves), a farm (where town-dwellers may sniff country odours), a 40-acre cycle circuit, a sports centre, an ice-skating rink and a nine-hole golf course.

In Epping Forest guided walks start from a Conservation Centre. At the Chiltern Open Air Museum, near Chalfont St Giles, an Iron-Age house has been reconstructed. At Wisley and St Albans our national preoccupation with gardening is indulged by parks and gardens outdoing each other with rare species, all conveniently labelled so that plants may be purchased and carried home to Metroland.

To these manifestly healthy and instructive places may be added the rather more unusual attractions offered by the Chessington World of Adventures, where there is a Goldrush town and where a monorail carries visitors through the trees to observe wild animals. The central feature of Thorpe Park features world-famous buildings scaled down to one thirty-sixth of their original size, which for the Statue of Liberty sounds most necessary.

Offering as it does so many nature reserves, forests, theme parks, arboretums and botanic gardens, Outer London would appear to be banishing the spectre of a dark, satanic and unhygienic city which so haunts the minds of ecologists. While commercial pressures and social pleasures attract people into cities, most of us seem to want to live outside them. By expanding deeper into the countryside London is giving us the best of both worlds and more and more places for exploration.

Natural History

by Reg Jones

A capital city, built up and bristling with buildings, would seem to be the last place to attract wildlife. But living things are very adaptable and the most arid areas are rarely completely sterile. In addition, London is one of the greenest of the world's capitals. In the centre there are numerous residential squares with shrubberies and trees, while the Royal Parks are a special feature. In the suburbs, apart from domestic gardens, there are heaths and commons, and many man-made sites often prove to be congenial habitats. Reservoirs, gravel pits, sewage plants and rubbish dumps all sustain distinctive communities.

Feral pigeons and sparrows are in evidence almost everywhere in central London. Both are scavengers which have prospered in urban surroundings. The feral pigeon is a descendant of the rock dove, which is normally found on rocky coasts, roosting in sea caves and on cliff ledges. In London the bird finds shelter in church towers, in lofts, under bridges or on any perch offering some cover. Sparrows, although numerous, are said to be less plentiful than in the days of horse traffic when spilled grain from the horses' feed was much appreciated. While pigeons and sparrows are present at all times, other species demand our attention. The mass roosting of starlings in selected parts of London is a special feature of late autumn evenings, flight after flight descending from

the sky, settling on buildings, the birds standing closely together in serried ranks throughout the night. Also, as atmospheric pollution has been reduced, some long-absent species have been tempted to return. A small number of house martins and swifts are summer residents.

The tree which has been most successful in the city is the London plane. Shedding bark periodically in flakes, the trunk and larger branches appear almost piebald, patches of fresh yellow bark contrasting with older, greyer material. Never found in the wild, this is the tree which lines thorough-fares. In residential squares it may be accompanied by sycamores and horse chestnuts to form sheltered havens. Recently cleared ground, left bare for any appreciable length of time, is soon populated. Yellow-flowered ragwort and pink willowherb appear as if by magic. They are host to a number of insects and their seeds soon attract finches. Sometimes there are real surprises. During the last war, when there was much exposed ground with many shattered buildings, a rare bird, the black redstart, became well established, feeding on the insect life and nesting in the damaged brickwork. Nowadays, with the devastation largely eliminated, the bird is more typical of industrial sites such as power stations away from the city centre.

The Royal Parks form an essential part of the lungs of the capital. In the West End, a band of greenery extends from St James's Park, through Green Park to Hyde Park and Kensington Gardens, while to the north is Regent's Park. Most of the parks have stretches of water which provide the main interest. There has been a collection of

Fallow deer in Richmond Park

Great crested grebe — a feature of the Serpentine

waterfowl in St James' Park since the 17th century. There is another collection in Regent's Park and although the birds are pinioned, they attract many others. Pochard and tufted duck are very prominent together with a large flock of Canada geese. But there are species other than ducks and geese. Moorhens and coots, renowned for their shyness, have joined the throng and great crested grebes breed on the Serpentine and on the lake in Regent's Park, the latter having a number of islands which form valuable refuges. On one is a small heronry and the sight of a solitary heron by the water's edge is not unusual. Numerous gulls are present in winter and the nesting of one or two pairs of herring gulls in the vicinity is a recent development. Apart from birds associated with water, there are others which nest in the trees. They include wood pigeon, stock dove, jay and magpie, all of which, in the countryside, tend to avoid man.

Richmond Park is the largest of the Royal Parks. In this more expansive setting there is much of interest. First, there are the herds of red and fallow deer, seen at their best in the autumn. Grey squirrels are common and the presence of a colony of badgers so close to the metropolis surprises many people. Within the park there is appreciable habitat diversity including a number of woodland plantations made up of a variety of trees, which in turn harbour a good selection of woodland birds. In addition, there are several ponds, the Pen Ponds being the largest, with great crested

grebes and tufted ducks nesting from time to time.

For those interested in wildfowl there are several places to visit. The River Thames, now much cleaner than in former years, carries large numbers of duck in winter. In the lower reaches, between Woolwich and Rainham Marsh, sizeable flocks of mallard, shelduck, teal, pintail and wigeon are present, though most of them leave in the spring.

Several man-made sites are also renowned for the wildlife they attract, the reservoirs at Staines being particularly well known. The variety of birds seen here over the year is truly impressive. Viewing is possible from the causeway which runs between the reservoirs. In winter, apart from the more familiar ducks, species such as goosander, red-breasted merganser, smew and goldeneye may occur, while flocks of gulls descend from the sky in the late afternoon to roost. A variety of waders may be seen in spring and in autumn. They will be passing through and are often accompanied by several species of tern. Other reservoirs have their specialities. At Walthamstow there is the largest heronry in the area with around 100 nests. Elsewhere, common terns have nested successfully in recent years.

Finally, for those who wish to explore more natural habitats, there is considerable choice ranging from Epping Forest in the north to Box Hill, a classic chalk downland site, in the south.

Advice for Visitors

Tourist Information

There is a wealth of information available, but here are the principal Tourist Information Centres (TICs) at your disposal with map references to the Inner London Atlas Section on pages 181—191 where applicable.

Inner London
The London Tourist Board & Convention Bureau TIC, Victoria Station Forecourt (5 B-4). Open: Apr-Nov. Daily 0900-2030 (extended hours in July & Aug); Nov-Easter Mon-Sat 0900-1900; Sun 0900-1700. *Tel: 01-730-3488; (Riverboat Information: 01-730-4812).* **British Travel Centre**, 12 Lower Regent Street (5 C-1). Open: Mon-Sat 0900-1830, Sun 1000-1600. *Tel: 01-730-3400.* **City Information Centre**, St Paul's Churchyard (3 C-4). Open: (Apr-Oct) Daily 0930-1700, (Nov-Mar) Mon-Fri 0930-1700, Sat 0930-1300. *Tel: 01-606-3030.* **Clerkenwell Heritage Centre**, 33 St John's Square (3 B-1). Open: (Apr-Sept) Mon-Fri 0900-1800, Sat & Sun 1400-1700. (Oct-Mar) Mon-Fri 1000-1700. **Harrods TIC**, Harrods, Knightsbridge (4 E-3). Open: During store hours. **Selfridges TIC**, Selfridges, Oxford Street (1 F-5). Open: During store hours. **H M Tower of London TIC**, West Gate, Tower of London (3 F-5). Open: (Apr-Oct) Daily 1000-1800.

Outer London
Croydon TIC, Katharine St, Croydon. Open: Mon 0930-1900, Tue-Fri 0930-1800; Sat 0900-1700. *Tel: 01-760-5400 X 2984/2985, or 01-760-5630.* **Greenwich TIC**, Cutty Sark Gardens, Greenwich. Open: (Apr & May) Daily 1100-1600; (June-Aug) Daily 1100-1730; (Sept & Oct) Daily 1100-1630; (Nov-Mar) Sun 1100-1600. *Tel: 01-858-6376.* **Harrow TIC**, Civic Centre, Station Rd., Harrow. Open: Mon-Fri 0900-1700. *Tel: 01-863-5611 X 2102/2103.* **Heathrow TIC, Terminal 1, 2 & 3**, Underground Station Concourse, Heathrow Airport. Open: Daily 0900-1800. **Heathrow TIC, Terminal 2 Arrivals**, Heathrow Airport. Open: Daily 0800-2000. **Hillingdon TIC**, 22 High St., Uxbridge. Open: Mon-Fri 0930-2000; Sat 0930-1700. *Tel: 0895-50706.* **Kingston upon Thames TIC**, Heritage Centre, Fairfield West, Kingston upon Thames. Open: Mon-Sat 1000-1700. *Tel: 01-546-5386.* **Lewisham TIC**, Borough Mall, Lewisham Centre. Open: Mon-Fri 0915-1715. *Tel: 01-318-5421/2.* **Richmond TIC**, Old Town Hall, Whittaker Avenue, Richmond. Open: Mon, Tu, Thur, Fri 1000-1800; Sat 1000-1700; Wed 1000-2000; Sun (Summer only) 1015-1615. *Tel: 01-940-9125.* **Tower Hamlets TIC**, 88 Roman Road. Open: Mon-Fri 0900-1730. *Tel: 01-980-3749.* **Twickenham TIC**, District Library, Garfield Road, Twickenham. Open: Mon, Thur, Fri 1000-1800; Tue 1000-2000; Wed & Sat 1000-1700. *Tel: 01-892-0032.* **Windsor TIC**, Central Station, Windsor. Open: Easter — end Oct, daily 0900-1830; rest of year, Mon-Sat·0930-1800; Sun 1000-1600. *Tel: 0753 852010.*

Special Events
From April each year the London Tourist Board publishes a useful fortnightly news sheet entitled *Events in London*, listing such diverse events as Pancake Day Races, visits by foreign heads of state, exhibitions, trade fairs, sporting events, and many ceremonial occasions.

Here is a brief list of some of the major events, but for details, see *Events in London* or Tel: 01-730-3488.

January The 'January Sales' are held in almost all London's large stores. International Boat Show, Earl's Court. Chinese New Year celebrated in Gerrard Street, Soho (in Jan or Feb).

February St James's Antiques Fair, Piccadilly Hotel. Cruft's Dog Show, Earl's Court. English Folk Dance and Song Festival, Albert Hall (Easter Weekend).

March Antiques Fair, Chelsea Old Town Hall. Ideal Homes Exhibition, Earl's Court. Country Music Festival, Wembley.

March or April Oxford & Cambridge University Boat Race (on the Thames between Putney & Mortlake). Easter Parade in Battersea Park (Easter Sun). Harness Horse Parade in Regent's Park (Easter Mon). Fair on Hampstead Heath (Easter Mon).

April RHS Spring Flower Show, RHS Westminster. The Queen's Birthday (21st April) with gun salutes from Hyde Park and the Tower. London Marathon (a Sun in April or early May).

May Royal Windsor Horse Show, Windsor Great Park. Soccer Cup Final at Wembley (usually 2nd Sat). Chelsea Flower Show (usually in 3rd week).

May or June Royal Academy Summer Exhibition at Burlington House opens.

June Trooping the Colour ceremony (at Horse Guards) (Sat nearest 11th June to mark the Queen's official birthday). Grosvenor House Antiques Fair. Derby Day on 1st Wed. Royal Ascot (race meeting). Wimbledon Lawn Tennis Championships (last week June, 1st week July).

July Henry Wood Promenade Concerts at Royal Albert Hall (until mid-September). Royal Regatta, Henley-on-Thames (1st week). Royal Tournament, Earl's Court.

August London Riding Horse Parade, Rotten Row, Hyde Park. West Indian Carnival, Notting Hill (Bank Holiday last weekend in month). Fairs on Hampstead Heath and Blackheath (same weekend).

September Autumn Antiques Fair, Chelsea Old Town Hall (last two weeks).

October Horse of the Year Show, Wembley. Opening of Royal Courts of Justice (1st Oct or 1st Mon). State Opening of Parliament (Oct or Nov). Trafalgar Day service and parade, Nelson's Column, Trafalgar Square.

November London to Brighton Veteran Car Run (starts from Hyde Park Corner) (usually on 1st Sun). State Opening of Parliament (or late Oct). Guy Fawkes Day (5th Nov) (fireworks at numerous locations, especially at Alexandra Park, Wood Green). Festival of Remembrance, Royal Albert Hall. Remembrance Sunday (nearest to 11th Nov) at the Cenotaph, Whitehall. Lord Mayor's Procession and Show (from Guildhall to the Law Courts) (2nd Sat). Caravan & Camping Show, Earl's Court.

December Royal Smithfield Livestock & Agricultural Show, Earl's Court. Lighting of the Norwegian Christmas Tree in Trafalgar Square (mid-month), with carols nightly.

Getting around London

Walking is by far the best way to explore London and we have therefore included no less than twenty walks in this book. However, if you wish to walk with an experienced guide, there are several services available. Details are advertised in publications like *Time Out*, *What's on in London* and on the back page of *The Times*. For further information *Tel: 01-730-3488.*

Underground Trains usually offer the easiest and quickest method of transport for any distance over two miles. For details of its network see the map on page 208, but if you ever find yourself without the book a similar map will be found at every station, and there is a useful extract displayed inside all the trains' coaches. Individual tickets may be purchased from machines or the booking office, but it is also possible to buy *London Explorer* tickets which offer unlimited travel for 1, 3, 4 and 7 days, not only on the Underground but also on the red London buses. This latter facility also includes discount vouchers for attractions like the London Transport Museum, the London Zoo, Madame Tussauds and the Guinness World of Records. These and details of other special tickets, including Capital Cards, which combine British Rail, Underground and bus, are available from any Underground station ticket office, and from London Regional Transport Offices at the following Underground stations: Victoria, St James's Park, King's Cross, Oxford Circus, Piccadilly Circus, Euston and Heathrow Central.

Buses are the best method of transport for short journeys although their network is not so easy to follow as the Underground. A journey on one of the red double-decker buses is an experience in itself, especially if you find a seat on the upper deck. The route number and final destination is boldly displayed on the front of each bus, and the bus number required can be worked out by referring to the panels displayed at each bus stop. Journeys to places on the outskirts of London may be taken on Green Line buses, although they have a limited number of stops in Central London. The most important ones are at Baker Street Station, Hyde Park Corner, Marble Arch — Park Lane, Eccleston Bridge near Victoria Station, and Aldgate. Further details of all bus services may be obtained from any London Regional Transport Office (See the end of the article above).

Guided Coach Tours for half a day or a day are offered by London Regional Transport and by a number of private companies such as London Pride *(Tel: 01-629-4999)* and Cityrama *(Tel: 01-720-6663).* Some of these services combine with a riverboat trip. For further details contact one of the TICs, who can also provide details of guided tours to such places as Greenwich, Windsor, Oxford or Stratford-upon-Avon.

Bus Tours are offered by London Regional Transport. These last about 1½ hours and provide a recorded commentary. They depart hourly from Marble Arch — Park Lane, Grosvenor Gardens, near Victoria Station, Baker Street Underground Station forecourt, and from Piccadilly Circus (Haymarket). Advance booking is not required.

Taxis. The conventional London cabs are reasonably good value when two or more passengers are involved. Their metered charges are tightly regulated, and many of their highly knowledgeable drivers can be very helpful. Unless specifically asked not to do so, they are required by law to take the most direct route. Their illuminated 'for hire' sign indicates when they are available. Radio-linked taxis and minicabs, which operate under a different set of regulations, must be ordered by phone, and it is wise to agree the approximate fare in advance. Phone numbers may be found in the Yellow Pages Directory.

River and Canal Trips. A free leaflet, *River Thames*, is available from the London Tourist Board's Information Centre at Victoria Station *(Tel: 01-730-3488)*, and the London Tourist Board's special recorded Riverboat Enquiry telephone service *(Tel: 01-730-4812)* provides details of the frequent riverboat services operating from Westminster, Charing Cross and Tower Piers. There are services to the Tower of London, Greenwich and the Thames Barrier throughout the year *(see London's River on page 178)*, and in the summer and on weekends in the spring and autumn, boats also go upstream from Westminster Pier to Kew, Richmond and Hampton Court. Information from each pier may be obtained on the following telephone numbers: *Westminster (downstream): 01-930-4097; Westminster (upstream): 01-930-2062; Charing Cross: 01-930-0971; Tower: 01-488-0344.*

Several of London's almost forgotten **canals** have come to life again, and waterbuses now ply along the Regent's Canal between Little Venice, London Zoo and Camden Lock. (Daily in summer and at weekends in winter; for details, *Tel: 01-482-2550).* Also for detail of traditional narrowboat trips *Tel: 01-286-3428, and/or 01-485-4433.*

Police

To contact the police in an emergency dial 999 from any telephone. Police Stations in the City and Central London are located as follows (references are to Atlas Section at rear): New Scotland Yard, Broadway SW1 (5 C-4); 26 Old Jewry, EC2 (City of London Police) (3 D-3); Bow St, WC2 (2 E-5); 70 Theobalds Rd, WC1 (2 F-3); Hyde Park, W2 (north of the Serpentine) (4 D-1); 72 Earl's Court Rd, W8 (to west of 4 A-5); 1, Seymour St, W1 (1 E-5); 63 Rochester Row, SW1 (5 C-5); 56 Tottenham Court Rd, W1 (2 C-3); 10 Vine St, W1 (5 C-1); 27 Savile Row, W1 (2 B-5).

Ordnance Survey Agents

The London Map Centre, 22-24, Caxton Street, London SW1H 0QU *Tel: 01-222-2466-7*
Edward Stanford Ltd., 12-14, Long Acre, London WC2E 9LP *Tel: 01-836-1321*
Hammicks Bookshops, King Edward Court, Windsor SL4 1TF *Tel: 0753-856-456*
W.H.Smith, Thames Street, Windsor SL4 3LD *Tel: 0753-869-678*

Places of Interest — A Summary List

Art Galleries and Art Complexes
Barbican Centre 20
British Museum 24
Courtauld Institute Galleries 32
Percival David Foundation 33
Dulwich Picture Gallery 104
Forty Hall, Enfield 105
Hall Place, Bexley 110
Hayward Gallery 40
Institute for Contemporary
  Arts 53
Leighton House 48
The Mall Galleries 53
National Gallery 57
National Portrait Gallery 57 – 58
Old Battersea House 95
Orleans House 123
Queen's Gallery 63 – 64
Royal Academy of Arts 66
Serpentine Gallery 44
Tate Gallery 83
Victoria & Albert Museum 88
Wallace Collection 89
Waterman's Art Centre 97
Whitechapel Art Gallery 128
Windsor Castle — Exhibition
  of Drawings 133
Zamana Art Gallery 42

Cemeteries
Highgate 115
Kensal Green 116 – 117

Churches
(A list largely confined to Inner London)
All Hallows by the Tower 19
All Souls, Langham Place 19
Brompton Oratory 24 – 25
Chapel Royal 27
Chelsea Old Church 28
Christchurch, Spitalfields 30
Guards Chapel 38
Queen's Chapel 63
St Andrew's, Holborn 71
St Andrew Undershaft 71
St Bartholomew-the-
  Great 71 – 72
St Bride's 72
St Clement Danes 72
St Etheldreda's 72 – 73
St George's Chapel,
  Windsor 132,133
St George's, Hanover
  Square 73
St James's, Piccadilly 74
St John the Evangelist 74 – 75
St John's, Smith Square 75
St Lawrence Jewry 75
St Margaret's, Westminster 75
St Martin-in-the-Fields 75 – 76
St Mary-le-Bow 76
St Mary Woolnoth 50
St Paul's Cathedral 76 – 77
St Paul's, Covent Garden 77
St Peter ad Vincula 77
St Sepulchre-without-
  Newgate 77 – 78
St Stephen Walbrook 78
Savoy Chapel 78

Southwark Cathedral 81 – 82
Temple Church 84
Westminster Abbey 90
Westminster Cathedral 91

City Livery Company Halls
Apothecaries' 19
Drapers' 35
Dyers' 33
Fishmongers' 35
Goldsmiths' 36
Grocers' 37
Haberdashers' 39
Mercers' 54 – 55
Merchant Taylors' 55
Painter-Stainers' 60
Skinners' 33 – 34
Tallow Chandlers' 33
Vintners' 88

Clubs
Athenaeum 61
Boodles 73
Brook's 73
Carlton 73
Clermont 22
Garrick 36
Naval & Military 59
Reform 61

Guildhall

Royal Automobile 61
Travellers' 61
Turf 26
United Oxford & Cambridge 61
United Services 61
White's 73

Colleges and Schools
Dulwich College 104
Eton College 106
Guildhall School of Music 21
Harrow School 113
Imperial College 42
Royal Academy of Dramatic
  Art 66
Royal Academy of
  Music 66 – 67
Royal Ballet School 125
Royal College of Art 67
Royal College of Music 67 – 68
Royal Military School of
  Music 125
Royal Naval College 126
University of London 88
Westminster School 91 – 93

Country Parks
(See also Parks and Gardens)
Aldenham 94

Places of Entertainment

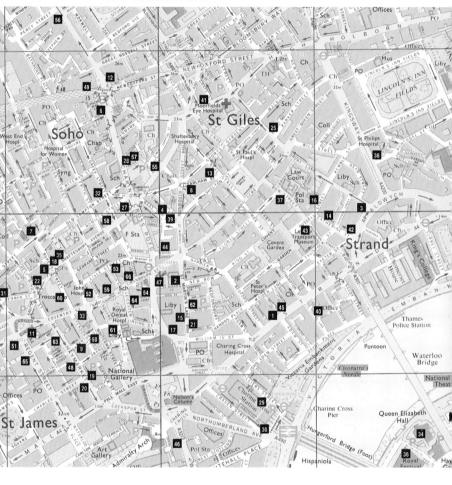

THEATRES & CONCERT HALLS

9 COMEDY	17 GARRICK	25 NEW LONDON	33 PRINCE OF WALES	40 SAVOY
10 COTTESLOE (NAT. THEATRE)	18 GLOBE	26 OLIVIER (NAT. THEATRE)	34 QUEEN ELIZABETH HALL	41 SHAFTESBURY
11 CRITERION	19 HAYMARKET THEATRE ROYAL	27 PALACE	35 QUEEN'S	42 STRAND
12 DOMINION	20 HER MAJESTY'S	28 PHOENIX	36 ROYAL FESTIVAL HALL	43 THEATRE MUSEUM
13 DONMAR WAREHOUSE	21 LONDON COLISEUM	29 PLAYER'S	37 ROYAL OPERA HOUSE	(COVENT GARDEN)
14 DRURY LANE THEATRE ROYAL	22 LYRIC	30 PLAYHOUSE	COVENT GARDEN	44 UNICORN
15 DUKE OF YORK'S	23 LYTTLETON (NAT. THEATRE)	31 PICCADILLY	38 ROYALTY	45 VAUDEVILLE
16 FORTUNE	24 NATIONAL FILM THEATRE	32 PRINCE EDWARD	39 ST MARTIN'S	46 WHITEHALL
				47 WYNDHAM'S

CINEMAS

52 CANNON (PREMIERE)	55 CANNON (SHAFTESBURY AVE)	58 CURZON (WEST END)	61 LEICESTER SQUARE THEATRE	64 ODEON (LEICESTER SQ.)
53 CANNON (PRINCE CHARLES)	56 CANNON (TOTTENHAM CT RD)	59 EMPIRE	62 LUMIERE	65 PLAZA
54 CANNON (ROYAL)	57 CURZON (PHOENIX)	60 METRO	63 ODEON (HAYMARKET)	66 WARNER (WEST END)

Places of Special Interest — Inner London

Admiralty Arch

London consists of 32 boroughs and the City. For the purposes of this guide, Inner London covers the City, Westminster, Kensington and Chelsea and also includes some places in Camden, Tower Hamlets, Islington, Southwark and Lambeth. Almost all places in this section are situated in the area covered by the Atlas section on pages 181 — 191, and may be located by the map reference provided. If you do not find a place you are looking for listed alphabetically, it may be in the Outer London section which commences on page 94.

Abbey Road *To immediate north of 1 B-1.* The name of this road in St John's Wood stems from the fact that it once led to the mediaeval Kilburn Priory. Its modern interest derives from the Beatles, who made many albums in the 1960s at the EMI Recording Studios. These included 'Abbey Road' which had a sleeve showing the four Liverpool lads outside on the pedestrian crossing. Occasionally the studios are open to the public by prior arrangement. *(Tel: 01-286-1161.)*

Adelphi (5 E-1) An imposing development of terrace houses between the Strand ★ and Embankment Gardens. Designed and built by the four Adam brothers from Scotland (Adelphi is Greek for brothers), work began in 1772. Inspiration for the Royal Terrace came from the Palace of Diocletian at Split, and for the vaults under the embankment of arches from the Etruscan Cloaca of ancient Rome. The main elevated terrace overlooking the Thames was demolished in 1936 but a few remaining houses are elegant reminders of what has been lost: the Royal Society of Arts ★ in John Adam Street, a fine building of classical proportions, has a lecture hall famed for its six huge paintings by James Barry, and No. 7 Adam Street is most attractive.

Admiralty, *Whitehall* (5 D-2) Set back in a courtyard almost hidden from public view by a Robert Adam screen topped with sea horses lies the Admiralty building put up by Thomas Ripley in 1722. Known as the Old Admiralty, the gracious rooms behind the classical portico are richly decorated with fine carvings, some of which came from Wren's earlier building. Flanking it and behind a double tier of railings is S.P. Cockerell's 1786 Admiralty House. The warm red-brick additions which overlook both Horse Guards and The Mall were put up a century later.

Admiralty Arch (5 D-1) *(See map on page 87)* The massive triumphal arch at the Trafalgar Square ★ entrance to The Mall ★, designed by Sir Aston Webb, was erected in 1911 as part of a national memorial to Queen Victoria. Each of the three arches has wrought iron gates but the central pair are opened only on ceremonial occasions.

Beyond the arch, outside the Admiralty building, is a statue of Captain Cook. The great explorer looks a little uncomfortable standing with one foot on a coil of rope. Facing him is a memorial (1903) to the Royal Marines, a defiant Marine defending his fallen companion.

Albany (5 B-1) Exclusive residential chambers, originally for bachelors only, set back in a courtyard on the north side of Piccadilly. Albany was built in 1771-75 by Sir William Chambers for Sir Peniston Lamb, first Viscount Melbourne and father of Queen Victoria's Prime Minister. In 1791 the Lambs moved to Whitehall, exchanging houses with George III's second son, Frederick Duke of York and Albany. The house got its name from the Duke's second title. The Duke, Commander-in-Chief of the British Army (immortalised in the nursery rhyme as 'the grand old Duke of York'), lived in Albany until 1800. Many past residents have had literary connections. Lord Byron occupied No. 1a in 1814 and was harrassed by wild, unexpected visits from his former mistress, Lady Caroline Lamb. Bulwer-Lytton, Macaulay, Gladstone and Aldous Huxley had chambers, and in more recent times Terence Rattigan, Malcolm Muggeridge, J.B. Priestley and Harold Nicolson carried on the literary tradition. There are now 69 chambers.

Albert Hall *See Royal Albert Hall ★*

Albert Memorial (4 B-3) *(See map on page 67)* In Kensington Gardens the national tribute to Prince Albert (1819-61), Queen Victoria's husband, stands like a Gothic altarpiece facing the Royal Albert Hall ★. The Prince always feared his memorial would be 'an artistic monstrosity' and, before it was decided to put up Sir Gilbert Scott's design, Queen Victoria rejected plans for several statues in classical surroundings and one, a reminder of the Crystal Palace, in a Gothic glasshouse. Work began on what Osbert Sitwell described as 'the wistful unique monument of widowhood' in 1864 and was finally completed at a cost of £120,000 when J.H. Foley's statue of the Prince was unveiled in 1876. On the four corners of the steps leading up to the memorial are marble groups representing Europe, Asia, Africa

The Albert Memorial

nd America. The podium is covered by a fine frieze f white marble on which there are 169 full-size igures. These are the men (and one woman) onsidered by the Victorians to be the greatest ainters, sculptors, architects, poets and musicians f history. Giotto and Michelangelo appear twice, nd the only woman, Nitocris, possibly never lived. he is among the architects on the north side: she is upposed to have built a pyramid, which sits in her ap. Above the frieze are large groups representing Agriculture, Manufacture, Commerce and Engineering. Statues ascend — seven tiers in all — ver the spire, becoming holier as they get higher, Scott said. The spire, surmounted by a cross, rises o a height of 175 ft. Prince Albert sits beneath the anopy, which is inlaid with mosaics, enamels and olished stones. In his right hand the Prince holds he Great Exhibition catalogue.

Aldwych (2 F-5) Crescent-shaped thoroughfare hat links the Strand ★ with Kingsway. Until 1900 ne southern end of Drury Lane was surrounded by arrow streets with overhanging Tudor houses which were all demolished to make way for the new oad. The name comes from a colony of Danes who ame to the area ('ald wic') in the 10th century. The rincipal buildings on the central island are Australia House, Bush House ★, India House, which is richly decorated inside, and a bank which stands on the ite of the Gaiety Theatre.

All Hallows by the Tower (3 F-5) A church with a istory that predates the Tower of London ★ which overlooks. There is firm evidence of the Saxon hurch and Roman remains may be seen in the ndercroft. Portions of the Norman and later 15th-entury church are incorporated in the fabric of the resent building, and the tower from where Pepys watched the Great Fire is the only example of romwellian church architecture in London. The rompt action of Admiral William Penn saved All Hallows in 1666: he had all the houses in the area estroyed to halt the Great Fire. Enemy action in 940 caused considerable damage.

All Hallows has rich historical associations, espe-cially with the Tower of London. The headless bodies of Bishop Fisher, the poet Thomas Howard and Archbishop Laud are among those which lay in the church after execution.

Admiral Penn's son William, who later founded Pennsylvania, was baptised here and received his early education in the parish schoolroom. The sixth President of the USA, John Quincy Adams, married Louisa Johnson at All Hallows in 1797. It is the Guild church of Toc H whose founder, the Rev. Tubby Clayton, became vicar in 1922.

The finely carved Grinling Gibbons font cover is of particular interest, and in the undercroft, besides the Roman and Saxon archaeological remains, there is an altar dating from the time of the Crusades: it came from Richard Coeur de Lion's castle in Palestine. The undercroft is open except during services. *(Tel: 01-481-2928.)*

All Soul's, Langham Place (2 B-4) At the north end of Regent Street, this is one of the few remaining Nash churches in the country. When John Nash planned his magnificent thoroughfare from Carlton House to Regent's Park ★ he wanted to continue the vista but was hindered by a sharp corner. He resolved the problem by making a wide sweep at Langham Place and putting the church with its classical portico and Gothic spire on a curve where it appeared as the climax of a vista. It is one of the few buildings to survive from his Grand Scheme.

Apothecaries' Hall, *Black Friars Lane* (3 B-4) The present building, the livery hall of the Apothecaries' Society, was designed by Thomas Locke between 1669-84 after the Great Fire destroyed the mediaeval house once owned by Lady Howard of Effingham. The brickwork on the east side rests partly on the guest house of the Black Friars monastery. Minor alterations were made in 1779 and 1927, but the house retains a good deal of its Carolean detail. The staircase with balusters twisting into vase-like bases is exceptionally fine; so are the wood-panelled Court room and library. The Society owns portraits of James I, Charles I, John Keats, a Reynolds sketch of John Hunter and a bust of Gideon de Laune, Anne of Denmark's apothecary and father of 37 children. The hall is occasionally open. The City Information Centre will have details. *(Tel: 01-606-3030.)*

Apsley House (4 F-2) The London home of the victorious commander at Waterloo, the 1st Duke of Wellington, is now a museum. Popularly known as 'No. 1 London', it is isolated on an island at Hyde Park Corner. Robert Adam, one of the four famous Scottish brothers, built the house in the 1770s for Henry Bathurst, Baron Apsley. The Marquess of Wellesley bought it in 1805 and twelve years later sold it to his brother Arthur, 1st Duke of Wellington. Most of Adam's work was covered over when Benjamin Dean Wyatt refaced the house for the Duke when he became Prime Minister in 1828, and added the portico and Waterloo Gallery.

Though the present Duke maintains a flat at the top of the house, since 1947 it has been owned by the nation and was opened as a museum in 1952. There are many mementoes associated with the Iron Duke's campaigns, especially the Battle of Waterloo.

Besides excellent examples of Meissen and Sèvres porcelain, and a superb Portuguese dinner service, the most surprising acquisitions in the house are paintings from the Spanish Royal Collection. One hundred and sixty-five pictures by such artists as Rubens, Vermeer, Murillo and Brueghel were discovered, minus their frames and stretchers, in the carriage of Napoleon Bonaparte's brother Joseph, ex-King of Spain, when he was fleeing from the Battle of Vitoria. The Duke had them restored and offered them back to Spain but the King, not wishing to deprive him of 'that which has come into your possession by means as just as they are honourable', requested they remain in London. The house is open. *(Tel: 01-499-5676.)*

Baker Street (1 F-3, etc.) A busy thoroughfare connecting Oxford Street with Regent's Park ★. Originally laid out in the mid-18th century by a speculative builder named William Baker, it is now lined with modern shops and office blocks. The street's most famous 'resident' was the invention of Sir Arthur Conan Doyle, whose detective Sherlock Holmes lived at 221b (a number which did not exist in Victorian times). In 1985 a plaque was put at the entrance to the building society that today bears the immortal number.

Bank of England (3 D-3) The central bank of the country lies on an irregularly shaped three-acre site with a frontage in Threadneedle Street. Founded in 1694 to raise money during the French-Dutch war, and nationalised since 1945, it acts for the Government and clearing banks, and issues all banknotes. At the end of the 18th century the then existing building was largely demolished to make way for Sir John Soane's replacement, a neo-classical building surrounded by a windowless wall to give the impression of impregnable strength. Though Soane's walls were retained, the bank was rebuilt

The Bank of England and the Royal Exchange

again in 1924 by Sir Herbert Baker. There are seven storeys above ground and three below. Baker, like Soane before him, retained Robert Taylor's Court Room where the directors still meet. This elegant, classical room on the first floor above ground overlooks the grass courtyard where Wren's church of St Christopher le Stock stood until 1782. 'The Old Lady of Threadneedle Street', the name coined for the bank by Richard Brinsley Sheridan, is not open to the public but special arrangements for party tours will be considered on receipt of written applications.

Bankside (3 C-5) In mediaeval times 'stews' (brothels) proliferated in the narrow streets beside the waterfront on the south bank of the river between today's Blackfriars and Southwark Bridges. Their opening hours were at one time regulated by the bishops of Winchester. Henry VIII closed them down but, by the end of the 16th century, when a number of theatres had been put up in the area, the ladies of ill repute were again doing flourishing business, and the buildings along the waterfront were described as 'a continual row of alehouses'. Among the playhouses were the Rose, the Swan and, the most famous of all, the Globe in Park Street. Shakespeare acted at this 'wooden O' and it is known that *Richard II, Romeo and Juliet, King Lear, Othello* and *Macbeth* were performed here. During a performance of *Henry VIII* in 1613 a cannon set fire to the thatch, and the Globe burnt down. Its replacement was demolished in 1644 shortly after the Puritans closed it. The American actor/director Sam Wanamaker is building a replica near the original site.

The ***Bear Gardens Museum***, in a 19th-century warehouse in Bear Gardens, is on the site of the Hope Theatre where Ben Jonson's *Bartholomew Fair* was first performed. The museum is devoted to Elizabethan and Jacobean theatre. *(Tel. 01-928-6342.)*

Banqueting House, Whitehall (5 D-2) *(See map on page 92)* The first classical building in London, a landmark in British architecture, it is the only surviving part of the Palace of Whitehall, which flourished from the mid-16th century to the reign of William and Mary. Miraculously it escaped the 1698 fire that destroyed the royal residence where Henry VIII died. The Banqueting House was, however, a Stuart addition to the straggling Tudor palace. Inigo Jones, Surveyor of the Royal Works, began work in 1619 and completed it three years later. The marvellous ceiling, commissioned by Charles I, was painted by Peter Paul Rubens, who received a knighthood and £3,000 for the murals that belong to mainstream European painting. The central panel shows the apotheosis of James I.

One of the most ignominious events in British history happened on the cold January morning in 1649 when Charles I walked from St James's Palace ★ to the Banqueting House and stepped from a first-floor window onto the scaffold where he was executed. Forty years later, after James II had fled to France, the crown was offered to Mary II and William of Orange in the Banqueting House.

The hall is frequently used for Government receptions and musical soirées: otherwise it is open to the public. *(Tel: 01-930-4179.)*

Barbican Centre (3 C-2) The largest arts complex in Europe lies to the north of London Wall. Commissioned by the City of London, which maintains it financially, it cost over £150 million, and was officially opened by Queen Elizabeth II on 3 March 1982. While the brutal exterior architecture and confusing split levels inside have invited criticism, the centre has been an enormous artistic success. Two theatres, the Barbican (seating 1,169) and the Pit, a studio space, are the London base of the Royal Shakespeare Company, whose worldwide reputation attracts record-breaking attendances for the repertoire of Shakespeare, classical and modern plays. The wood-panelled concert hall

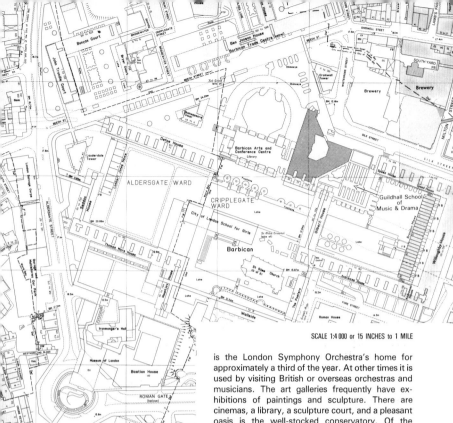

SCALE 1:4 000 or 15 INCHES to 1 MILE

is the London Symphony Orchestra's home for approximately a third of the year. At other times it is used by visiting British or overseas orchestras and musicians. The art galleries frequently have exhibitions of paintings and sculpture. There are cinemas, a library, a sculpture court, and a pleasant oasis is the well-stocked conservatory. Of the several restaurants, one overlooks an artifical lake: in good weather a meal on the terrace makes it easy to forget that one is surrounded by huge concrete buildings in a pulsating city. *(Tel: 01-638-4141.)*

The Guildhall School of Music and Drama adjoins the Centre, and in Golden Lane the Barbican Exhibition Halls are used for public and trade exhibitions and conferences.

HMS Belfast (3 F-5) This, the largest cruiser ever built for the Royal Navy, is permanently anchored in the Pool of London. The 11,500-ton ship took part in the last naval action in European waters in the Second World War. She is now a floating naval museum, the responsiblity of the Imperial War Museum ★. Access is via Tooley Street and Vine Lane. *(Tel: 01-407-6434.)*

HMS *Belfast and Tower Bridge*

The Barbican Centre and the Museum of London

The Barbican Centre

The Grenadier in Wilton Row

Belgravia (5 A-5, 4 F-3, etc.) A most fashionable residential area developed during 1825-36 by Richard, 1st Marquess of Westminster, and the builder Thomas Cubitt. Inspiration for the wide streets and squares with large stuccoed houses came from the work of John Nash, George IV's favourite architect. Today a large number of embassies occupy the pride of the development — Belgrave Square (4 F-3). Behind several of the gracious streets lie less grand Georgian terraces and charming mews. In Wilton Row the Grenadier public house, which claims a ghost, was formerly an officers' mess for the Duke of Wellington.

Berkeley Square (5 A-1) Famous people of the past, a play, a film and a suspect nightingale have lent the square a romantic aura which its modern appearance hardly sustains. As Max Beerbohm pointed out, it isn't even a true square. It is an oblong area surrounded by buildings of varying architectural merit from different centuries. The Square takes its name from Lord Berkeley of Stratton, the Royalist Commander during the Civil War of 1645. He built a house (later known as Devonshire House and demolished in 1924) on the south side, facing Piccadilly. When the square was laid out in the 1730s houses were built on the east and west sides only: all on the east have gone, including Horace Walpole's at No. 11, but the plane trees, planted by his neighbour, Mr Bouverie, still spread over the faded grass. Several original houses survive on the west side, among them No. 44, described by Sir Nikolaus Pevsner as 'the finest terrace house in London'. Built in 1742-44 for Lady Isabella Finch, it is now the Clermont Club and to see the elaborate staircase one has to be a member or guest.

Big Ben (5 E-3) The name given to the Clock Tower of the Houses of Parliament★, though it really should only be applied to the bell. No one is sure whether 'Ben' is Benjamin Caunt, a famous boxer, or Sir Benjamin Hall, the Commissioner of Works when the bell was winched into position. During the Second World War the hours struck on Big Ben and broadcast over the BBC acted as a morale booster to the nation and helped allay fears that London had been destroyed by bombing raids.

Billingsgate (3 E-5) The wharf on the riverside at Lower Thames Street was used for landing fish from about the 9th century, and eventually became a market. Until 1982, when the market was moved to the Isle of Dogs, every kind of fish had been sold here for centuries. The 1875 brick market building, by Horace Jones, had arcades of cast-iron pillars and has been converted for an American bank by Richard Rogers. On the adjoining site in 1984, beneath the new blue-glass building, extensive excavations revealed Roman and mediaeval remains, and a pre-Fire church. On the opposite side of the street, on the corner of St Mary at Hill, a Roman bath was discovered when the Victorian Coal Exchange was regrettably, in many people's opinion, pulled down in 1968.

Almost obscured by office blocks is the church of St Magnus the Martyr, its spire (along with the Monument★) once a landmark for watermen approaching London Bridge. Built in 1671-76 by Sir Christopher Wren, inside it is an 'inexplicable splendour of Ionian white and gold' according to T.S. Eliot. Miles Coverdale, the rector between 1564 and 1566 of an earlier church on the site, translated the first English version of the Bible. His body was reburied in the church in 1840. Remnants of the mediaeval London Bridge and the Roman wharf are in the churchyard. To the east of the old fishmarket is the Custom House★.

Blackfriars (3 B-4) Dominican monks who founded a monastery near the river's edge just south of St Paul's★ in the late 13th century give the area its name. From the 14th to the 16th centuries the monastery buildings were sometimes used as courts of justice or for parliamentary purposes. Playhouse Yard marks the site of the Blackfriars Playhouse which Richard Burbage ran with Shakespeare as one of his partners. The theatre was demolished in 1655.

Blackfriars Bridge was the third to span the river. It was put up in 1760-69 when Robert Mylne, an unknown young Scot in his mid-twenties, won the prize to design it, in competition with over 60 established engineers. The present bridge was opened exactly a century later by Queen Victoria.

Blewcoat School, *23 Caxton Street* (5 C-3) Originally a charity school for 50 poor boys from the parish of St Margaret's Westminster★, today it is an information centre and shop for the National Trust. William Green, a local brewer, provided the money to build the school in 1709 and it continued as a school until 1926. The National Trust bought it in 1954 and restored it in 1975. *(Tel: 01-222-2877.)*

Bloomsbury (2 D-3, etc.) The once fashionable district to the east of Tottenham Court Road attracted artists and writers in the early years of the 20th century. They became known as the Bloomsbury Group, its most eminent members — Virginia Woolf and Lytton Strachey — living in Gordon Square. In previous centuries the area abounded in great houses of the nobility — the Montagus, Southamptons, Russells. Through advantageous marriages much of the land was inherited by the Russell family who developed it, creating at the end of the 18th century a series of pleasant tree-lined streets and squares with well-proportioned terrace houses. Many of these terraces have given way to

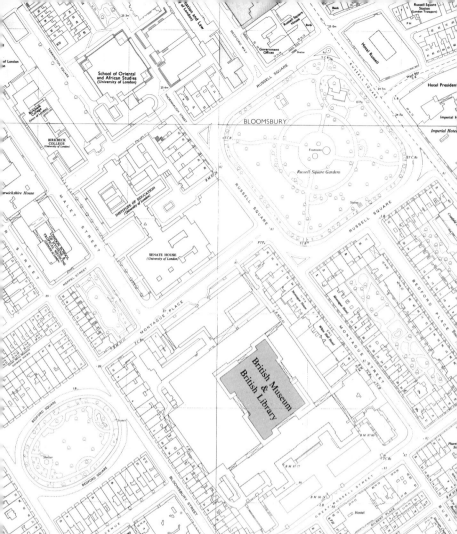

Bloomsbury and the British Museum

SCALE 1:4 000 or 15 INCHES to 1 MILE

the modern blocks of London University but Bedford Square survives as London's best example of a Georgian square. With a background of well-known writers, many publishing houses, several museums and a large university, Bloomsbury retains an atmosphere of literature and learning.

Bond Street (2 B-5, 5 B-1, etc.) The fashionable street of exclusive shops running between Piccadilly and Oxford Street celebrated its tercentenary in 1986. The south end was planned by Sir Thomas Bond and given the prefix 'Old' when the street was extended to the north early in the 18th century, the extension becoming known as New Bond Street. Sotheby's ★, the internationally renowned art auctioneers founded in 1744, has its headquarters at No. 35. While the street has always been occupied by art dealers, specialist shops and such fine goldsmiths and jewellers as Asprey's (No. 34), it was once partly residential and lived in by Laurence Sterne, Dean Swift, James Boswell, Lady Hamilton and Sir Henry Irving.

Asprey's — one of Bond Street's exclusive shops

The British Library (2 D-3) *(See map on page 23)*
Repository of over 10,000,000 books and manuscripts, at present housed within the British Museum ★ in Great Russell Street. It was formed by Act of Parliament in 1973 when the British Museum Library, the National Central Library and the National Lending Library for Science and Technology were amalgamated. It is one of the three largest libraries in the world. A copy of every book, newspaper and magazine published in the United Kingdom has to be deposited by law. The book collections, maps, government papers and stamps are stored all over London and have to be called up daily by scholars, many of whom use the circular Reading Room with its wide dome. Admission to the Reading Room, where Karl Marx sat in Row G writing *Das Kapital*, is by ticket only, though it may be seen as part of a guided tour.

The Grenville Room and the King's Library are both open and house historical manuscripts and such famous items as Magna Carta, the Gutenberg Bible and the autographs of Queen Elizabeth I and William Shakespeare.

To cope with the ever-increasing number of books (2 miles of new shelves are needed every year) a new British Library is being built at St Pancras and by the beginning of the 1990s the first stage should be completed. *(Tel: 01-636-1555.)*

The British Museum (2 D-3) *(See map on page 23)* One of the most varied museums in the world is in Gt Russell Street at the top of the narrow streets north of New Oxford Street. Behind the great Ionic portico, surmounted by a pediment with allegorical reliefs, lies a fabulous collection of Greek and Roman antiquities, and archaeological discoveries from the ancient worlds of Assyria, Egypt and China. There are priceless Prehistoric and Romano-British antiquities such as the Celtic decorated Battersea Shield (1st century BC), the 4th-century Roman silver found at Mildenhall and the 7th-century royal burial ship excavated at Sutton Hoo in East Anglia in 1939.

The Museum was formed when Sir Hans Sloane, antiquary and royal physician, died in 1753 and left his 'cabinet of curiosities' and 'chamber of rarities' to the nation. Manuscripts collected by Robert Harley, Earl of Oxford, and Sir Robert Cotton were added to Sloane's books, manuscripts, paintings, Greek and Roman marbles and natural-history specimens. George II presented the 9,000 books belonging to the old Royal Library. All these formed the nucleus of the collection opened to the public in Montagu House, Bloomsbury, in 1759.

By the middle of the 19th century Montagu House was bursting at the seams following the arrival of colossal statues which came from Egypt after the Napoleonic campaign, the acquisition of the Elgin Marbles from the Parthenon, and libraries presented by the statesman Thomas Grenville and George IV. It was finally pulled down in 1845 as Robert Smirke's neo-classical building went up around it. The new building was then ready to receive the trophies of what became known as the age of 'battleship archaeology'. The Navy helped to bring back monuments from Asia and the Middle East. While the Crimean War raged C.T. Newton shipped home the sculptures from Halicarnassus and Cnidus; Sir Charles Fellows sent the Nereid Monument from Turkey, and Sir Henry Layard's Assyrian antiquities, including the massive winged lion, arrived from Nineveh.

Space in the Reading Room became congested in the years after the passing of the Copyright Act of 1851, which required that a copy of every book published in Britain be deposited in the Museum. The building in 1857 of Antonio Panizzi's circular Reading Room, its dome the second widest in the world, eased the situation in what is now the British Library ★ and the plans to move the Library by 1991 will give the museum much-needed space to show collections normally in store. Selections from the unseen hoards are displayed in frequent theme exhibitions devoted to such diverse subjects as coins, sculpture, jewellery, glass, prints and drawings or archaeology. *(Tel: 01-636-1555.)*

The British Telecom Tower (2 B-3) Better known as the Post Office Tower, at a lean 619 ft high it is one of London's tallest buildings and was completed in 1964. Its many aerials are used for transmitting and receiving television and satellite broadcasts. After a bomb incident in 1975 the viewing platform and revolving restaurant were closed but there are plans to re-open them.

The British Telecom Tower

Broadcasting House (2 B-4) The headquarters of the British Broadcasting Corporation's internal radio services have been housed in G. Val Myers's stately building in Portland Place since 1932. The sculpture over the main door is by Eric Gill who saw Shakespeare's Ariel as the symbol of broadcasting: it shows Prospero sending Ariel out into the world. Though Broadcasting House was badly damaged twice during the Second World War, programmes continued even when a bomb which killed seven people landed in the building during the Nine O'Clock News.

Brompton Oratory (4 C-4 & 4 D-4) After Westminster Cathedral this ornate Italian-style building, opened in 1884, is London's most important Roman Catholic church. It is served by priests of the

Institute of the Oratory, an order founded by St Philip Neri in 1575. They were brought to Brompton in 1848 by John Henry, Cardinal Newman, whose statue by Chavalliaud is to the left of the entrance. The Baroque two-storey façade with pillars, a portico and pediment resembling a Florentine building, was designed by Herbert Gribble. The elaborate Italianate interior, richly adorned with marble and statuary, boasts a nave wider than St Paul's Cathedral ★. The glorious mosaic decorations were added in the 1930s. The larger-than-life statues of the Apostles by Giuseppe Mazzuoli (1644-1725) were abandoned by Siena Cathedral after two centuries, rescued from a warehouse in Genoa, and brought to London. The high altar in St Wilfrid's Chapel came from St Servatius at Maastricht in Holland, and the Renaissance altar in the Lady Chapel, by Francisco Corbarelli and his sons, was saved when a church in Brescia was demolished in 1885. The high standard of the Oratory choir draws a congregation from all over London. (Tel: 01-589-4811.)

Buckingham Palace (5 B-3) The London home of the Queen and the Duke of Edinburgh. Compared with Schönbrunn or the Palacio Real at Madrid, it is a modest royal palace, but, commanding such a magnificent view of St James's Park, Queen Anne noted with annoyance that it gave the presumptuous appearance of owning all it surveyed. 'Buck House' was built in her reign, in 1703, for John Sheffield, Duke of Buckingham, and did not become a royal residence until 1762 when George III bought it for Queen Charlotte. It owes much of its present appearance to their eldest son.

In 1820 when George IV came to the throne he commissioned John Nash to turn Buckingham House into a home fit for a king. In the rebuilding orgy that followed, the florid Renaissance-style house was demolished to make way for the sumptuous splendours of the Blue Drawing Room and the Music Room. Both master and architect died before the work was finished. It was continued by the thriftier Edward Blore who made an inner courtyard (not visible to the public) by placing a dull

Buckingham Palace

SCALE 1:4 000 or 15 INCHES to 1 MILE

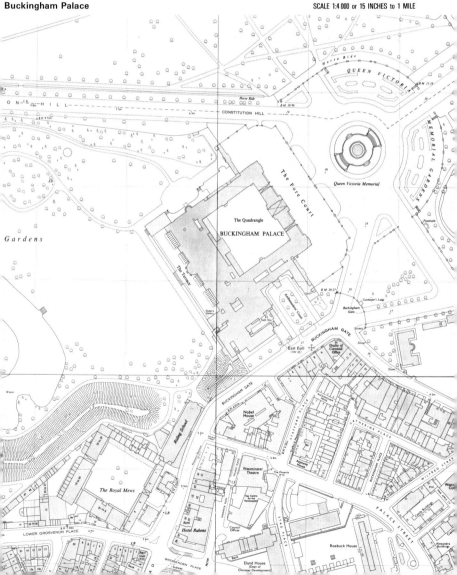

Buckingham Palace

wing on the front side. He also banished Nash's triumphal gateway to Marble Arch ★. Later a large ballroom was added but rarely used in Queen Victoria's reign. Edward VII and Queen Alexandra made up for the lacklustre years. It was said that not even the Czar's receptions at St Petersburg could rival their glittering State Balls.

George V and Queen Mary asked Sir Aston Webb to give the Palace a more imposing façade and the present front facing down The Mall, with its balcony looking across to the Queen Victoria Memorial ★, was added in 1913.

During the Second World War George VI and Queen Elizabeth steadfastly remained at the palace. It was hit by bombs nine times and they narrowly escaped death. Damage to her home prompted Queen Elizabeth to confess: 'I'm almost comforted that we've been hit. It makes me feel I can look the blitzed East End in the face.'

Although the Queen, the Duke of Edinburgh and some other members of the Royal Family have their own suites, most of the 600 rooms are used as offices for the Royal Household and as domestic quarters. When the Queen is in the palace the Royal Standard (her personal flag) flies from the mast. The ceremony of Changing the Guard takes place in the forecourt every morning during the summer and on alternate mornings from mid-August to April. The Palace is not open to the public, though two side sections are — the Queen's Gallery ★ and the Royal Mews ★.

Burlington Arcade (5 B-1) *(See map on page 62)* This covered passageway, filled with tempting shops, on the north side of Piccadilly was built during the Regency to prevent passers-by tossing their litter into Lord George Cavendish's Burlington House ★ garden. Behind the glass-fronted windows lies a cornucopia of expensive goods. Beadles patrol the arcade to make sure the rules forbidding singing, running or carrying an open umbrella are obeyed.

Burlington House (5 B-1) *(See map on page 62)* This former private house in Piccadilly is today the home of the Royal Academy of Arts ★. Originally built in 1665, it was inherited by Richard Boyle, 3rd Earl of Burlington (1695-1753), the enthusiastic art lover. A devoted admirer of Palladio, he redesigned the house with the aid of Colen Campbell, William Kent and James Gibbs. When Lord Burlington died the house passed to the Cavendish

family who sold it to the Government in 1854. After the Royal Academy of Arts took possession in 1869 extensive alterations were carried out. In the courtyard the great gateway, Gibbs's colonnade and the stable blocks were all torn down and replaced by the present solid Victorian buildings. These provide accommodation for the Linnaean Society, the Society of Antiquaries and other learned bodies.

Bush House (2 F-5) The headquarters of the British Broadcasting Corporation's External Services. Programmes are transmitted in a large number of languages to all parts of the world, and in English on the World Service. The building, between Australia House and India House, on Aldwych ★, is named after the American who planned it, Irving Bush. The entrance looking towards Kingsway has a huge arch surmounted by a group of statues that represents England and America holding between them a torch of freedom. During the blitz a bomb broke off the American's arm (several people were killed). The arm was left unrepaired as a memorial to those who perished in the air raids. However, in 1977, to mark the Queen's Silver Jubilee, the Indiana Limestone Company, which originally made Malvina Hoffman's sculpture, replaced the arm.

The Cabinet War Rooms (5 D-3) The fortified offices occupied over 3 acres beneath the Government buildings that stretch from King Charles Street to Parliament Square. They were dug out in the basement prior to the Second World War and protected by a vast area of concrete reinforced to withstand bombs. Nineteen of the rooms — only a small part — have been left as they were in 1945. These include the sound-proofed one where the War Cabinet met, Churchill's sparse bedroom, the tiny telephone room which had a direct line to President Roosevelt and the Map Room that Churchill, after he became Prime Minister, visited every day when he was in London. The rooms, maintained by the Imperial War Museum ★, are open to the public. The entrance is from Horse Guards Road. *(Tel: 01-930-6961.)*

Carlton House Terrace (5 D-1 & C-2) The two magnificent terraces in cream stucco overlooking the north side of The Mall ★ were built by John Nash in 1827-32 on the site of the Prince Regent's exotic Carlton House. The latter had been pulled down when the Prince, by then George IV, decided to remodel Buckingham Palace ★ instead. Nash's original intention had been to use Regent Street ★, his magnificent thoroughfare, to connect the Prince's Carlton House and a summer palace planned for Regent's Park ★. In the event, one was demolished and the other remained a dream.

Such eminent statesmen as Lord Palmerston, Gladstone, Lord Curzon and Earl Grey have lived in the very grand mansions which today house the Foreign Secretary's official residence, the Royal Society (No. 6), the Turf Club (No. 5), the Institute of Contemporary Arts and similar bodies. The Tuscan granite Duke of York's Column ★ is between the terraces, at the top of the steps leading down to The Mall.

Carlyle's House, *24 Cheyne Row, Chelsea (See map on page 29)* Thomas Carlyle, the most venerated literary man of his day, and his wife Jane, moved to the modest Queen Anne terrace in 1834. No house in London gives a better picture of the way ordinary middle-class Victorians lived. In the drawing room, dull by modern standards, Mrs Carlyle received the men of letters who came to discuss issues of importance with her husband — Dickens, Emerson, Ruskin, Chopin. Here too she received her émigré admirers — Cavaignac and Mazzini. It was also in the drawing room that her husband listened to a breathless John Stuart Mill's calamitous news: Mills confessed that his maid had accidentally put on the fire the borrowed manuscript of volume one of Carlyle's *The French Revolution*. Carlyle had to sit down and start all over again. He rewrote the attic study where he could escape the noise of passing traffic and the neighbours' clucking hens. He was soon complaining about the hooters on boats plying their trade on the Thames.

The full flavour of the Victorian era is captured in the kitchen. It is almost exactly as it was during the Carlyles' long occupation. There are no household gadgets, no modern appliances. Up to the time Jane died in 1866 the maid had to sleep in the cold, forbidding kitchen. Often she was kept up late as Carlyle, banned from smoking upstairs, used to slip down to have his pipe in peace, forcing the poor girl to sit up in the scullery.

Thomas Carlyle died in his most comfortable chair, placed today where it was in February 1881. Fourteen years later the house was purchased by subscription and opened to the public. Many of the personal possessions removed were returned, and now with its sombre heavy furniture, it is almost exactly as it was 100 years ago. It is advisable to visit it on a bright day: there was no electricity in Carlyle's day and some rooms are still without it. In the care of the National Trust. *(Tel: 01-352-7087.)*

The Cenotaph (5 D-2) This deceptively simple monument in Whitehall ★ is the national memorial to 'The Glorious Dead' of two World Wars who are buried elsewhere (the name means an 'empty tomb'). Originally a temporary wooden structure for the peace celebrations in the summer of 1919, to honour the men and women of the British Empire who fell in the Great War, Sir Edwin Lutyens's monument was then constructed in stone and unveiled for the second anniversary of the Armistice on 11 November 1920. Although it appears to be composed of straight lines, it is an illusion. A triumph of stone-cutting, every surface is curved for optical effect. In 1946 the inscription honouring the dead of the Second World War was added. Each year in November on the Sunday nearest to the 11th the Queen, members of the Royal Family, the Government, the Opposition, Commonwealth and Diplomatic representatives lay poppy wreaths around the base, and two minutes' silence is observed.

Central Criminal Court (3 B-3) More popularly known as the Old Bailey, this is where all serious criminal offences committed in the Greater London area are tried. Infamous murderers like Crippen and Christie were brought to justice here and sentenced to death. The neo-English-Baroque building, with a curving façade and a dome derived from Greenwich, dates from the early 20th century, but some of the stonework came from the earlier

Central Criminal Court — the Old Bailey

prison, George Dance's formidable Newgate, which for centuries had been the principal prison in London and a place of execution when hanging was discontinued at Tyburn in the 18th century.

Inside there are a number of fine 17th-century statues, among them Charles I, Charles II and Thomas Gresham — all by John Bushnell and taken from the old Royal Exchange ★. The statues of sovereigns in the entrance hall are all Victorian. There are six courts in the section entered from Newgate Street and 12 in the 1970 extension. Anyone over the age of 14 may sit in the public galleries to hear the trials.

Central Hall, Westminster (5 D-3) The Methodist headquarters at Storey's Gate, built in an ornate French Renaissance style, was opened in 1912. When not in use for church services, it is often a venue for concerts and public meetings, and is where the first assembly of the United Nations was held in 1946.

The Chapel Royal at *St James's Palace* ★ (5 C-2) *(See map on page 73)* A surviving example of Henry VIII's royal palace, the chapel has been altered only once since Tudor times. The painted roof is attributed to Holbein, but the rest of the décor was carried out in the reign of William IV in the 1830s. From early in the 18th century, when Queen Anne moved the sovereign's choir to St James's, it has been noted for its music. Thomas Tallis, William Byrd and Henry Purcell are among its famous organists. The choristers comprise six 'Gentlemen', and ten boys who wear Court dress.

Until the 20th century, when royal weddings have been solemnised at Westminster Abbey or St Paul's, the Chapel Royal was frequently where sovereigns or princes and princesses were united, among them William III to his first cousin, Mary II, in 1677, Queen Victoria to Prince Albert (1840), and the future George V to Princess May of Teck, later Queen Mary, in 1893. On the Sundays when there are morning services, visitors may attend.

Chancery Lane (2 F-4 & 3 A-3) A street with long legal associations, linking Holborn to Fleet Street. It takes its name from mediaeval times when the House for Converted Jews was given to the Keeper of the Rolls of Chancery. Until the 17th century there were nine Inns of Chancery where students of law went before graduating to the higher Inns of Court. One of the latter, Lincoln's Inn★, lies to the west. The London Silver Vaults★ are on the east of the street, a short distance from the Patent Office whose library, a division of the British Library★, contains the best collection of scientific and technical books in the country. The Public Record Office★, on the site of the old Rolls Chapel, is almost opposite the headquarters of the Law Society, a massive building designed by Lewis Vulliamy in 1831 for this voluntary body which controls the education and discipline of solicitors.

Charing Cross (5 D-1 & E-1) *(See map on page 87)* The centre of London, the place from where all distances used to be measured, and a railway terminus. The actual spot is marked by a plaque, although this is not in front of the station but on the south side of Trafalgar Square★ where the statue of Charles I looks down Whitehall. Here in 1291 Edward I put the last of the twelve crosses that marked the resting places of his beloved wife Eleanor's funeral cortège on its way from Lincolnshire to Westminster Abbey. The original Eleanor's Cross was demolished by the Puritans in 1647 during the period of Cromwell's rule. E.M. Barry's replica, based on imprecise prints, was erected in the forecourt of the station in 1855. The eight figures of Eleanor were the work of Thomas Earp.

When Dr Johnson said 'I think the full tide of human existence is at Charing Cross', he was speaking almost a century before Barry's second and much larger piece of ornamented Victoriana — the Charing Cross Hotel — went up over the station. In the good doctor's day proclamations were read out at Charing Cross, and people were put in pillories. An earlier recorder of London life, the diarist Pepys, recalled the execution of one of the eight regicides who had signed Charles I's death warrant: 'I went out to Charing Cross to see Major-General Harrison hanged, drawn, and quartered — which was done there — he looked as cheerfully as any man could do in that condition.'

The railway station is a major terminus for trains from SE London, Kent and East Sussex.

Charing Cross Road (2 D-5 etc.) The creation of this street linking Trafalgar Square to Oxford Street involved the demolition of notorious slums in the 1870s. Throughout this century booksellers have occupied a great number of the shops. Foyle's, founded in 1906 by two brothers and run today by the daughter of one of them, claims to be 'the world's largest bookshop'. Several other shops in the north section of the street stock new titles, many specialising in 'remaindered' books. Only a few of the secondhand and antiquarian bookshops remain. These are to be found south of Cambridge Circus and in Cecil Court. Marks & Co., made famous by Helene Hanff in her book *84 Charing Cross Road*, was by Cambridge Circus, opposite the Palace Theatre. Wyndham's, the Phoenix and the Astoria are other theatres on the street.

Chelsea *(See map on facing page)* A delightful, largely residential part of London, traditionally associated with artists, with little streets of charming terraced houses much coveted by the discerning. Until Sir Thomas More built his country house

Charing Cross Road   SCALE 1:4 000 or 15 INCHES to 1 MILE

near the river early in the 16th-century, Chelsea was a small hamlet. Within a short time it became known as a 'Village of Palaces'. This was after Henry VIII incarcerated More, his Chancellor, in the Tower and then had him executed. The King built himself a manor house on land adjoining More's Beaufort House, much to the annoyance of the dead man's family. More's house was demolished in 1740 by Sir Hans Sloane. Its Inigo Jones' gateway survives and is now in the grounds of Chiswick House★. More has not been forgotten: his statue is outside Chelsea Old Church★ where he worshipped, and Crosby Hall★, a house he owned in the City, was taken down and re-erected in a corner of his old garden. The King's house, where Anne of Cleves died and the future Queen Elizabeth I spent some of her youth, has also disappeared. A number of the large mansions on Cheyne Walk ★ cover the site.

Charles II left a more permanent mark on the district which, a century after Henry VIII's death, was still a village even though several noblemen had built fine houses. Inspired by *Les Invalides* in Paris, Charles founded the Royal Hospital ★ for old soldiers. The Chelsea Pensioners, often seen walking around in their scarlet uniforms, provide a colourful contrast to the trendy youths who since the 1960s have treated the King's Road ★ as a parade ground for the pop-culture movement.

Ranelagh Gardens, fashionable pleasure gardens frequented by the *beau monde* in the 18th century, now form part of the Royal Hospital grounds, where the Chelsea Flower Show is held each May. To the west of the Hospital are the National Army Museum ★ and the Physic Gardens ★, from where the cotton seeds were taken to found the American plantations.

Chelsea has attracted famous artists and writers, many of whom lived on Cheyne Walk. James McNeil Whistler, who died at No. 101 had earlier lived at No. 96 with his mistress. He had also occupied a house and studio (Tower House) in Tite Street where his neighbour at No. 34 was Oscar Wilde, whom he introduced into London society. Leigh Hunt and his unruly family occupied 22 Upper Cheyne Row for a while, a short distance from Carlyle's House ★ at 24 Cheyne Row. After a visit to Jane Carlyle, Leigh Hunt went home and wrote his poem 'Jenny kissed me when we met, Jumping from the chair she sat in'. The chair Jane rose from to greet him is still at No. 24. William de Morgan, painter, novelist and potter, and his artist wife Evelyn, lived at 127 Old Church Street, and the explorer Captain Robert Falcon Scott at 56 Oakley Street.

Wellington Square, Paultons Square and Carlyle Square — all off the King's Road — are pleasant examples of three styles of late Georgian architecture to survive almost unaltered.

Chelsea Old Church *(See map below)* On the Embankment, the Church of All Saints was founded in the 12th century. Two landmines caused such devastation on an April night in 1941 that it was

thought nothing could be salvaged. Miraculously the 1325 chapel, restored by Sir Thomas More in 1528 and now bearing his name, escaped serious damage. So did the statue of Lady Jane Cheyne (remembered by Cheyne Walk) which was flung through the air but only broke its toe and is now back in place. The rest of the church was rebuilt and rededicated in 1958. In the More Chapel is the canopied, but badly war-scarred, memorial to the Duchess of Northumberland who died in 1555. Her son the Earl of Leicester was Elizabeth I's favourite, her grandson the Elizabethan golden boy — Sir Philip Sidney — and a daughter-in-law was the ill-fated Lady Jane Grey. The church possesses some of the finest Tudor monuments in London, excellent wall cartouches and tablets. The chained books, presented by Sir Hans Sloane, are the only such examples in a London church. They include two volumes of Foxe's *Book of Martyrs*.

Chelsea Physic Gardens, *66 Royal Hospital Road (See map on page 140)* The oldest botanic garden in England after Oxford was established in 1673 by the Apothecaries' Company, which was later given the land by Sir Hans Sloane. His statue by Michael Rysbrack is in the centre surrounded by rare and unusual plants, exotic trees and shrubs, and a herb garden with historical and modern medicinal plants. There is a water garden and the oldest rock garden in the country. The earliest cedar of Lebanon trees planted in Britain have not survived. In 1732 cotton seed was sent from here to a colonist in Georgia to help him start the industry in America. The gardens are open approximately twice a week between April and October. (*Tel: 01-352-5646.*)

Cheyne Walk *(See map on this page)* Called after the Cheyne family who were lords of the manor in the late 17th century, this road with beautiful Queen Anne and later Georgian houses overlooking the Thames at Chelsea has attracted

Cheyne Row, Chelsea

Old Chelsea, including Carlyle's House and Cheyne Walk SCALE 1:4 000 or 15 INCHES to 1 MILE

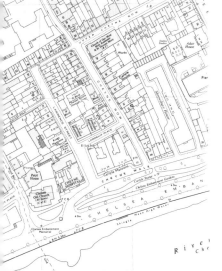

famous residents, among them the eccentric and bohemian. Artists lured by the changing light from the river and writers seeking inspiration have given the tree-lined byroad a colourful past. George Eliot, thinking the air would prove beneficial, came to No. 4. She died a month later. This house was also the home of the artists William Dyce and Daniel Maclise, Dickens's life-long friend. It has lovely wrought-iron work, as does No. 5 where the well-known miser James Cameron Neild lived. When he died in 1852 he left his fortune to Queen Victoria. Equally fine gates adorn the Queen's House, No. 16. Here, much to the consternation of his neighbours, Dante Gabriel Rossetti kept a small menagerie. The wombat, armadillos, and other animals frequently escaped. Rossetti's legacy to all later tenants is a clause in the leases banning wild animals! Rossetti, who shared the house for a time with Algernon Swinburne, is commemorated in Ford Madox Brown's bronze medallion on the fountain in the gardens facing the house. Bram Stoker, creator of Dracula, lived at No. 27, Henry James in Carlyle Mansions, and the Victorian novelist Mrs Gaskell was born at No 93. Sir Marc Brunel and his son Isambard Kingdom were at No. 98, once part of 17th-century Lindsey House. Whistler, who resided in several of the houses, died at No. 101, a few yards from Hilaire Belloc's home at No. 104. Turner's house, No. 119 at the west end, no longer stands, but one bearing his name is on the site.

Beyond Chelsea Old Church★, on the corner of Danvers Street is Crosby Hall★.

Christ Church, Spitalfields *(To immediate east of Map 3 F-2)* The vast church overlooking Commercial Street is one of six built in London by Nicholas

Christ Church, Spitalfields

Hawksmoor, 'domestic clerk' to Wren, and also Vanbrugh's assistant for a time. It was put up between 1714 and 1729 to serve the needs of the refugee French Huguenot silkweavers who had settled in Spitalfields★. The fortunes of the neigh-

bourhood declined after the Industrial Revolution and the parish could not afford to maintain the church. By the middle of the 20th-century it was so dilapidated that it was closed. However, fund-raising efforts by the Friends of Christ Church Spitalfields have, in recent years, financed extensive restoration work. An annual festival of music and various theatrical presentations have been held in the church whose interior Sir John Betjeman described as 'massive, simple and gigantic'.

Christie's, *8 King Street, St James's* (5 C-2) Founded by James Christie in 1766, the fine-art auctioneers have been at this address since they moved from Pall Mall in 1823. In the early days bric-a-brac was sold but Christie's friendship with his Pall Mall neighbour Gainsborough, and with Reynolds, Sheridan and Garrick, soon changed the auction rooms to a fashionable and reputable place for fine art. The building was severely damaged during the Second World War and has been reconstructed. Sales take place from October to July. Experts are on hand to give free valuations and opinions on art and antiques brought in. (*Tel: 01-839-9060.*)

City of London (3 D-4 etc.) The oldest part of London, one of the most important business centres in the world. Ironically, in view of its 2,000 years of history, the 'square mile' is full of modern glass and concrete buildings. Since 1215 when King John granted the citizens the right to elect a Mayor and Corporation, the 677 acres (just over a square mile) to the north of the Thames between Tower Bridge★ and Temple★ have been ruled by an annually elected chief citizen — the Lord Mayor — and governing body comprising sheriffs, aldermen and members of the Court of Common Council. The area over which they have jurisdiction was originally defined by the Romans who colonised 'Londinium' in AD 43-50. They built a 3¼-mile wall (fragments can still be seen) with six gates and the first London Bridge★ to link the City with the main road to the English Channel.

Little is known about London after the Romans departed in AD 410, although Ethelbert, the King of Kent, is credited with founding St Paul's Cathedral★ in AD 607 on the site of a Roman temple dedicated to Diana.

During the Middle Ages the guilds of craftsmen, predecessors of the City Livery Companies, represented the people in the choice of Mayor (the prefix 'Lord' did not come into use until after 1414). They met at Guildhall★ and their efficient way of governing the City was copied by guilds, burghers and administrators in other towns and boroughs, notably at Westminster★ in 1585.

After the Dissolution of the Monasteries there was much unemployment which the financier and builder Sir Thomas Gresham sought to counteract by setting up the Royal Exchange★ as a launching-place for City merchants to start export businesses. Great trading companies were born and fleets of ships sailed the oceans selling English goods. The most famous of these was the East India Company.

The rambling mediaeval City which was so lovingly recorded by John Stow in his *Survey* was hit by two enormous tragedies in the middle of the 17th century. In 1665 the Great Plague claimed many victims. About 110,000 are assumed to have died.

The second disaster, which altered the City for all time, happened on the night of 2 September 1666 when a fire broke out in Thomas Farrinor's bakery in Pudding Lane. It raged for four days, destroyed 84 parish churches and 13,200 homes. 100,000 people were homeless. Five-sixths of the City were laid waste. Fortunately only eight people died. Until the Second World War the City knew no greater period of change.

In the years after the Fire, which is commemorated by the Monument ★, Christopher Wren built fifty-one new churches and his masterpiece, St Paul's Cathedral. Many great City institutions were founded — among them the Bank of England ★, Lloyd's ★ and the Stock Exchange ★. More buildings went up in the 18th century to cope with the increasing commercial demands. By early Victorian times more bridges were needed and new roads were cut through the narrow post-Fire streets.

The bombs of the Second World War devastated an area equal to that of the Fire, and it has taken far longer to rebuild. While a great number of the Wren churches have been reconstructed and several of the City Livery halls restored, the City's quaint alleyways and historic courts have largely disappeared. Their replacements have been faceless glass and concrete blocks, although the planners may be having a change of heart in the 1980s mainly influenced by public opinion. While the Museum of London ★ has been acclaimed and awarded prizes for its interior layout, other new buildings like the artistically successful Barbican Centre ★ have been criticised for a lack of decorative refinement.

Although approximately 360,000 people work in the City, fewer than 6,000 live there. The City is still ruled by its councillors (The Court of Common Council meetings at Guildhall are open to the public), and each year in the autumn a new Lord Mayor is elected. On the second Saturday in November the annual Lord Mayor's Procession, whose origins lie back in the mid-16th century, goes from Mansion House ★ to the Royal Courts of Justice ★.

The City Information Centre in St Paul's Churchyard gives detailed information on everything going on in the City of London. *(Tel: 01-606-3030.)*.

Clarence House (5 C-2) *(See map on page 73)* The London home of Queen Elizabeth the Queen

Clarence House

Mother adjoins St James's Palace ★. John Nash built it in 1825-27 for the Duke of Clarence, later William IV. Subsequently it was occupied by Queen Victoria's son Alfred, Duke of Edinburgh. After extensive restoration in 1949 Princess Elizabeth and the Duke of Edinburgh moved in, and here, the following year, Princess Anne was born. The Queen Mother, widowed in 1952, has lived in this cream stuccoed house overlooking The Mall ★ since the accession of her daughter, Elizabeth II.

Cleopatra's Needle (5 E-1) On the day in 1878 when the rose-pink granite obelisk was placed on the Thames Embankment, an onlooker observed it was 'the oldest thing in London'. The 60-ft-high column, carved with dedications to the gods, is more than 3,000 years old. It was floated down the Nile from quarries at Aswan in 1475 BC and erected at Heliopolis where it remained for twelve hundred years. Then it was moved to Alexandria. Tradition — probably untrue — says that this was done by Cleopatra and that she installed it as a memorial to her dead son by Julius Caesar: hence the name. After the Napoleonic campaigns the Turkish viceroy of Egypt presented it to Britain, but it was more than 50 years before it was placed in an iron cylinder and floated — not without incident and loss of life — to the Thames. Entombed under it is a selection of objects to bemuse future archaeologists. These include coins, the newspapers for 12 September 1878, hairpins, a razor, photographs of 12 pretty women and a copy of *Bradshaw's Railway Guide of the World*.

Clerkenwell (3 B-1 etc.) A historic village to the northeast of the City, hidden from the traffic of the modern world behind undistinguished buildings. The name refers to springs. Beside them parish clerks performed Mystery Plays in the Middle Ages. The 'Well of the Clerks' is inside the offices of the *New Statesman* magazine (14 -16 Farringdon Lane). A few yards away, facing Clerkenwell Green, is the Marx Memorial Library and the old Middlesex Court of Sessions. Behind the library, by the Georgian church of St James's, recent archaeological excavations revealed portions of the mediaeval nunnery of St Mary's and of the great house owned by the dukes of Newcastle. This was one of several Tudor mansions built by the nobility on monastic land given to them after the Dissolution of the Monasteries. Here had been the Priory of St John of Jerusalem, the headquarters of the Knights Hospitallers. The outline of the round nave of the church built in 1125 can still be seen in St John's Square and the Norman crypt survives under the church of the revived Protestant Order, the Most Venerable Order of the Hospital of St John of Jerusalem, whose museum is across the road in St John's Gate ★.

The great 14th-century Carthusian monastery of **Charterhouse** lay to the south of the Gate. It, too, passed to the nobility but in 1611 Thomas Sutton, 'the richest commoner in England' bought it and founded a school for poor boys and a hospital for indigent gentlemen. The school later took fee-paying pupils. Among its students were the poet Richard Lovelace, John Wesley and the novelist Thackeray. It moved to Godalming in the middle of the last century, and although the Medical School of St Bartholomew's Hospital ★ has been built over the Great Cloisters, pensioners still live in surrounding buildings, some of which retain their 14th-century walls.

Warehouses near St James's Church have been converted into studios for specialist tradesmen and manufacturing craftsmen.

Sadler's Wells Theatre ★ and the Greater London Record Office and History Archives ★ are among other places of special interest.

The Clerkenwell Heritage Centre at 33 St John's Square provides information on this hidden village, and organises regular guided walking tours. (*Tel: 01-250-1039.*)

The Clink (3 D-5) Close by Southwark Cathedral ★, near the ancient dock of St Mary Overie, stood the notorious Clink prison of Tudor times which gave rise to the expression 'in the clink'. Burned down during the Gordon Riots, the prison was covered over by 19th-century warehouses which are being restored for commercial use. The narrow cobble-stoned streets have attracted a number of producers making films about the seamier sides of Victorian London. The *Kathleen & May*, the last remaining wooden three-masted topsail schooner, permanently anchored in the dock, is open to the public. An exhibition on board traces her history as a coastal trader. (*Tel: 01-403-3965.*)

College of Arms, *Queen Victoria Street* (3 C-4) The heralds of the sovereign, who are members of the Royal Household, have had their headquarters on this site since 1555 when Queen Mary I granted them a charter — although they had been incorporated originally by Richard III in 1484. The three kings of arms (Garter, Clarenceux, and Norrey and Ulster) are authorised to grant arms to suitable eminent people (they refused Shakespeare's father), subject to approval by the hereditary Earl Marshal, the Duke of Norfolk. The building, put up shortly after the Great Fire of 1666, has survived but its gates were sent for scrap metal during the Second World War. The present gates, the gift of Blevins Davis of the USA, came from Goodrich Court in Herefordshire. Open to the public. *(Tel: 01-248-2762.)*

Commonwealth Institute, *Kensington High Street (To west of Map 4 A-3)* The national centre for information on every aspect of the 49 countries that make up the British Commonwealth. The startling building, with its copper, space-age parabolic roof, was built in 1960-62 and replaced the old Imperial Institute, off Exhibition Road. The well-laid-out interior leads from one exciting exhibition area to another, each explaining the life, culture, history, landscape, natural resources and industries of the countries. Regular changing programmes of music, dance and drama illustrate the performing arts of the Commonwealth. There is a cinema, good reference library, art gallery and restaurant. The centre is very popular with children. (*Tel: 01-603-4535 or recorded 24-hour information on 01-602-3257.*)

Thomas Coram Foundation for Children, *40 Brunswick Square* (2 E-2) In 1739 Thomas Coram, a merchant sailor, opened a Foundling Hospital which stood in the adjacent **Coram Fields** from 1742 until 1926, when the building was demolished and the children moved to Berkhamsted. The fields, still

with the Georgian entrance colonnades, are preserved as a playground for children: adults may only enter if they have a young escort.

When the Hospital moved, the original plaster ceiling was put up in the Court Room of the present house. This room, an exact replica of the Governors' Room in the old Hospital, is hung with paintings given to Captain Coram by a number of his contemporaries. Impressed by the work he was undertaking for abandoned babies, they helped him raise money by giving him examples of their work. The collection comprises 120 paintings and sculptures by Hogarth, Gainsborough, Reynolds, Roubiliac and other artists. Handel, a great believer in the work Coram was doing, became a supporter. He presented an organ (now looked after by the Church of St Andrew, Holborn ★, where Coram is buried) on which he regularly gave recitals, and he left them a fair copy of the *Messiah* in his will. Open to the public. (*Tel: 01-278-2424.*)

County Hall (5 F-3) The administrative headquarters of the London County Council, and then of its successor, the Greater London Council, until it was abolished in 1986. At the time of writing, the future of the Renaissance-style building, erected 1912-22, had not been decided.

Courtauld Institute Galleries *Woburn Square* (2 D-2) One of London's most charming galleries where every painting and drawing — each a bequest — is of major importance. The Courtauld Institute of Art (its teaching section is in Portman Square) was founded by the millionaire industrialist Samuel Courtauld in 1931. The idea was suggested to him by Viscount Lee of Fareham and both men left their collections to it. Courtauld's was rich in French Impressionists; Lee had works by Rubens, Velasquez, Bellini and Botticelli. The collection of the art critic Roger Fry was added when he died in 1933 and the death of Sir Robert Witt brought Old Master drawings. In 1978 Count Antoine Seilern bequeathed a remarkable collection which includes 32 paintings and 23 drawings by Rubens and six sheets of drawings by Michelangelo. There are plans to move this delightful gallery to Somerset House ★. (*Tel: 01-580-1015.*)

Covent Garden (2 E-5) A lively, busy area north of the Strand ★, with wine bars, theatres, specialist shops and restaurants, and the Piazza and covered Central Market at its hub. The name comes from pre-Reformation times when the land formed the convent garden of Westminster Abbey. After the Dissolution of the Monasteries it came into the possession of the Russell family, successively earls and then dukes of Bedford. Francis Russell, the 4th Earl, employed the King's architect, Inigo Jones, to develop the land. It was the first planned layout in London and resulted in the Italian-inspired piazza and the church of St Paul's ★. In the surrounding streets 'houses and buildings fitt for the habitacons of Gentlemen and men of ability' went up, supervised by Jones. Around the Piazza traders began to set up stalls and the 5th Earl took out a licence in 1670 for a produce market. This became the biggest market for fruit, vegetables and flowers in England and lasted until 1974 when it was moved to Nine Elms, near Vauxhall. The Duke of Bedford sold the estate in 1918, but the family are remembered in the

Covent Garden

names of nearby streets, and in the Theatre Royal Drury Lane ★ the family crest adorns one of the stage boxes.

After the market moved, the neo-classical central buildings were restored. With period-style shop fronts and hanging signs, the market now looks much as it would have done when it opened in 1830.

The east exit from the Central Market leads into Russell Street, where Boswell first met Dr Johnson in a bookseller's. Around the corner in Bow Street, opposite the police station, is another theatre of importance, the Royal Opera House, Covent Garden ★, home of the Royal Ballet and the Royal Opera. A few yards away, in the basement of the old Flower Market building is the new Theatre Museum ★. Entrance to the London Transport Museum ★, housed in same building, is from the Piazza.

Crosby Hall *(See map on page 140)* A 15th-century building, now the headquarters of the Federation of University Women, it was brought from the City and re-erected on Chelsea Embankment in 1908. By an interesting twist of fate, the 15th-century house on the corner of Danvers Street now stands in a part of what was Sir Thomas More's garden. The house, which was in Bishopsgate, had been owned by Sir Thomas from 1532-54, although he never lived in it. Built originally in 1466 for Sir John Crosby, Lord Mayor of London, it was leased to the Duke of Gloucester and here in 1483 he accepted the Crown as Richard III. At one time in the 17th century it was the headquarters of the East India Company. The doors to the main hall are often left open in the afternoon at weekends to enable passers-by to see the superb timber roof.

Custom House (3 E-5) Since 1382 a Custom House, set up to levy duty on goods landed from ships in the Upper Pool of the Thames, has stood to the east of old Billingsgate ★ fishmarket. Four previous buildings were destroyed by fire and the present classical building, largely the work of Robert Smirke, was built 1815-28. Austere and cold on the Lower Thames Street side, the Portland-stone front with three porticoes facing the river is imposing, especially when viewed from London Bridge City ★.

Percival David Foundation of Chinese Art, *53 Gordon Square* (2 D-2) Sir Percival David, a member of the Sassoon family, presented his library and unique collection of Chinese ceramics to the University of London in 1951. Porcelain of the Sung, Yuan, Ming and Ch'ing dynasties is displayed on three floors, all extremely well documented. A number of the pieces, which come from the 10th-18th centuries, were owned by Chinese emperors and have imperial inscriptions. Scholars may use the library on application. Open to the public. *(Tel: 01-387-3909.)*

Dean's Yard (5 D-3) Behind Westminster Abbey, through the archway beyond the Great West Door is a square containing a number of mediaeval monastic buildings. Westminster School ★ and the entrance to the Cloisters are on one side, across from the Abbey Choir School, whose pupils share the central green with the school. The building on the south is Church House, designed by Sir Herbert Baker in 1937 as headquarters for the Canterbury Houses of Convocation and more than 50 other Church societies.

Dickens' House, *48 Doughty Street* (2 F-2) Home of the great Victorian novelist from 1837-39 and now a museum. Charles Dickens lived in a number of houses from the time of his arrival in London in 1822 at the age of 10 until he bought Gad's Hill, near Rochester in Kent, in 1856. A year after his marriage he moved to Doughty Street where he wrote *Nicholas Nickleby*, *Pickwick Papers* and *Oliver Twist*. Shortly after he took this house, in which two of his children were born, Dickens was unable to write for several weeks because of his distress at the death of his 17-year-old sister-in-law Mary Hogarth on 7 May 1837. Publication of *Pickwick* and *Oliver* had to be suspended for a month. He spent 33 months here before settling with his increasing family in a larger Regent's Park establishment.

In 1925, when demolition seemed inevitable, the Dickens Fellowship bought the house and turned it into a museum which now contains the most comprehensive Dickens library in the world. There are also first editions of his books, portraits, illustrations, personal ephemera and the desk on which he wrote two letters the day before he died in 1870. Upstairs is the Dickensiana collected by the late Comte Alain de Suzannet, and a reproduction of the *Dingley Dell* kitchen is in the basement. The study and drawing room are arranged as they would have been during the author's tenancy. *(Tel: 01-405-2127.)*

Dowgate Hill (3 D-4) On the west of the street the halls of three City Livery Companies survive, the oldest being the **Tallow Chandlers'** at No. 4. The Company, granted its charter in 1462, purchased the site fourteen years later, but the hall was destroyed in the Great Fire. Much of the next hall, which was rebuilt in 1670-72, is intact, including the panelling in the parlour and the Court Room which has its original seating. Other parts of the hall, like the Italianate courtyard, are the result of Victorian restoration, and repairs carried out after Second World War bomb damage.

The Skinners' Company at No. 8 is one of the twelve Great Livery Companies — ranking at sixth or seventh in alternate years (giving rise to the term 'at sixes and sevens') because of an argument with the Merchant Taylors about precedence in the late 15th century. The Company's first charter dates from 1327 and it has had a hall on Dowgate Hill since c. 1380. The post-Great-Fire hall was refronted in 1790 and extensive remodelling to the building has occurred at later dates, though the old Court Room has its 1670 woodwork. The Skinners own some exceptionally fine plate.

The Dyers at No. 10 are able to trace their history back to 1188 and were granted a charter in 1471. With the Vintners they have the privilege of owning the swans on the Thames and each year in July, in a ceremony known as Swan Upping, all cygnets are marked. When the second of their halls in Upper Thames Street fell down in 1731 they moved to Dowgate Hill. The present building of yellow brick, erected in 1839-42, has proved more durable. The entrance through a glass-vaulted corridor has wall paintings of birds by Sir Peter Scott.

The Livery Halls are occasionally open. The City Information Centre will have dates and times. (*Tel: 01-606-3030.*)

Downing Street (5 D-2) *(See map on page 92)* A narrow cul-de-sac off Whitehall ★ containing the official residence of the Prime Minister. Running between tall Government offices, the narrow street

No. 10 Downing Street

was built in 1683-86 by the second man to graduate from Harvard, Sir George Downing. No. 10, eventually the property of the Crown, was offered by George II to the First Lord of the Treasury, Sir Robert Walpole, who accepted in that capacity. For two-and-a-half centuries it has been the office and home of Prime Ministers. The interior, redesigned by William Kent, was altered by Sir John Soane. Since 1805 No. 11 has been the residence of the Chancellor of the Exchequer and No. 12 is the office of the Government Party Whips. For security reasons the street is normally cordoned off.

Drapers' Hall (3 E-3) *Throgmorton Street* The hall of the third of the City's Great Livery Companies is on the site of land purchased by Henry VIII. The

front of the present spacious mansion was put up by the Adam brothers after a fire in 1772 destroyed most of the late 17th-century hall. The Court Dining Room with a fine plaster ceiling was saved. The garden, with mulberry trees, is a tiny portion of the original Drapers' Gardens which once stretched to London Wall. The City Information Office will have the dates and times the hall is open. (*Tel: 01-606-3030.*)

The Duke of York's Column (5 C-1) The memorial to George IV's spendthrift brother stands at the top of the steps leading from Waterloo Place to The Mall ★. It was designed by Benjamin Wyatt and the bronze statue on top is by Richard Westmacott. The Duke of York was Commander-in-Chief of the British Army but was dismissed from office for a few short years when it was discovered that his mistress, Mary Anne Clarke, had sold army commissions. Every soldier had to contribute a day's pay towards the cost of the memorial. The wags of the day said the lightning conductor was put up to pin his bills on!

Earl's Court *(To SW of Map 4 A-5)* The district takes it name from the courthouse of the earls of Warwick and Holland, and was a small village until the Underground was built. The exhibition hall, opposite the Warwick Road entrance to the station, covers 12 acres and hosts such large-scale annual events as the Boat Show, the Royal Smithfield Show and the Royal Tournament.

Ely Place (3 A-2) A few yards from the bustle of Holborn Circus, protected from Charterhouse Street by heavy iron gates, is a short road in which a few tall Georgian houses still remain. These were built in 1772 on the site of the bishops of Ely's London house, where John of Gaunt took refuge from Wat Tyler's Peasants' Revolt in 1381 and where he died 18 years later. Gaunt was at Ely House when Shakespeare (in *Richard II*) had him reflect about 'This royal throne of kings, this sceptered isle...This blessed plot, this earth, this realm, this England'. Shakespeare wrote of Ely House again in *Richard III* when Gloucester asked the Bishop to bring him strawberries from the garden. The request was a ruse: next day the Bishop was gaoled.

Elizabeth I sequestered the house and gatehouse for one of her favourite courtiers, Sir Christopher Hatton. Nearby Hatton Garden ★ is called after him. The Queen is said to have danced with him around a cherry tree in the garden. The trunk of the tree is preserved in a corner of Ye Olde Mitre Tavern in Ely Court, an 18th-century public house on the site of an earlier 16th-century one. The entrance, easily missed, is through a narrow alley between Nos 9-10 Ely Place.

A small part of the bishops' house survives in Ely Chapel — St Etheldreda's ★, a place of worship since 1251. In 1879 it became the first pre-Reformation church in London to return to Roman Catholicism.

Ely Place is a private road administered by six elected commissioners, and until 1948 held ancient rights and privileges as a sanctuary exempt from police patrol.

Embankment (5 E-2 etc.) The walls enclosing the river between Blackfriars Bridge and Chelsea.

Although Sir Christopher Wren and, much later, in the early 19th century, Colonel Sir Frederick Trench proposed embanking the Thames, little was done until 1858 when, after successive outbreaks of cholera and, finally, a dreadful smell in the Houses of Parliament, the authorities were forced to take action. Sir Joseph Bazalgette, a noted engineer, supervised the construction of the three embankments — Victoria on the north bank between 1864-70; Albert south of the river in 1866-69; and Chelsea in 1871-74. The 3½ miles of walls, parapets and landing stages are all faced in granite quarried on Lundy Island.

Eros, *Piccadilly Circus* (5 C-1) When Alfred Gilbert was invited to design a memorial to the philanthropic 7th Earl of Shaftesbury, he was determined to create an artistic symbol which would capture the spirit of Lord Shaftesbury's work for poor children. Gilbert's Cupid represents 'blindfolded love sending forth indiscriminately, yet with purpose, his missiles of kindness'. Although the naked winged youth firing arrows provoked much criticism when unveiled in 1893, Eros has become a much-loved memorial. In the autumn of 1984 it was taken to Edinburgh for repair, and aluminium on the delicately balanced foot was strengthened. Meanwhile the fountain was moved several yards to a pedestrian area and Eros was put back on top in March 1986.

Euston (2 C-1 etc.) A fairly undistinguished area on the north side of Bloomsbury, developed in the 18th century by the Fitzroy family — earls of Euston and dukes of Grafton. The Euston Road was created in 1756 (then known as the New Road and renamed a century later) to link Islington with Paddington. Euston Station is a main line terminus for trains from the Midlands and the north of England. The classical entrance arch was demolished, despite public opposition, when the Victorian station was rebuilt in the 1960s. In the windy quadrangle there is a bronze statue of the engineer Robert Stephenson (son of George Stephenson of *Rocket* renown). He planned the original station in 1836. Two other railway termini loom over the Euston Road — St Pancras★ and King's Cross★.

Farringdon Road (3 A-1 etc.) A main road leading from Ludgate Circus to King's Cross★. When it was laid out in 1845-46 some of the worst slums in the City disappeared. On the east side, near Seacoal Lane, the notorious Fleet Prison had stood until closed in 1842. It had been a gaol since the Middle Ages, first for persons committed there by the Court of Chancery, then for those convicted by the Star Chamber, and for debtors. Clergymen imprisoned for debt performed the clandestine 'Fleet Marriages' until they were banned in 1763. Dickens' Mr Pickwick did time in the Fleet.

Smithfield Market★ lies to the east of the road and just beyond the junction with Clerkenwell Road, at Nos. 14-16 Farringdon Lane, is the Clerk's Well (see Clerkenwell★).

Fitzrovia (2 B-2 & B-3) Fitzroy Square, called after Henry Fitzroy, son of Charles II by Barbara Castlemaine, gives the surrounding area its name, which was only coined c.1940. Henry became Earl of Euston and Duke of Grafton. The second Duke built

Euston Road★ and a later descendant created the square, a good example of Georgian architecture. In Victorian times many of the houses in the square were the homes of artists — Sir Charles Eastlake at No. 7 and Ford Madox Brown at No. 37, where he gave Dante Gabriel Rossetti painting lessons and kept open house for drunken local artists. George Bernard Shaw lived for a while at No. 29. In the 19th century a number of houses of ill repute were to be found in the neighbourhood, and around the time of the Oscar Wilde court cases several attracted well-documented scandals.

Fishmongers' Hall (3 D-5) On the north side of London Bridge★, the Fishmongers' Company is one of the twelve Great Livery Companies, and one of the few still performing its original function. Officials ensure that all fish sold in the City is fit for human consumption. Its first charter was granted in 1272. A hall has been on the present site since 1434. Severe bomb damage necessitated extensive restoration of the late-Georgian building, which has a pleasant classical façade overlooking the Thames. The Company, one of the richest, owns a fine collection of 17th- and 18th-century plate, the dagger which Mayor William Walworth (a fishmonger) used to kill Wat Tyler in 1381 at Smithfield★, paintings by Romney, and Annigoni's famous portrait of Queen Elizabeth II. The Company organises the annual Doggett's Coat and Badge Race — the world's oldest boat race — for apprentice watermen. This has taken place from London Bridge to Cadogan Pier, Chelsea, every July since 1715.

Fleet Street (3 A-4) From the time Caxton's assistant Wynkyn de Worde moved here c.1500, the 'Street of Ink' (or 'of Shame' according to a modern satirical magazine) has been associated with the printed word and until very recently was the heart of the newspaper industry. In the 1980s a number of papers, long established in the area, have moved to new premises in Docklands.

Linking Ludgate Hill with the Strand★, the mediaeval street, named after the river that now flows underground, was once lined with the houses of bishops. Salisbury Court and Peterborough Court (within the old *Daily Telegraph* building at No. 135) are reminders of the prelates. Of the two churches, Wren's St Bride's★ can claim to have been in almost continuous use for about 1,500 years while **St Dunstan's in the West**, no longer a parish, can trace its origins to the 12th century. It has a number of well-made monuments, and interesting early American associations. The bracket clock at St Dunstan's was made in 1671. The two figures who strike out the bells at the hour are assumed to be the legendary giants Gog and Magog. It is mentioned in Goldsmith's *Vicar of Wakefield*, Dickens' *Barnaby Rudge*, and the eight bells were the chimes in *A Christmas Carol*. Next door to the church Sweeney Todd, the fictitious barber who cut up his customers and made them into pies, had his shop.

Several narrow alleys have literary connections, among them Bolt Court leading to Dr Johnson's House★ in Gough Square, and Wine Office Court where the Cheshire Cheese, a restaurant and pub rebuilt in 1667, is situated. The good doctor, Boswell, and Goldsmith are said to have met here.

Temple Bar★, marked by a monument in the

Fleet Street

middle of the road, is the boundary between the City of London and the City of Westminster. To the south is the Temple ★.

Fortnum and Mason (5 B-1) The luxurious store on Piccadilly was founded in the reign of Queen Anne by William Fortnum, one of her footmen, and his friend Mason. The exotic foods imported from abroad established their reputation as high-quality grocers, and officers serving overseas relied on supplies being sent out to them. During the Great Exhibition of 1851 hampers were prepared for visitors, a service which still exists, especially at Christmas and for social occasions like Royal Ascot. In the 20th century the business has expanded to sell men's and women's fashions. The clock over the front door, put up in 1964, has the figures of Mr Fortnum and Mr Mason bowing to each other on the hour.

Garrick Club, *Garrick Street* (2 D-5) One of the few gentlemen's clubs not in the region of St James's ★. The members mostly come from the world of the theatre or film, literature or the law. The club has an exceptionally good collection of theatrical paintings and sculpture.

Geological Museum, *Exhibition Road* (4 C-4) *(See map on page 59)* A national museum illustrating the general principles of geology and the mineral resources of the world. The plain building gives no indication that it houses a most magnificent collection of precious gemstones in cut and uncut form — rubies, diamonds, sapphires, emeralds. A permanent audiovisual show, set up in a simulated Scottish cliff, explains the story of the earth. On the floor devoted to the regional geology of Great Britain are some remarkable fossils. There is an excellent library. (*Tel: 01-589-3444.*)

Gerrard Street (2 D-5) At the southern end of Soho ★, parallel with Shaftesbury Avenue ★, the bilingual street signs — in English and Chinese — signal that one is entering London's Chinatown. At both entrances to the pedestrian precinct are large red and gold metal Chinese arches. Dryden, who is

commemorated by a plaque on No. 43, where he lived 1687-1700, would certainly not recognise the street, now full of Chinese restaurants and supermarkets.

Globe Theatre, *Park Street, Southwark* (3 C-5) There is only a plaque on the wall to mark the *approximate* site of the theatre built on Bankside ★ in 1599 by Richard Burbage, his brother and a syndicate of five, of whom one was Shakespeare. This was the 'wooden O', referred to in the Prologue of *Henry V*, possibly the first of many of his plays produced here. Cylindrical in shape, open to the sky, it had tiered seats round a jutting stage. The theatre had a short life. It burned down in 1613 when cannon set light to the thatch during a performance of *Henry VIII*. The Puritans closed down its successor. The American actor/director Sam Wanamaker is building a replica.

Goldsmiths' Hall, *Foster Lane* (3 C-3) The Goldsmiths', like the Fishmongers' ★, is one of the twelve Great Livery Companies still with a role to perform. Founded late in the 12th century and granted its first charter in 1327, its hall has been in this narrow street for six centuries. The present Renaissance-style building was erected in 1829-35 and has wood panelling from the post-Fire hall in the Court Room. Extensive restoration took place after the Second World War. All gold, silver and platinum made in London is assayed and hallmarked by the Company which also determines that the metal content of coins does not fall below the legally prescribed minima. This latter ceremony — known as the Trial of the Pyx — has taken place annually since 1248. The Company owns a rich collection of plate which is displayed in the occasional exhibitions mounted during the year. The City Information Centre will have details of the exhibitions and times when the Hall is open. (*Tel: 01-606-3030.*)

Gray's Inn (2 F-3) One of the four Inns of Court with the right to call men and women to the English bar. It was established in the 14th century and once owned by the de Gray family. Each Inn has its own Great Hall, where the members (benchers,

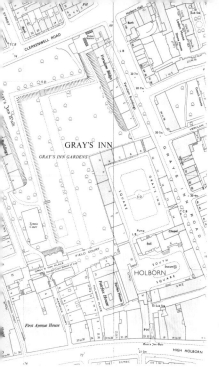

GRAY'S INN

Gray's Inn

barristers or students) are required to dine several times a year, a church and library.

The hall, built in 1560, has a beautiful carved screen and some early stained glass. Shakespeare's *Comedy of Errors* was given its first performance here in 1594. The hammer-beam roof was largely restored after a bomb fell in 1941 severely damaging the hall, the chapel and library where 30,000 books were destroyed. The gardens are said to have been laid out by Sir Francis Bacon who, like Sir Philip Sidney and Sir Francis Walsingham, was a member of the Inn. A statue of Sir Francis is on the lawn in one of the several courtyards, around which legal chambers are ranged. The hall and chapel are open when not in use. Inquire at the porter's lodge.

Gray's Inn

Grocers' Hall, *Prince's Street* (3 D-3) In order of importance the Grocers' is the second of the twelve Great Livery Companies, having been first mentioned as the Pepperers' Company in 1180. The present hall, set back from the street, is the fifth on the site since 1431 and is modern. It largely dates from 1970, after a fire destroyed its predecessor. Some 17th-century ironwork is preserved inside. Contact the City Information Centre for opening hours. *(Tel: 01-606-3030.).*

Grosvenor House, *Park Lane* (4 F-1) Now a hotel on the site of the town house of the dukes of Westminster. The previous house had been occupied by George III's uncle, the Duke of Cumberland (the 'Butcher of Culloden') and then by the King's brother, the Duke of Gloucester, when it was known as Gloucester House. It was sold to Lord Grosvenor (whose descendants became dukes of Westminster) and remained in the family's ownership until 1924, when purchased by Lord Leverhulme. He died shortly afterwards and his executors sold it to property developers who demolished it. The building that went up in its place was in part designed by Sir Edwin Lutyens, who incorporated a reminder of the 1842 Doric screen that had been on the former house. The Great Room of the hotel is used for large banquets and for the annual Grosvenor House Antiques Fair.

Grosvenor Square (1 F-5) One of Mayfair's two squares. Developed by Sir Richard Grosvenor, whose mother Mary Davies had been a considerable heiress. The first houses went up c. 1725 (the last of the spacious 18th-century homes — No. 44 — stood until 1968). The fashionable residential area attracted the rich and famous.

For two centuries the square has had strong links with North America. John Adams, the first minister from the United States to the Court of St James and later the second President, lived in the northeast corner between 1785 and 1788. The Pierpont Morgans' London home was at No. 12 and the Canadian pioneer Donald Alexander Smith, 1st Lord Strathcona and Mount Royal, occupied what is now No. 28. The American associations continued during the Second World War when the square became affectionately known as Eisenhower Platz. The US Army Headquarters were at No. 20, where General Eisenhower had his offices, the Navy was next door and other departments in other buildings.

With all the square's American connections it was appropriate that the memorial to Franklin Delano Roosevelt should be put up here. It was unveiled by the wartime President's widow, Mrs Eleanor Roosevelt, in the presence of George VI and Queen Elizabeth in 1948 and paid for by public subscription. The Embassy of the United States of America, designed by Eero Saarinen and surmounted by a golden eagle poised to swoop, occupies the entire west side of the square.

Greater London Record Office and History Archives, *Northampton Road, Clerkenwell* (3 A-1) The archives, maps and photographs available to researchers are an invaluable source of information on London's history. The 13 miles of bookshelves contain such diverse material as school lists, workhouse records, church registers, directories and magazines. Over 500 requests are dealt with in the search-room every day by a staff able immediately to requisition items from the strong-rooms. A number of the old prints and maps of London have been reproduced and are on sale. Until the abolition of the Greater London Council, the Record Office was in its care. That responsibility has now been taken over by the Corporation of the City of London which also looks after the excellent and not dissimilar Guildhall Library ★ . (*Tel: 01-633-7193.*)

Great Ormond Street (2 E-3) The Bloomsbury street, named after the Royalist Commander James Butler, Duke of Ormonde, is renowned for the Hospital for Sick Children, the first of its kind in England and established in 1851 at a time when more than a third of those who died in London were children under ten. In 1929 the playwright J.M. Barrie gave the copyright of his immortal *Peter Pan* to the Hospital which has benefited financially from all subsequent productions.

Green Park (5 B-2 etc.) A pleasant green oasis between Piccadilly ★ and Constitution Hill. The 53 acres of grass and trees have been a royal park since the reign of Charles II. The mound opposite No. 119 Piccadilly covers the ice house the King had built to keep drinks cool during the summer. The paved path on the east is known as The Queen's Walk after George II's consort Caroline, who had it prepared in 1730 so the Royal Family would not be disturbed when they went out to take the air. The Dominion gateway, opposite the Queen Victoria Memorial ★ , leads into the Broad Walk which runs to the fine 18th-century ornamental wrought-iron gates on Piccadilly. These came from Devonshire House (nearly opposite the Ritz Hotel) when it was demolished in the 1920s.

Handel's *Music for the Royal Fireworks*, written to celebrate the Treaty of Aix-la-Chapelle, was performed in the Park in April 1749. The Temple of Peace ordered by George II caught fire as the fireworks exploded, three people died and a drunk fell into a pond. More pyrotechnics were ordered 65 years later by the Prince Regent for the meeting of allied sovereigns. The star attraction at these junketings, which continued across the road in Hyde Park ★ , was the balloon ascent of John Sadler.

The Park is a popular picnic spot for office workers at lunchtime. On Sundays the railings on Piccadilly become an open-air art gallery for painters of variable quality.

Guards' Chapel (5 C-3) The Royal Military Chapel at Wellington Barracks ★ was opened in 1838, greatly altered forty years later and largely destroyed by a flying bomb during morning service on 18 June 1944 when 121 people were killed and many more injured. The apse escaped and six silver candlesticks, the gift of George VI, continued to flicker on the altar. A new chapel was built in 1963 incorporating the beautiful mosaics that survived in the apse. The approach, a memorial cloister dating from 1956, honours the members of the Household Brigade killed in the Second World War. Outside is a statue of Earl Alexander of Tunis by James Butler. It was unveiled in 1985. The chapel is open to the public.

Guildhall (3 D-3) The administrative headquarters of the City of London from the 12th century to

Guildhall and part of the City
SCALE 1:4 000 or 15 INCHES to 1 MILE

today — although little is known about the earliest hall, where meetings of the ancient Court of Husting were held. The present buildings are a happy marriage of work begun in 1411, substantially altered or restored over the centuries and added to as recently as 1974.

The Great Hall, the scene of the annual Lord Mayor's Banquet, when the Prime Minister delivers a 'state of the nation' speech, has witnessed many historic occasions. Lady Jane Grey and her husband, Lord Guildford Dudley, were condemned to death here in 1553 and, in the same year, the trial of Archbishop Cranmer took place. Visiting Heads of State are entertained by the Lord Mayor and Corporation of the City, and the City has also given banquets for the Coronation of the Queen and on the occasion of Her Majesty's Silver Jubilee in 1977.

One of the very few mediaeval buildings in London to survive, the Great Hall is 152 ft long and 49 ft wide. Only Westminster Hall, ★ with which it may be compared, is larger. Most of what is visible is the work of George Dance Jr. in 1788-89, the earlier 12th-13th-century remains being the lower part of the hall, the crypts and the porch. The Great Fire of 1666 took its toll: only the walls stood when Wren put in a new roof, which remained until 1862-63 when the City architect Horace Jones replaced it with hammerbeams. This lasted until 29 December 1940, when the roof had again to be renewed, this time by Sir Giles Gilbert Scott, although the walls and east crypt had withstood the Luftwaffe assault.

Several interesting statues are in the hall, among them the legendary giants Gog and Magog, which oversee proceedings from the balcony. These are 20th-century replacements carved by David Evans to replace the 15th-century pageantry figures destroyed in 1940. Other monuments and statues commemorate William Beckford, the Lord Mayor who took George III to task over an election, William Pitt the elder and the younger, the Duke of

Wellington and Winston Churchill.

A stone and concrete cloister, built in 1974, connects the old Guildhall to a new office block.

Guildhall Library ★, with an extensive maps and prints department, can be reached by a corridor from the porch or from the main entrance in Aldermanbury.

Information on opening hours, meetings of the Court of Common Council or such ceremonies as the elections of Sheriffs or the Lord Mayor may be obtained from the City Information Centre (*Tel: 01-606-3030.*)

Guildhall Library, *Aldermanbury* (3 D-3) The library has a huge collection of material on the history of London, its people, businesses and buildings. Together with the Greater London Record Office and History Archives ★, it is the place anyone researching London's past should start. The map collection exceeds 28,000; its topographical prints and drawings — over 30,000 — are unsurpassed. The library also owns portraits, paintings, and ephemera, some of which are on display in small exhibitions.

Within the building is the **Guildhall Clock Museum** where the collection of the Clockmakers' Company is housed. This was given to the City and is probably the best horological collection in the world. It comprises some 700 items. (*Tel: 01-606-3030.*)

Guy's Hospital, *Thomas Street, London Bridge* (To south of Map 3 E-5) Founded in 1721 by Thomas Guy, a governor of St Thomas's, to alleviate overcrowding in that hospital, Guy's was ingeniously designed with a central colonnade to provide covered access to the other buildings. Guy, a rich bookseller and publisher, died before the first patients were admitted in 1726 but his fortune, which the epitaph on his memorial in the hospital's chapel says 'rivalled the Endowment of Kings', went towards the upkeep of the twelve wards.

Richard Bright, Thomas Addison and Thomas Hodgkin (all of whom have had diseases named after them) worked at the hospital. Guy's was the first London hospital to have a dental surgeon, and its dentistry school still exists.

Following extensive damage during the Second

Guy's Hospital

World War, there has been extensive rebuilding, including a massive tower block in 1963. Guy's, its medical school famous all over the world, has 894 beds.

Haberdashers' Hall, *Gresham Street, but entrance from Staining Lane* (3 C-3) The Haberdashers' first hall was built here in 1478, about 100 years after the Company's foundation. The second, designed by Christopher Wren in 1668, survived two severe fires but was eventually destroyed by a German bomb in 1940. The new hall, with some early 18th-century panelling, was incorporated into an apartment block in 1956. The Company has a particularly good collection of plate. For occasional times of opening, contact the City Information Centre. (*Tel: 01-606-3030.*)

Harrods, *Knightsbridge* (4 E-3) It is often said that this luxurious department store, one of the largest in the world, sells everything 'from a pin to an elephant'. This particular claim really belonged to the now vanished Whiteley's in Bayswater. But Harrods, which invites its customers to 'enter a different world' can supply everything, including houses and pets, from the cradle to the grave. In the Food Halls, Art Nouveau tiles depict the delicacies available on the counters. The dull terracotta building, its outline picked out in tiny lights at night, was put up in 1905 on the site of a small grocery shop bought in 1849 by a City tea merchant, Henry Charles Harrod. Rapid expansion and the sale of a great many other goods prompted the boast in late Victorian times that 'Harrods serves the world'.

An innovation which fascinated customers was the installation of an escalator in 1898, the first in London. An assistant, with brandy and sal-volatile at the ready, stood at the top waiting to calm those of a nervous disposition.

Harrods — 'a different world'

Hatton Garden (3 A-2) The centre of the diamond trade. The street's name derives from Hatton House, home of Elizabeth I's Chancellor, Sir Christopher Hatton, who was given episcopal land in Ely Place ★ by his Queen. Until the early 19th century it was a residential street, once lived in by the playwright William Wycherley and Thomas Coram.

Silversmiths were in business in the street by the early 1830s and gradually diamond merchants moved in. De Beers, who handle 80 per cent of the output from the world's diamond mines, have their London headquarters nearby on Holborn Viaduct.

Haymarket (5 C-1) The road connecting Piccadilly Circus with Pall Mall. Until 1830 straw and hay were sold in the street that had in the 18th and early 19th centuries achieved a reputation as a 'parade ground of abandoned women'. There are two important theatres facing each other — the Theatre Royal, Haymarket★ and Her Majesty's. The Haymarket Theatre built by Nash is one of the most charming theatres in London, its classical façade and portico complementing the other Nash buildings that run into Suffolk Place. Her Majesty's, the fourth theatre on the site, has had a distinguished past. The first theatre was built by Sir John Vanbrugh in 1705 and was managed by him and William Congreve. Most of Handel's oratorios and operas were first produced here. Opera was the staple fare of the second and third theatres where Jenny Lind sang and Bizet's *Carmen* and Wagner's *Ring* received their first English performances. The present building dates from the end of the 19th century and was financed by Sir Herbert Beerbohm Tree. The repertoire in modern times has mostly been musicals or melodramas.

The Royal Opera Arcade at the back of Her Majesty's was designed by John Nash and G.S. Repton in 1816-18. It is the oldest arcade in London and, with its bow-fronted windows and glass roof, most attractive.

Hayward Gallery, *South Bank* (5 F-2) The spacious concrete art gallery on the South Bank was opened in 1968 and named after Sir Isaac Hayward, a leading figure in local government in the years the arts complex was conceived. Large temporary art or architectural exhibitions are staged throughout the year. (*Tel: 01-928-3144.*)

Holborn (3 A-2 etc.) The Hole-borne, part of the river Fleet, gives its name to the street and surrounding area which runs from the Central Criminal Court★, or Old Bailey, to New Oxford Street. Those condemned to hang at Tyburn travelled in carts from Newgate, to the great enjoyment of large crowds, until the last years of the 18th century. At the Church of St Sepulchre★, on the corner of Holborn Viaduct and Giltspur Street, nosegays were handed to each condemned prisoner.

At Holborn Circus, with his back to the *Daily Mirror* building, the bronze figure of Prince Albert on his charger doffs his plumed hat to the Church of St Andrew★, where Thomas Coram is buried. Within sight of his left eye is Charterhouse Street and the entrance to Ely Place★. Beyond Hatton Garden★ the Gothic red-brick building is Alfred Waterhouse's headquarters for the Prudential Assurance Company. Opposite, just by the corner of Fetter Lane, is Barnard's Hall, now a restaurant, the oldest secular building in the City.

Facing the Gray's Inn Road is the half-timbered front of Staple Inn★, originally a hostel for woolstaplers and, from the time of Henry VIII, one of the nine Inns of Chancery. The War Memorial in the centre of the road commemorates the Royal Fusiliers, and the obelisks on the pavement mark the City boundary.

Two of the Inns of Court★ lie behind High Holborn, Gray's Inn★ to the north and Lincoln's Inn★ to the south.

Horse Guards (5 D-2) *(See map on page 92)* The military offices on Whitehall★ where two mounted troopers of the Life Guards or the Blues and Royals are posted daily. The west, and more architecturally interesting side, overlooks *Horse Guards Parade*, a square parade ground where the ceremony of Trooping the Colour, the Queen's Birthday Parade, takes place on a Saturday every June.

The central stone building stands on the site of an earlier guard house erected in the tiltyard of the old Palace of Whitehall. The present London District

The Whitehall entrance to Horse Guards

army headquarters were begun by William Kent in 1745 and completed after his death by John Vardy. The first-floor room overlooking the Parade, under the clock, was the Duke of Wellington's office — his desk is still in use.

Around the Parade are a number of elegant buildings. The Citadel, covered in Virginia Creeper, was a communications centre in the Second World War. Along from it is the bright red-brick New Admiralty and, in the corner, the plain mellow-bricked Paymaster-General's Office. The rear of Dover House (formerly Melbourne House and today the Scottish Office) with the Venetian window immediately to the south of Horse Guards, was where Lady Caroline Lamb in the scandalous pursuit of Lord Byron entertained the 'mad, bad and dangerous to know' poet in the spring of 1812. The trees in front of the south wall screen the gardens of Downing Street★.

Almost all the statues commemorate military men

— Lord Kitchener, Lord Roberts, and the most recent — the Allied Commander in SE Asia in the Second World War — Lord Mountbatten.

House of St Barnabas-in-Soho, *1 Greek Street* (2 D-4) A charity house for the destitute. The plain exterior gives no hint of the magnificence inside. The early Georgian house on the corner of Soho Square was the home of Richard Beckford, an East India merchant and uncle of William Beckford, owner of the fantastic folly of Fonthill Abbey. Beckford came here in 1754 and probably commissioned the splendid rococo plasterwork — the best in London — fine woodwork and metal balustrades. After Beckford's death, subsequent owners little altered the building. In 1861 the house was sold to the charity. A small chapel was built at the rear. In the courtyard at the back the meeting took place between Dr Manette and Sidney Carton in Dickens' *A Tale of Two Cities*. The house is open for a limited number of hours twice a week. (*Tel: 01-437-1894.*)

Houses of Parliament or **the Palace of Westminster** (5 E-3). *(See map on page 92)* The seat of government and officially a royal palace. Although a sovereign has not lived here since Henry VIII moved to Whitehall Palace after a fire in 1532, the building remains the responsibility of the Lord Great Chamberlain. In two chambers the country's business is debated, its laws enacted by elected representatives of the people in the House of Commons, and by hereditary and life peers in the House of Lords who must approve all bills, except financial, before they become statutory. The House of Lords is also the highest court in the country to which, in extreme circumstances, appeals may be made.

Each year, usually in November, the monarch opens a new session of Parliament, and goes in procession from the Sovereign's Robing Room through the Royal Gallery to the House of Lords: no monarch has entered the House of Commons since 1642 when Charles I tried to arrest five members. Before the sovereign arrives there is a ceremonial search of the House, a reminder of the check made in 1605 when Guy Fawkes' plan to blow up James I was discovered. The members of the House of Commons are then summoned to the bar of the Upper House to listen to the speech from the throne in which the sovereign outlines the government's proposed legislation for the forthcoming session of Parliament.

The country has been ruled from Westminster since the 11th century, and from the present building since the middle of the 19th century. The Gothic-style Houses of Parliament were designed by Sir Charles Barry and decorated by Augustus Pugin after a fire in 1834 destroyed all but Westminster Hall★, and the undercroft and cloisters of St Stephen's Chapel. A light shining from the clock tower known as Big Ben★, and the Union Jack flying on top of the Victoria Tower indicate that Parliament is sitting. The Victoria Tower houses important archives. Among them are all Acts of Parliament, of which some, going back to 1497, were previously kept across the road in the Jewel Tower★. Leading off New Palace Yard — below Big Ben — is the Speaker's House and Westminster Hall.

The chamber of the House of Commons, destroyed during the Second World War, was com-

The Houses of Parliament

pletely rebuilt by Giles Gilbert Scott and furnished by countries who looked on Westminster as 'the Mother of Parliaments'. The Speaker's Chair was the gift of Australia, the despatch boxes of New Zealand, the table of Canada. In the Commons Lobby, immediately outside the chamber, members meet to discuss parliamentary business, and in the Central Lobby members of either house can meet each other, interview constituents, see groups who come to 'lobby' Parliament, and talk to Lobby Correspondents.

The Peers' Lobby, where the Lords vote, leads to the Upper chamber and Royal Gallery where Daniel Maclise's huge murals depict the Death of Nelson and Blücher after Waterloo. There are also portraits of kings and queens, beginning with Victoria.

A six-year cleaning programme in the 1980s has removed a century's grime and restored the exterior of Charles Barry's Victorian Gothic building to its original mellow honey colour.

Public access to the Houses of Parliament has been restricted in recent years. Tours and tickets for debates must be arranged with a Member of the House, but a limited number of people who queue at St Stephen's entrance are allowed into the Visitors' Gallery when the Houses are sitting.

Hunterian Museum, *Royal College of Surgeons, Lincoln's Inn Fields* (2 F-4) An important medical museum which lost a large number of its specimens during the Second World War. The nucleus of the anatomy collection was formed by the Scottish surgeon John Hunter, and six years after his death in 1739 it was purchased for the nation. Open only by written application to the curator. (*Tel: 01-405-3474.*)

Hyde Park (4 E-2 etc.) One of London's several 'lungs', the royal park, bounded on the east by Park Lane★, covers 360 acres and measures 3½ miles round. With adjacent Kensington Gardens there are 600 acres of continuous parkland. In spring the flowers make a colourful splash. Horsemen from the stables in the mews south of Knightsbridge ride daily along Rotten Row, a sandtrack for riders. Soldiers of the Household Cavalry stationed at Knightsbridge Barracks also exercise their horses here. Rotten Row and the lawns by the so-called Statue of Achilles were frequented by society ladies as well as courtesans throughout the 19th century.

Spring in Hyde Park

On Sundays Speakers' Corner ★ attracts orators whose views are often extreme. Bathers swim in the Serpentine, an artificial lake in the centre of the park created for Queen Caroline, the wife of George II, in 1730. Originally the park belonged to the monks of Westminster. It was seized by Henry VIII at the Dissolution of the Monasteries and converted into a royal hunting ground where deer hunting continued until the middle of the 18th century. Charles II made it a fashionable meeting place. It was also a favourite place for duels, especially during the reign of William and Mary. In 1814 the Prince Regent, to celebrate the Hanoverian centenary and victory over both the French and the Americans, had a 'Great Fair' in the park during which a mock sea battle was staged on the Serpentine. Prince Albert chose a large area overlooking the Kensington Road as the site for the Great Exhibition of 1851 when more than six million people came to Joseph Paxton's Crystal Palace to see the 'Works of Industry of All Nations'.

On the birthdays of the Queen, the Duke of Edinburgh and Queen Elizabeth the Queen Mother, and other important royal anniversaries, gun salutes are fired at noon by the King's Troop, the Royal Horse Artillery, from a position opposite the Dorchester Hotel.

Hyde Park Corner (4 F-2)

At the south-east entrance to Hyde Park ★ is a very large roundabout fed by six roads — among them Park Lane from the north and Piccadilly from the east. This was once the main entrance into London from the West of England, and there was a tollgate here until early in the 18th century. Beside Apsley House ★ is the screen, designed by Decimus Burton in 1825, originally intended to be sited as a noble approach to Buckingham Palace from Hyde Park. Constitution Arch, originally Wellington Arch, now on the central island, was once beside the Ionic columns of the screen. On the island are a number of monuments, among them the Duke of Wellington on his horse Copenhagen by Edgar Boehm, the Royal Artillery Memorial and the Machine Gun Corps Memorial.

Imperial College, *Exhibition Road* (4 C-3)

Now part of the University of London. Colleges of Science and Technology occupy both sides of the road and are built on the land bought with the profits of the Great Exhibition of 1851.

The Queen's Tower by the faculty buildings is all that remains of the old Imperial Institute — forerunner of the Commonwealth Institute ★. Almost 300 ft high and with 324 steps, it was put up by Thomas Collcutt in 1887, the year of Queen Victoria's Golden Jubilee, to celebrate the British Empire. From the top of the tower there are splendid, panoramic views across London. Open during the tourist season. (*Tel: 01-589-5111.*)

Imperial War Museum, *Lambeth Road (To east of Map 5 F-4)*

A national museum principally concerned with the history of the First and Second World Wars. Britain's involvement in war is recreated in atmospheric displays recalling the hardship endured by servicemen and civilians in battle and on the home front. The museum has an excellent collection of paintings and drawings, many of them by official war artists, and a good photographic records department. Changing exhibitions devoted to specific social or military aspects of war are often mounted. Audiovisual shows and dioramas are aimed at young visitors. On the front lawn huge 15-inch naval guns from the battleships 'Ramillies' and 'Revolution', cast in 1915 and 1916, greet visitors. The museum's name is a reminder that the British Empire had not faded when it was established in 1920. At first housed at Crystal Palace and then until 1936 at the Imperial Institute, it has since occupied the former Bedlam Asylum.

The present building has almost come to the end of its useful life: after the success of a public appeal in 1985 plans to renovate and add to the museum will involve considerable alterations to the layout of the exhibits for a few years. The library and photographic records may be seen by appointment. Excellent educational facilities are available for children, and there are frequent film shows. The obelisk in the grounds was on St George's Circus from 1771 until re-sited here in 1907. (*Tel: 01-735-8922.*)

Inner Temple (3 A-4)

This Inn of Court is generally referred to as the Temple ★, sharing a church and gateway with Middle Temple ★.

Ismaili Cultural Centre, *Cromwell Gardens* (4 C-4)

Opposite the Victoria and Albert Museum. Designed by Sir Hugh Casson and his partners for the Aga Khan's London community, its pale polished stone and windows suggest an eastern influence. Inside the Centre is the **Zamana Art Gallery** which mounts interesting exhibitions devoted to the art and culture of Islam. (*Tel: 01-584-6612.*)

Jermyn Street (5 C-1) *(See map on page 62)*

From its earliest days, although in part residential, Jermyn Street has attracted fashionable, and often specialist shopkeepers who, until Simpson's introduced women's wear, largely catered to gentlemen. One of the first streets to be built in the West End of London, it bears the name of Henry Jermyn, created Earl of St Albans at the request of Henrietta Maria at the Restoration. A diplomat who lived in France for many years, he was granted the lease of Pall Mall Fields, laid out St James's Square ★ and was responsible for developing the area. On the corner of Bury Street there is a relief showing Jermyn being handed the deeds by Charles II. In 1676 he laid the foundation stone of St James's Piccadilly ★, the Wren church he largely financed.

One shop with a long history is Floris at No. 89. Founded in 1730 as a perfumery, it has been ere ever since, one of the few businesses in London still in the ownership of the original family. The fine mahogany showcases came from the Great Exhibition of 1851. A few doors away (No. 93) is Paxton and Whitfield, a long-established cheesemonger.

The Cavendish Hotel, whose flamboyant Edwardian manager, Rosa Lewis, was immortalised in a television serial and in the books of Evelyn Waugh, has been rebuilt.

Before the street became almost entirely commercial, private houses provided lodgings for such eminent men as Benjamin Franklin in 1725, Bishop Berkeley, the metaphysician, and William Pitt. Other residents included the poet Thomas Gray and Sir Thomas Lawrence, the Regency portrait painter.

The Jewel Tower, *Abingdon Street* (5 D-3) *(See map on page 92)* Built in 1365 as a repository for Edward III's valuables, the moated three-storey royal treasure-house is a survival of the mediaeval Palace of Westminster. From 1621 Parliamentary records were stored here, but in 1864 they were removed to the Victoria Tower of the Houses of Parliament★. An assay section of the Weights and Measures Office was then in the tower until 1938. One of the country's important historic monuments, and in continual use for almost 600 years, it has been open to the public since repairs were carried out after Second World War damage. (*Tel: 1-222-2219.*)

The Jewish Museum, *Woburn House, Tavistock Square* (2 D-2) The collections of over 1,300 ritual objects illustrate Jewish life, its history and religion, notably in Britain. Synagogue and domestic items are displayed with Torah scrolls, an elaborate 16th-century Ark of the Covenant carved in Italy, and a Byzantine gold plaque with symbols. An audiovisual show explains Jewish rituals. (*Tel: 01-388-4525.*)

Dr Johnson's House, *Gough Square, off Fleet Street* (3 A-3) The only London house lived in by Dr Samuel Johnson that still exists, and open to the public since before the First World War when it was bought, renovated and presented to the nation by Cecil Harmsworth, a brother of the famous newspaper barons. It is administered by a Trust and has been refurnished in 18th-century style over the years.

Dr Johnson came here in 1748 and during his eleven years' occupation he compiled his Dictionary in the attic. His wife Tetty, 'always drunk and reading romances in bed', according to one of his friends, killed herself taking opium here in 1752. The doctor's friends — David Garrick, Oliver Goldsmith, Dr Burney and Joshua Reynolds — and aspiring writers were frequent visitors. There are many portraits of Johnson and his circle, a first edition of the Dictionary and personal ephemera. (*Tel: 1-353-3745.*)

Kensington (4 A-3 etc.) Created a royal borough at the wish of Queen Victoria in 1901, and now combined with Chelsea, Kensington is a busy residential, commercial and shopping centre, and the home of royalty for 300 years. Even before a fire destroyed the Palace of Whitehall★ in 1698, William and Mary had settled in Nottingham House and renamed it Kensington Palace★, and while

sovereigns have not lived here since George II's death in 1760, the palace's private apartments, where Queen Victoria was born in 1819, have been occupied by various members of the royal family ever since.

In the Domesday Book Kensington appears as Chensit, probably a farm near the present church of St Mary Abbott. The area was settled by the Norman family of de Vere (later earls of Oxford). By the early 17th century large country mansions belonging to noblemen had been put up to the north of Kensington High Street. There were so many grand houses in 1851 that Leigh Hunt christened the roads around the palace 'the Old Court Suburb'. The best known was **Holland House**, a large Jacobean mansion which had been bought by Henry Fox, 1st Baron Holland. Its considerable reputation as a social centre for Whig politicians in the 18th and 19th century was largely influenced by Charles James Fox who had been brought up here. Badly damaged during the Second World War, only a small portion of the house was saved. The gate piers designed by Inigo Jones and carved by Nicholas Stone, survived. The formal gardens are open, and during the summer the former terrace of the house is used for open-air concerts or theatrical performances. Art exhibitions are sometimes held in the Orangery.

In front of Holland House is the Commonwealth Institute★, a magnet for children, and nearby are two Victorian residences of note — 12 Holland Park Road, the exotic Leighton House★, built by the artist Frederic, Lord Leighton, and 18 Stafford Terrace, the Linley Sambourne House★, which remains almost exactly as it was in the 1890s.

Melbury Road★ has seen several famous residents in houses built by well-known architects.

The small, attractive terrace houses in Edwardes Square were built in 1812 by a Frenchman who reputedly planned to use them as quarters for Napoleon's officers of lower ranks when the French Emperor occupied London. Leigh Hunt, who later spent eleven years looking across to the small Tuscan-temple summer-house in the central garden, said the square offered 'cheap lodgings and *fête champêtre* combined; here economy in-doors and Watteau without; here repose after victory…a French Arcadia. So runs tradition…'

The huge Albert Memorial★ stands in Kensington Gardens★, across the main Kensington Road from the Royal Albert Hall★, two of many tributes to Queen Victoria's husband, who was the instigator of the museums, institutes and centres of learning that proliferate in the area and run through to South Kensington★.

Two of London's largest exhibition complexes are in the borough: Earls Court★, just south of Kensington High Street, and Olympia at its western end.

Kensington Gardens (4 B-2 etc.) The royal park, separated from Hyde Park★ by the Long Water and the Serpentine, was laid out for William and Mary and extended by Queen Anne, who had the red-brick Orangery put up for summer supper parties. But the greatest embellishments were inspired by George II's wife, Caroline of Anspach, a dedicated landscape gardener. In consultation with the royal gardener Charles Bridgeman, she had trees planted on avenues she decreed should be wide and straight. Near the Broad Walk (her idea) she had a basin excavated and filled with water — known now

Kensington Palace and Kensington Gardens

SCALE 1:4 000 or 15 INCHES to 1 MILE

as the Round Pond. Queen Caroline's most ambitious scheme was to create the ornamental lake by joining up various pools of the river Westbourne to form the Long Water and the Serpentine. The King believed Caroline paid for the improvements herself. He discovered only after her death in 1737 that she had persuaded Sir Robert Walpole, First Lord of the Treasury, to finance her projects.

The presence of royalty did not deter criminals from visiting the park and the King was once held up by a highwayman when he was out for his morning stroll.

After the defeat of the French at Montreal in 1760 there were scenes of rejoicing in Kensington Gardens and George II reviewed Colonel Burgoyne's Regiment of Light Horse. Two days later the King died of a heart attack as he was about to take his daily constitutional.

Although the gardens' best known monument is Queen Victoria's contribution — the enormous Albert Memorial ★ — the most loved is the statue of Peter Pan, whose creator J.M. Barrie considered the gardens an ideal place for nannies to perambulate with their small charges. Barrie presented the original swings in the playground at the north end of the Broad Walk.

The Serpentine Gallery — administered by the Arts Council — has frequent exhibitions of modern art and sculpture. (*Tel:* 01-402-6075.)

Kensington Palace (4 A-2) A royal palace since 1689, its State Apartments have been open to the public since 1899. The private rooms have been divided into apartments and provide London homes for the Prince and Princess of Wales, Princess Margaret, the Duke and Duchess of Gloucester and Prince and Princess Michael of Kent. William and Mary bought what was Nottingham House when they came to Kensington from Whitehall ★ to escape the damp river air that brought on the King's asthmatic attacks. Sir Christopher Wren was asked to extend the house and later monarchs employed Hawksmoor and William Kent to carry out further additions and alterations. Until George III came to the throne in 1760 it was one of the sovereign's principal homes. William and Mary, her sister Queen Anne, and George II all died here. Although George III lived at Kew ★ and Windsor ★, several of his children came to Kensington when the palace was divided into apartments, and his granddaughter, Princess Victoria of Kent, was born in the northeast corner room on the ground floor (below the State Apartments). Eighteen years later she awoke on a June morning to be told she was Queen. During her reign another Queen was born at the Palace — May of Teck who became George V's consort.

One of the splendours of the State Apartments is Wren's staircase with William Kent's murals show

Kensington Palace

ing members of the Royal Household looking down on those coming up the stairs. It is Kent's best work and his self-portrait has him holding a palette. The fine marble busts of eminent men — among them Handel and Garrick — were commissioned by George II's wife Caroline, whose influence and taste is still evident in the palace. The furniture and valuable paintings, many here for centuries, are all from the royal collections.

The large Carrara marble figure of Queen Victoria outside the palace on the Broad Walk in Kensington Gardens ★ was sculpted in 1893 by her daughter Princess Louise, Duchess of Argyll.

The State Apartments, extensively renovated in 1975, are open throughout the year and there is a separate exhibition of Court dresses. (*Tel: 01-937-9561.*)

King's Cross *(To north of Map 2, E-1)* The shabby, mean streets and railway yards get their name from a monument to George IV which stood for a brief fifteen years from 1830 where the Euston Road met Pentonville Road. The entrance to the station, built in 1851-52 by Thomas Cubitt's brother Lewis, has recently undergone a facelift that is not in keeping with the Victorian brickwork. The clock in the tower between the trainsheds came from the Great Exhibition of 1851. The legend that Queen Boudicca's burial place is under Platform 19 is most unreliable. The station is the terminus for trains from the north-east and Scotland.

King's Road, *Chelsea (To south of Map 4, D-5)* Since the 1960s a trendy street full of boutiques catering to followers of various pop-culture movements who parade up and down on Saturdays in colourful garments with exotic coiffures to match. Until 1830 the eastern part of Chelsea's principal street was a private road, once used by Charles II on his journeys to the west, and the public had to obtain a copper pass to use it. This was stamped with the words 'The King's Private Roads' and had his monogram on the other side. The Duke of York's Barracks is on the south side, and many attractive roads and squares lead off to the right and left.

Kingsway (2 E-4 etc.) The thoroughfare connecting the Strand and Holborn was cut through at the beginning of the 20th century when mechanised transport demanded wider roads. Twenty-eight acres that included some Tudor streets and a number of famous theatres, among them the old Gaiety, were demolished for the street which now has an underpass from Waterloo Bridge ★ leading into it.

Knightsbridge (4 E-3 etc.) An affluent residential and shopping area. The name appears to derive from the village on the edge of Hyde Park ★ where, in the 11th century, legend claims that two knights fought a battle on a bridge. In the 16th and 17th centuries there were a large number of inns in the district: the diarist Pepys frequented one, and his contemporary, the Restoration playwright Thomas Otway, mentions another, the Swan, in his play *The Soldier's Fortune.*

Harrods ★, the famous department store which invites customers to 'enter a different world', is the most luxurious of the several large shops in the area.

Along the road which links Piccadilly with Kensington there are a number of notable buildings. At Albert Gate one of the two large houses built by Thomas Cubitt is now the French Embassy. When they were erected in 1854 they were known as 'the two Gibraltars', because it was said they would never be taken. Knightsbridge Barracks, rebuilt by Sir Basil Spence in 1970 on the site of former Horse Guards premises, incongruously retains its Victorian pediment on the Hyde Park side. The barracks accommodate over 500 soldiers, and horses, of the Household Cavalry.

In the King's Road, Chelsea

Knightsbridge

Knightsbridge

SCALE 1:4 000 or 15 INCHES to 1 MILE

Lambeth (5 F-3 etc.) The modern borough stretching back from the Thames to far-off Streatham has little of the wealth and grandeur of Westminster, which it faces. The village the borough is named after is the area nearest the river, a place known to the Romans. Current and proposed archaeological excavations may soon reveal more about their occupation. With the exception of the Archbishop of Canterbury's official residence at Lambeth Palace ★, nothing earlier than the tightly packed Victorian streets filled with terrace houses survives, and many of these have recently been rebuilt. An example is Lambeth Walk — made famous in the song — now an unattractive pedestrian shopping precinct with upper level flats. Enormous redevelopment programmes have taken place on the waterfront since the Second World War. A large arts complex on the South Bank ★, begun in 1951 when the Royal Festival Hall ★ was built, should be complete when the Museum of Moving Image ★ opens (probably in the winter of 1987-88). The National Theatre ★, the National Film Theatre ★ and the Hayward Gallery ★ form part of the complex. They are not, however, Lambeth's only centres of culture.

This century *The Old Vic Theatre,* in the Waterloo Road, under the management of the indomitable Lilian Baylis, gave birth to The National Theatre which was housed here from 1963-76, and to the embryo ballet and opera companies known today as the Royal Ballet and English National Opera. Miss Baylis, who took over running the theatre which had been established as the Royal Coburg in 1818, brought Shakespeare into the repertoire in 1914, and employed for small salaries some of the country's best actors. She encouraged Ninette de Valois to put on ballet, and mounted opera productions in English.

Lambeth has no large museums, but smaller ones include the Museum of Garden History ★ and the Museum of the Pharmaceutical Society of Great Britain at 1 Lambeth High Street, which is open only by appointment. (*Tel: 01-735-9141.*)

Lambeth Bridge crosses the Thames at a spot where there was a horse ferry from the 16th century until a bridge was built in 1861. Hence Horseferry Road at the west end. The present five-span bridge dates from 1932. Between Westminster Bridge ★

and Lambeth Bridge lies St Thomas's Hospital ★. Modern operating theatres and wards are gradually replacing the Victorian hospital where Florence Nightingale founded a nursing school. Waterloo Station ★ is the terminus for trains from the southwest of England.

Lambeth Palace (5 F-4) The London residence of the Archbishop of Canterbury, and the oldest building in Lambeth. The land was bought in 1190 and a house erected seven years later. Nothing remains of this building, but the vaulted crypt under the present chapel survives from the 13th century. The red-brick Tudor gatehouse, where 'the dole' was handed out to the local poor until the middle of the last century, was built by Henry VII's devoted Cardinal-Archbishop John Morton. The Great Hall, 'a new old-fashioned Hall' according to Pepys, went up in 1663 after the palace was damaged during the Commonwealth. Although its style is Gothic, the decorative carvings are classical. The rebuilt Guard Room, where Thomas More was examined by Thomas Cromwell when he refused to take the Oath of Supremacy in 1534, retains its 14th-century timber roof. The Archbishop's offices and private apartments are in Edward Blore's 1829 neo-Tudor building.

The palace has witnessed numerous historic scenes, among them John Wyclif's trial for 'propositions, clearly heretical and depraved' in 1378, and Matthew Parker's consecration in December 1559 as the first truly Anglican Archbishop.

The Library, founded in 1610 by Archbishop Bancroft, claims to be the oldest public library in the country. It is now open only by appointment. (*Tel: 01-928-6222.*) It contains over 1,300 manuscripts, and such treasures as 9th-century Gospels, illuminated Bibles and the St Alban's Chronicle, a beautifully illustrated 15th-century history of England.

The Palace is very occasionally shown to parties, who must apply in writing. The gardens at the rear, known as Archbishop's Park (entrance in Carlisle Street), are open to the public.

Lancaster House, *Stable Yard, St James's* (5 B-2) *(See map on page 73)* The best example in London of an early 19th-century mansion; often used for Government receptions. It was first called York House, after the extravagant 'grand old Duke of York' who became heir presumptive in 1820 when his father George III died. His new status, he felt, required a grand house. Godolphin House was pulled down so Robert Smirke could build a massive palace between St James's Palace ★ and Buckingham Palace ★. The Duke, whose mistress Elizabeth, Duchess of Rutland, had very definite ideas about design, quarrelled with the architect and this ied to the appointment of Benjamin Wyatt in 1825. But the Duke died two years later, leaving an unfinished house and huge debts.

It became Stafford House when the Marquess of Stafford (later created Duke of Sutherland) bought it in 1827, employed Smirke to finish it and Sir Charles Barry to decorate part of the inside. Harriet, wife of the 2nd Duke, a great social and political hostess, was a close friend of Queen Victoria. The Queen, who came here many times, is reported to have once said: 'I have come from my house to your palace.' The 3rd Duke was a keen supporter of Garibaldi. When the Italian leader came to stay at Stafford House he was cheered through the streets. Millicent, the 4th Duchess, carried on the traditions of a society hostess, but this ceased in 1912 when the Duke disposed of the house to Lord Leverhulme who renamed it after his native royal duchy — Lancaster. Later he consigned the lease to the Government for the London Museum (housed here for some years) and a hospitality centre.

The plain exterior, of Bath stone with a Corinthian portico and *porte-cochère,* has a very splendid interior. The Staircase Hall is the best of its kind and date in the country. It rises to the roof, is lit by a huge clerestory, its patterned ceiling supported by enormous black caryatids. The walls of imitation marble have copies of paintings by Veronese. The State Rooms are open at weekends from Easter to autumn when not in use. (*Tel: 01-212-4784.*)

Leadenhall (3 E-4 etc.) In or leading off Leadenhall Street, which connects Aldgate to Cornhill and Mansion House ★, there are a number of important City institutions. The Baltic Exchange, where brokers deal in cargoes of grain, timber, oil and other commodities, is in St Mary Axe. The huge tower block belonging to an insurance company and the smaller P & O building are in a piazza, and looming over the area is Richard Rogers's new building for Lloyd's of London ★. Nearby is the London Metal Exchange.

The entrance to **Leadenhall Market**, where Pepys bought 'a leg of beef, a good one, for sixpence' in 1663, is in Whittington Street. The late-Victorian market building, with its elaborate arcades, follows the mediaeval street plan. It is a busy market, which has recently been renovated. Although many of the traditional shops selling fish, poultry, game and other delicacies are still here, souvenir shops and a wine bar have been opened to cater for the growing number of tourists.

When the present market was built in 1882 part of what appeared to be a substantial Roman public building was discovered. Later archaeological digs, including one in 1986 immediately to the north on the corner of Gracechurch Street, have provided firm evidence of a large basilica and forum covering nearly 8 acres. This most important area of the Roman city, dating from the end of the 1st century AD, extended to Cornhill.

Leicester Square (5 D-1) Lined with restaurants and large cinemas, and closed to traffic, the square is associated with leisure pursuits. In the middle of the 19th century, when many of the residents moved away, theatres, pleasure domes, museums and hotels took their place. Leicester Fields, as it was called in the 17th century, has changed a great deal since Robert Sidney, 2nd Earl of Leicester, was granted permission to build himself a mansion to the north of the Royal Mews (now Trafalgar Square) in 1631. The square came into being about 40 years later when houses were erected around the fields. Leicester House became a royal residence in 1717 when the Prince of Wales (later George II) moved out of St James's Palace after a quarrel with his father. His son Frederick, Prince of Wales, died here in 1751 after receiving a blow from a cricket ball. The house ceased to have royal connections in 1767 and became a natural history museum before demolition in 1791. The Empire Cinema is on the site today.

The houses around the square were initially

occupied by aristocratic families. Artists and writers arrived in later years. They included Hogarth, Sir Joshua Reynolds and John Singleton Copley. Another resident was the surgeon John Hunter, whose collection of physiological specimens forms the nucleus of the Hunterian Museum ★ .

The most spectacular place of entertainment in the square was the Great Globe built in 1851 by the geographer James Wyld. Here 'the congregation in London of the different nations and races of our empire' could view from a four-tiered gallery 'the physical features of the earth, the horizontal surface being on the scale of an inch to ten miles, and mountains, shown by mechanical devices, on thrice that scale...' Maps, atlases and globes were also displayed. Although it was a great attraction, the Globe was sold eleven years later and demolished.

The gardens were in private ownership until Albert Grant, an MP of dubious distinction, presented them to the Board of Works in 1874. Before he did so he commissioned James Knowles to lay them out. Knowles designed the marble statue of Shakespeare, and was also responsible for placing stone busts of former residents in each corner — Reynolds with his hat at a rakish angle, the lampooning artist William Hogarth, the surgeon John Hunter, and Isaac Newton who lived in nearby St Martin's Street.

By the beginning of the 20th century three famous theatres had been built around the square — the Alhambra, the Empire, and Daly's (where Lehar's *The Merry Widow* was first produced in England). These were all pulled down between the wars and replaced respectively by the present Odeon, Empire and Warner cinemas. The Society of West End Theatre's half-price ticket booth (for day of performance only) is on the west side of the square, a few yards from the captivating statue of Charlie Chaplin as the tramp.

Leighton House, *12 Holland Park Road, Kensington (To west of Map 4)* A museum and art gallery with a permanent display of High Victorian art. The plain brick façade gives no clue that the inside is one of the most exotic in London. The house was designed by Frederic Leighton, President of the Royal Academy, with the help of his architect friend George Aitchison. Leighton wanted a spacious studio and an out-of-the-ordinary setting where he could entertain his many friends. On the ground floor is the Arab Hall with a small fountain. The walls are lined with rich dark-blue tiles brought from Damascus, Cairo and Rhodes. The painter moved in during 1866 and died here 30 years later, exactly a month after he became Lord Leighton, the only English artist to be created a peer. Besides his own works, the collection contains paintings, drawings and sculpture by Leighton's friends and contemporaries — Burne-Jones, Alma-Tadema, Millais, Poynter and Watts. (*Tel: 01-602-3316.*)

Lincoln's Inn (2 F-4) One of the four Inns of Court where eminent lawyers have their chambers and student lawyers train for their profession. The Honourable Society of Lincoln's Inn has occupied the present site to the west of Chancery Lane since the 15th century, although the society has been in

Lincoln's Inn and Lincoln's Inn Fields

SCALE 1:4 000 or 15 INCHES to 1 MILE

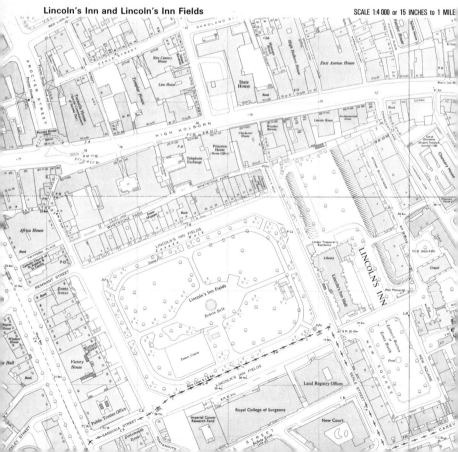

Lincoln's Inn

existence since 1292. The name derives either from the title of Henry de Lacy, Earl of Lincoln, one of Edward I's advisers, or from Thomas de Lincoln, the King's Serjeant (principal law officer) at Holborn. Above the gatehouse on Chancery Lane are the arms of Henry VIII, the Earl of Lincoln, and Sir Thomas Lovell, who is thought to have built it in 1518. The Old Hall, put up between 1490 and 1520, was used as the Court of Chancery from 1733 to 1837 and was the fictional setting for the case of Jarndyce v. Jarndyce in Dickens' *Bleak House*. Although Inigo Jones is sometimes credited with building the Chapel — raised on vaulted arches under which people can walk — early in the 17th century, it is almost certainly by John Clarke. Other buildings have been added for the lawyers in later centuries. These include the chambers in New Square c.1690, the classical Stone Buildings in 1774-80, and the New Hall and Library in 1843. This hall houses many legal portraits and G.F. Watts' mural, *Justice — a Hemicycle of Lawgivers*, which depicts 33 great lawyers of history. The library, the oldest in London, was founded in 1497 and contains over 70,000 law books and is the most comprehensive legal library in the country. Only members of the Inn may use it. Past distinguished members of the Inn have been Sir Thomas More; John Donne; the historian Thomas Babbington Macaulay; John Henry, Cardinal Newman; and seven Prime Ministers, among them Robert Walpole, Benjamin Disraeli and Lord Melbourne. The Inn suffered little damage during the Second World War. It is usually possible for visitors to see the chapels and halls by asking at the Porter's Lodge (11a New Square) for permission. (*Tel: 01-405-6360.*)

Lincoln's Inn Fields (2 F-4) An archway leads from New Square, Lincoln's Inn, onto a large grass expanse with fine plane trees. Inigo Jones is thought to have laid out the square and to have been responsible for a number of the houses; one, possibly by him, survives, No. 59-60. Next door a very similar building — No. 57-58 — was built a century later in 1730 by Henry Joynes. Newcastle House on the northwest corner was rebuilt this century by Sir Edwin Lutyens, who retained the style of the old house, part of which was attributed to Wren. The Royal College of Surgeons occupies the south side, its classical façade the work of Sir Charles Barry in 1835-37. The interior, which houses the Hunterian Museum★, was partially reconstructed after the Second World War. The College

owns Holbein's cartoon of Henry VIII granting a charter to the Company of Barber-Surgeons (from which the College separated in 1745): the panel itself is in the Company's livery hall. In the middle of the north side, No. 13 is of great interest to architects and architectural historians — the Sir John Soane's Museum★. This was the home of Soane, architect of the Bank of England, who left his house and collections to the nation when he died in 1837, stipulating that everything should be preserved exactly as he left it. Among its treasures are eight in the series of Hogarth paintings *The Rake's Progress.*

Linley Sambourne House, *18 Stafford Terrace, Kensington (To west of Map 4, A-3)* The most perfectly preserved Victorian house in London. From 1874 until his death in 1910 it was the home of Linley Sambourne, the artist and political cartoonist of *Punch*. His descendants — among them the theatre designer Oliver Messel — took great care to ensure the wall hangings, decoration, furniture and pictures remained as in the 1890s. In 1980 they presented the house to the nation. The Victorian Society is responsible for its upkeep. Open about twice a week between March and October. (*Tel: 01-994-1019.*)

Little Venice, *Paddington* (1 A-3 & B-3) The tree-lined streets and wide expanse of water at the

Little Venice

Little Venice   SCALE 1:4 000 or 15 INCHES to 1 MILE

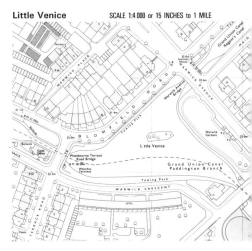

eastern section of the Regent's Canal★ were likened to Venice by Robert Browning, but the name 'Little Venice' was coined for the neighbourhood by an enterprising estate agent only in the 1950s. The area has attracted many artists to the houseboats and tall Victorian houses along the canal banks. Canal cruises and waterbuses leave from Blomfield Road and Warwick Crescent for Camden Town or London Zoo★.

Lloyd's of London (3 E-4) The world's largest single insurance market occupies a revolutionary new building on the corner of Leadenhall Street and Lime Street. Designed by Richard Rogers and Partners as a simple rectangle with walls of sparkling glass, it opened in 1986. Six towers contain all services such as lavatories and heating plants. The external glass lifts, the first of their kind in London, carry staff and visitors to each of the galleries that look down on the market where

Lloyd's of London

business is conducted. This Underwriting Room, where there is an income of over £20 million in premiums every working day, is on the ground floor. Although the ultra-modern new room incorporates all the features of the computer age, the Casualty Book and Lutine Bell are its focal point. The bell, recovered from a ship which sank in 1799, is rung on ceremonial occasions or to announce important news: two peals for good news, one for bad. It is nowadays rarely rung when a ship is lost at sea. The Adam Room, where the Council of Lloyd's meets, is over 200 years old. It came originally from a house in Wiltshire to the old Lime Street building and has been re-erected on the eleventh gallery.

Business at Lloyd's is transacted by nearly 29,000 members grouped into 370 syndicates. Members accept insurance risks for their own profit or loss and are liable to the full extent of their personal wealth to meet their insurance commitment. Trading began in 1688 in Edward Lloyd's coffee house in Tower Street where shipowners and merchants met to exchange news. It was soon recognised as a place to obtain marine insurance, and gradually expanded to accept other business. Almost anything from fleets of ships, aircraft and satellites to nuclear power stations, racehorses and mundane household contents can be insured here.

A viewing area has been opened on gallery four. For the first time in 300 years the public can see how the market works. An exhibition, complete with a recreation of Edward Lloyd's coffee house, traces the history of the society and insurance, and leads onto a gallery which overlooks the Underwriting Room. The entrance is in Lime Street. (*Tel: 01-623-7100 X 3786.*)

Lombard Street (3 D-4 & E-4) Ever since merchants from Lombardy set up in business as moneylenders in this street in the 13th century, it has been the banking centre of London. The decorative bank signs — copies of mediaeval ones — were put up to celebrate the coronation of Edward VII in 1902: prior to this they had been banned for over 200 years because Charles II feared they might fall on pedestrians. Several of the bank buildings are of architectural interest. On the corner facing the Mansion House★ is the church of **St Mary Woolnoth** which has withstood many attempts by developers to demolish it. Built by Nicholas Hawksmoor in 1716-27, its lofty interior, planned like a Roman atrium, is a pleasing contrast to the highly original but formidable exterior.

London Bridge (3 D-5) The bridge is a few yards upstream from the site of London's earliest known Thames crossing, a Roman one. The 1973 bridge, of three spans with six lanes, was needed to cope with the increased flow of traffic. Rennie's bridge, put up 150 years earlier, was dismantled at the same time and sold to Lake Havasu City in Arizona for $1 million. Neither of these bridges, however, can compare with the elaborately ornamented mediaeval London Bridge which took 30 years to construct in the 12th century. Rents from the houses and shops built over the nineteen piers contributed to its maintenance. Of all the sumptuous buildings, the most remarkable was Nonsuch House, 'a beautiful and chargeable piece of work' according to the Elizabethan chronicler John Stow. In the middle of the 14th century there were 198 houses on the bridge, and all trade from the Continent was channelled over it. 'Comparable in itself to a little City', noted the royal surveyor John Norden, it brought prosperity to the City and in gratitude a number of merchants made bequests in their wills to 'God and the Bridge'. All subsequent City bridges have been maintained from these early endowments.

Between the Roman bridge, thought to have been erected about AD 50, and the famous mediaeval one, there were probably several wooden bridges, including one pulled down by invading Vikings, giving rise to the nursery rhyme: 'London bridge is falling down...'

London Bridge City (3 E-5 etc.) On the south bank between Tower Bridge and London Bridge, crumbling Victorian warehouses backing onto Tooley Street have been renovated or replaced in a multimillion pound development financed by Kuwaiti interests. A private hospital and offices, some with a shiny cream cladding or glass panels, blend with mellow brickwork on the restored buildings and brighten up what was a dark, dull district. A galleria, with shops, restaurants and bars, under an iron and glass domed arch, resembles the former Crystal Palace. A river path is also planned. The grey bulk of HMS Belfast ★ looks a little sombre against the sunny new buildings.

London Coliseum (5 D-1)

Home of English National Opera (formerly Sadler's Wells Opera) since 1968. The theatre — 'the house that Stoll built' — was designed by Frank Matcham for the impresario Sir Oswald Stoll and opened in 1903 with a variety show that caused a sensation. On the revolving stage — the first in England — Stoll 'ran' the Derby: the spectacle of six horses being urged on by their jockeys was a theatrical triumph. Many great artists from Grock, Sir Henry Wood and Sarah Bernhardt to the members of Diaghilev's Ballet Company, John Gielgud and Noël Coward have appeared on its stage. In the 1940s the theatre became a home for American musicals, and was briefly a cinema. The richly decorated interior with classical emblems in relief, massive gold leaf sculptures and beautiful mosaics is most impressive. English National Opera, whose wide repertoire is performed in English, are in residence from August until May. The theatre — London's largest with 2,358 seats — is usually rented to London Festival Ballet and foreign ballet companies for the remaining months.

London Dungeon, *28-34 Tooley Street* (3 E-5) The seamier side of London's past is set out in a series of gruesome displays showing mediaeval tortures, executions and the horrors of the plague. The cold, damp railway arches under London Bridge station lend atmosphere to the morbid but evocative tableaux which fascinate children. Young children and those of a nervous disposition who may find the rats and skeletons frightening are duly warned. (*Tel: 01-403-0606.*)

London Library, *14 St James's Square* (5 C-1) A subscription library founded in 1841 by Thomas Carlyle, who 'ignited' a group of eminent men to help him start it. Carlyle, annoyed at the hours he had to wait for books at the British Museum, determined to have a library where a gentleman could borrow books not normally available in circulating libraries. Subscribers today have immediate access to over one million books. Some were published centuries ago; others are brand new. It is especially strong on history and topography. Light literature and scientific and medical books will not be found on the shelves. The original aim of the library to supply 'good books in all departments of knowledge' is still adhered to. New members are always welcome. (*Tel: 01-930-7705.*)

London Palladium, *Argyll Street* (2 B-5) The decline of the music hall has seen this theatre's long association with variety give way to musicals in the 1980s, although occasional international stars (Shirley Maclaine and the late Bing Crosby in recent years) have followed in the footsteps of Palladium 'immortals' like Judy Garland and Danny Kaye. Designed by Frank Matcham for the impresario Walter Gibbons, who wanted to out-do his rivals at the London Coliseum ★, the Palace and the Hippodrome, it opened with a variety programme in

December 1910. The classic façade and interior with brilliant colouring and features like the Palm Court at the back of the stalls were considered the height of luxury in their day, as was the installation of box-to-box telephones: a great talking point. These have long since gone but the foyer, auditorium and first-floor bar retain the air of Edwardian splendour.

London Planetarium, *Marylebone Road* (1 F-3) A popular tourist attraction, next door to Madame Tussauds. Shows illustrating the stars in the universe take place during the day. The Zeiss projector has 20,000 separate parts capable of

In the London Planetarium

creating 9,000 stars on the domed ceiling. In the evenings the building is used as a Laserium: shows with pop and classical music augment the laser beam displays. (*Tel: 01-486-1121.*)

London Silver Vaults, *Chancery House, 53-64 Chancery Lane* (2 F-4) A vast quantity of antique silver is stored, put on display by retailers and sold in underground vaults which until a few decades ago were private safe deposits. The present premises with shops were rebuilt in 1953 as the result of bomb damage.

London Transport Museum, *The Piazza, Covent Garden* (2 E-5) Public transport from 1830 to today is illustrated with examples of buses and underground trains, beginning with a replica of George Shillibeer's Horse Omnibus which initiated London's first public bus service. There are several Victorian horse-drawn buses, a tram, early motor buses and their more modern successors. The underground train on view was in use in the 1860s. Visitors may board most of the vehicles, and operate the controls. The museum has a collection of posters, photographs, maps and records concerning the development of transport in London. (*Tel: 01-379-6344.*)

London Wall (3 D-3 etc.) A street running from Broad Street to Aldersgate along the line of the City's Roman wall. Severe damage during the Second World War necessitated the complete rebuilding of the street, which is now lined with modern office blocks. A remnant of the wall with mediaeval additions stands on the corner of Noble Street. This is almost opposite the Museum of

London ★ in whose garden there is visible evidence of a Roman fort.

London Zoo, *Regent's Park (To north of Map 1, F-1)* The gardens of the Zoological Society of London, whose headquarters are here, contain a large collection of animals, birds and reptiles. This, the world's oldest zoo, was laid out in 1826 by Decimus Burton for the Society which had just been founded by Sir Stamford Raffles and Sir Humphry Davy, and it has expanded from an original 5 acres to 35. The initial intake of animals included those given by George IV, who arranged for the royal menagerie to be transferred to the park. Two years later an elephant, an anaconda, 100 rattlesnakes and other creatures which had been on show at the Tower of London were also moved here. In Victorian days a reptile house, an aquarium and an insect house were added, each being the first in the world. Other new buildings and terraces have been constructed throughout the zoo's history, principally to provide better conditions for the growing numbers of animals, reptiles and birds and to make the surroundings in which they are seen more like their natural environments. The feeding of the sealions, the elephants' bath time, the nocturnal animals in the Clore Pavilion's Moonlight World, and the Snowdon aviary are always popular. In the Children's Zoo, the animals may be handled.

The Zoological Society still maintains the aims set out in its original royal charter to further 'the advancements of Zoology and Animal Physiology' and to introduce 'new and curious subjects of the Animal Kingdom'. It is a major centre for research, and there is an animal hospital in the grounds.

At London Zoo

London Zoo attracts many visitors. Its upkeep is very expensive and for the first time in its history has recently received financial assistance from the government to better the facilities for animals and visitors, and for redevelopment plans. Open all year round. (*Tel: 01-722-3333.*)

Lord's Cricket Ground, *St John's Wood* (1 C-1) Headquarters of the Marylebone Cricket Club (MCC) and now of the Cricket Council, which has governed the game since 1970 when it took over from the MCC; also the grounds of the Middlesex County Cricket Club. In 1787 Thomas Lord enclosed 7 acres of fields behind his back garden. This is now

Dorset Square but a plaque commemorates that it was here the MCC was formed. Increased rents forced the club to play at several places until 1813 when the present grounds at St John's Wood were taken. Each time Thomas Lord moved the club the turf went too, so that 'the noblemen and Gentlemen of the MCC should be able to play on the same footing as before'. The club bought the freehold in 1866 and erected a grandstand; 11 years later the Middlesex County Cricket Club made Lord's its grounds. The first test match here, when England beat the Australians, was in 1884; the first against the West Indies in 1928, New Zealand in 1931, India the next year and Pakistan in 1958. New stands, a tavern and a block of flats have been put up around the grounds.

The Cricket Memorial Gallery has a unique collection of pictures, trophies and ephemera illustrating the history of cricket. The Ashes are kept in the gallery. It is open on match days; otherwise by appointment. (*Tel: 01-289-1611.*)

'Henry VIII and his Six Wives' — at Madame Tussaud's

Madame Tussaud's, *Marylebone Road* (1 F-3) The famous waxworks museum has been one of London's greatest attractions for over 150 years. Madame Tussaud, an art tutor at the court of Louis XVI, came to England in 1802 when attendances at the exhibition of lifesize wax models she had inherited fell off after the French Revolution. She brought with her the death masks of guillotined heads she had made, and after successfully touring the country for years opened a display of tableaux in Baker Street in 1835. Her grandchildren moved to the present site in 1884. Though the original collection was largely destroyed by fire in 1925, some of the death masks, including Marat's with the mark of Charlotte Corday's fatal knife wound, are in the Chamber of Horrors, alongside notorious murderers and macabre items like the gallows used at Hertford Gaol until the abolition of hanging in 1965, and the bell from Newgate, tolled to summon Londoners to executions. Less gruesome tableaux feature lifesize models of royalty, politicians, film stars, pop singers and people whose names are frequently in the news. (*Tel: 01-935-6861.*)

The Mall (5 C-2) The broad avenue with its distinctive red asphalt makes a regal approach to Buckingham Palace ★, especially on state occasions when flags fly between the double rows of plane trees. It is, however, a more modern road than the one laid out after the Restoration as an avenue to St James's Palace. This had an alley

Marble Arch and Speakers' Corner

SCALE 1:4 000 or 15 INCHES to 1 MILE

where the game 'paille mail', a type of croquet, was played. A popular place for royalty and fashionable London to promenade in the 17th century, it also attracted the courtesans. The garden of the most celebrated, Charles II's Nell Gwyn, overlooked The Mall. The line of the old Mall can still be seen in the horse ride that runs below Carlton House Terrace ★.

The present wide road was opened in 1911. With Admiralty Arch ★ and the Queen Victoria Memorial ★ it forms part of the national tribute to the Queen-Empress who died in 1901. Each of the long line of lamp posts on the processional route is topped with a sailing ship — not Nelson's fleet so he can look down on it from his column (as some like to imagine), but old-fashioned galleons. Near the Admiralty there are statues commemorating Captain Cook and the Royal Marines. Two entrances on Carlton House Terrace ★ to the east of the steps to the Duke of York's Column ★ lead to the **Institute for Contemporary Arts** (Tel: 01-930-0493), where there is a theatre, cinemas, art gallery and restaurant, and to The Mall Galleries where regular changing art exhibitions are held. A statue to George VI is further along the terrace. On the wall of Marlborough House ★ the plaque commemorating Queen Mary was unveiled in 1967. St James's Palace ★ and Clarence House ★, the London home of Queen Elizabeth the Queen Mother, look across to St James's Park which runs almost the entire length of the southern approach to Buckingham Palace.

Mansion House (3 D-4) The official residence and office of the Lord Mayor of London during his or her year of office. George Dance the elder's well-proportioned classical building, incorporating a great hall 'built after the Egyptian manner', is London's original Mansion House. Until it was completed the Lord Mayor lived in his private house and entertained the City's guests at his livery company's hall. The house was erected on land leased in perpetuity from the church of St Mary Woolnoth, which receives £10 a year from the Corporation. Dance, who drew his inspiration from Colen Campbell's *Vitruvius Britannicus* and Inigo Jones, spent over 15 years working on the building. On 9 November 1752, following a ball at Guildhall after the Lord Mayor's Banquet, Lord Mayor Alderman Crisp Gascoyne became the first resident. The majority of the sumptuously decorated state rooms were then finished, the exception being the Egyptian Hall with its colonnade of forty Corinthian columns and a clerestory of 40 windows. Work continued here for a further seven years, and although the ceiling has been altered a number of times the present barrel-vaulted one, restored in 1931, is based on the 1759 designs. The niches were filled with marble statues a century later. Large banquets, balls, receptions and public meetings are frequently held here. The state rooms are shown to visitors on certain Saturdays in the year. Written application should be made to the Secretary.

It is likely that the vista from the portico of the Mansion House will radically change in the near future. There are plans to redevelop the triangle between Poultry and Queen Victoria Street.

Marble Arch (1 E-5) At the northern end of Park Lane is John Nash's triumphal entrance, originally

Marble Arch

sited in front of Buckingham Palace. Designed to resemble the Arch of Constantine in Rome, it was placed outside the palace in 1828 and moved to its present site 22 years later. Richard Westmacott sculpted the relief on the north side, E.H. Baily those on the south. A statue of George IV, intended to go on top, was put up instead in Trafalgar Square. Only senior members of the royal family and the King's Troop, the Royal Horse Artillery, may pass through its gates.

Marlborough House (5 C-2) *(See map on page 73)* The large red-brick mansion on The Mall was handed over to the Commonwealth Secretariat in 1959 and is now used by the countries of the Commonwealth for conferences and receptions. Before this it had been a London residence of members of the royal family since 1817 when the lease granted to the Churchill family ran out. Sarah, Duchess of Marlborough, acquired the lease in 1709 and employed Sir Christopher Wren — to build her 'a strong, plain and convenient' home but she fell out with 'the poor old man', and sent for Louis Laguerre to paint the walls. The irascible Sarah, Queen Anne's friend and wife of John Churchill, the 1st Duke, died here in 1744.

When Princess Charlotte, the only child of the Prince Regent, married Prince Leopold of Saxe-Coburg, the house was renovated for them, but Charlotte died in childbirth in November 1817 and the Prince (Queen Victoria's Uncle Leopold) occupied it until he became King of the Belgians in 1831. Queen Adelaide made it her home after William IV died.

The most memorable resident was the future Edward VII. Queen Victoria's heir ordered extensive alterations when he and his bride, Princess Alexandra of Denmark, made this their London home in 1863. To the chagrin of his mother, the lavish entertainment offered to fashionable society at 'the best kept house in London' was the talk of the town. To belong to 'the Marlborough House Set' meant one had arrived socially. The Queen frowned on some of the Prince of Wales's friends, who comprised not only the aristocracy but bankers, businessmen and the odd raffish figure that 'Bertie' liked around him. George V, born here in 1865, returned as Prince of Wales during his father's reign. Queen Alexandra spent her 15 years as a widow in the house that had been her London home for almost 40 years, and it was also where Queen Mary came when George V died.

The murals commissioned by Sarah, Duchess of Marlborough, to depict Churchill's victories at Blenheim and Ramillies are among the many fine features of the house. There is a ceiling by Gentileschi, painted for the Queen's House at Greenwich ★ and taken from there by Sarah with Queen Anne's consent. The house is occasionally open to the public by prior arrangement if not in use; guided tours may be arranged. *(Tel: 01-930-9249.)*

Marylebone or *St Mary-le-bone* (2 B-4 etc.) The district north of Oxford Street takes its name from a church dedicated to Our Lady which stood on the edge of a stream called the Bourne. The church was moved from what is now Oxford Street c. 1400 and rebuilt where the present parish church stands in Marylebone Road. Opposite it, at the top of Marylebone High Street, was the manor house.

Early in the 18th century this was owned by Edward Harley, Earl of Oxford and Mortimer. He developed the land, building square blocks of large houses, many of which became the consulting rooms of the medical profession. Margaret Cavendish Harley, who inherited the estate, married William Bentinck, 2nd Duke of Portman, and continued to build, giving all the streets and squares family names. Marylebone High Street, despite a lot of rebuilding, retains a village atmosphere.

The creation of Regent's Park ★ prompted more development north of the Marylebone Road, where today one finds Madame Tussauds ★ and the London Planetarium ★, the Royal Academy of Music ★ and Marylebone Station, a terminus for trains from Oxford and Buckinghamshire. Further south the Wigmore Hall ★ and the Wallace Collection ★ are important artistic centres in the area. The late Victorian Gothic Roman Catholic church of St James's Spanish Place in George Street replaces the chapel used by the Spanish ambassador when he occupied Manchester House (see the Wallace Collection ★).

Mayfair (5 A-1 etc.) A fashionable residential area with smart shops and business premises between Regent Street ★ and Park Lane ★. The name comes from a fair held for 15 days each May on land south of modern Curzon Street. As the Court moved west from Whitehall to St James's Palace, the area was developed by wealthy members of the aristocracy who built themselves large mansions. The family which contributed most were the Grosvenors (later dukes of Westminster). They laid out Grosvenor Square ★ and the present Duke is landlord of a great deal of Mayfair property.

Shepherd Market, where the May Fair was held in the 17th century until notoriety caused its suppression, was laid out by Edward Shepherd c. 1735. Many of the buildings in the narrow streets and passageways have been rebuilt but the 'village in Mayfair' has managed to keep the atmosphere of another century. Several streets near the market retain their Georgian houses, and one or two mews still exist, although the stables have been converted to expensive bijou homes.

In Bond Street ★, with its specialist shops, it is not hard to imagine the days when it catered exclusively to the carriage trade.

Melbury Road, *Kensington (To west of Map 4, A-3)* The curving road west of the Commonwealth Institute ★ had several famous residents and has some houses of great architectural interest, the most extraordinary being Tower House at No. 29. This was designed in 1880 by the mediaevalist William Burges 'as a model residence of the 15th century' when he wanted a fantastic retreat. G.F. Watts, the painter, lived at No. 6 in a Norman Shaw house; Luke Fildes in another (now No. 31). Shaw, architect of New Scotland Yard ★, designed a number of houses in the street, including No. 8, the home of Marcus Stone, who illustrated many of Dickens's works. The Pre-Raphaelite artist Holman Hunt was at No. 18 and the sculptor Sir William Thornycroft at No. 29.

Mercers' Hall, *Becket House, Ironmonger Lane* (3 D-3) In order of precedence the Mercers' are the first of the twelve Great Livery Companies, and their hall — part of an office block — is one of the newest, being rebuilt in 1955 to replace its predecessor which was destroyed in the Second World War. The chapel (the only one in a livery hall) and hall contain some woodwork and stained glass from the old building, and carvings in the panelled court room and dining room are attributed to Grinling Gibbons. The Mercers', originally merchants trading principally in textiles, are extremely wealthy and have since 1509 administered St Paul's School, now at Barnes. They also maintain St Paul's Girl's School, Whittington College and the Trinity Almshouses at Greenwich ★. Contact the City Information Centre for occasional opening times. (*Tel: 01-606-3030.*)

Merchant Taylors' Hall, *30 Threadneedle Street* (3 E-3) The largest of all the livery halls. The company, which ranks either sixth or seventh (see Dowgate Hill ★ for explanation), has been on this site for over six centuries. Although extensive restoration was necessary after the roof was burnt in the Great Fire, and there was severe bomb damage in 1940, small sections of the library, court room and great kitchen can claim to have been in continuous use since early in the 15th century. Some pieces of the mediaeval and later building have been left uncovered for visitors to see. The company entertained James I when he arrived in London from Scotland, and in the hall it is thought the National Anthem was sung for the first time in 1607. The historian John Stow and Sir Christopher Wren were members of the company which today, having no connection with its former trades, maintains almshouses, governs a number of schools and awards scholarships at Oxford and Cambridge. The company owns several prized manuscripts. Occasional opening times from the City Information Centre. (*Tel: 01-606-3030.*)

Middlesex Guildhall, *Broad Sanctuary* (5 D-3) The assertively Gothic building facing Parliament Square was put up in 1913 as civic headquarters for the County of Middlesex, which was absorbed into the now disbanded Greater London Council in 1965. The Crown Court for the area covered by Middlesex is still here.

Middle Temple (3 A-4) One of the four Inns of Court, it has common entrances with Inner Temple with which it shares Temple Church ★. Although quite separate the precincts of the two Inns are referred to as the Temple ★.

Millbank (5 E-5) The wide road between Great College Street and Vauxhall Bridge on which tall modern buildings and the classical façade of the Tate Gallery ★ face the Thames. They are a good deal more impressive than anything here in previous centuries. Originally on the riverside road (named after a mill which stood opposite Victoria Tower Gardens) there was a large 19th-century penitentiary and some houses put up by Thomas Cubitt. These have been replaced by buildings which are examples of different styles of 20th-century architecture.

Minories (3 F-4) A street of little distinction today. It is the terminus of the Docklands Light Railway.

Until a bomb destroyed it in 1940, the church of the Holy Trinity of the Minoresses (hence the name) stood on the site of a convent which belonged to the nuns of the order of St Clare up to the reign of Henry VIII. During an excavation in Clare Street in 1964 archaeologists found the tomb of Anne Mowbray, the wife of Richard Duke of York, who died in 1481 and was buried at the convent. The area was associated with gunsmiths until the 18th century. The banker Nathan Meyer Rothschild, founder of the English Rothschild bank, lived at No. 100 early in the 19th century.

The Monument, *Monument Street* (3 E-4) When the City was rebuilt in the 17th century, it was decided to commemorate the Great Fire, not at the

The Monument

spot in Cock Lane where it ended but near Thomas Farrinor's bakery in Pudding Lane where it started. After a number of proposals by Christopher Wren, his idea for a flaming gilded urn above a fluted Doric column was erected. It is 202 ft. high, and panels on the base are inscribed with descriptions of what happened on the night of 2 September 1666. A spiral staircase of 311 steps leads to a platform beneath the urn from where there are good views of the City. (*Tel: 01-626-2717.*)

Museum of Garden History, *St Mary-at-Lambeth* (5 E-4) The world's first museum devoted to the history of gardening. Displays explain the work of the 17th-century explorers who sailed the seas in search of plants, and show the flowers and trees they brought back. Appropriately, the museum is housed in the redundant parish church where John Tradescant and his son (also John), gardeners to Charles I and Henrietta Maria, are buried. They both travelled extensively in Europe, Russia and Virginia, gathering plants which they introduced to England. Their tomb in the churchyard lies beside that of another traveller who went to the Pacific in search of plants — Bligh of the *Bounty.*

The church was saved from demolition in 1977 by the Tradescant Trust which runs the museum and is gradually turning the old churchyard into a historical garden with a 17th-century flavour. (*Tel: 01-261-1891.*)

Museum of London, *London Wall* (3 C-3) *(See map on page 21)* The history of London and its people chronologically set out in imaginative and fascinating displays. Opened in December 1976 in a building conceived to house the amalgamated collections of the old London Museum and Guildhall Museum, its design has been praised and won awards. The entrance, partly built over a traffic roundabout, is from a walkway high above street level. The first displays cover prehistoric times and lead into a section on Londinium (Roman London). Here on Roman pavements discovered in the City archaeological finds have been used to reconstruct rooms of houses in the 1st and 4th centuries AD. A small viewing platform looks down on a garden where a section of a Roman fort survives.

The development of London is illustrated in a number of ways: occasionally in models as with the Tower of London. Something of the enormity of the Great Fire of 1666 can be appreciated in an audiovisual show. Georgian, Victorian and modern London are recreated in room settings, and a typical street of shops gives an indication of how Londoners lived and worked in the 18th, 19th and 20th centuries. Even some Art Deco lifts from Selfridges have been preserved to jog memories and bring atmosphere to the sections covering the past 50 years. The Lord Mayor's sumptuously decorated coach with its beautifully painted panels is on permanent exhibition in the museum, except on the second Saturday in November when it is used in the Lord Mayor's show. The history of certain districts, of subjects like the music hall or cinemas, or of specific industries, are often the subject of special displays, and the museum also mounts larger theme exhibitions. There are few aspects of London not covered in this exciting, very popular museum.

The museum's Department of Urban Archaeology, responsible for archaeological excavations in the City, has its headquarters here. There are regular lectures and films, education programmes for schools, research departments, a library,

A room setting in the Museum of London

conservation departments and good collections of costumes, London maps, paintings, drawings and prints. (*Tel: 01-600-3699.*)

Museum of Mankind, *Burlington Gardens* (5 B-1) *(See map on page 62)* The Ethnography Department of the British Museum. The collections devoted to the different races of man and their various environments are displayed in temporary, atmospheric settings which evoke tribal villages and their indigenous populations. Certain treasures like the Mayan turquoise masks and crystal skull are permanently on view. The museum's holdings of material from West Africa, the Americas and the South Seas is especially fine. Until 1970 the collections were at the British Museum but for more display space were moved to Sir James Pennethorne's large, airy building, originally built 1866-69 for the University of London. The museum has research facilities, and programmes of lectures. (*Tel: 01-437-2224.*)

Museum of Moving Image (5 F-2) Next door to the National Film Theatre ★ and forming part of the South Bank arts complex, the museum devoted to the history and development of the film industry is scheduled to open in the winter of 1987-88. Twenty sections in the permanent collection will cover the earliest days of cinema, its progress, production techniques, the story of television and an animation workshop. Live shows, lectures, screenings of classic films from the National Film Archive and exhibitions during the year are also planned. (*Tel: 01-928-3232.*)

Museum of Order of St John, *St John's Gate* (3 B-1) A small museum maintained by the Most Venerable Order of the Hospital of St John, an English Protestant revival of the mediaeval Order which came to Clerkenwell ★ and founded a priory c. 1140. On show are items relating to the Order of St John outside Malta. These include a 15th-century Flemish triptych, books and manuscripts, and there are objects relating to aspects of the ecclesiastical, medical and military life of the Order. In the section devoted to the history of the St John Ambulance is the uniform of Queen Elizabeth the Queen Mother. The Gatehouse, built in 1504, is on the site of an earlier gateway, once the main entrance to the Priory of Clerkenwell. The Order acquired it in 1874. The Grand Priory Church in St John's Square has been destroyed and rebuilt several times, but the late-Norman crypt has miraculously survived the Peasants' Revolt, the Reformation, fires and bomb damage. Visitors to the museum may also take guided tours of the church and gatehouse. The reference library is open by appointment. (*Tel: 01-253-6644.*)

National Army Museum, *Royal Hospital Road* *(See map on page 69)* The history of the British army from the reign of Henry VIII until the 1982 campaign in the Falkland Islands. A number of tanks and two 5.51 guns on carriages are on the pavement outside the building. Some of the collections came from Sandhurst when the museum opened in 1971, and further material is on semi-permanent loan. The corridors leading to the chronological displays are lined with standards, guidons and colours of the British Army. In rooms on two floors the campaigns and functions of the army are illustrated with models, contemporary equipment and personal ephemera that show the changing nature of war. The large number of guns on display is impressive. On a separate floor army uniforms from different periods are complemented by a small amount of furniture and pictures. The decorations of famous field-marshals (Gough, Wolseley, Kitchener and Roberts) and their wives are in frames along one wall. The museum has collections of paintings and prints that include works by Romney, Reynolds and Lawrence, and an art gallery. There is a reference library (open by written appointment) with over 20,000 books and the archives of a number of important commanders, and a lecture theatre. (*Tel: 01-730-0717.*)

National Film Theatre, *South Bank* (5 F-1) *(See map on page 80)* Founded in 1953 by the British Film Institute and moved to its present site under Waterloo Bridge in 1958. Films from the beginning of the cinema to the latest blockbuster are shown in two theatres. A third small cinema is often pressed into use if, say, an international film star or director is lecturing in the large hall. Programmes usually change every day. Each November the London Film Festival, which lasts approximately 2½ weeks, is held here. There is a restaurant, bar and film bookshop. Temporary as well as annual membership is available. (*Tel: 01-928-3232.*)

National Gallery, *Trafalgar Square* (5 D-1) *(See map on page 87)* The national collection of Old Masters. A representative selection of masterpieces from every major European school with works by artists from Giotto to Van Gogh. The gallery owes its existence to George IV who, in 1824, helped by his friend Sir George Beaumont, persuaded the government to buy 38 valuable paintings owned by Sir John Julius Angerstein who had just died. These included works by Raphael, Rembrandt and Van Dyck. A further 16 pictures — by Claude, Rubens and Wilkie and others — were given by the government and by Sir George Beaumont. These were the nucleus of a collection now numbering over 2,000. Astute purchases have enriched it over a century and a half. The first director, Sir Charles Eastlake, travelled widely in Italy where he was able to acquire fine Renaissance pictures, and major works from Flemish, Dutch and Spanish masters were added in the 1870s. A large collection of paintings by British artists was transferred to the Tate Gallery★ when it was opened in 1897. The collections of each school are kept together and shown in adjoining rooms.

The gallery is maintained by public funds and receives an annual purchase grant from the government, but this is rarely sufficient to meet increasingly high costs of buying major works of art. However, a generous gift from the American philanthropist John Paul Getty has greatly eased the gallery's problems.

Until William Wilkins's gallery was built the paintings were on view in Angerstein's house in Pall Mall. Wilkins's building, put up between 1832-38, incorporates a lasting reminder of George IV. The columns on the portico came from the former Prince Regent's Carlton House which had been demolished after a fire. There have been a number of extensions to the gallery, enabling many pictures normally stored to be exhibited. Work on a further extension, financed by the Sainsbury family, began in 1987.

Exhibitions of works borrowed from private and public collections at home and overseas are occasionally mounted. There are guided tours, lectures, film shows and educational facilities. (*Tel: 01-839-3321.*)

National Monuments Record Office, *Fortress House, Savile Row* (2 B-5) A large library comprising more than one million photographs and drawings recording the architectural history of England. There are also archaeological records and aerial photographs of sites. Open for research and study purposes. (*Tel: 01-734-6010.*)

National Portrait Gallery, *St Martin's Place* (5 D-1) *(See map on page 87)* Adjoining the National Gallery a separate building displays portraits of the men and women who from Tudor times until today have made major contributions to the country. The paintings, supplemented by drawings, sculptures and photographs, are a historical record of the faces of royalty, politicians, artists, scientists and people in the news. The collection, which now comprises over 10,000 works, was founded in 1856 and has been in the present building — the gift of William Henry Alexander — since 1896. An extension, financed by the art dealer Lord Duveen, was built in 1937, but so much has now been acquired that only a small selection of the gallery's holdings is on view.

The paintings are arranged chronologically, beginning with the Tudors on the top floor and

The National Gallery

In the National Portrait Gallery

57

ending near ground level with recent acquisitions such as the Princess of Wales by Brian Organ, portraits of Queen Elizabeth II, and such men of our times as Sir Robin Day. Each period room has wall hangings, specially reproduced to look like contemporary backgrounds. The earliest portrait is of Henry VII by Michel Sittow, and there is Holbein's life-size cartoon of Henry VIII, the icon of Elizabeth I painted by Gheeraerts, and the only known contemporary portrait of Shakespeare by J. Taylor. The reign of George III leading into the Regency is particularly well represented with portraits by Reynolds and Lawrence.

In the 20th century Sir Winston Churchill was painted by Walter Sickert and in his later years by Graham Sutherland: only the sketch for the Sutherland exists as Lady Churchill, who didn't like it, burnt the portrait.

The gallery provides educational facilities, has a programme of lectures and mounts temporary exhibitions. (*Tel: 01-930-1552.*)

National Postal Museum, *King Edward Building, King Edward Street* (3 C-3) The Post Office Collections of British postage stamps includes almost every stamp issued by the Post Office in the United Kingdom and those overseas countries once in its control. The museum, which occupies a small section at the south-east corner of the Post Office, was founded in 1965 by Reginald Phillips, who contributed a large sum for its support as well as donating his own collection, one of great philatelic and historic importance. There is also an extensive collection of stamps from foreign countries, and the philatelic archives of the firm of Thomas De La Rue & Co., which has printed stamps for countries all over the world. The reference library is extensive. (*Tel: 01-432-3851.*)

National Theatre (5 F-1) *(See map on page 80)* One of the country's most important theatres, with three auditoriums in a new building overlooking the Thames. The theatre company, under its then artistic director, Sir Laurence Olivier (now Lord Olivier), gave its first performance in 1963 at the Old Vic Theatre and remained there until Sir Denys Lasdun's new building was completed in 1976. The first public performances were given in the Lyttelton auditorium on 16 March 1976, and the theatre was officially opened the following October by Queen Elizabeth II, who recalled in her speech that the idea of a National Theatre had first been proposed in Queen Victoria's reign — in 1848 by Effingham Wilson, a London publisher.

The three theatres have a total seating capacity of over 2,400, the largest being the fan-shaped Olivier. The Lyttelton, a conventional proscenium arch theatre, seats 890 and the Cottesloe, intended as an experimental studio, can accommodate up to 400. The repertoire is varied, ranging from Greek tragedy to modern comedies, from Shakespeare and Restoration dramatists to the occasional musical.

This somewhat fortress-like structure of grey concrete has several terraces, including one for light meals in good weather. There are bars, buffets, a restaurant and bookshops. Live music is performed in the foyer in the early evening and there are frequent exhibitions of paintings or photographs. A rich collection of theatrical paintings bequeathed by Somerset Maugham is on permanent view in the foyers. Conducted tours of the front-of-house and backstage take place on weekdays. (*Tel: 01-633-0880.*)

National Westminster Bank Tower, *Old Broad Street* (3 E-3) The bank headquarters designed by Richard Seifert rise 52 storeys to a height of 600 ft, making it, at least for a short time, the highest office block in Europe. The viewing platform is only open to invited customers and guests.

Natural History Museum, *Cromwell Road* (4 C-4) This Romanesque building, where the national holdings of fossils and living plants are to be found, is officially the British Museum (Natural History), but is always known by its descriptive name. Divided into five departments — Zoology, Entomology, Palaeontology, Mineralogy and Botany — the museum places an emphasis on biology and man. It also serves as an important research centre. One of London's most popular places to visit, it is a special favourite with children. The dinosaurs, including reconstructions of the head of a Tyrannosaurus Rex

Entrance to the Natural History Museum

and flying reptiles, are big attractions. Rooms with butterflies, stuffed birds, and skeletons of whales, and the hall showing the growth of man also compete for attention.

The museum's origins lie in the bequest of the antiquary Sir Hans Sloane. On his death in 1753 he left his 'cabinet of curiosities' to the nation. This formed the nucleus of the British Museum ★. When space at Bloomsbury became a problem there were proposals for a separate building to house the natural history collection. Land acquired with profits from the Great Exhibition of 1851 was available and the impressive new museum was erected. Designed by Alfred Waterhouse, who incorporated carvings of flowers and fauna in the stonework, it opened in 1881.

During school holidays imaginative programmes are arranged for children. There are lectures all year round, changing exhibitions and film shows. (*Tel: 01-589-6323.*)

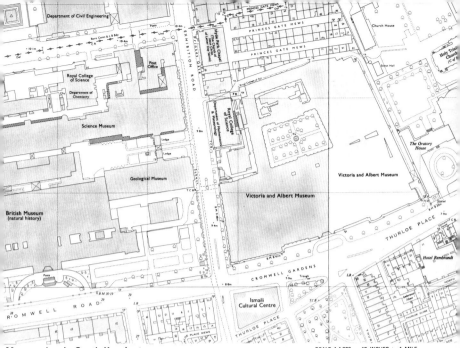

Museum Land – South Kensington

SCALE 1:4 000 or 15 INCHES to 1 MILE

Naval and Military Club, *94 Piccadilly* (5 A-2) A private club in a building popularly known as the In and Out because of the directions on the stone gateposts. The club, founded by five army officers in 1862, acquired the premises three years later when its owner, the Prime Minister, Lord Palmerston died. Before Palmerston came here the house was a royal residence, the home of George III's youngest son, Adolphus Duke of Cambridge. Queen Victoria, on a visit to her uncle, was once attacked in the courtyard by a lunatic. The house, a fine example of a large 18th-century mansion, was designed by Matthew Brettingham in 1756 for Lord Egremont. It is not open to the public.

Nelson's Column, *Trafalgar Square* (5 D-1) The monument to commemorate Admiral Lord Nelson who died at the Battle of Trafalgar in 1805. The idea of erecting a 'Nelson Testimonial' in the square named in honour of his last naval victory was first aired in a letter to *The Times* in 1837. This was after Dublin had put up a pillar and Great Yarmouth a column. 120 designs and forty models were submitted to a committee headed by the Duke of Wellington before William Railton's 170-ft Corinthian column was chosen. Completed in 1843, it is surmounted with E.H. Baily's stone statue of England's most popular hero in his admiral's uniform. Reliefs at the base, fashioned from captured cannon, depict scenes from Nelson's victories — at the Nile, Copenhagen, St Vincent. A fourth, on the Whitehall side, shows his death at Cape Trafalgar.

New Scotland Yard, *Victoria Embankment* (5 E-3) Opposite Westminster Pier, Members of Parliament today occupy offices in the sombre granite and red-brick building which Norman Shaw designed as police headquarters in 1888. An overlarge plaque on the wall commemorates the architect. The police

moved in 1967 to a new building — which confusingly carries the same name — between Victoria Street and Broadway.

Old Bailey (3 B-3) The name of this street is derived from the defensive city wall which surrounded a prison known as Newgate in the 12th century. The notorious prison, rebuilt several times, was finally demolished in 1902 to make way for the Central Criminal Court★, commonly known as the Old Bailey.

Old Curiosity Shop, *Portsmouth Street* (2 F-4) This souvenir shop takes its name from Dickens's book and is supposed to be his model for Little Nell's home. The shop, in a house dating from c. 1567, claims to be the oldest in London.

Old Jewry (3 D-3) The name of this street is a reminder of the 13th century when rich Jewish merchants settled in West Cheape, near present-day Gresham Street. Their fine mansions and ever-increasing prosperity caused envy among Christians, who were forbidden by the Church to make money by usury. Acquisition of land through mortgages was alleged to be a threat to the Crown. Over 700 Jews were murdered by Simon de Montfort at the Jewry in 1262 when one money-lender demanded more interest from a Christian than was legally permitted. Many persecutions followed and the Jews were expelled in 1290 by Edward I who 'made a mighty mass of money of their houses' according to the historian John Stow. They were not permitted to return to England for 365 years.

Oxford Circus (2 B-4) So 'that the sensation of having passed Oxford-street will be entirely done away', John Nash solved the problem as he had

Oxford Circus   SCALE 1:4 000 or 15 INCHES to 1 MILE

done at Piccadilly by creating a circus. Known as Regent Circus North until the end of the 19th century, the stores on the four crescents that formed the circus were demolished before the First World War and rebuilt to retain the shaped curve.

Oxford Street (2 A-5 etc.) This busy thoroughfare, closed to private motorists, is lined with shops and department stores whose variety and quality of goods range from the exclusive and expensive to the cheap and nasty. Following the line of a Roman road, this has always been the main route from London to the West, changing its name a number of times until the 18th century when the 2nd Earl of Oxford occupied a house in Marylebone ★. Development began c. 1740, and by the end of the century several places of entertainment had been established between St Giles Circus and Marble Arch ★ to cater to the growing number of residents. The Pantheon, where masquerades, fêtes and concerts were held, was, said Horace Walpole, 'the most beautiful edifice in England'. But when the popularity of the assemblies waned, it became an exhibition hall, a theatre and finally a bazaar. The name, however, lives on in the rebuilt store on the corner of Poland Street: the Pantheon branch of Marks and Spencer.

Many small 19th-century shops were replaced by department stores — the largest, Selfridge's, was opened in 1909 by Gordon Selfridge of Chicago. There have been many changes in the street in the last 20 years, the more affluent stores giving way to

Selfridge's, Oxford Street

chain stores of variable quality. While quite a number of the street traders have licences to sell from stalls, less scrupulous operators are liable to disappear in a hurry if a policeman appears.

Paddington (1 B-3 etc.) A district of immense variety whose population of about 100,000 occupy houses ranging from grand mansions to shabby tenements. A borough until 1965 when it was incorporated into the City of Westminster, it has a long history. Lying to the west of Edgware Road (on the line of Watling Street, the Roman road to the north), and stretching to West Kilburn, it is bounded on the south by the Bayswater Road (the Roman road to Silchester). At the apex of the two roads, a plaque (on the island to the side of the Marble Arch) records that this was *Tyburn,* the site of the three-legged gallows where public executions took place from 1196 until 1783. Today, in a convent, a few yards away on the Edgware Road, nuns still pray for all those martyred.

Little remains of Paddington Green and the village whose rural isolation first attracted Huguenot refugees in the 18th century. In later years artists and aristocrats moved in but the peaceful atmosphere was disturbed early in the 19th century when the Church of England, which owned a vast area of surrounding land, sold leases for development. Houses were built around a series of squares; the Bishop of London granted the lease for the extension of the Grand Union Canal ★, and more property was put up near its banks. The Church's modern successors, the Church Commissioners, still administer some of the property although in the 1980s the freeholds in Maida Vale are being sold. Paddington Green today nestles uncomfortably under the Westway flyover.

Paddington Station, opened in 1838, was redesigned in the year of the Great Exhibition by Isambard Kingdom Brunel, who took his inspiration from Paxton's Crystal Palace. It is the terminus for trains from the West of England.

Painter-Stainers' Hall, *Little Trinity Lane* (3 C-4) This livery company has had a hall on this site since the reign of Henry VIII. Although Charles II is reputed to have watched the approaching Great Fire from the hall, it did not escape, and was rebuilt in 1670. This building in turn was destroyed in 1941. In the new hall, erected in 1961, the company has a fine collection of plate, some dating from the early 17th century, and a series of paintings on wood executed c.1705. Contact the City Information Centre for occasional open days. (*Tel: 01-606-3030.*)

Palladium *See London Palladium ★*

Pall Mall (5 C-2) The wide street connecting Trafalgar Square ★ and St James's ★ has many fine buildings, a number of them gentlemen's clubs, specialist shops and business premises. The strangely foreign name derives from an Italian game which was played here until moved for convenience to The Mall ★. Called 'pelemele' by Pepys who first saw the Duke of York playing it in April 1661, it was a form of croquet popular with Charles II and his mistresses. When the road was laid out in 1661 it was first known as Catherine Street but the more popularly known name has come down the centuries — Pall Mall.

The large houses that went up attracted royal, fashionable and sometimes notorious residents. Charles II's mistress Nell Gwyn was set up in a house and granted a Crown lease. This she refused to accept until it was consigned to her free by Parliament, giving as her reason that she had 'always conveyed free under the Crown'. To this day No. 79 is the only freehold property on the south of the street. In 1766 George III's brother, the Duke of Gloucester, married the Countess Waldegrave here, one of the marriages that led to the Royal Marriage Act of 1772. Next door Schomberg House was divided in three, one section being Gainsborough's studio. William Augustus, Duke of Cumberland — the 'Butcher of Culloden' — was another resident, and it was also where the notorious quack Dr James Graham kept his grand celestial bed, and his 'Temple of Health and Hymen' with the assistance of young Emma Hart (the future Lady Hamilton). Queen Victoria's daughter Princess Christian of Schleswig-Holstein occupied the house early this century, and her daughters, Princess Helena Victoria and Princess Marie Louise, remained here until after the Second World War. The interior of Schomberg House has been rebuilt.

In the 18th century many coffee houses in the street became gentlemen's clubs but some of these have disappeared or amalgamated after 200 years. The United Services Club, on the corner of Waterloo Place, was built by John Nash in 1827 when Carlton House was demolished and remodelled in 1842 by Decimus Burton. Today it is the Institute of Directors. Facing it is the Athenaeum, still an elite club, designed in Grecian style by Burton in 1828. The Doric porch is surmounted by the gilded figure of Pallas Athene and the blue and white frieze resembles that on the Parthenon. The Italian Renaissance-style Travellers' (No. 106) and the Reform (Nos. 104-105) were both designed by Charles Barry in the 1830s. Among the other clubs are the Royal Automobile Club (No. 89) and the United Oxford and Cambridge University Club (No. 71).

Park Lane (4 F-1) Six prestigious hotels overlook the six-lane carriageway that runs along the east side of Hyde Park. Grosvenor House Hotel★, the Dorchester and the Londonderry have each been built on the sites of large mansions that belonged to aristocrats or rich businessmen. The Inn on the Park and the Inter-Continental were put up when the road, south of the Hilton Hotel, was extended in the 1960s. Although Park Lane has a fashionable reputation, this was not achieved until the 19th century: even then many of the fine houses only backed onto the road. Very few of the splendid mid-Victorian homes of the wealthy and titled residents — of whom Trollope wrote — survive.

Parliament Square (5 D-3) The tree-lined square by the side of Westminster Abbey★ was laid out in 1868 by Sir Charles Barry to give a clear, unimpeded approach to the Houses of Parliament★. On state occasions flags fly from between the trees on the central island where, with one exception, the statues are of 19th- and 20th-century British statesmen — Sir Robert Peel, Benjamin Disraeli, the 14th Earl of Derby, Lord Palmerston and Sir Winston Churchill. The only foreigner is the South African leader Field-Marshal Jan Smuts. Two statues, outside Middlesex Guildhall and the Royal Institu-

tion of Chartered Surveyors, face the square — the American President Abraham Lincoln, and George IV's Prime Minister, George Canning.

Petticoat Lane, *Spitalfields* (3 F-3) A Sunday morning street market in Middlesex Street and spilling into adjacent roads. Early in the 17th century secondhand clothes were sold in 'Peticote' Lane

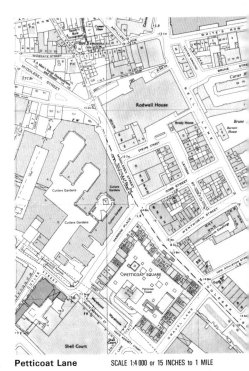

Petticoat Lane   SCALE 1:4 000 or 15 INCHES to 1 MILE

and although the street was renamed Middlesex Street over a century ago the old name has stuck. Despite attempts to close the market — enormously popular in Victorian times — its future was secured by an Act of Parliament in 1936. At least half the stalls still sell clothes but hardware, jewellery and other goods are also to be found.

Physic Gardens See Chelsea Physic Gardens★

Piccadilly (5 B-1 etc.) The broad street extending from Piccadilly Circus★ to Hyde Park★ follows the line of one of the two main roads (Oxford Street is the other) from London to the West. At Hyde Park Corner★ there was a toll gate until early Georgian times. The strange name is assumed to derive from Robert Baker's shop (near Great Windmill Street) where pickadils — frills for collars — were sold at the beginning of the 17th century. From the circus to Green Park the buildings on both sides are occupied by a variety of commercial organisations, among them hotels, airline offices, shops and the affluent stores of Simpson of Piccadilly and Fortnum and Mason★. The Wren church of St James's★, the exclusive residential chambers of

Albany ★, and Burlington House, home of the Royal Academy of Arts ★, are also in this east section. While the houses west of the Ritz Hotel all overlook Green Park ★ and give the appearance of being residential, most are offices and clubs.

The street was developed in the 17th century. After the Restoration when the Court moved to St James's and the King to Kensington a number of large mansions were built on Piccadilly. Of these only Burlington House ★ remains. Albany, the Naval and Military Club ★, and the house now occupied by the Arts Council (No. 105 — largely rebuilt) were erected for the nobility in Georgian and Regency times when it was fashionable to live on Piccadilly. Residents have included the Duke of York and the Duke of Cambridge (sons of George III), their sister the Duchess of Gloucester, and more recently at the now demolished No. 145 the future Elizabeth II. Among other renowned people who lived here were Sir William and Lady Hamilton, Lord Byron, the Marquess of Queensbury (who had a reputation for spotting passing pretty girls from his windows), Lord Elgin (of the Marbles) and the dukes of Devonshire, whose mansion opposite the Ritz was demolished in the 1920s.

Piccadilly Circus

Piccadilly Circus (5 C-1) Considered in days gone by as the hub of the Empire, the oddly shaped junction today has lost many of its recognisable features and some of its character. Intended as an axis on the magnificent thoroughfare John Nash created from Carlton House to Regent's Park, it was completed in 1821 when only four roads led into it. Since then there have been numerous alterations. Shaftesbury Avenue was cut through in 1886, and Eros ★, the statue commemorating the philanthropist Lord Shaftesbury, placed on an island site seven years later. This was moved to a pedestrian area outside the Criterion building in 1986. Swan and Edgar, the department store that opened as a haberdasher's on the corner of Piccadilly and Regent Street in 1811, closed down in 1982. The interior has been relaid out and is now a record shop. Most of the famous neon signs on the site of the old Del Monico restaurant have gone, and the

London Pavilion is at present being redeveloped partly to house a pop music waxworks branch of Madame Tussauds. The future of the Criterion is constantly being discussed but the famous theatre seems secure. The County Fire Office, erected in 1817 and rebuilt in 1924 to bear some resemblance to the original building, still occupies the offices it moved into when Nash built the circus.

Pimlico (5 C-5 etc.) This largely residential area has a faded look. Stretching from the river to Victoria Station, it lies between Vauxhall Bridge and Chelsea Bridge. Laid out in the 1830s by Thomas Cubitt for the Grosvenor family, the terraces of stucco houses, many of them small hotels today, have never been as smart as those he built in adjacent Belgravia ★.

Dolphin Square, a huge 1930s development with over 1,200 apartments, faces the Thames on Grosvenor Road. In Pimlico Gardens, opposite, there is a statue to the man with the dubious distinction of being the first person killed by a train (Stephenson's *Rocket* in 1830). The unfortunate

Piccadilly and Piccadilly Circus

SCALE 1:4 000 or 15 INCHES to 1 MILE

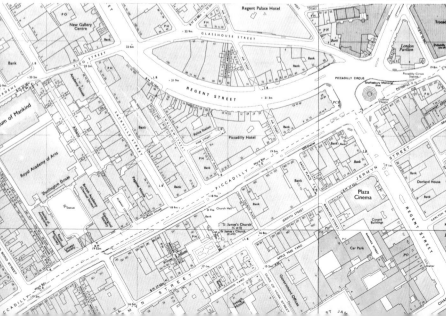

William Huskisson M.P., dressed in a toga by the sculptor, caused Osbert Sitwell to describe the statue as 'boredom rising from a bath'.

Planetarium See London Planetarium ★

Portland Place (2 A-3) The elegant, spacious street, once the widest in London, retains its 18th-century proportions. Laid out c. 1774 by Robert and John Adam on land owned by the Duke of Portland, it was lined with fine neo-classical houses. A large number of the original buildings fell into the hands of Victorian developers who destroyed them, but a few survive, notably between Weymouth Street and New Cavendish Street. Nos. 46 and 48 are good examples. Most of the country's national radio programmes are transmitted from Broadcasting House ★, the BBC's building on the corner of Langham Place.

A street of such distinction has inevitably had many famous residents. Lord Byron courted his future wife Annabella Milbanke at No. 63, Field-Marshal Lord Roberts, the Commander-in-Chief in India, Ireland and South Africa, lived at No. 47, John Buchan at No. 76. The historian Henry Brook Adams worked at No. 98 when it was the U.S. Embassy and his father was Abraham Lincoln's ambassador in London.

The Royal Institute of British Architects has its headquarters at 66 Portland Place where exhibitions are often held in the gallery. The British Architectural Library is open by arrangement. A small shop on the ground floor has an excellent selection of books on architecture. (Tel: 01-580-5533.). The Institute is also responsible for the RIBA Heinz Gallery at 21 Portman Square where small exhibitions are mounted, and there are facilities for those who wish to examine the drawings collections (which may possibly move back to Portland Place in the future).

The statues in the centre of the street commemorate Quintin Hogg, founder of the Polytechnic, the surgeon Joseph Lister who discovered antiseptics, and Field-Marshal Sir George White, a forgotten hero today who achieved the remarkable distinction of winning the Victoria Cross twice.

Prince Henry's Room, 17 Fleet Street (3 A-4) Over the Inner Temple Gateway is a half-timbered house with a room named after James I's eldest son Henry, Prince of Wales. Formerly the Hand Inn, the name was changed to the Prince's Arms when the publican extended the premises in 1610. The room has fine panelled walls and a highly decorative ceiling. Mrs Salmon's waxworks (inspiration for Dickens in the Old Curiosity Shop) were once exhibited here. A small collection of material relating to Samuel Pepys is on display. (Tel: 01-353-7323).

Printing House Square, Blackfriars (3 B-4) A courtyard in front of a modern office block and the name are the only reminders that in the 17th century on part of the site of old Blackfriars Monastery dozens of small printers were in business here, among them the King's printers. From 1785 until 1974 the headquarters of The Times were here.

Public Record Office, Chancery Lane (3 A-3) The principal repository of the state archives of the country from 1066 to modern times, although a large proportion of government papers have been removed to a new building in Ruskin Avenue, Kew. (Tel: 01-876-3444.). An Act of Parliament established the office in 1838. On the completion of Sir James Pennethorne's Tudor-style building in 1856 archives from the Tower of London were brought here so all the legal, judicial and state papers could be in one place. The Domesday Book is kept in a small museum together with Magna Carta, Shakespeare's will, other documents of international importance, and royal signatures from the Black Prince in the 14th century to Queen Elizabeth II. An arch from the Rolls Chapel — founded in 1232 — has been incorporated into the fabric of the building. In an attempt to convert Jews to Christianity the chapel, financed by Henry III, was intended as a 'Domus Conversorum'. Readers' tickets are necessary to examine the records, and the museum is only open at certain times of the year. (Tel: 01-405-0741.)

Queen Anne's Gate (5 C-3) A street of unusual charm with a number of delightful houses built c. 1704 by Charles Shales. The statue of Queen Anne in the wall of No. 13 was erected in her lifetime. The carved faces on the keystones and the decorated wooden canopies over the doorways are very unusual. Lord Palmerston, the Victorian Prime Minister, was born at No. 20. Jeremy Bentham and later John Stuart Mill lived at No. 40. The National Trust headquarters are at No. 36.

Queen Elizabeth Hall (5 F-1) (See map on page 80) A concert hall, part of the arts complex on the South Bank ★. The hall, opened in 1967, is used by chamber orchestras, for small-scale opera performances, recitals and occasionally film shows or conferences. It seats 1,100 and, with the smaller adjacent **Purcell Room** and Royal Festival Hall ★, is administered by the South Bank Concert Board.

The Queen's Chapel, Marlborough House (5 C-2) (See map on page 73) A delightful small classical church, once part of St James's Palace but separated from it when Marlborough Road was laid out. Inigo Jones's first ecclesiastical building was begun in 1623 when Charles I was engaged to the Catholic Infanta of Spain and completed four years later for his eventual bride, Henrietta Maria. With a Venetian window, coffered ceiling and Palladian detail, it was an architectural innovation for England. The green and white walls and 17th-century furniture have altered little since the chapel was renovated after the Restoration for Charles II's Queen, Catherine of Braganza. Details of Sunday morning services (open to visitors) during the summer months are announced in The Times the previous day.

The Queen's Gallery, Buckingham Palace (5 B-3) (See map on page 25) A gallery where temporary exhibitions of treasures from the royal collections are displayed. Built on the site of the palace chapel which was largely destroyed by a bomb during the Second World War, it opened in 1962. The variety of the changing exhibitions, each lasting approximately a year, has ranged from displays of Sèvres porcelain to the drawings of Leonardo da Vinci,

The Music Lesson *by Vermeer – a painting from The Queen's Gallery (Reproduced by gracious permission of Her Majesty the Queen)*

from paintings purchased by past and present members of the royal family to the Fabergé collection amassed by Queen Alexandra and added to by Queen Mary and her descendants. *(Tel: 01-930-4832 ext. 351.)*

Queen Victoria Memorial (5 B-3) *(See map on page 25)* In front of Buckingham Palace ★, the 82ft-high marble memorial to Queen Victoria was unveiled by her grandson George V in 1911, although it was not completed until 1921. The gilded winged figure of Victory looking down The Mall ★ is high above the seated statue of the Queen-Empress. A rather large figure with three children, symbolising motherhood, faces the palace. Other representational figures are Courage and Constancy, with Progress, Peace, Agriculture and Manufacture by the side of the bronze lions guarding the steps between the fountains.

Regent's Canal (1 B-3 etc.) The canal runs from the Thames at Limehouse to Little Venice ★ where it joins the Grand Union Canal ★. Opened in 1820, it was the last canal link between London and Birmingham, and was part of John Nash's grand plan of improvements in London. Going through several tunnels on an eastward journey, the canal skirts the edge of Regent's Park ★ and passes London Zoo ★. Considerable damage was caused to the canal, and nearby houses were blown up, when one of a convoy of barges laden with sugar, petroleum and gunpowder caught fire and exploded under Macclesfield Bridge by the North Gate in October 1874.

The Regent's Canal Information Centre, 289 Camden High Street, in the former Hampstead Road Lock cottage, has a historical exhibition of paintings and drawings illustrating the changes that have occurred from the time the canal carried freight to the present day when it is almost exclusively plied for pleasure. The Centre, overlooking Camden Lock Market, has maps, guides and general information on other British canals as well as full details about special events on the canal in London. Boat trips start either at Camden Town or Little Venice. *(Tel: 01-482 0523 or 01-482-2550.)*

Regent's Park (1 F-1 etc.) Surrounded by magnificent stucco terraces and further enhanced by Regency villas, this is one of London's prettiest and most elegant parks. Almost round, the 487 acres are bounded by the Outer Circle, a road which, with the exception of the northern arc, is ringed by ten terraces of fine houses, all conceived as part of John Nash's grand scheme of metropolitan improvements. Appropriately the park is named after

Regent's Park

SCALE 1:25 000 or 2½ INCHES to 1 MILE

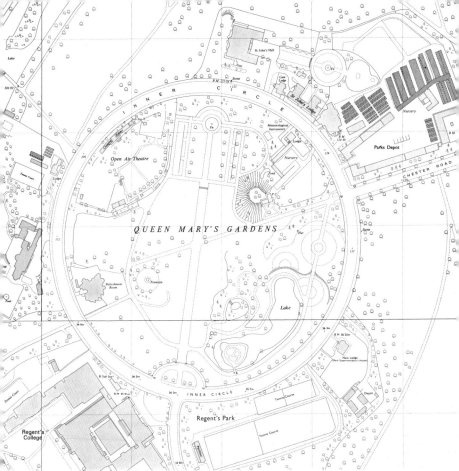

Queen Mary's Gardens, Regent's Park

SCALE 1:4 000 or 15 INCHES to 1 MILE

the Prince Regent (later George IV) who supported his architect through numerous difficulties which happened while London's only town planning on a large scale was carried out. Work took place from 1812-42 on land that had once been a forest and then, after the Dissolution of the Monasteries, a park where Elizabeth I hunted.

The Inner Circle, where there are a number of

Queen Mary's Gardens, Regent's Park

charming Regency villas, surrounds the beautiful rose gardens named after Queen Mary, wife of George V. She took a keen interest in their upkeep when they became the responsibility of the Royal Parks Department in 1932. In the same year *Twelfth Night* was performed by Nigel Playfair and Phyllis Neilson-Terry in a roped-off enclosure of the gardens, and this led to the foundation of the Open Air Theatre, where plays by Shakespeare and Shaw are given against an enchanting background on fine evenings for three months each summer.

Following a heavy frost in 1867, forty people in a huge crowd skating on the attractive boating lake fell through and drowned. Later on, the lake's depth was considerably reduced. A second disaster occurred seven years later on the Regent's Canal ★ when a barge carrying gunpowder blew up killing three men.

In 1826 the recently formed Zoological Society was offered a 5-acre site where its collection of animals became known as London Zoo ★ . Over half a century later when an elderly elephant was sold to Barnum's Circus in America, public outcry whipped up by some enterprising journalists brought such large crowds to see 'Jumbo' that receipts enabled the Society to built a reptile house.

The terraces and villas in the park, planned by Nash and largely designed by him or members of the Burton family, have mostly survived and been restored to their original splendour in recent years. Inside Hanover Gate, an exotic new building is the London Mosque, an all-white edifice save for the gilded minarets and dome.

Regent Street (2 B-5 etc.) This wide street with a sweeping curve is one of London's most important shopping thoroughfares. Stores such as Liberty's, Jaeger, Dickins and Jones, Hedges and Butler, Hamley's and Aquascutum have been here since the last century. Planned and laid out between 1811 and 1825 by the Prince Regent's favourite architect, John Nash, it was envisaged as a fashionable rendezvous 'for those who have nothing to do but walk about and amuse themselves'. The original intention was to connect the Prince's Carlton House with a proposed palace in Regent's Park ★ but the house at the bottom of Lower Regent Street was demolished before the street was completed and the palace in the park forgotten. Between Piccadilly Circus ★ and Vigo Street Nash put up the Quadrant, a covered arc of colonnades on either side of the street. These he thought would provide shelter on rainy days for the gentry. Quite a different sort of street walker was attracted to the arcades, an excuse for removing them in 1848.

The curve of the street was retained at the insistence of George V, after a number of the original stucco buildings were demolished before the First World War. Eventually all were replaced by shops faced in Portland stone and the transformation was completed about 1926. One of the most impressive of the new stores was put up by Liberty's, who also have a Tudor-style annexe in Gt Marlborough Street connected by a bridge to Regent Street. The timbers for this extension, its interior described as 'a Chinese puzzle conceived by a mediaeval mind', came from two old ships.

While the street has lost some of its exclusivity, and is no longer *the* place to celebrate national events as in Victorian days, it still attracts a wealthy clientele, and the annual Christmas lights cause endless traffic jams.

Liberty's, Regent Street

Royal Academy of Arts, *Burlington House, Piccadilly* ★ (5 B-1) *(See map on page 62)* The country's oldest and most highly regarded society devoted to the fine arts. The Academy runs art schools and organises important changing exhibitions, the most famous being the Summer

The Royal Academy of Arts, Burlington House

Exhibition of paintings, drawings, sculpture and architectural models by living artists. This annual show has been held without a break since the Academy was founded in 1768 by Sir Joshua Reynolds, the first President. Other founder members included the architect William Chambers and the painters Benjamin West, Thomas Gainsborough and Paul Sandby. There are 40 Academicians (RA) and 30 Associates (ARA), each of whom is elected by the whole membership when a vacancy occurs. The present premises have been occupied by the Royal Academy since 1868 when they moved from the National Gallery. Before this they were first in Pall Mall and then at Somerset House ★. In the forecourt the statue of Joshua Reynolds shows him holding a conventional palette, quite unlike the shovel-shaped ones he actually used, of which the Academy owns two.

Besides the priceless Michelangelo *Tondo*, usually on display in the private rooms, the Academy has a superb collection of paintings and sculpture; each Academician is required to present 'a Picture, Bas-relief, or other specimen of his abilities'. A small selection of these often hang on the staircase and corridor walls in Burlington House but normally the collection is hidden from public view and can only be seen by special arrangement, the galleries being reserved for impressive, major loan exhibitions from all over the world. There is a fine arts library, open to research scholars. The Royal Academy of Arts is generally open daily. (*Tel: 01-734-9052.*)

Royal Academy of Dramatic Art, *62-64 Gower Street* (2 C-2) The country's leading drama school. Founded in 1904 by Sir Herbert Beerbohm Tree, and granted a royal charter by George V in 1920, the Academy is managed by a council of distinguished people in the theatrical field. A large percentage of Britain's best known actors were trained at RADA. At the Vanbrugh Theatre in Malet Street the students regularly give performances which are open to the public. In the main Gower Street building there is the smaller GBS Theatre, named after George Bernard Shaw who was an active member of the council. In his will he left RADA a third of his royalties.

Royal Academy of Music, *Marylebone Road* (1 F-2) The oldest conservatory in the country teachng advanced musical courses. Founded in 1822 under the patronage of George IV, the academy offers full-time professional training in all aspects of performance at undergraduate and postgraduate levels. In 1986 it announced an ambitious plan to transform the academy into an international institution and established five international chairs: Anne-Sophie Mutter is the first holder of the chair of violin studies; Hans Werner Henze the chair of composition and contemporary studies; and Robert Tear of vocal studies. Several times a year student orchestral concerts and opera productions are open to the public in the theatre. The library, begun in 1823, has a large stock of books, important early editions, manuscripts and priceless musical instruments. Its own resources of orchestral music have been augmented by Sir Henry Wood's collection.

Royal Albert Hall, *Kensington Gore* (4 B-3) The huge concert hall, an amphitheatre capable of

The Royal Albert Hall

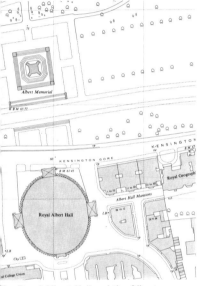

The Royal Albert Hall and the Albert Memorial   SCALE 1:4 000 or 15 INCHES to 1 MILE

accommodating approximately 8,000 people, is also used for public meetings, fashion shows, boxing matches and balls. After the Great Exhibition of 1851 Queen Victoria's husband suggested that land on which he envisaged museums and centres of learning be bought with the profits. Gore House was purchased, and then demolished, and although two architects submitted plans for a hall the project was in abeyance when Prince Albert died in 1861. The idea was revived as a memorial by Henry Cole, who with the Prince had been the driving force behind the Crystal Palace★. He proposed a scheme for raising the money by leasing 1,300 seats at £100 each. This entitled investors to attend every performance free for 999 years. This arrangement still exists, and today the descendants of the leaseholders negotiate to let their seats each year. The foundation stone of what was to be known as the Hall of Arts and Sciences was laid by Queen Victoria in 1867. On this occasion she announced the wished the prefix Royal Albert to be given to the

building. At the opening ceremony in 1871 the Queen was too distressed to speak and the Prince of Wales deputised for her.

Orchestras of international repute, conductors, singers and choirs have always appeared at the hall and continue to come. Richard Wagner conducted a festival of his own compositions in 1877. Bruckner inaugurated the famous Willis organ. The cream of the music world appear here. Singers, whether opera divas like Adelina Patti in the last century and Jessye Norman today or modern vocalists like Frank Sinatra and Shirley Bassey, have drawn huge crowds. From mid-July to early September the Sir Henry Wood Promenade Concerts — the Proms — take place almost every night. A celebration of orchestral music, they attract large crowds, especially of young people. They have been held here since a bomb destroyed the Queen's Hall in 1941. Founded by the conductor Sir Henry Wood in 1895, responsibility for organising the concerts was assumed by the BBC in 1927.

It is occasionally possible to tour the building when concerts or rehearsals are not in progress. (*Tel: 01-589-8212.*)

Royal College of Art, *Kensington Gore* (4 B-3) Beside the Royal Albert Hall★, an undergraduate and post-graduate college awarding degrees in art and industrial design. The college moved to the eight-storey modern building of grey glass and concrete designed by Sir Hugh Casson in 1962. Originally the School of Design, founded in 1837, it developed its practical art department at the suggestion of Prince Albert's friend Henry Cole in 1852. For many years it was closely associated with the Museum of Ornamental Art, the forerunner of the Victoria and Albert Museum★, and shared the same buildings. Queen Victoria granted it royal status in 1896. Exhibitions are occasionally held here.

Royal College of Music, *Prince Consort Road* (4 B-3) The college provides musical training for undergraduate and postgraduate students wishing to become performers, teachers or composers. Past pupils have included the composers Ralph Vaughan

Williams and Benjamin Britten and opera's 'La Stupenda' — Dame Joan Sutherland.

At the back of the Royal Albert Hall, the college founded in 1882 by the Prince of Wales (the future Edward VII) was granted a royal charter a year later. The present purpose-built red-brick college, with a charming statue of Queen Alexandra in the porch, was completed in 1894 and has been extended several times, the most recent addition being the Britten Opera Theatre opened by the Queen in November 1986. The first director George Grove, compiler of the music dictionary, was succeeded by Sir Charles Parry. Jenny Lind was once a professor here. The college owns the exceptionally fine Donaldson collection of old musical instruments (this may be seen by appointment), and has a new spacious library with an extensive collection of books and music and a collection of portraits and ephemera with musical associations.

Royal Courts of Justice, *Strand* (2 F-5) The principal courts in the country for hearing civil cases consist of the Court of Appeal, the High Court (made up of the Queen's Bench Division, the Chancery Division and Family Division), and the Crown Court. Judges of the Queen's Bench are empowered to preside over criminal cases, some of which are now held in the new Queen's Building when the Old Bailey ★ lists are full.

In 1857 lack of adequate court space persuaded the government to purchase land south of Lincoln's Inn. G.E. Street's long, dignified Gothic building, with more than 1,000 rooms and 3½ miles of corridors, took ten years to complete and was formally opened by Queen Victoria in 1882. In the impressive entrance there are statues of Christ, King Alfred and biblical figures. Near the main hall, in the centre of the building, there is a small museum devoted to changing fashions in legal dress. Gothic arches lead to the various courts — over 60 in total, some in the original building, and a dozen in the 1968 extension. The Bankruptcy and Company Courts are in the Thomas More Building in Carey Street, which has led to the phrase 'in Carey Street', meaning in financial difficulties.

Royal Exchange (3 D-4) On a triangular site between Threadneedle Street and Cornhill with the Mansion House almost directly opposite, the present building with its elaborate columned portico is the third exchange to have been built since Sir Thomas Gresham established a meeting place for merchants in 1570, a function which ceased in 1939. The interior has been reconstructed to house temporarily the London International Financial Futures Exchange whose transactions may be viewed at certain hours from a visitors' gallery.

The first exchange, modelled on the bourse at Antwerp, was declared 'royal' by Queen Elizabeth I when she visited it in 1571. There were a hundred shops ranged around the colonnaded piazza — goldsmiths, apothecaries and traders in materials, glassware, armour and books. It became the commercial centre of the world, the competition resulting in the foundation of many overseas trading companies.

Niches above the columns held statues of Tudor monarchs: ironically, although Nicholas Stone's statue of Elizabeth I was rejected, it, unlike the others, survived the Great Fire and is today at Guildhall Library ★. The second Royal Exchange, opened in 1669, was also destroyed by fire but some of the John Bushnell statuary was saved and is now at the Central Criminal Court ★.

Sir Edward Tite's third exchange, opened by Queen Victoria in 1844, has an imposing pediment with sculpture by Richard Westmacott the younger depicting Commerce. The more important statues facing the Mansion House are the Duke of Wellington by Chantrey, and a war memorial by Aston Webb with figures by Alfred Drury. Gresham's Turkey paving which was retained is difficult to see today, but the courtyard walls, later adorned with paintings by such artists as Lord Leighton and Sigismund Goetze, may be seen by prior application to London International Financial Futures Exchange. (*Tel: 01-623-0444.*)

Royal Festival Hall (5 F-2) *(See map on page 80.)* One of London's most important concert halls and the largest of three halls that form the South Bank Concert Halls complex. It was the first major building to emerge out of the Festival of Britain in 1951, although it wasn't completed until 1965. Over 3,000 can be accommodated for large orchestral concerts; slightly less for the ballet seasons at Christmas and in the summer when a special proscenium arch is put up. The hall plays host to all the world's major orchestras, as well as the principal home orchestras, choirs, choral societies and solo artists. Art exhibitions frequently occupy part of the spacious foyers, and there are bars and restaurants.

Royal Horticultural Society Halls, *Vincent Square and Greycoat Street* (5 C-4) The two halls which back onto each other, are used regularly by the Royal Horticultural Society for flower shows, competitions and displays, and at other times hired to various commercial organisations for exhibitions. The Chelsea Flower Show, organised by the Society, is too large to be accommodated here and is held in the grounds of the Royal Hospital, Chelsea ★.

Royal Hospital, Chelsea *(See map on facing page)* Begun in 1682 at the instigation of Charles II, the hospital opened ten years later as a home for old and disabled soldiers. It has continued as such ever since. The Chelsea Pensioners, of whom there are over 400 today, wear distinctive scarlet coats and tricorn hats, an adaptation of uniforms worn in

The Royal Hospital, Chelsea

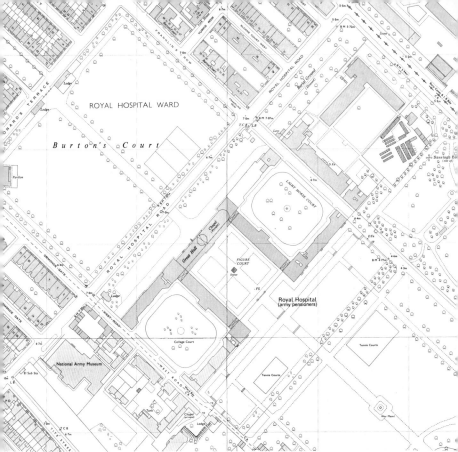

The Royal Hospital, Chelsea

SCALE 1:4 000 or 15 INCHES to 1 MILE

Marlborough's day. The idea for the home, inspired by the *Hôtel des Invalides* in Paris, followed the building of a hospital in Dublin and is the military predecessor of the similar institution for sailors at Greenwich ★. Nell Gwyn is often credited with suggesting it to the King — and a plaque acknowledging her benefaction is in the Great Hall — but it was the Paymaster-General, Sir Stephen Fox, who first outlined the plans to the King and financed them himself. John Evelyn supplied advice and Christopher Wren, invited to design it, set the red-brick building around three courtyards where the old soldiers could sit in sheltered sunlight.

Except for minor alterations the buildings, in which the Chelsea Pensioners sleep in dormitories, have little changed. The north wing contains the Great Hall, where the soldiers dine each day. This is hung with flags and portraits of military heroes, and at the west end hangs Verrio's huge portrait of Charles II on horseback. The Chapel has elaborate carvings in oak, and the half-dome of the apse is decorated with a fresco of the Resurrection by Sebastian Ricci. The Council Chamber (normally open only on Sunday afternoons) has some fine military trophies and a number of portraits of the Stuart monarchs, including a Charles I family group by Van Dyck. On the lawn in the Figure Court is Grinling Gibbons's fine contemporary bronze of Charles II, presented to the hospital in 1692. Each year on a date near Oak Apple Day (29 May), when the old soldiers parade and enjoy double rations, the

King's statue is decorated with oak leaves to commemorate his refuge in an oak tree after his defeat by the Roundheads at Worcester in 1651. The Hall, Chapel and a small museum are usually open 10 am – noon and 2 pm – 4 pm. (*Tel: 01-730-0161.*)

Royal Mews, *Buckingham Palace Road* (5 B-3) *(See map on page 25)* The state coaches, carriage horses and cars used by the Queen and members of the royal family are kept in the 18th-century Riding House built by William Chambers and later altered

The Royal Mews

69

by John Nash, which is open to the public twice a week (except during Royal Ascot week and on state occasions). The most splendid vehicle is the Gold State Coach designed for George III by Chambers in 1761 with painted side panels by Cipriani. Normally seen only at coronations, it was used by Queen Elizabeth II in the drive to St Paul's for her Silver Jubilee celebrations in 1977. The Irish State Coach, also on show, was ordered in Dublin by Queen Victoria in 1852 when she wanted a special coach for the State Opening of Parliament. George V bought the Glass Coach for royal weddings in 1910. Photographs depicting the royal family's keen interest in horses are on view. (*Tel: 01-930-4832 x 249.*)

Royal Opera House, *Covent Garden* (2 E-5) One of the great opera houses of the world, and the home

The Royal Opera House

of two internationally famous companies — the Royal Opera and the Royal Ballet. The opera company was formed after the Second World War from a number of existing companies. All performances are given in the original language and leading opera singers of every nationality appear in lavishly staged productions which alternate with the ballet. The Royal Ballet, founded by Dame Ninette de Valois at Sadler's Wells Theatre ★ in 1931, came to Covent Garden in 1946.

The origins of the Theatre Royal Covent Garden (as it was known) lie in one of two royal patents Charles II granted in 1662 allowing playhouses to perform legitimate drama. One went to Thomas Killigrew of the Theatre Royal Drury Lane ★, the other to Sir William Davenant of the Duke's Theatre, Lincoln's Inn. This latter patent was eventually owned by John Rich, who made history by producing 'the first English opera', John Gay's *The Beggar's Opera*. The profits enabled him to open his new theatre in Covent Garden four years later, on 7 December 1732, with a revival of Congreve's *The Way of the World*, closely followed by the opera which had brought him wealth. For

many years plays alternated with opera and ballet, and a number of Handel's works received their first performances here. Continuous rivalry with Drury Lane did not stop an interchange of performers such as Peg Woffington and David Garrick. The first productions of both Goldsmith's *She Stoops to Conquer* and Sheridan's *The Rivals* were at Covent Garden.

The first theatre (which had housed Handel's organ), burned down in 1808 and was replaced in under four months by Robert Smirke's classical building which had a frieze of literary figures, sculpted by Flaxman, under the portico. It was here the famous Mrs Siddons made her farewell in 1812, and in 1833 Edmund Kean collapsed while appearing in *Othello* and died shortly afterwards. The first performances in England of several Mozart, Rossini and Verdi operas took place here.

Smirke's building was destroyed by fire and replaced by Edward Barry's present theatre in which the Flaxman sculptures have been incorporated. The sumptuous red and gold auditorium is exceptionally well suited to royal galas and state occasions. A large extension has recently been added and a further £55 million rebuilding plan, scheduled to begin in 1988, will include development of the site at the side of the Opera House.

Royal Society of Arts, *8 John Adam Street* (5 E-1) A very pleasing building and one of the few surviving houses in the Adam brothers' Adelphi ★ scheme. Founded in 1754 as the Society for the Encouragement of Arts, Manufactures and Commerce, the Society was the first occupant in 1774 and has remained ever since. The words 'Arts and Commerce Promoted' on the frieze under the pediment succinctly describe the role of the society which played a large role in organising the Great Exhibition of 1851 and many subsequent exhibitions including the Festival of Britain in 1951. The first plaques commemorating the famous residents of London houses were put up by the society. The lecture hall is decorated with six huge murals by the Cork painter James Barry who took no payment. Many of his contemporaries — Dr Burney, Dr Johnson, Edmund Burke, Barry himself, Dr John Hunter and members of the RSA are depicted. The hall is occasionally shown to visitors who should apply in advance. (*Tel: 01-930-5115.*)

Sadler's Wells Theatre, *Rosebery Avenue (To north of Map 3 A-1)* Although some distance from the West End, this theatre in Islington ★ has been associated with opera and dance for the past half-century and is an important temporary home for touring companies, especially from overseas. The present theatre owes its existence to Lilian Baylis who took over the derelict previously famous playhouse and re-opened it in 1931. The Royal Ballet, founded by Dame Ninette de Valois, performed here from 1931 until they moved to the Royal Opera House ★ after the Second World War, but the theatre is today the headquarters of its touring company — known as the Sadler's Wells Royal Ballet. The opera company founded by Lilian Baylis in 1931, has been renamed English National Opera and since 1968 has performed at the London Coliseum ★. The recently formed New Sadler's Wells Opera Company gives short seasons of popular operettas by Lehar, Kalman, and Gilbert and Sullivan.

A 'musick' house, a side attraction to a medicinal well (now under the stalls), was first opened here by Thomas Sadler in 1683. For 300 years its fortunes have varied, with its greatest periods at the beginning of the 19th century and in mid-Victorian times. In 1781 Joseph Grimaldi, the greatest of all theatre clowns, made his first appearance in the playhouse with which he was associated for almost fifty years. Edmund Kean appeared as a boy actor in 1804. When the theatre monopoly of Covent Garden and Drury Lane was broken in 1843 the manager, Samuel Phelps, mounted 34 Shakespeare plays, an undertaking not surpassed until Lilian Baylis produced all the plays in the First Folio at the Old Vic 70 years later.

St Andrew's Holborn, *Holborn Viaduct* (3 A-3) A
church has been on the top of Holborn Hill for over a thousand years but the mediaeval church re-modelled by Christopher Wren in 1684 was — with the exception of the tower and outer walls — destroyed during the Second World War. The reconstruction was more faithful to the Victorians than to Wren. Some furnishings came from the chapel of the Thomas Coram Foundation★, among them the richly gilded organ case which once held the Renatus Harris instrument on which Handel gave recitals, and the hexagonal pulpit. In a recess is the tomb of Captain Coram. Samuel Wesley, father of John and Charles, was ordained here in 1689, and Benjamin Disraeli was baptised here when his Jewish father, annoyed at being fined for refusing to take office at the Bevis Marks Syna-gogue, had his 12 year-old son christened in protest.

St Andrew Undershaft (3 E-4) On the corner of
Leadenhall Street and St Mary Axe, Stow's 'fair and beautiful church of St Andrew the Apostle' was one of the few City churches to escape serious damage during the Second World War. The name Undershaft refers to a shaft or maypole put up on May Days for a celebration which was discontinued in 1517 after a riot directed against foreigners caused several deaths. The church, first mentioned in 1268, was rebuilt in the 14th century and has undergone five restorations, the most recent after a fire in 1976. The exterior and north-west doorway still retain their Tudor appearance. The church's best known memorial is to John Stow, the Eliza-bethan chronicler whose *Survey of London* is an invaluable record of the City from the late Plan-tagenets to the end of the Tudors. Stow died in poverty in 1605 at the age of 80 when his widow had the marble and alabaster monument put up. Every year on a date near to his birthday (5 April) the Lord Mayor attends a service and renews the quill pen Stow holds in his hand.

St Bartholomew's Hospital, *West Smithfield* (3 B-3) The oldest hospital in London, with many
specialist departments and a reputation as one of the best medical schools in the country. Granted a charter by Henry VIII, whose statue — the only one of him in London — is over the gateway, 'Barts' retained its Board of Governors until 1974.

The hospital was founded in 1123 after Rahere, court jester to Henry I, contracted malaria on a journey to Rome. He vowed if his life was saved he would establish a hospital for the poor on his return,

and the King granted him the land. From the adjacent Augustinian priory, which he also founded, he was able to see the nuns 'wait upon the sick with diligence and care in all gentleness'. Wat Tyler, however, was dragged from his hospital bed and immediately executed when he was admitted in 1381 after Mayor Walworth had stabbed him during the Peasants' Revolt. A later and better-known mayor, Dick Whittington, left money for repairs.to be carried out when he died in 1423.

At the Dissolution of the Monasteries the hospital managed to keep going and was re-founded by Henry VIII at the instigation of Sir Richard Gresham, and four years later in 1548 the City assumed responsibility for appointing governors. The most impressive room in the present buildings, designed by James Gibbs in 1729 around a quadrangle, is the Great Hall. This nobly proportioned hall has a double tier of windows (one of 17th-century stained glass shows Henry VIII granting the charter) and a ceiling with delicate lacy plasterwork. The public are admitted to see the hall and staircase.

St Bartholomew the Less, a small octagonal church in the grounds, was rebuilt in 1825 retaining the 15th-century tower and west wall.

St Bartholomew-the-Great, *West Smithfield* (3 C-2) In the oldest parish church in London it is still
possible to see traces of the Norman columns and arches of the Augustinian priory founded by Rahere (Henry I's fool or *jongleur*) in 1123 at the same time as he established the adjacent St Bartholomew's Hospital★. Rahere's tomb lies in the chancel.

Although there have been additions and much restoration, the transition from Norman to Gothic is visible in the crossing, which has round arches on the east and west and the later pointed ones on the

The Church of St Bartholomew-the-Great

other sides. Prior Bolton, who was in charge of the monastery from 1500 to 1532, put in the beautiful oriel window on the south of the chancel. This enabled him to hear masses without leaving his rooms. After the Dissolution the nave was de-molished but the chancel was saved. The entrance to the church is through a small gateway which has a half-timbered Elizabethan façade. The porch is Victorian but the tower rising from it was erected in 1628, its five bells a century older. Dereliction occurred in the late 18th century when parts of the church were rented out as stables, a school and a blacksmith's; the 14th-century Lady Chapel was once a tenement and a print shop where Benjamin Franklin worked in 1725; but the Victorians saved St Bartholomew's from complete delapidation. In 1887 the rector invited Sir Aston Webb to begin the restoration which lasted well into the present century.

St Bride's, *Fleet Street* (3 B-4) Often called 'the wedding cake church' because its tiered spire is said to have inspired William Rich, a baker on Ludgate Hill, to make 'bride cakes' resembling it, this is one of the few City churches with an active ministry and services on Sundays. Fleet Street's own parish church is in constant contact with newspapers, printing and publicity organisations.

St Bride's, named after the 5th-century Irish saint, is possibly the oldest Christian place of worship in London. Standing on the site of a Roman house, the church built by Christopher Wren in 1683-87 was the fifth on the site and was one of his largest and most expensive. On the night of 29 December 1940 it was almost totally destroyed, although the lectern (said to have been rescued previously in 1666) was saved and the steeple remained standing even though the bells fell in molten ruin. Before the rebuilding — largely financed by the newspaper industry — archaeologists were able to discover evidence of the earlier churches. The finds are now on display in the crypt (open daily) where the development of printing in Fleet Street is also illustrated.

St Bride's associations with the printed word began when Caxton's assistant Wynkyn de Worde, who was buried in the church, set up his press next door. The diarist Samuel Pepys was christened here and John Dryden, John Milton, Dr Johnson, James Boswell, Oliver Goldsmith, David Garrick, and

St Bride's Church

Edmund Burke are among the many literary figures who lived within 100 yards. The parish records reveal that parents of Edward Winslow — one of the Pilgrim Fathers and Governor of Plymouth, Massachusetts — were married here and that the parents of Virginia Dare — the first English child born in America — were parishioners.

St Clement Danes (2 F-5) The central church of the Royal Air Force on an island in the Strand. Reconstructed by Christopher Wren after the Great Fire, it was destroyed by the Luftwaffe in 1941. Its second rebuilding was financed by contributions

St Clement Danes Church

from the Royal Air Force, and the Commonwealth and Allied air forces. The organ was the gift of the United States Air Force, the lectern of the Australian Air Force. This is the church of the nursery rhyme 'Oranges and Lemons', although the song is also attributed to St Clement Eastcheap. Bells, hung in 1957, play the tune four times a day.

Almost nothing is known about the 9th-century Danish church (hence the 'Danes') dedicated to the patron saint of sailors, but Wren incorporated remnants of the AD 1022 stone building into the tower when he demolished St Clement's and put up a new one. The tower, with 1719 additions by James Gibbs, withstood the air raids.

Ann Donne, wife of Dr John Donne, the poet and Dean of St Paul's, was buried here but her tomb was destroyed in 1941. Dr Johnson, whose statue is outside, worshipped here regularly, and in the list of rectors on the south wall can be seen the name of Dr William Webb-Ellis, who as a schoolboy 'first took the ball in his arms and ran with it', thus initiating the game of rugby football.

St Etheldreda's Ely Place (3 A-2) The oldest Catholic church in Britain, and the oldest building in Holborn. A small chapel built in 1251 on the site of the present crypt became the property of the Bishop of Ely in 1286. The great mediaeval church went up a few years later. The Black Prince, who lodged at nearby Ely House, and John of Gaunt, who also lived there, were regular worshippers. When Henry VIII and Catherine of Aragon came to a great five-day feast in 1531 the knights and squires lodged in the church and cloister. After the King's quarrel with Rome the Catholic tradition at St Etheldreda's finally lapsed in 1570.

A sudden change of wind saved the church at the Great Fire, and again it survived when Ely Place ★ was redeveloped in 1772. It was bought by the Rosminians in 1873, and restored to the Roman Catholic church. There are daily services.

St George's Hanover Square (2 B-5) Built in 1713-24 to cater for the growing population in Mayfair ★, its most impressive feature is the portico, the first on a London church. St George's has always been fashionable for weddings and the register records the marriages of Sir William Hamilton and Emma Hart, Disraeli and Mrs Wyndham Lewis, and confirmation of Shelley's Scottish marriage to Harriet Westbrook.

George Frederic Handel, the composer, who lived close by in Brook Street, worshipped here for 34 years. An annual festival of music is held in his memory.

St James's (5 C-1 etc.) A not clearly defined district on both sides of St James's Street between Piccadilly and St James's Palace. In the broadest sense it may be said to encompass St James's Park ★, Buckingham Palace ★ and Clarence House ★. St James's became a fashionable area soon after the Restoration when the Court officially moved to St James's Palace ★. A number of grand houses between St James's and Green Park have given it a distinguished air which is increased by gentlemen's clubs and old-established businesses in the street itself.

The area to the east, stretching as far as Lower Regent Street, was developed by Henry Jermyn, Earl of St Albans, who, granted a lease by Charles II, laid out St James's Square ★ and several surrounding streets, including the one bearing his name. He also put up money for Wren to build St James's Church, Piccadilly ★.

Although there have been extensive alterations over 300 years, St James's has maintained its elegant air and it is still possible to experience the atmosphere of bygone days. In St James's Street several Georgian shops survive and an alleyway at the bottom of the street leads into a courtyard where Texas had an embassy before it became part of the United States. White's, one of the most famous clubs, founded in 1674, is at Nos. 37-38, its distinctive bow window dating from 1811; Boodle's is at No. 28, the Carlton at No. 69 and Brook's is on the corner of Park Place. The hexagonal building set back from the road at No. 25 is the office of the *Economist* magazine.

St James's Palace (5 C-2) The principal royal residence from 1698 when the Palace of Whitehall burnt down until the reign of George IV. While no sovereign has lived here for 150 years this is officially the palace where new sovereigns are proclaimed. All foreign envoys are accredited to the Court of St James's. The State Apartments are now used only for private receptions. In other sections of the palace there are the offices of the Lord Chamberlain and residences of court officials, and the Duke and Duchess of Kent occupy the apartments known as York House.

A hospital for female lepers stood on the site from the 12th century until Henry VIII exchanged it in 1532 for land in Suffolk. The inmates were given annuities, the buildings razed and a new palace erected. The gateway facing up St James's Street and the Chapel Royal are Tudor survivals. State Apartments were added by Christopher Wren for William III after the Whitehall fire but Wren's external work is only evident today on the south side of Engine Court. In the Throne Room there are fine Grinling Gibbons carvings. Other public rooms were further embellished by William Kent. In 1825 Nash added a dwelling to the southwest end of the State Apartments for George IV's brother the Duke of Clarence. This is today the Queen Mother's home.

Charles II's favourite palace has witnessed many notable historical events. The saddest was when his father Charles I, who spent his last days here, walked from the palace to the scene of his execution in Whitehall ★ in January 1649. Earlier, Mary Tudor died here. Queen Anne and the first

St James's Palace

SCALE 1:4 000 or 15 INCHES to 1 MILE

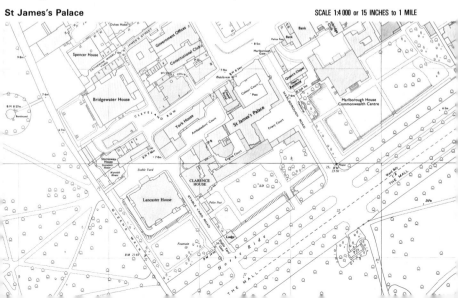

St James's Palace

three Hanoverian kings were frequently in residence.

The palace is not open to the public (except for the Chapel Royal ★ on certain Sundays for services) but as it stands directly on the street three of the four courts are visible. The fourth, Colour Court, lies inside the Tudor gateway where there are guards posted. The Changing of the Guard takes place in Ambassadors' Court after a detachment arrives from Buckingham Palace ★ .

St James's Park (5 C-3 etc.) The prettiest and most royal of royal parks is surrounded by palaces, former palaces and the houses of past and present members of the royal family. With its curving lake, sloping lawns, magnificent trees, carefully-tended flower beds, and rare wildfowl, this is the loveliest oasis in London.

The marshy land of the hospital Henry VIII acquired in 1532 was drained to create a deer park with a rural garden — Spring Garden ★ — in the northeast corner. Over a century later, inspired by the gardens at Versailles, Charles II removed the surrounding walls. The King, his spaniels at his heels and accompanied by one of his mistresses, would stroll to feed the ducks on the long ornamental canal that had been laid out for him (possibly by Le Nôtre), or walk to inspect the long range of aviaries at the south of the park — hence Birdcage Walk. Wishing to see and be seen by his people, Charles II had the park opened for the public.

Drastic changes were made to the layout in 1770 by Capability Brown, and even greater alterations

St James's Park

carried out by John Nash on the orders of the Prince Regent (George IV). He changed the shape of Charles II's canal, and the peninsula he created became known as Duck Island. In 1957 the present slender bridge replaced the graceful suspension bridge across the lake — despite many protests in The Times. The Guards Memorial, facing Horse Guards Parade, commemorates the officers and men of the Grenadier Guards, and of the Scots, Welsh, Irish and Coldstream Guards who were killed in the First World War.

St James's, Piccadilly (5 C-1) (See map on page 62) One of only two Wren churches outside the City, and the only one he erected where no previous church had stood. Largely financed by Henry Jermyn, Earl of St Albans, to serve the estate he was developing, St James's was consecrated in 1684. The spacious interior, with Corinthian pillars rising to the roof from the balconies, contains some fine carvings by Grinling Gibbons and the organ case he made for the Palace of Whitehall. This was given to the church by Queen Mary II. Extensive restoration work at St James's in 1937 was erased by a bomb in 1940. The damage was repaired but further restoration work is essential and a million-pound appeal was launched in the autumn of 1986.

St James's Square (5 C-1) At the heart of St James's ★ lies the aristocratic square laid out by the Earl of St Albans who intended it to be surrounded by the palaces of noblemen. Jermyn had to settle for grand mansions and, although none of the original houses remain, the uniformity of elevation and varied façades reflect some of the character of the earlier houses. Until this century the square was largely residential and attracted the aristocracy and prominent gentlemen as Jermyn intended. Two of James II's mistresses — Arabella Churchill and Catherine Sedley — were early occupiers of No. 21. Now rebuilt, the house is united with No. 20, the childhood home of Queen Elizabeth the Queen Mother early this century. Frances Stewart, Duchess of Richmond, the virtuous mistress of Charles II whose face was the model for Britannia on coins, lived at No. 15. Three Prime Ministers — Pitt, Derby and Gladstone — resided at No. 10. The tall façade in the northwest corner — No. 14 — is the London Library ★ . The oldest house in the square now is No. 5 (from where the shot killing WPC Yvonne Fletcher was fired at the start of the Libyan Peoples' Bureau siege in 1984). Norfolk House, Henry Jermyn's own home, was standing until 1938 when the present apartment block was erected: the music room was saved and recon-structed at the Victoria and Albert Museum ★ . General Eisenhower had headquarters here during the Second World War. The equestrian statue in the gardens is of William III in Roman dress.

St John the Evangelist, Tower of London (3 F-5) The chapel dedicated to St John is the oldest Norman ecclesiastical building in London, having been built in 1078 at the same time as the White Tower, in which it stands. William the Conqueror came here to worship. Henry VI is said to have lain here after his murder, and Henry VII's wife, Elizabeth of York, lay in state after her death. It was the scene of the proxy betrothal between Mary Tudor and Philip of Spain. From the 17th to the 19th century archives were stored in the chapel and services were discontinued until restoration took place in 1968. Once again it is a place of worship, used for Free Church services.

St John's Gate, Clerkenwell (3 B-2)

St John's Gate, *Clerkenwell* (3 B-2) The gatehouse, built in 1504, stands at the original entrance to the Priory of Clerkenwell where the Knights Templar founded a branch of the Order of St John c. 1140. The Order was suppressed at the Dissolution of the Monasteries but Prior Thomas Docwra's

St John's Gate, Clerkenwell

gatehouse, then new, was left standing and became the office of Elizabeth I's Master of Revels. In the 18th century it was the offices of the publisher of *The Gentleman's Magazine* which Dr Johnson, David Garrick and Oliver Goldsmith came to visit. Later it became an inn. The gate is now occupied by the Most Venerable Order of the Hospital of St John of Jerusalem, the revived Protestant Order. The Museum of the Order of St John ★ adjoins the gatehouse.

St John's, Smith Square (5 D-4)

St John's, Smith Square (5 D-4) This baroque church with its four distinctive towers is today a popular concert hall. Badly damaged in 1941, the church was sold to a Trust which restored the gutted interior. The 1713 design is supposed to have been inspired by Queen Anne who kicked over a footstool and told Thomas Archer to build a church like it. The name 'Queen Anne's footstool' has stuck. More probably the architect designed the four towers so that if the church sank in the then marshy ground it would do so evenly. The controversial style has often been criticised, notably by Dickens (in *Our Mutual Friend*) who wrote that it resembled 'some petrified monster, frightful and gigantic, on its back with its legs in the air'.

St Katharine Docks

St Katharine Docks *(See map on page 86)* A most attractive yacht haven with private moorings surrounded by restored 19th-century warehouses, a modern hotel and a trade centre. The dock is on the site of the ancient hospice of St Katharine, founded in 1146 and the only ecclesiastical establishment governed directly by the queens of England. Early in the 19th century the hospice moved to Regent's Park ★ and the area became a dock, the import centre for the wine, spices, tea and ivory trades. Extensive restoration and redevelopment in recent times have transformed a shabby dock into a thriving commercial and leisure complex with restaurants, an 'old-world' pub and other attractions. The hundreds of yachts provide a permanent, floating boat show.

St Lawrence Jewry, Guildhall Yard (3 D-3)

St Lawrence Jewry, *Guildhall Yard* (3 D-3) The guild church of the Corporation of the City of London derives the latter part of its name from the Jews who lived nearby until expelled by Edward I in 1291. The 12th-century mediaeval building was burnt down in the Great Fire. In 1677 Charles II attended the consecration of the new church, one of Wren's most expensive creations. Gutted in December 1940, the church has been restored, and Wren's elaborate plasterwork and reredos copied. The Commonwealth Chapel is regarded as one of the most beautiful restored interiors in London. The occasions when the civic dignitaries come to worship are particularly splendid. Regular lunchtime organ recitals are given in the church.

St Margaret's, Westminster, Parliament Square (5 D-3)

St Margaret's, Westminster, *Parliament Square* (5 D-3) Standing at the side of Westminster Abbey, in whose care it was placed by a special Act of Parliament in 1973, this is the parish church of the House of Commons. This association began in 1614 when the Puritan movement was spreading and the Commons, wishing to dissociate themselves from High Church practices, assembled in the church rather than the Abbey for corporate communion on Palm Sunday.

The present building, consecrated in 1523, is the third since the parish was founded in the 11th century to cater for the tradesmen and craftsmen who lived in the village around the Palace and Abbey. Although extensively restored, some of its mediaeval style has been retained, and the glass, furniture and funeral monuments are especially fine. Immediately below the east window the exceptional reredos, carved in limewood in 1753, has a centrepiece based on Titian's painting *The Supper at Emmaus*. The 19th-century west window, has a portrait of Sir Walter Raleigh whose headless body was buried under the high altar after his execution. Around the walls the most fascinating memorials are those of Tudor courtiers, and the artist Wenceslaus Hollar.

St Margaret's has many famous connections and for centuries has been popular for fashionable weddings — Samuel Pepys, Winston Churchill and Lord Louis Mountbatten are among those who were married here. Despite being at the side of the great Abbey, the church has its own congregation, and a choir supplied by Westminster City School.

St Martin-in-the-Fields, Trafalgar Square (5 D-1)

St Martin-in-the-Fields, *Trafalgar Square* (5 D-1) *(See map on page 87)* One of London's best-known landmarks, the church has only enjoyed its magnificent setting since the 1820s when the square was laid out. Built in 1722-24 by the architect James Gibbs, it was previously hemmed in by 'vile houses' at the lower end of St Martin's Lane. These were

St Martin-in-the-Fields from Trafalgar Square

demolished to create the present vista. A steep flight of steps leads up to the impressive pedimented portico with the tower and steeple rising up immediately behind the entrance.

This is the third church on the site since the 13th century. In the Tudor church (pulled down as unsafe in 1721) Charles II was baptised. His mistress Nell Gwyn was buried in the churchyard when she died in 1687 at the age of 38 but her tomb has long since disappeared. The royal associations with St Martin's are still maintained. Buckingham Palace and St James's Palace come within the parish and the boxes by the chancel are reserved for the royal family.

The crypt, a refuge for homeless soldiers during the First World War, became a shelter for down-and-outs between the wars, a ministry continued to this day. Restored after use as an air raid shelter when a bomb hit it, it is now occasionally the scene of opera productions and concerts.

St Mary le Bow, *Cheapside* (3 C-4) One of the most famous and oldest parochial churches in London with a Norman crypt where the stone arches or bows — hence the name — had capitals decorated with spearheads. Here the Court of Arches met to settle matters of ecclesiastical discipline. The twelve church bells — Bow Bells — are celebrated in the legendary story of Dick Whittington turning when he heard them, whereupon he returned to become Lord Mayor three times. They are also referred to in the nursery rhyme 'Oranges and Lemons', and to be a true Cockney one must be born within the sound of them.

The history of the Norman church is packed with incident. At various times the roof has been blown off and the tower has toppled down, on each occasion killing people. In 1196 a rabble-rousing agitator, William Fitz-Osbert, barricaded himself in and had to be smoked out.

Incendiary bombs engulfed the church in flames in May 1941 and although the undercroft and walls withstood the enemy action, the famous peal of bells crashed to the ground. Recast from the old metal, they were not heard again until 1961, when the rebuilding was nearing completion. The statue outside the church is of Captain John Smith, who led the expedition to Virginia in 1606.

St Pancras (2 E-1) The British Rail terminus and Sir George Gilbert Scott's huge Gothic hotel dominate the drab neighbourhood at the east end of the Euston Road. There is only partial truth in the story that Scott used his rejected designs for the Foreign Office for the sombre building which, after being offices, may again become a hotel. To the immediate west another large building is under construction. This, due to open early in the 1990s, will house the British Library ★ which is moving from the British Museum. Scholars and researchers will then have faster access to the 250 miles of books presently stored in 15 buildings around London.

St Paul's Cathedral (3 C-4) Sir Christopher Wren's masterpiece, the cathedral church of the Bishop of London, a landmark and national symbol, this is one of the country's principal tourist attractions. Since Wren completed it in 1709, 33 years after the foundation stone was laid, it has been the scene of great state occasions: the jubilee services of sovereigns, services of thanksgiving after battles won and the funerals of such national heroes as Nelson, Wellington and Winston Churchill. In 1981 the marriage of Prince Charles to Lady Diana Spencer was the first wedding at St Paul's of a Prince of Wales since Henry VII's eldest son Arthur married Catherine of Aragon at the old cathedral in November 1501.

Old St Paul's, built according to tradition on the site of a Roman temple, was the successor to the 7th-century church endowed by Ethelbert, King of Kent. Neglected and used for stabling during the Civil War, it was engulfed by flames at the Great Fire, the ruins later demolished by gunpowder. Wren submitted a model in oak for the new cathedral (this is now displayed in the crypt) but this and his subsequent 'Nightmare' design were rejected. Work began on the present building in 1675, financed by public subscription and by a coal tax in London. Long before the great dome was

St Paul's Cathedral

St Paul's Cathdral   SCALE 1:4 000 or 15 INCHES to 1 MILE

finished the first services were held. The dome, painted by Sir James Thornhill with scenes from the life of St Paul, is not the one visible from outside. Above the paintings there is an inner conical brick dome with projecting timbers supporting the exterior metal tureen. The elegant lantern and cross, weighing 700 tons, are secured by encircling iron chains.

The only substantial remnant of the old cathedral is the monument to Dr John Donne, the poet and preacher who became Dean of St Paul's. As memorials were not permitted until 1790 in Wren's building, it is the oldest by far, but has been joined by many since, among them those to Sir Joshua Reynolds and Dr Johnson.

In the crypt, said to be the largest in Europe, lies the tomb of Wren. The famous epitaph composed by his son, is on the stone, the last line reading: *Lector, si monumentum requiris, Circumspice.* (Reader, if you seek a monument, look around you.) Exactly beneath the centre of the dome, a black marble sarcophagus holds the coffin of Admiral Lord Nelson; originally intended for Cardinal Wolsey, it lay unoccupied at Windsor for over 250 years. The Duke of Wellington is in a huge sarcophagus of Cornish porphyry. Nearby are memorials to the ten field marshals of the Second World War.

In 'Painters' Corner' graves and memorials commemorate artists, including Van Dyck, Lord Leighton, the Regency portraitist Sir Thomas Lawrence, Benjamin West (the American painter who became second President of the Royal Academy), John Constable, the architect Sir Edwin Lutyens and Holman Hunt, a copy of whose *The Light of the World* hangs in the south aisle.

A staircase in the south aisle leads to the Whispering Gallery, the best place to see Thornhill's paintings. Here words whispered against the wall can be heard quite distinctly on the other side of the gallery. There are extensive views over London from the Stone Gallery, and even more dramatic ones from the Golden Gallery which involves a climb of 627 steps.

Although St Paul's was hit twice by bombs during the Second World War, causing damage to the North Transept and east end, it was saved largely by the brave efforts of the nightly firewatchers.

The Cathedral is open daily, and there are frequent services. A small chapel is set aside for those who wish to pray undisturbed by tourists. (*Tel: 01-248-2705.*)

St Paul's, Covent Garden (2 E-5) The portico overlooking the piazza of Covent Garden is the setting at the beginning of *Pygmalion* (and in the musical version — *My Fair Lady*) but the stage associations of Inigo Jones's church pre-date George Bernard Shaw by several centuries. Rather as happens today, Samuel Pepys watched a Punch and Judy show near the porch in May 1662. Known as the Actors' Church, memorial services for famous players are held frequently. Many performers have been buried in the vaults and churchyard. Numerous tablets on the walls commemorate such stage personalities as Charles Macklin, who was reputed to be 107 when he died in 1797 (though the coffin plate says 97), and Dame Ellen Terry, whose ashes are in a casket in the south wall.

St Paul's, completed in 1633, was the second city church to be built after the Reformation. Francis Russell, 4th Earl of Bedford, engaged Inigo Jones to develop the Covent Garden piazza, but as the church would produce little income the architect was instructed to keep it simple — 'not much better than a barn'. This prompted Jones's celebrated reply: 'Well then, you shall have the handsomest barn in England.' In order to give an imposing façade, Jones built a great portico facing the square, but this is a fake because behind it is the altar and people have to enter by the smaller west door.

St Peter ad Vincula, *Tower of London* (3 F-5) In the inner ward, this chapel built in the 16th century on the site of two previous ones faced Tower Green and the scaffold on which Lady Jane Grey and two of Henry VIII's wives (Anne Boleyn and Catherine Howard) were executed. The bodies were unceremoniously buried beneath the nave along with those of Thomas More, John Fisher and Simon Fraser, and Lord Lovat, the last man in England to die by the axe. Along with other illustrious people who were executed, they were only given proper burials in 1876 and are now under stones bearing their coats of arms in the chancel. A number of fine monuments commemorate citizens who died of natural causes but none was as important as the beheaded. There is free access to the Tower for those attending services.

St Sepulchre-without-Newgate, *Holborn Viaduct* (3 B-3) The largest of the City's parish churches, with strong musical associations. The Chapel of St Stephen is dedicated to musicians. A window commemorates Sir Henry Wood, the founder of the promenade concerts. The conductor was assistant organist here at the age of fourteen. On the Sunday after the Last Night of the Proms the wreath is removed from his bust in the Royal Albert Hall ★ and placed here. Another window depicts Dame Nellie Melba and has peaches in one corner, a reminder of the dessert named after her. The blue carpets were given in memory of another famous Proms conductor, Sir Malcolm Sargent. Each year on the feast of St Cecilia (22 November) the choirs of St Paul's Cathedral, Westminster Abbey, Canterbury Cathedral and the Chapel Royal take part in a musical service honouring the patron saint of music.

After the Great Fire the parishioners were in such a hurry to rebuild that they started before Wren arrived with the result that some of the mediaeval building was retained. St Sepulchre's peal of ten bells are the 'Bells of Old Bailey' whose Great Bell was tolled during executions outside Newgate Gaol.

The prison, where the Central Criminal Court ★ now stands, has grim associations with the church. Through a door-head, still visible, the sexton went down an underground passage to the prison to see the condemned before they went to their executions.

St Stephen Walbrook (3 D-4) The dull exterior, completely overshadowed by the Mansion House ★, gives little indication that the interior is Wren's best parish church, and the model for St Paul's. Bands of Corinthian columns are cleverly arranged to form a Greek cross and appear to have little to do with the dome they support. Although the building was damaged by bombs in 1941, most of the furnishings were saved. The west lobby with the organ gallery, the pulpit and reredos are all 17th century. The headquarters of the Samaritans, the association founded by the rector the Rev. Dr Chad Varah to give comfort to those who cannot cope with life, are in the crypt. Extensive restoration work is in progress and the central altar, designed by Henry Moore, excited controversy when installed.

St Thomas's Hospital, *Lambeth Palace Road* (5 E-3) The large teaching hospital with approximately 1,000 beds is gradually being modernised. Overlooking the Thames, the turreted Continental-style Victorian buildings where Florence Nightingale established her school of nursing are being replaced by Eugene Rosenberg's glass blocks. The hospital, founded early in the 12th century, was in Southwark until 1856, across the road from Guy's Hospital ★. The development of the railway brought about the move to the present site. However, in St Thomas Street, below London Bridge Station the **Old Operating Theatre** is in part of a Georgian terrace. It is open to the public. (*Tel: 01-407-7600.*)

Savoy Chapel (2 E-5) The full name of this little chapel with many royal associations is the Queen's Chapel of the Savoy. Since 1937 it has been the chapel of the Royal Victorian Order, founded by Queen Victoria to recognise personal service to the sovereign. Earlier this century it was one of the few churches where divorced couples could be remarried, thanks to the rector's beliefs in divorce reform.

The chapel was built early in the 16th century as part of the hospital Henry VII established on the site of the Palace of Savoy. This palace was inherited by John of Gaunt who had to flee when it was sacked in 1381 by Wat Tyler. The dull exterior of the church gives no indication of the rich interior, which has been heavily restored. The Tudor roof (a Victorian copy) is decorated with quatrefoils and royal shields, the walls panelled. The sixteen stalls belong to knights of the Royal Victorian Order whose arms are emblazoned on copper plates. Services noted for their high music standards are held every Sunday except in August and September.

Savoy Hotel, *Strand* (5 E-1) The hotel built in 1884 by Richard D'Oyly Carte adjoins the theatre he had put up three years earlier to house the operas of Gilbert and Sullivan. Almost from the beginning each bedroom had its own bathroom, an unheard-of luxury at the turn of the century. The first manager and chef, César Ritz and Auguste Escoffier, established standards the hotel has always tried to maintain. The Grill Room and River Restaurant are among the best restaurants in London. Unlike that of some large modern chain hotels, the decor and furnishings in soft colours suggest Edwardian comfort.

Science Museum, *Exhibition Road* (4 C-4) This foremost museum in the country devoted to science and industry attracts over 3 million visitors a year. They come to learn about the scientific principles that govern the world and outer space. There are remarkable collections of machines, industrial plant, medical equipment and scientific apparatus which explain the mechanics of manufacture, their discovery and invention.

In a room named Synopsis display cases are filled with objects and explanatory panels: these give brief resumés of what the visitor may expect in the museum's 50 or more galleries. Every first-time visitor should begin here before going to the Centre Hall where there are railway trains, among them *Puffing Billy*, the world's oldest locomotive, and Stephenson's *Rocket*. Far more sophisticated rockets are in the halls devoted to the exploration of space. There are early motorcars on show. Explanations are provided about nuclear power, and the development of computers. Photography and astronomy are on the same floor as the aeronautics gallery. Here is the first plane to cross the Atlantic, that flown by the British pilots Alcock and Brown in 1919. Part of the Wellcome Museum of Medical History ★ is on the top floor. The collections illustrate the progress of medicine.

A number of the museum's exhibits were bought at the Great Exhibition and subsequent purchases, such as the collection owned by the Patent Office, were originally housed with the fine arts acquisitions at the the Museum of Ornamental Art (later the Victoria and Albert Museum ★). The arts and sciences were separated at the turn of the century and the present museum opened in 1913. The national library devoted to pure and applied sciences is open to research scholars. The museum's education department organises lectures, demonstrations and film shows. (*Tel: 01-589-3456.*)

Seven Dials (2 D-5) Seven roads lead into the tiny roundabout where Earlham Street crosses Monmouth Street. A column which had a clock with seven faces — hence the name — was put up here in 1694 and removed in 1773 when a rumour spread that money was secreted in the base. It is due to be replaced in the late 1980s. The surrounding area, intended as a fashionable residential district, achieved a notorious reputation in the 19th century as the haunt of crooks and thieves.

Shaftesbury Avenue (2 C-5, D-4 & D-5) Five theatres and two large cinemas are in the street that cuts through Soho. The Apollo, Lyric, Globe and Queen's are the four nearest Piccadilly Circus ★, each staging a mixture of straight drama, comedies and the occasional musical. The casts are invariably headed by well-known actors. The Palace, facing Cambridge Circus, is now owned by Andrew Lloyd Webber who continues the policy of presenting musicals. The Curzon West End, the cinema on the corner of Frith Street, screens serious films, some by foreign directors. Further along on the way towards High Holborn, the Cannon normally shows popular Hollywood movies.

The street is named after the philanthropic 7th Earl of Shaftesbury who helped the poor in the neighbourhood; its creation in 1886 resulted in the clearance of some squalid slums. Although shops and offices mingle with restaurants and places of entertainment the avenue has never been noted as a main shopping area.

Shell Centre, *South Bank* (5 F-2) The international oil company's offices are in two massive blocks on either side of Hungerford Bridge. Linked by an underground tunnel, they cover 7 ½ acres, making them one of the largest office complexes in Europe. In the central courtyard of the upstream building (part of which rises to 25 storeys) there is a fountain of bronze shells piled on top of each other, down which the water cascades.

Silver Vaults *See London Silver Vaults ★*

Smithfield (3 B-2 etc.) One of the most unusual areas in London with a well-documented history of a gory past and where buildings known to mediaeval generations still survive. South of Charterhouse Street is London's main meat market. Poultry and provisions are also sold here in vast buildings with nearly 2 miles of selling space. Over 3,000 people work here and more than 350,000 tons of meat are sold annually.

In 1173 William FitzStephen, Thomas Becket's clerk, noted it was 'A smoth field where every Friday there is a celebrated rendezvous of fine horses to be sold'. Within a hundred years a live cattle market was established. This remained until 1855, after which only slaughtered meat was sold. The present covered central meat market was erected in 1866-67, and the poultry market in 1963. Smithfield is at its busiest from 8 pm when large refrigerated lorries begin offloading carcasses for the 5 am trading start. By midday, silence prevails.

Being just outside the City walls the 'smoth field' (hence the name) was convenient for jousting, and a royal tournament held in 1384 lasted seven days. For four centuries the open space was also a place of execution. Wat Tyler, who was stabbed by Mayor Walworth while addressing Richard II, died later in front of St Bartholomew's Hospital ★. The most appalling burnings and hangings occurred during the religious persecutions after the Reformation. Of the 270 Protestants executed during Mary I's reign, 43 were hanged or put on the fire in front of the hospital. Memorials on the wall commemorate the Smithfield Martyrs.

In Bartholomew Close the satirical painter William Hogarth was born, and Benjamin Franklin lived close by when he was employed at printing works next door in the church of St Bartholomew the Great ★. In Cloth Fair, beside the church, drapers set up their stalls for St Bartholomew's Fair, held annually at Smithfield for over 700 years, and immortalised in Ben Jonson's play *Bartholomew Fair*. In its last years a reputation for debauchery and bawdiness resulted in the fair's suppression in 1855. There have been attempts to revive it in recent years. Two Jacobean houses (Nos. 41 and 42 Cloth Fair) survived the Great Fire and have been well restored. Pye Corner, the furthest extent of the fire of 1666, is marked by a small gilt statue of a boy on the corner of Giltspur Street and Cock Lane.

Sir John Soane's Museum, *13 Lincoln's Inn Fields* (2 F-4) This little-known museum which deserves wider recognition typifies the curious taste of an eminent, somewhat eccentric Georgian gentleman. When Sir John Soane, architect of the Bank of England, died in 1837 at the age of 84 he left instructions that his collections were not to be touched. To this day the house (actually three adjoining houses) remains undisturbed. The effect of space in the small rooms is achieved by the ingenious use of mirrors and such devices as a shallow-domed ceiling in the breakfast room.

The museum has a wealth of antiquities and art bought by Soane, fine period furniture and a world-famous collection of architectural drawings. The drawings include George Dance's 52 designs for the Mansion House, drawings by Piranesi, and nearly 9,000 designs from the office of Robert and John Adam. Among the paintings are Hogarth's *Rake's Progress* and *The Election.*

In 1825 Soane held a three-day reception to show off his acquisition of the alabaster sarcophagus of Seti I from the Valley of the Kings in Egypt. He bought it after the British Museum declined to pay the asking price of £2,000.

To ensure the future of the house and its treasures before he died, Soane obtained an Act of Parliament preserving them for the nation. Part of No. 12 is a library where students may study the drawings collection. (*Tel: 01-405-2107.*)

Soho (2 C-4 etc.) Restaurants, patisseries, charcuteries, delicatessens, many run by foreigners, and the market in Berwick Street lend this district a cosmopolitan atmosphere. Westminster City Council has tried to clean up the strip clubs, sex shops and illegal drinking clubs that proliferated in the 1970s but many continue to operate. Their neon signs add a garish touch to a neighbourhood which has acquired a shady reputation. Wardour Street is the centre of the film industry, and there are also a number of recording studios used by the music industry.

The name is assumed to come from a cry — 'So-Ho' — used by huntsmen riding over the land before it was developed in the 17th century. Charles II's natural son, the Duke of Monmouth, had a fine mansion in Soho Square. This and adjacent Carlisle House — a temple of festivities — have gone, but one particularly fine building, the House of St Barnabas ★, survives on the corner of the Square and Greek Street.

Berwick Street Market, Soho

From its earliest days foreigners were attracted to the narrow streets of terrace houses. French Huguenot refugees settled close to their chapel near Greek Street. They were followed by a large number of immigrants from Europe, and recently by the Chinese who have taken over Gerrard Street ★. The foreign population has drastically declined since the Second World War, and a large number of the shops they ran have disappeared. Most of the now-shabby Georgian houses that have not been demolished have been turned into offices with shops at street level.

Somerset House, *Strand* (2 F-5) William Chambers's large Palladian building, set around a courtyard, was erected with an impressive frontage onto the Thames at the end of the 18th century for learned societies and government bodies. The Board of the Inland Revenue occupy one wing but the Registry of Births, Marriages and Deaths, kept here for over a century, moved out in 1973 leaving only the Principal Probate Registry, where copies of all wills since 1858 are filed. The State Rooms, which housed the Royal Academy until 1836, have been restored and there are plans to move the Courtauld Institute Galleries ★ here before the end of the 1980s.

The present building stands on the site of the mediaeval London houses of the Bishops of Worcester and Chester. These were demolished by the Lord Protector Somerset for whom a palace was being built when he was executed in 1552. The palace became a Crown possession, providing a home for Elizabeth I before she came to the throne, and was later the residence of the queens consort until Queen Charlotte preferred Buckingham House.

Sotheby's, *34-35 New Bond Street* (2 B-5) Until they moved to their present salerooms just before the First World War the international fine art auctioneers specialised in books. Founded in 1744

Sotheby's

by Samuel Baker, a bookseller, who took his nephew John Sotheby into the partnership 32 years later, the firm remained in the family for a hundred years. The acquisition of Parke Bernet in 1964 gave the auctioneers a major American outlet, and in 1983 the firm was bought by an American.

South Bank (5 F-2 etc.) The riverside between Waterloo Bridge and Westminster Bridge has undergone enormous changes since the Festival of Britain was held on wasteland in 1951. The Royal Festival Hall ★ was the first of the many buildings devoted to the arts that sprang up afterwards. Two further concert halls — the Queen Elizabeth Hall ★ and the Purcell Room — are by its side, and the Hayward Gallery ★ is squeezed up by the side of Waterloo Bridge. Immediately below the gallery is the National Film Theatre ★, beside which the Museum of Moving Image ★ is under construction. The National Theatre ★, opened in 1976, with three auditoriums, is east of the bridge. A river walk runs from the theatre in front of the concert halls to Jubilee Gardens and beyond to the front of County Hall.

South Bank

SCALE 1:4 000 or 15 INCHES to 1 MILE

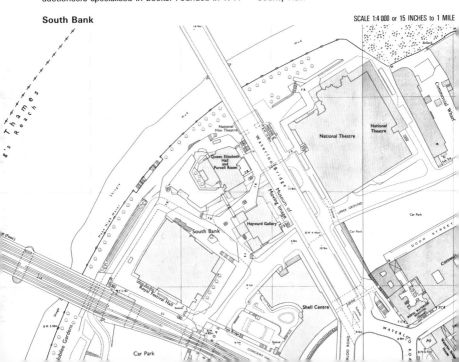

South Kensington (4 C-4 etc.) The museum and residential area to the south of Hyde Park. On either side of Exhibition Road the museums and colleges of further education are monuments to the success of the Great Exhibition held in the Crystal Palace in Hyde Park in 1851. The surplus profit of £186,000 was used to purchase two estates south of Kensington Road and 87 acres 'safe for future years amidst the growth of the metropclis'. Over the next 50 years were built the institutes and training colleges where Prince Albert envisaged art and science applied to manufacture being created. The first building to go up was the South Kensington Museum — later renamed the Victoria and Albert ★ — and this was followed by the Natural History Museum ★, the Royal College of Science, the Imperial Institute, Geological Museum ★ and Science Museum ★.

Southwark (3 D-5 etc.) The workaday borough across the river from the City today stretches south to more prosperous Dulwich ★; but Southwark itself, which possesses 2,000 years of history, lies near the river where dull, drab Victorian houses and rundown corner shops hardly illustrate a notable past. Occasional surface evidence is visible to the keen-eyed explorer. Archaeological excavations in the 1980s have proved Southwark the oldest suburb in the metropolis. Beneath the centuries of neglect are traces of the mediaeval and Tudor years when the neighbourhood had a palace, famous inns, playhouses and distinguished residences.

Being on the south side of London Bridge ★ — the only Thames crossing until 1750 — this was a thriving commercial district, and the 1980s replacement of dingy dilapidated Victorian warehouses by the modern glass and brick façades indicates that before long Southwark may soon be the important and busy neighbourhood it once was.

Two great Roman roads met south of the bridge. As this was the entrance to the City from the south there were a number of coaching inns. Of these *The George Inn* at 77 Borough High Street still exists. The only galleried inn left in London, and dating from 1676, it is on the site of a mediaeval tavern. In the care of the National Trust, it still serves refreshments to weary travellers. (*Tel: 01-407-2056.*) Nearby a tablet in Talbot Yard, Borough High Street, recalls the site of the Tabard, the inn where the pilgrims met, as recalled in Chaucer's *The Canterbury Tales*. The Tabard stood until late in the 19th century.

The 9th-century church of St Saviour and St Mary Overie, known today as Southwark Cathedral ★, was until 1897 within the diocese of the Bishop of Winchester whose residence was close by. Vestiges of the mediaeval Winchester Palace are to be seen in Clink Street where there is a single wall with the outline of a rose window. In 1642 the palace became a prison, providing yet another gaol for a rowdy area that boasted seven. Recent rebuilding has left little evidence of the most famous, the Clink prison ★, which gave rise not only to the expression 'in the Clink' but to the colloquialism 'on the fiddle' after the sign with a violin hanging outside the gaol.

To the west of Southwark Bridge is Bankside ★, famous in the 16th century for its numerous playhouses including Shakespeare's Globe, and at one time for its alehouses and 'stews'. The latter were brothels on land owned by the Bishop of

Winchester to whom they paid rents and fines; the ladies of dubious virtue thus acquired the name 'Winchester Geese'.

Southwark Cathedral (3 D-5) The Cathedral of St Saviour and Collegiate Church of St Mary Overie; the seat of the Bishop of Southwark since 1905. Known to be the fourth church on the site, the first being the 7th-century nunnery of St Mary Overie (over-the-le: le being water), this later became an Augustinian monastery. In 1106 a church (traces of which remain) was built by the canons who also administered St Thomas's Hospital ★. After a fire it was largely rebuilt in 1206 and the choir and other

Southwark Cathedral

Southwark Cathedral SCALE 1:4 000 or 15 INCHES to 1 MILE

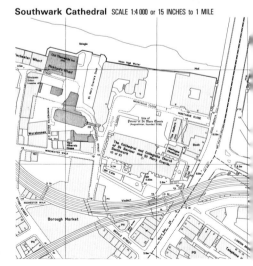

parts of London's first Gothic church survive. A 13th-century arch in the north choir aisle leads to the Harvard Chapel, which commemorates John Harvard who was baptised in 1607 at St Saviour's before emigrating to Massachusetts where he founded the university that bears his name. There are some fine monuments, a few remembering the thespians of Bankside★ including the reclining figure of Shakespeare. The bard's playwright brother Edmund was buried in the church and so were the dramatists Philip Massinger and John Fletcher. A more modern note is struck by a memorial to Oscar Hammerstein, the lyricist who died in 1960.

Speakers' Corner (1 E-5) A forum for free speech at the Marble Arch end of Hyde Park where orators assemble every Sunday to assail the crowds on public, political and religious issues. One or two godly souls try to win over the faithful. It is far from being a hotbed of sedition: most of the speakers

At Speakers' Corner

express strongly worded reactionary views. The law hovers in case it may be needed to bring calm to overwrought extremists. The right of assembly but not the absolute right (as is sometimes supposed) to say anything prevails.

Spitalfields (3 F-2 etc.) The name derives from the mediaeval Augustinian Priory and Hospital of St Mary Spital, around which Roman Catholic recusants and refugees from the Continent settled after the Reformation. Huguenots who fled from France after the Revocation of the Edict of Nantes in 1685 formed a large community in the area and established an extensive silkweaving business. As they prospered and moved elsewhere, immigrants arrived from East Europe. Today this rundown area east of Bishopsgate is fast losing former affiliations as later immigrants from Asia replace the French churches and period terrace houses. As recently as 1986 the furnishings and beautiful plaster interior of a Huguenot church were taken out and burnt to make way for the furnishings of a modern mosque. Christ Church, Spitalfields★, has been saved and renovated. A few of the early-18th-century houses of the Huguenot silk weavers are to be found in Fournier Street, Elder Street and Artillery Lane. The busy Sunday market in Middlesex Street — more commonly known as Petticoat Lane★ — hides the severe, sooty shops and tenements.

Spring Gardens (5 D-1) At the side of Admiralty Arch★ the narrow right-angled thoroughfare connecting Cockspur Street and The Mall★ retains the name acquired when a fountain was put in this part of the royal gardens during the reign of Queen Elizabeth I. This private garden — part of the land belonging to St James's Palace — also had a pond for bathing, and the fountain, with hidden jets, sprayed the unwary. Early in the 17th century the royal menagerie was put here. Today only the name survives. The sculpture outside the offices of the British Council is by Henry Moore.

Staple Inn, *Holborn* (3 A-3) The gabled and half-timbered Tudor building with oriel windows overhanging the street is one of the few of its kind in London. Formerly a meeting place where wool-staplers conducted their trade, it was an Inn of Chancery from the 15th century to 1884 when the Institute of Actuaries acquired and restored it. A hall with a hammer-beam roof was added in 1580 and although this and the 18th-century houses around two quadrangles were largely destroyed in 1944 the Holborn buildings survived. The Institute rebuilt the hall using the original materials. Dr Johnson lived in a house here in 1759-60 and wrote *Rasselas* in the evenings of a single week to pay for his mother's funeral. Visitors may enter the courtyard.

Stock Exchange, *Old Broad Street* (3 E-3) In the tall modern block behind the Bank of England brokers buy and sell shares. The present building, on the site occupied by the Exchange since 1802, is equipped with the latest electronic and computerised systems, enabling brokers to have instant access to clients and markets around the world. There is a Visitors' Gallery for the public and a cinema where the intricacies of the Stock Exchange are explained in a film. (*Tel: 01-588-2355.*)

Strand (2 E-5 etc.) The street running from Trafalgar Square to Temple Bar takes its name from days when it was a riverside walk between Westminster and the City. Today the mixture of 19th and 20th-century shops and houses has none of the grandeur of mediaeval and later Tudor times when it was lined with the Thameside London residences of bishops and the nobility. These great houses and their occupants are remembered in the names of the streets that run south to the river. George Villiers, Duke of Buckingham, who owned a large mansion near present day Charing Cross Station, even had the 'of' in his title commemorated by Of Alley (now York Place). At Adelphi★ Durham House Street recalls the house of the bishops of Durham. The site of John of Gaunt's Savoy Palace, destroyed in the Peasants' Revolt in 1381, is occupied by a hill, a hotel, theatre, street and chapel all bearing the name Savoy. East of Somerset House★ was Arundel House, the London residence of the Howard family — dukes of Norfolk. The house of Robert Devereux, Earl of Essex, stood where Essex Street is today.

Facing the Royal Courts of Justice★, at 216 Strand, is the tea and coffee shop of *Twining's*. Thomas Twining opened a coffee house in 1706 in Devereux Court and shortly after acquired the premises next door (the present shop). Street numbering was then unknown and he chose the sign of the Golden Lion as his symbol of identification. The oldest ratepayer in Westminster, Twining's is probably the oldest business in London still run by the same family, and selling the same products from the same premises. At the back of the shop a small museum traces the history of tea and explains the firm's long association with it. (*Tel: 01-353-3511.*)

On the island in the middle of the road, a few yards from Twining's, is St Clement Danes★, the official church of the Royal Air Force. On another island, opposite the entrance to King's College, stands the church of St Mary-le-Strand completed in 1717 by James Gibbs.

Tate Gallery, *Millbank* (5 D-5) The national collection of modern art and the national collection of historic British art are in this neo-classical building named after Sir Henry Tate, the sugar millionaire, who gave the gallery to the nation. Although the National Gallery★ has a representative holding of 18th- and 19th-century British masterpieces, the major works of the best known British painters such as Hogarth, Constable, Gainsborough, Blake and Reynolds are here as well as paintings by the Impressionists, Post-Impressionists and Pre-Raphaelites.

Using its government purchase grant and bequests, the gallery regularly adds to the modern collection of paintings, recently buying works by such artists as David Hockney, Jackson Pollock, Andy Warhol and Francis Bacon. There is also a large sculpture collection which, besides pieces by Auguste Rodin, Henry Moore and Elizabeth Frink, has controversial works like the much-criticised 'Tate bricks'.

Since 1897 when it opened, there have been a number of extensions, three financed by the art dealer Sir Joseph Duveen and his son Lord Duveen. A further gallery, named in memory of the industrialist Sir Charles Clore, is devoted to the Turner Bequest which comprises 100 paintings, 182 unfinished ones and over 19,000 drawings.

There is an excellent restaurant, decorated with Rex Whistler's delightful mural, *The Pursuit of Rare Meats,* a cafeteria, lecture rooms where there are daily programmes of educational talks and films, and a bookshop. Frequent changing exhibitions, often devoted to a major artist or school, are held throughout the year. (*Tel: 01-821-1313.*)

Temple (3 A-4) A delightful backwater between Fleet Street and the Thames with small squares and Georgian buildings where lawyers have their chambers and where some live. Although the two Inns of Court — the Inner Temple and the Middle Temple — are quite separate, the area is known as the Temple. The main entrance to Inner Temple is through the Tudor gateway in Fleet Street. Middle Temple Lane (still illuminated by gas lights which are lit manually at dusk) divides the Inns — the Inner Temple to the east and Middle Temple on the west, but they share the historic Temple Church★.

Before it became associated with lawyers, the Knights Templar had established their Order here, built the church in 1185 and later a Great Hall. When the Order was dissolved in 1312 the Knights of St John took over the buildings, leasing some to lawyers who formed an Inn c. 1450. Eventually the land was granted to the benchers in perpetuity by James I.

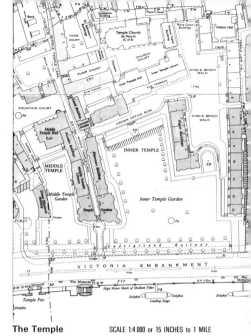

The Temple SCALE 1:4 000 or 15 INCHES to 1 MILE

Outside the church is a loggia, a modern reconstruction of a destroyed original by Wren. This leads to Inner Temple Hall, a replacement for the hall also destroyed in 1941. A buttery and crypt, however, are 14th century. Beyond the arches is King's Bench Walk where Nos 4 and 5 are believed to be by Wren. The terrace leads to the separate gardens of the Inner and Middle Temple in one of which, according to Shakespeare, Richard Plantagenet and the Earl of Somerset plucked the white and red roses that were to become the symbols of the Wars of the Roses (*Henry VI, Part I*, act II, scene IV).

This is by no means the only Shakespearian connection. In **Middle Temple Hall**, a glorious building with the finest hammer-beam roof in the country, Shakespeare is said to have performed his new play, *Twelfth Night,* before Queen Elizabeth I. Badly damaged in the Second World War, the hall has been carefully restored. Of particular note is the magnificent screen and the benchers' table. This was carved from a single oak from Windsor. The table below was made from the timbers of Sir Francis Drake's *Golden Hind.* The hall is usually open on weekdays. (*Tel: 01-353-4355.*)

Both inns have remarkably good libraries. The

The Middle Temple

chambers have been occupied by many distinguished men, among them Oliver Goldsmith, Charles Lamb, Dr Johnson at 1 Inner Temple Lane (demolished), and William Makepeace Thackeray. The Inns are private property and there is no public right of way but visitors are allowed to stroll around and admire the beautiful buildings; the porters will advise which may be entered.

Temple Bar (3 A-4) The boundary between Westminster and the City is marked by a monument where the Strand meets Fleet Street. Surmounted by a bronze griffin and bearing statues of Queen Victoria and the Prince of Wales (Edward VII), it marks the site of Temple Bar which straddled the street and was designed by Wren to replace a wooden Tudor gateway. The heads of such traitors as those who took part in the '45 Rebellion were exhibited on spikes on the top. The gate was removed in 1878 and is now at Theobalds Park, near Waltham Cross. Plans are constantly put forward to bring it back to the City. On state visits the ancient custom of the sovereign asking permission from the Lord Mayor 'to pass Temple Bar' is still observed.

Temple Church (3 A-4) An exceptionally fine and interesting round church on the floor of which are memorials to the illustrious crusaders who were associated with the Order of Knights Templar. The Order was founded in 1118 to protect pilgrims on the way to Jerusalem and the church, built by the Knights, was consecrated in 1185 by the Patriarch of the Church of the Holy Sepulchre in Jerusalem (see the inscription over the main door) on whose church the circular building was modelled. After the suppression of the monasteries the church became Crown property. The freeholds of the Temple and the church were given to the benchers of Inner and Middle Temple by James I in 1608. Since then it has been a royal 'peculiar', subject only to the jurisdiction of the sovereign and the Archbishop of Canterbury. The roof caved in during the Blitz in 1941, when considerable damage was also caused to the fascinating effigies of the 13th-century knights in armour. These and the church have been sympathetically restored. A narrow staircase where the Round Church meets the choir of the later adjoining building leads to a cell where templars adjudged guilty of sin did penance.

Temple of Mithras, *Bucklersbury House, Queen Victoria Street* (3 D-4) In 1954 a Roman temple dedicated to the god Mithras and a group of sculptures were discovered during redevelopment. Built at the end of the 1st century AD, the temple was nearly 60 ft long. The sculptures included the heads of Minerva, Mithras and Serapis, the god of the underworld. The publicity given to the find resulted in what little remained of the Mithraium being reconstructed — not entirely successfully — in front of Temple House. The sculptures and a model of what the temple probably looked like 2,000 years ago are in the Museum of London.

Theatre Museum, *Covent Garden* (2 E-5) The extensive collections previously at the Victoria and Albert Museum ★ have been moved to this new museum where they are shown in changing exhibitions. The nucleus is the collection given by Mrs Gabrielle Enthoven in 1924. This chronicles the history of the English stage from the 17th century in playbills, programmes, newspaper cuttings, texts, music scores and manuscripts. This archive is kept up to date and material about each new production in the UK is added daily. Among the museum's acquisitions are Diaghilev ballet costumes and scenic backdrops, the important Dame Bridget D'Oyly Carte collection relating to the Gilbert and Sullivan operas, and a growing amount of pop and rock 'n' roll material. Items from these are shown in semi-permanent displays devoted to the story of the performing arts. Two galleries, one named after Sir John Gielgud, are for temporary exhibitions, and there is also a room of theatrical paintings. The new museum, open on certain evenings until 'curtain-up' time in nearby theatres, has excellent research facilities for students. (*Tel: 01-836-7891.*)

Theatre Royal Drury Lane, *Catherine Street* (2 E-5) Large-scale musicals, many originating on Broadway, are staged in this most historical of all London theatres. The present building is the fourth on the site. Granted a royal patent by Charles II in 1662, it was one of two theatres legally entitled to mount plays and operas, the other being the Theatre Royal Covent Garden (see Royal Opera House). The history of the English theatre from the Restoration to the early 19th century virtually centres on Drury Lane, where Nell Gwyn made her first appearance in 1665. A great era began after David Garrick's first performance in 1742. Within five years he had acquired the patent and employed the Adam brothers to decorate the interior. When he retired Richard Brinsley Sheridan assumed command and produced his *The School for Scandal* to great acclaim. During the tenure of John Philip Kemble, Wren's 1672 building was demolished and when the new one, by Henry Holland, was destroyed by a fire in 1809, it was replaced by Benjamin Wyatt's present theatre. Today's theatre is the one for which Byron wrote the opening prologue in 1812. Edmund Kean, Grimaldi and Charles Macready were all associated with Drury Lane in the first half of the 19th century. Later the theatre was renowned for spectacular Christmas pantomimes starring Dan Leno, and in 1905 Sir Henry Irving gave his last season here. During the twenties and thirties musicals by Jerome Kern, Noël Coward and Ivor Novello were popular successes, succeeded after the Second World War by such American shows as *Kiss Me Kate* and *My Fair Lady*.

Theatre Royal Haymarket (5 D-1) One of the most charming theatres in London with a general policy of presenting star names in conventional plays or social comedies, and many revivals of classics. The interior is decorated in Louis XIV style. When the doors opened in 1720 only two theatres were licensed to stage plays. The Haymarket defied the law, and incurred considerable difficulties until 1766 when it was granted a patent for performances during the summer months only and adopted the prefix Theatre Royal. The present theatre, designed by John Nash, is the second on the site. It opened in 1821 with Sheridan's *The Rivals*.

Threadneedle Street (3 D-4 & E-3) The windowless, fortress-like wall of the Bank of England occupies a large section of the street. Here, too, are the headquarters of other banks, the Royal

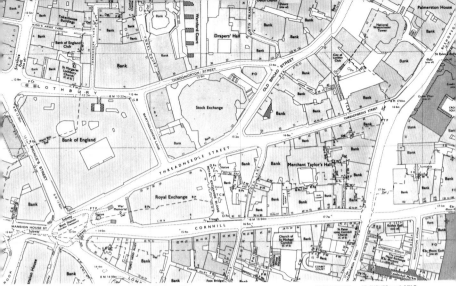

Threadneedle Street — the heart of the City

SCALE 1:4 000 or 15 INCHES to 1 MILE

Exchange★ and part of the Stock Exchange★. The origin of the name of London's most important financial street is assumed to come either from the emblem of the Merchant Taylors' or from the three needles of the Needlemakers' Company.

Tower Bridge (3 F-5) The most elaborate of all the Thames bridges is clearly recognisable from the twin towers rising from massive piers connected at the top by a footbridge. Opened in 1894 to relieve congestion on other City crossings, the construction had to be such that large vessels could enter the Upper Pool. The designers hit on the idea of raising the middle section of the roadway by means of a double-drawbridge. Two bascules, each weighing over a thousand tons, lift into the air in 90 seconds, allowing ships through the bridge. The hydraulic machines were powered by steam engines until 1975 when electric motors were installed in the Gothic-style towers. An exhibition tells the story of the bridge and its history, drawings explain the mechanism, and there is a display about the City's other bridges. The entrance to the *Tower Bridge Walkway* is in the north-west tower where a lift or stairs take visitors 60 ft above ground. (*Tel: 01-403-3761.*)

Tower Bridge

Tower of London (3 F-5) The great fortress of London has been inextricably linked with English history for 900 years. Officially a royal palace, but rarely used as a residence since mediaeval times, the Tower today is largely a museum reflecting the many aspects of its great and notorious past. Each year millions of tourists come to hear the Yeomen Warders recount the grisly details of the executions on Tower Hill or Tower Green; of the disappearance of the little Princes; and of the horrific tortures. The Beefeaters standing guard over the Tower's star attraction, the Crown Jewels, patiently repeat the tale of how Colonel Blood nearly escaped with them in 1671.

In the reign of Elizabeth I John Stow described the tower as 'a citadel to defend or command the city...a royal palace for assemblies or treaties; a prison of state for the most dangerous offenders; the only place of coinage for all England...the armoury for warlike provision; the treasury of the ornaments and jewels of the crown; and general conserver of the most records of the queen's courts of justice'. These were its functions for hundreds of years, and while changes occurred early in the 19th century and again in the last 50 years, many of its uses, customs and ceremonies survive to this day.

The Tower is still a garrisoned fortress although the military presence is now only a small detachment assigned for guard duty and ceremonial occasions.

The Royal Armouries, since 1985 a national museum in its own right, are kept in four separate buildings. The early collections of tournament, mediaeval, Renaissance, Tudor and Stuart arms and armour are in the White Tower, 18th- and 19th-century British military collections in the New Armouries, Oriental armoury in the Waterloo Barracks and instruments of torture and punishment in the Bowyer Tower.

The Crown Jewels are in the Jewel House in the Waterloo Block, guarded in an underground chamber to deter any latter-day Colonel Blood. The royal regalia has not been allowed to leave the country since Edward III took the Crown Jewels to the Low Countries and tried to pawn them. Among the many crowns on display, the most famous is the King Edward Crown used at the moment of

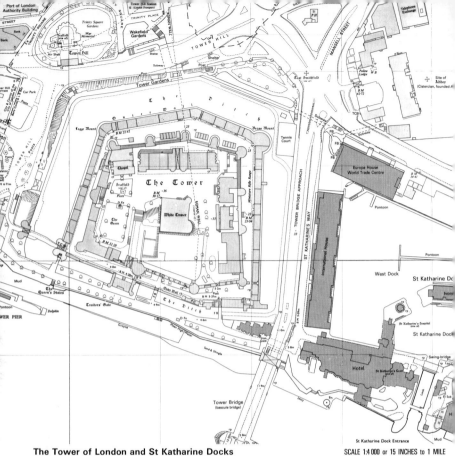

The Tower of London and St Katharine Docks

SCALE 1:4 000 or 15 INCHES to 1 MILE

crowning only and the Imperial State Crown which is worn at other times during a Coronation, and at the State Opening of Parliament.

During the two World Wars the Tower again became a prison and place of execution. Eleven convicted German spies were shot by firing squad between 1914 and 1916, and Sir Roger Casement was held here before his trial for treason. The last prisoner received at the Tower was Hitler's deputy, Rudolf Hess, who was brought to London and spent four days in the Queen's House after his dramatic parachute landing in Scotland in 1941. It was not long after this that the last execution by firing squad took place here — when a German spy suffered the same fate as his First World War counterparts.

The Tower was one of three strongholds built in London by William of Normandy after the Conquest in 1066, ostensibly to ward off Danish invaders. The White Tower was started in 1078 on William's order, the massive keep of white Caen stone being intended to house the King, his family and the royal treasury. A staircase led to state apartments and to the King's private chapel of St John the Evangelist ★. Successive kings added the surrounding buildings, almost all of which survive, but of the wall-towers only the Bell Tower remains. Henry III, who chose to live at the Tower rather than at Westminster, added the inner curtain wall with its dozen small towers, and had his own private oratory in the Wakefield Tower. The outer defences including the Middle Tower were added by his son Edward I.

From earliest times the Tower had a lurid reputation. William FitzStephen, friend and clerk to Thomas Becket, noted that the citizens believed the stones of the White Tower were cemented with the blood of wild animals — to put ferocious strength into the walls. A prison as early as 1100, it frequently housed malcontents and dissenters. The most famous prisoners were the ill-fated little Princes — Edward V and his brother — sent to the Tower for protection by their uncle the Duke of Gloucester who took the crown for himself as Richard III in 1483. The unproven story is that Richard ordered their murder in the Bloody Tower. Two of Henry VIII's wives, Anne Boleyn and Catherine Howard, tried and condemned on charges of adultery and treason, were executed on Tower Green. In 1554 Lady Jane Grey watched the return of her husband's body from Tower Hill before she was executed the same day. Sir Thomas More, confined to the Bell Tower in 1535 for refusing to acknowledge Henry VIII as head of the church, was convicted on false evidence and executed. Nearly 20 years later Henry's daughter Elizabeth was taken downriver, through Traitor's Gate, and also imprisoned in the Bell Tower by her sister Mary.

When Sir Walter Raleigh was held in the Tower large crowds gathered to see him take his daily walk on the ramparts (now known as Raleigh's Walk). Accused of plotting against James I, Raleigh was condemned to death, reprieved and lived in the Bloody Tower for thirteen years before being released and later executed.

After the drama of the Tudor and Stuart periods, the Tower was a place where the routine duties of the Ordnance, the Army, the Royal Mint and Record Office were carried out in the 18th century. The first offices of the Ordnance Survey were also housed in the Tower (in the Long Armoury) from 1791 until their destruction by fire in 1841. Despite the changes that have occurred, the links with the past remain unbroken, and ancient customs such as the Ceremony of the Keys — the nightly routine of locking all the gates which began nearly nine centuries ago — continue to this day.

Special educational programmes are arranged for pre-booked school parties. The Tower of London is open throughout the year. (*Tel: 01-709-0765.*)

Trafalgar Square (5 D-1) The scene of occasional political demonstrations, and revelry on New Year's Eve, this large square in the centre of London is named after Admiral Lord Nelson's most famous naval victory. Until it was laid out to John Nash's plan by Sir Charles Barry in 1829, the royal mews had been on the site since the reign of Edward I. The centre of the square is dominated by Nelson's Column ★. The granite plinth on which the colossal statue stands is by William Railton, the statue the work of E.H. Baily, and the four bronze lions (with the paws of a cat) were modelled by Sir Edwin Landseer. Landseer's godson, the architect Sir Edwin Lutyens, re-designed the fountains in 1939 as memorials to Admirals Beatty and Jellicoe. The statues in the square are of Sir Charles James Napier and Sir Henry Havelock, generals who served in India. The equestrian statue of George IV by Sir Francis Chantrey was originally intended to top the Marble Arch but was placed here instead in 1843. On the north wall the standard linear measures — inch, foot and yard — are set out in metal.

Facing down Whitehall to the scene of his execution is the equestrian statue of Charles I by Hubert le Sueur. During the Civil War it was hidden by Royalists. After the Restoration the statue was recovered and sold to Charles II. At its base is a plaque marking the spot as the centre of London. It is also the site of the original Eleanor Cross, which gives Charing Cross ★ its name.

Trafalgar Square

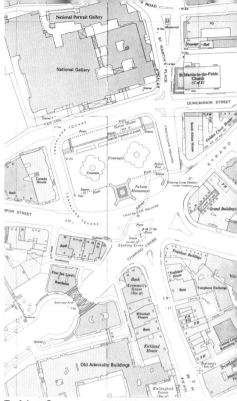

Trafalgar Square   SCALE 1:4 000 or 15 INCHES to 1 MILE

The building on the north of the square is the National Gallery ★. South Africa House, designed by Sir Herbert Baker, is on the east and Canada House on the west.

Transport Museum *See London Transport Museum ★*

Trocadero (2 C-5 & 5 C-1) A new commercial venture comprised of shops, restaurants, leisure attractions and a cinema on the block between Shaftesbury Avenue and Coventry Street. The adjacent London Pavilion site will form part of the redevelopment. The Trocadero is open daily, and besides the many shops selling clothes and souvenirs, there is the ***Guinness World of Records*** where superlatives and record-breaking achievements are illustrated in displays, videos and microcomputers. (*Tel: 01-439-7331.*)

At the Guinness World of Records

In *The London Experience*, a small theatre, a multi-screen presentation, complete with special effects, tells the history of London with a slight emphasis on the gory, seamier and more dramatic moments of the past. (*Tel: 01-439-4938.*)

University of London, *Malet Street, Bloomsbury* (2 D-3 etc.) Various faculties of the university are in numerous buildings all over London but here is the main campus where the original classical-style college faces onto Gower Street. The Bloomsbury site is dominated by the tall white Senate House where there are administrative offices, library and the Institute of Historical Research. The School of Hygiene and Tropical Medicine, the School of Oriental and African Studies and other colleges are close by.

Granted its charter in 1836, ten years after a group of eminent men established it as non-denominational, the university rapidly expanded. Today it appoints teachers and professors to the medical schools of the principal London hospitals, and such institutions as the Imperial College of Science and Technology. The London School of Economics and Political Science, Birkbeck College and Goldsmiths' College all come under its aegis.

Victoria (5 B-4 etc.) The district to the east of Belgravia was given its name to honour the reigning queen. When Victoria Street was laid out in 1851, it cut through slums, providing a more dignified approach to Westminster Abbey ★ and the Houses of Parliament ★. Victoria Station, a terminus for trains from the Continent and the South Coast, was opened in 1860. Large-scale redevelopment in the 1960s and 1970s has removed most of the Victorian buildings in the vicinity of the station, and the street itself now has a number of tall, angular glass office blocks. A great improvement has been the creation of a piazza in front of Westminster Cathedral ★.

Victoria and Albert Museum, *South Kensington* (4 C-4) *(See map on page 59)* A very large national museum devoted to art and design with collections of many periods and styles from all countries. Numerous departments cover such diverse items as architectural details, embroideries, metalwork, porcelain, furniture, jewellery, prints, oil paintings, furniture and costumes.

Established after the Great Exhibition, the collections rapidly expanded. At the end of the 19th century the decision was made to separate the scientific departments (see the Science Museum) and concentrate on fine and applied art in a new building. Queen Victoria requested it should carry her and Prince Albert's names and on her last public engagement she laid the foundation stone in 1899. The present museum was opened by Edward VII ten years later.

The treasures, including carpets, furniture, stained glass, porcelain and paintings, illustrate selected periods — Gothic art in several rooms, Italian Renaissance in others, English art on the first floor. The Mediaeval Treasury, opened in 1986, is the first of a series of gallery refurbishments which will continue to the end of the century. The second is a gallery devoted to the finest collection in Europe of Japanese art.

In individual departments, visitors may examine the intricacies of lacework, textile printing and weaving. For students the prints and drawings department is of special importance.

The museum's most priceless exhibits are on loan from the Queen. These are seven of the ten Raphael Tapestry Cartoons. Drawn by Raphael for Pope Leo X in 1515-16, they were sent to Brussels as tapestry designs for the Sistine Chapel. The original tapestries are in the Vatican. The Music Room from Norfolk House in St James's Square ★ has been reconstructed in one gallery and the façade of Sir Paul Pindar's c. 1600 house from Bishopsgate in another. A number of carved doorways, fireplaces and fragments from fine period houses have also been preserved. The late 16th-century Great Bed of Ware, big enough to hold eight people and mentioned by Shakespeare and Ben Jonson, is in the English Art section.

In the Henry Cole Wing, named after the museum's first director, the museum's modern holdings of paintings, drawings, photography and sculpture are housed, and changing exhibitions of industrial design are also held here.

The National Art Library is also in the museum but readers' tickets must be obtained to use it regularly. The museum arranges a full programme of temporary exhibitions, lectures, gallery talks and film shows. There is a self-service restaurant, a craftshop and a book shop. (*Tel: 01-589-6371.*)

Victoria Embankment Gardens (5 E-1) In the gardens created below the now demolished Royal Terrace of Adelphi ★, the watergate of York House, dating from 1626, shows how wide the Thames was before it was embanked. This was formerly the river entrance to the Duke of Buckingham's great London house. Inigo Jones may have been the designer. Two fountains commemorate Henry Fawcett and Major General Lord Cheylesmore of the Grenadier Guards, a philanthropist. There is a statue of Robert Raikes, the founder of Sunday Schools, a massive bronze of Robert Burns and on a path an enchanting military memorial of a soldier on a camel: this commemorates the British, Australian, New Zealand and Indian men who died during the First World War in the Middle East.

During the summer concerts are often given on the bandstand.

Vintners' Hall, *Upper Thames Street* (3 D-4) The Vintners', one of the twelve Great Livery Companies, are still associated with their original trade and hold certain responsibilities for ensuring EEC wine laws are enforced. Granted a charter in the 14th century, they have occupied a hall on this site since 1446. The present premises were built in 1671 after the Great Fire. During the Second World War the hall suffered only minor damage. In 1948 the hall was restored to its former condition. The staircase with elaborate balusters carved with leaves and flowers is especially fine and the Court Room has wood panelling decorated with garlands. The company owns a Van Dyck painting, a rare 15th-century tapestry and a valuable collection of plate, some of it dating from the 16th century. With the Dyers' and the Crown, the Vintners' have right of ownership of all swans on the Thames, marking their cygnets with two nicks during the Swan Upping ceremony every July. The hall is occasionally open. Contact the City Information Centre for details. (*Tel: 01-606-3030.*)

Wallace Collection, *Hertford House, Manchester Square* (1 F-4) An enchanting national museum containing paintings and objets d'art given to the nation in 1897 by Lady Wallace, widow of Sir Richard Wallace, the natural son of the 4th Marquess of Hertford. The main influence is French, and there are paintings by Boucher and Watteau, superb Sèvres porcelain and rich furniture of the Louis XIV, Louis XV and Louis XVI periods.

The French paintings are of great importance, and eight Bouchers alone adorn the grand staircase and landing. There are also major works by Dutch, Flemish, Italian, Spanish and English artists. In the first room hang an outstanding number of portraits

The Laughing Cavalier, *by Frans Hals — one of the outstanding treasures of the Wallace Collection*

by Sir Joshua Reynolds and Sir Thomas Lawrence. Gallery 18, on the first floor, has the pride of the collection, the most famous being Frans Hals' *Laughing Cavalier*, and several examples of work by Velasquez and Murillo. A most attractive Lawrence portrait of George IV at one end of this long room is surrounded by three portraits of Mrs Robinson — one each by Gainsborough, Reynolds and Romney. She was the actress 'Perdita' with whom he was in love when he was a youthful Prince of Wales. In the hallway at the entrance to Gallery 15 there is a watercolour of Isabella, the 2nd Marchioness of Hertford, who, when he was her lover, regularly received the Prince Regent in the Oval Drawing Room.

One room is filled with Venetian views by Guardi and Canaletto. Other outstanding paintings in the collection are Van Dyck's *Philippe Le Roy, Seigneur de Ravels*, Rembrandt's portrait of his son *Titus*, Rubens' *The Rainbow Landscape*, and his sketch for the *The Adoration of the Magi*, now in King's College, Cambridge.

The Italian maiolica, Limoges and other ceramics are completely overshadowed by the Sèvres soft paste porcelain, one of the best collections in the country.

Several rooms house the European arms and armour purchased by Sir Richard Wallace in 1870 to join the collection of Oriental arms and armour formed by his father. (*Tel: 01-935-0687.*)

Waterloo Bridge (5 F-1) Completed under difficulties during the Second World War, the present crossing with five arches was the first concrete bridge in London. Designed by Sir Giles Gilbert Scott, it replaced Rennie's 1811-17 bridge, which the sculptor Canova thought the most beautiful in the world.

The Wellcome Institute for the History of Medicine, *183 Euston Road* (2 C-2) In 1982 the main collections of this museum, founded in 1913 by the pharmaceutical magnate Sir Henry Wellcome (1853-1936) and showing historic developments in medical science, were transferred to the top floor of the Science Museum ★. However a vast and precious collection comprising rare manuscripts, medical archives and drawings illustrating the history of medicine remain here. The extensive library may be used by doctors and research scholars on application, and occasional exhibitions are open to the public. (*Tel: 01-387-4477.*)

Wellington Barracks, *Birdcage Walk* (5 C-3) Built in 1833 for the Foot Guards, the barracks have recently undergone reconstruction and new buildings have been put up to accommodate the Grenadier Guards. Frequently the battalion which provides the guard at Buckingham Palace can be seen on the parade ground half-an-hour before the ceremony begins. The Guards Chapel ★, bombed with a tragic loss of life during the Second World War, contains some splendid mosaics that survived.

Westminster (5 D-3 etc.) *(See map on page 92)* The administrative and political centre of the country and principal home of the sovereigns since the 11th century, when Edward the Confessor moved his court here from the City. Beside the great cruciform church which the pious King ordered to replace a small Saxon church dedicated to St Peter, he built a palace from which he watched Westminster Abbey ★ take shape. The Abbey was consecrated late in 1065 and eight days later, in the New Year, Edward died and was buried in front of the high altar. No trace remains of his palace or of the additions carried out by his Norman successor, William the Conqueror, but the forerunner of Westminster Hall ★, built by the Conqueror's son William Rufus, is today incorporated into the Houses of Parliament ★.

In mediaeval times a thriving community grew up around the Palace of Westminster and the Abbey. Considerable jealousy existed between the traders in the City and the prosperous merchants who found favour at court and sought political favours. The increasing wealth of Westminster merchants brought a degree of vice to the area. In an effort to discipline the licentious elements an Act was passed in 1585 establishing a Court of Burgesses. The Court had power to 'punish all matters of incontinency, common scolds, inmates, common annoyances etc.', ensured that weights and measures were regulated, and kept the streets cleaned daily. This was the forerunner of Westminster Council which was granted the status of a city in 1900. In 1965 when the metropolitan boroughs were altered, Westminster City Council's boundaries were extended beyond the West End and Mayfair to take in Paddington, St John's Wood and West Kilburn.

Westminster Abbey (5 D-3) *(See map on page 92)*
Neither a cathedral nor a parish church, the Collegiate Church of St Peter was made a 'royal peculiar' by Elizabeth I and under the jurisdiction of a Dean and Chapter is subject only to the sovereign. Its long association with British history makes it perhaps the most important place in London to visit.

The exterior of the Abbey was extensively restored by Sir Christopher Wren at the start of the 18th century and completed by Nicholas Hawksmoor who designed the twin towers for the west front in 1734.

Immediately inside the Great West Door a green marble tablet in the floor commemorates Sir Winston Churchill. A few paces on, surrounded by poppies, is the tomb of the Unknown Warrior, an unidentified soldier of the First World War brought from Flanders and buried here in 1920. The Gothic nave, the highest in England, is filled with plaques, medallions, busts and monuments to a great number of eminent men and women. Politicians and important statesmen are commemorated in the North Transept, where there are three small chapels.

The South Transept is known as Poets' Corner. Geoffrey Chaucer was buried here in 1400, Edmund Spenser in 1599 and since then memorials have been put up to honour major poets, writers, composers and actors, many of whom are also buried in the Abbey, among them Ben Jonson, Handel, Dr Samuel Johnson, David Garrick, Charles Dickens and Rudyard Kipling. Shakespeare, who lies at Stratford-upon-Avon, is honoured by a full-length statue. Others like Keats, Shelley, Sir Walter Scott and more recently Noël Coward, Dylan Thomas and W.H. Auden were buried elsewhere but are remembered with busts or on tablets. The Australian poet Adam Lindsay Gordon and America's Henry Wadsworth Longfellow are among the foreign writers accorded tributes.

A door in the south choir aisle leads to the Cloisters which date from the 13th and 14th centuries. Entrance to the Chapter House, Library and Muniment Room, Chapel of the Pyx and the Norman Undercroft is from the East Walk. The Chapter House was used for meetings of the House of Commons from the reign of Edward III until 1547, and subsequently as a state archive. The Abbey Treasures and those of St Margaret's ★ are displayed in the Chapel of the Pyx, and there is also a museum where the wax effigies of Tudor and Stuart monarchs, and other illustrious subjects are preserved.

Since the death of Edward the Confessor in 1066 English monarchs have been crowned in the great Abbey he founded, and he was the first of 17 English sovereigns to be buried here. The mosaic-decorated marble tomb of King Edward, canonised in 1163, lies in a chapel at the back of the High Altar. Around this Shrine are a number of other magnificent tombs. The beautiful bronze effigy of Queen Eleanor, beloved wife of Edward I, shows her with flowing hair beneath a coronet. The Purbeck marble tomb of her father-in-law Henry III is surmounted by a gilt-bronze effigy of the King in his coronation robes and crown. Carvings on the 13th-century screen show events from the Confessor's life. The oak Coronation Chair was made to hold the Stone of Scone which was brought to the Abbey by Edward I who seized it in 1296 during his struggle to conquer the Scots. The Stone, on which the Scottish kings were crowned for centuries, is, according to legend, the pillow Jacob rested his

Westminster Abbey

head on at Bethel, and also reputed to be the Stone of Destiny from Tara, the seat of the Irish kings. It was stolen on Christmas Eve 1950 by Scottish Nationalists and recovered at Arbroath four months later.

Apart from the Undercroft and Chapel of the Pyx, built shortly after the Conquest, little of the 11th-century Benedictine Abbey remains. In 1245 Henry III started to rebuild the church as a memorial to the Confessor. Work took 25 years, and further additions, largely financed by Richard II, were made a century later.

In 1503 Henry VII began a burial chapel for himself, requesting that after his death masses should be sung for the salvation of his soul 'as long as the world shall endure'. The Henry VII Chapel with its sculpture, delicate lacework fan-vaulting and tracery is perhaps the finest example in the country of late mediaeval architecture. Work was not finished when the King died in 1509 but he left sufficient funds for its completion and he was buried behind the altar beside his wife Elizabeth of York. Their tomb, of black and white marble, with their effigies in gilt-bronze, was completed in 1518. The effigy on the tomb of his mother, Lady Margaret Beaufort, is one of the most important sculptures in the Abbey, her figure remarkably lifelike. A canopied tomb is shared by Mary I and her sister Elizabeth I. James I spent a meagre £765 on this memorial to his predecessors but was more generous with the grave of his mother, Mary, Queen of Scots. Among the many other important royal tombs in this magnificent chapel is the last sovereign buried in the Abbey, George II, in 1760. Since 1725 the Henry VII chapel has been the chapel of the Order of the Bath; the colourful banners of the knights hang above the stalls.

Unless closed for royal or state occasions, or for special services, the Abbey is open every day. A side chapel is reserved for private prayer. *(Tel: 01-222-7110.)*

Westminster Bridge (5 E-3) Until the reign of George II London Bridge ★ was the only one crossing the Thames. When a second was proposed at Westminster objections were raised by ferrymen, afraid of losing business. Despite protests Charles Labelye's Portland stone bridge of thirteen arches supported on piers embedded in the river went ahead and was opened in 1750. The engineering methods used were controversial at the time, and the critics were proved correct when old London Bridge was demolished in 1831. The increased flow of water seriously undermined the foundations of Labelye's bridge and it had to be replaced in 1862. The huge statue of Boudicca, Queen of the Iceni, faces Big Ben ★. At the top of the steps to the riverwalk leading to the Royal Festival Hall is the **South Bank Lion** which originally stood in front of the Old Lion Brewery near Waterloo Station. When this was demolished in 1950 the lion became a feature of the 1951 Festival of Britain and was afterwards preserved and put in its present position at the instigation of King George VI.

Westminster Cathedral, *Francis Street* (5 B-4)

The leading Roman Catholic church in England, and the diocesan seat of the Cardinal-Archbishop of Westminster. Designed by John Francis Bentley, the Cathedral, in contrasting bands of red brick and Portland stone, was consecrated in 1903. Whether so dominating a Romano-Byzantine building inspired by Siena Cathedral is suited to London is a matter of controversy and Baron Corvo (Frederick Rolfe) described the exterior as a 'pea-soup and streaky-bacon coloured caricature of an electric-light station'. The interior, which has taken most of this century to decorate and is not yet finished, is ornamented with over 100 different kinds of marble from all over the world. The nave, the widest in England, has eight columns of dark green marble. The stone Stations of the Cross on the piers, carved in low relief, are the work of Eric Gill. Side chapels, especially the Lady Chapel, are richly adorned with mosaics and marbles.

The Sanctuary, where the Archbishop's throne is a copy of the papal *cathedra* in the basilica of St John Lateran in Rome, has an altar table of Cornish granite under a white marble canopy on eight pillars of yellow marble from Verona.

When the Roman Catholic hierarchy was restored in England in 1850, more than 300 years after the Reformation, Cardinal Wiseman was appointed the first Archbishop of Westminster. On his death a memorial fund was established and his successor Cardinal Manning bought the site of the demolished

Tothill Fields Prison for the Cathedral in 1884. Ten years later work was instituted by Cardinal Vaughan. Several Cardinal-Archbishops are buried in the crypt which may be entered by asking permission at the Sacristy. The lift to the campanile — 284 ft high and with excellent views over London — is in the entrance porch. An open piazza giving a fine view of the front of the Cathedral was created during recent rebuilding in Victoria Street. Mass is celebrated several times every day. *(Tel: 01-834-7452.)*

Westminster Hall, *New Palace Yard* (5 E-3) *(See map on page 92)*

The great hall of the kings of England has been the scene of many decisive historic events. In modern times it has been used for the solemn lying-in-state of sovereigns and important statesmen, for foreign monarchs or heads of state to address Parliament and for very auspicious receptions.

Built by William the Conqueror's son, William Rufus, in 1097, it is one of the few surviving parts of the Palace of Westminster. With a height of 240 ft, it was probably the largest in Europe. Three centuries later in the reign of Richard II, the master mason Henry Yevele and carpenter Hugh Harland put in the magnificent oak hammer-beam roof.

Brass plaques and carvings in the floor or tablets on the wall commemorate some of the major events in the Hall's past — Edward I's abdication, the deposition of Richard II, and the door through which Charles I passed when he attempted to arrest five members of Parliament. Eight years later, in 1649, Charles I sat in an armchair of crimson velvet and faced the charge of treason for levying war 'against the parliament and kingdom of England'. Earlier, in 1535, the Hall was the scene of the trials of Sir Thomas More and John Fisher, Bishop of Rochester, of Sir Thomas Wyatt in 1554, the Earl of Essex in 1601 and Guy Fawkes in 1605.

An increased number of court cases necessitated the removal of the Royal Courts of Justice ★, which had met here for centuries, to new premises.

The Hall was also used for coronation banquets. In 1821 George IV colourfully decorated the hall through which the King's Champion rode on a white charger (borrowed from Astley's Circus) before throwing down the gauntlet and challenging all comers to impugn the King's title. This was the last occasion a coronation banquet was held in the Hall.

Westminster School, *Dean's Yard* (5 D-3)

A leading fee-paying public school providing education for approximately 400 boys and, in recent years, a small number of girls. The roll-call of former students includes the names of Ben Jonson, John Dryden, Sir Christopher Wren, Warren Hastings and more recently A.A. Milne, Sir John Gielgud and Peter Ustinov. The pupils have certain privileges connected with Westminster Abbey ★, one of which is shouting the 'Vivats' at coronations. Although a school was run by the Benedictine monks as early as the mid-14th century, the present school owes its foundation to Queen Elizabeth I in 1560 and is built around the mediaeval monks' quarters, of which some traces remain in Little Dean's Yard. The school hall had a fine hammer-beam roof, but most of the visible part was destroyed in wartime bombing. It dated from c.1090 when it was the monks' dormitory. The red-brick Ashburnham House, the Prior's Lodging in the

Westminster Cathedral

Westminster School

14th century and now the school library, was refaced and altered in 1660, possibly by Inigo Jones's assistant John Webb. For a time it was the home of the earls of Ashburnham. The rich interior has some fine plasterwork, an unusual staircase and a number of portraits, including one of Elizabeth I. Applications to view the school must be made to the bursar, and Ashburnham House is open during the Easter school holiday. (*Tel: 01-222-3116.*)

Whitehall (5 D-2 etc.) The broad avenue that runs from Trafalgar Square to Parliament Square has many government offices, and in the centre of the road a number of statues. The official buildings at the top of the street include the Old Admiralty, set back in a courtyard, its entrance screen topped by seahorses, and next to it the early Georgian mellow-brick façade of the Parliamentary Counsel, formerly the office of the Paymaster General. The street named Great Scotland Yard stands on the site of the mediaeval London residence of the kings of Scotland. Until 1891 the headquarters of the Metropolitan Police were here. Outside the Horse Guards★, mounted soldiers of the Life Guards or the Blues and Royals are posted daily. Next door, the Scottish Office, its portico and hall by Henry Holland, was the birthplace of Lord Melbourne. Gwydyr House, opposite, built in 1772, is now the Welsh Office. The Ministry of Defence occupies the large 1930s block that overlooks the river. The Prime Minister's residence and that of the Chancellor of the Exchequer are in Downing Street★, a turning off Whitehall. Almost opposite the Home Office is The Cenotaph★, the memorial to the dead of two World Wars. Richmond Terrace, put up in

the reign of George IV, has recently been gutted and rebuilt with the old façade retained. The Treasury and the Foreign and Commonwealth Office also face onto this wide street which takes its name from the Tudor Palace of Whitehall.

The Palace was originally York Place, the home of Thomas Wolsey when he was Archbishop of York. It was confiscated by Henry VIII in 1530 and became the principal London residence of the sovereign. Part of Henry VIII's wine cellar still exists beneath the Ministry of Defence, but is not open to the public. The Palace was the scene of great festivities during Henry's reign and again when Elizabeth I was on the throne. James I intended to have a new palace but only the Banqueting House★ was put up. Designed by Inigo Jones, it is the first and finest example of Palladian architecture in London. From a window of an annexe to this building Charles I walked to his execution in 1649. Oliver Cromwell died in the Palace in 1658. With the Restoration of Charles II royalty and revelry returned to Whitehall and were finally banished by a disastrous fire in 1698. Only the Banqueting House was left standing.

Wigmore Hall, *Wigmore Street* (2 A-4) A concert hall with excellent acoustics for recitals. Leading opera singers, instrumentalists, and ensemble groups are regular performers here and it is also often used for the London debut of young artists. It was built in 1901 by Friedrich Bechstein to adjoin his pianoforte showrooms and in common with many places with German names during the First World War changed its name from Bechstein to Wigmore when sold in 1917.

Zimbabwe House (5 E-1) The Zimbabwe High Commission offices on the corner of Agar Street and the Strand were designed by Charles Holden in 1908 for the British Medical Association. At the same time Epstein sculpted 18 figures whose nudity

Zimbabwe House — with mutilated Epstein figures

was immediately criticised — 'a form of statuary which no careful father would wish his daughter and no discriminating young man his fiancée to see,' said the *Evening Standard*. The statues were later subjected to severe amputations, leaving the present mutilated barely discernible frieze round the building.

Zoo See London Zoo★

Places of Special Interest —
Outer London

**Places of outstanding interest are printed in
blue. Places referred to in the text which are
covered by a separate entry in this section or
the Inner London Section are identified with
the symbol ' ★ '.**

*In this section of the guide will be found all
London's boroughs except the City, Westminster,
Kensington and Chelsea (for which see Inner
London) and places in them. A few important
places in Camden, Islington, Lambeth, Southwark
and Tower Hamlets — near the river or City
boundaries — are also in Inner London while places
situated further out in these boroughs will be found
on the pages that follow.*

*Outer London has also been liberally interpreted
as going outside the administrative Greater London
boundaries: to the north up to Hatfield and St
Albans; east to Brentwood; south to Westerham
and west to Windsor and Cliveden. Landranger
maps 166, 167, 175, 176, 186, 187 and 188 cover the
places listed in the following pages. The completion
of the M25 motorway (the 'London Orbital') has
brought many outlying places, houses and beauty
spots within easy range of the motorist setting out
from central London. A double-page map (page
134 – 135) shows some of the places to visit that lie
just off the M25 and which may be approached
from one or more of its 31 intersections. They are
described in their alphabetical place in this section
of the gazetteer.*

Aldenham Country Park (176) (TQ 16-95) *Near
Elstree, 12 mi. NW Central London.* Tucked in the
apex formed by the old Roman road of Watling
Street (the A5183) and the busy parallel roads to the
north (the M1 and the A41) this country park has
several acres of woodland and open spaces. An
attractive centrepiece is the lake. Created as a
reservoir by French prisoners of war during the
Napoleonic campaigns, it is now popular for sailing
and fishing. Numerous walks, a nature trail, informal glades, a pets' corner and adventure playground are other assets. Picnic sites. Open daily,
and an information desk supplies mapped-out
walks.

Alexandra Palace and Park (176) (TQ 29-89)
Wood Green, 6 mi. N Central London. For over 100
years the building and focal point of the 480-acre
park on Muswell Hill was an exhibition centre and
concert hall. The 'Palace' was named after the
Danish Princess who married the Prince of Wales in
1863. The first building burnt down 16 days after the
opening and was immediately replaced by an
unsightly edifice which lasted until July 1980 when
it, too, was largely destroyed by fire.

Intended as North London's answer to the Crystal
Palace ★ , it proved no rival for the attractions of its
Sydenham rival despite a racecourse in the park.
During the First World War it became a barracks
and transit camp for Belgian refugees. In 1936 the
BBC acquired part of the building for studios and
put up the world's first television transmitter. In

August 1936 a variety show was the first programme and regular TV services from 'Ally Pally'
began the following November. The first colour
tests were made in 1955, the year before the BBC
moved to Shepherd's Bush. Brass band championships used to be an annual feature in the concert
hall.

Major restoration work is being carried out and
up-to-date facilities for concerts, exhibitions and
sports events are being installed. The new Alexandra Palace is scheduled to open in the late 1980s.
(*Tel: 01-883-6477.*)

Amersham (176) (SU 96-98) *26 mi. NW Central
London.* The wide main street with its old red-brick
buildings of many periods makes this a charming
old town to visit. Timbered, shuttered and gabled
cottages and wide openings to courtyards where
once there were inns are characteristic of Amersham. The town hall, built on arches, and the 17th-
century almshouses are especially attractive. A
monument on top of the hill to the north of the
town commemorates the Lollards who were burned
here in 1414. Gulielma Springett, who became
William Penn's wife, lived at Bury Farm, at the foot
of the steep Gore Hill (176) (SU 95-96).

Barking and Dagenham (177) (TQ 44-84 etc.) *9
mi. E Central London.* This built-up eastern borough
of London with a population of 150,000 lies north of
the Thames. The coming of the railway brought a
rapid expansion of industry to what had previously
been a fishing community. Housing estates were
put up to accommodate the many factory
employees, the largest at Becontree where over
27,000 houses and cottages were built in the 1920s.
The biggest employer in the area is the Ford Motor
Company at Dagenham.

The ruins of the great Benedictine nunnery — the
Abbey of Barking — are in the grounds of St
Margaret's Church. The Abbey, where William the
Conqueror stayed after his coronation, owned large
tracts of land, including the church of All-Hallows-
by-the-Tower ★ . The Curfew Gate remains as the
entrance to St Margaret's, an interesting 13th-
century flint and ragstone church with a fine
modern carved screen. Depicted on the screen is
Captain James Cook who married Elizabeth Batts of
Barking in the church in 1762.

Valence House (177) (TQ 48-86) in Becontree
Avenue is the only house of any importance left in
Dagenham. Today a local history museum, it
houses 48 important portraits of the Fanshawe
family who lived nearby. (*Tel: 01-592-2211.*)

Barnet (176) (TQ 24-95) *11 mi. N Central London.*
For over seven miles the Edgware Road (which
follows the line of the Watling Street, the old
Roman road) forms the eastern boundary of this
large north London borough which opens onto
Green Belt country on the Hertfordshire side. Nearly
300,000 people live in the main dormitory towns of
Hendon, Mill Hill, Edgware ★ , Barnet and Finchley.

The Royal Air Force Museum ★ , with the Battle
of Britain and Bomber Command Museums in
adjacent buildings, is on the site of Hendon
Aerodrome, the scene of pioneer work in British
aviation.

The British Library Newspaper Collection in
Colindale Avenue (176) (TQ 21-89) is a division of

Battersea and Chelsea

SCALE 1:25 000 or 2½ INCHES to 1 MILE

the British Library ★. Daily and weekly newspapers from all over the country and dating back to 1801 are kept here as well as papers from the Commonwealth and other countries. Temporary daily tickets may be obtained. (*Tel: 01-200-5515.*)

Hampstead Garden Suburb (176) (TQ 25-88), on the border of Camden, is a remarkable 20th-century housing development, the brainchild of Dame Henrietta Barnett who believed the social classes should mingle and live side by side in well-planned surroundings with tree-lined streets and open spaces. The mixed architecture — from 16th-century style to folksy arts and crafts — blends harmoniously and complements the central feature, Sir Edwin Lutyens's 18th-century-style square with St Jude's Church as its focal point. The grounds of the nearby North London Crematorium (176) (TQ 25-88) at Golders Green were laid out by the gardener Gertrude Jekyll, Lutyens's collaborator on numerous projects.

Battersea (176) (TQ 28-76) *4 mi. S Central London.* Long before it became industrialised and full of Victorian terraces, this large section of Wandsworth ★ across the Thames from Chelsea, was a village, and a borough in its own right. Although mentioned in the Domesday Book, Battersea can trace its origins back to the Iron Age: a magnificent shield in the British Museum ★ proves it. The most distinctive landmark is the massive Power Station, a listed building, which generated electricity from 1934 until the early 1970s. Future plans indicate that Sir Giles Gilbert Scott's example of pre-war modern architecture with its four huge chimneys will soon become a leisure centre.

Between the Power Station and the old village is **Battersea Park**, created in 1853 on 200 acres of marshland. In the centre of the lake is a Barbara Hepworth sculpture, *Single Form.* It was placed there in 1963 as a memorial to UN Secretary-General Dag Hammarskjöld (a duplicate is in New York). In 1951 the amusement ground of the Festival of Britain was concentrated in the Park. On the river's edge a 110 ft Peace Pagoda, built by the Nippozan Myohoji sect of Buddhist monks, and richly decorated in gold leaf, was presented to London in 1985.

The famous Dogs' Home in Battersea Park Road was founded in 1860 as 'The Temporary Home for Lost and Starving Dogs'. Approximately 17,000 stray dogs are brought in each year. Cats have been accepted since 1882.

St Mary's Church in Old Battersea dates from 1777, when it was said to have 'the second best carriage congregation in London'; it is on the site of an 11th-century church. The St John family (Viscounts Bolingbroke) lived in the nearby manor house and their funeral monuments are the pride of the church.

Old Battersea House (176) (TQ 26-76), built in the style of Wren for Walter St John c. 1699, has recently been restored and contains a collection of paintings and ceramics which may be seen by appointment. *(Write to the De Morgan Trust, 21 St Margaret's Crescent, London SW15 6HL.)* The house serves as an example of the fashionable 17th-century village which, because of its accessibility to the City and West End, is fast becoming an increasingly popular residential area.

Bayhurst Wood Country Park (176) (TQ 06-89) *near Uxbridge, 16 mi. NW Central London.* On the link road between Ickenham and Harefield and opposite the quaintly named Mad Bess Wood, this country park has a number of bridle paths between copses. These are ideal for riders and walkers. Special areas are set aside for picnics and barbecues.

Bekonscot Model Village (175) (SU 93-91) *Warwick Road, Beaconsfield, 23 mi. W Central London.* This delightful miniature village, complete with model railway, captures the atmosphere of the 1930s. First opened in 1929, Bekonscot is an imaginary village with a zoo, a castle, lake and a flying club, and was the brainchild of Roland Callingham, a chartered accountant, who could not contain his hobby of model-making in his house. The cinema is showing *Snow White and the Seven Dwarfs* and some of the names on the shops are real — an interesting example of paid-for advertising benefiting the Church Army which has administered the village since 1978. Picnic facilities. Open daily March to October. (*Tel: Beaconsfield (049 46) 2919.*)

Bethnal Green Museum of Childhood (177) (TQ 35-82) *Cambridge Heath Road, 3 mi. NE Central London.* As the name indicates, almost everything in this charming museum is associated with children's toys and pleasures. Collections of dolls and dolls' houses date from the 17th century, and there are all types of playthings, board games, card games and Victorian model theatres. The museum also has a display of costumes; wedding dresses and glamorous gowns worn by royalty and society ladies are particularly elegant. Excellent examples of the delicate work of the Huguenot silkweavers of Spitalfields ★ are shown. The decorative arts from the early 19th century to the Art Nouveau movement are illustrated.

Part of the iron and glass building once formed a section of the Victoria and Albert Museum ★ of which the museum is a branch. It was brought here before the museum opened in 1877.

There are changing exhibitions, and a regular programme of lectures, and activities for children. (*Tel: 01-980-2415.*)

Bexley (177) (TQ 46-75) *14 mi. E Central London.* Between the Thames to the north and the main Maidstone road (the A20) to the south, almost ¼ million people live in this borough which has numerous parks and thousands of acres of Green Belt land. Before the railway encouraged the development of Sidcup, Bexleyheath, Crayford, Erith and Welling for London-bound commuters, Bexley had many large estates like Danson Park where a Palladian villa was set in grounds landscaped by Capability Brown. This is now a public park. The most magnificent of these country houses, Hall Place ★, was built in Henry VIII's reign and later altered.

The Red House (177) (TQ 48-75), a Gothic L-shaped building at 13 Red House Lane, Bexleyheath, was designed by Philip Webb for William Morris. With its turrets and gables, it excited much comment in 1860. Although Morris only lived in it for five years much of the decor carried out by him and his Pre-Raphaelite friends has been retained by subsequent owners. Guided tours take place by appointment once a month. (*Write to the above address.*)

The parish church of St Mary the Virgin in Bexley High Street dates from before the Conquest and a few 12th-century and pre-Reformation remnants can be seen among the Victorian restoration. St Paulinus in Crayford High Street is also a pre-Conquest foundation. Largely rebuilt after a fire in 1628, there are some traces of the Norman and 15th-century church. The monuments are especially fine.

Biggin Hill (177) (TQ 41-60) *18 mi. SE Central London.* Farms and woodland still surround this residential area of the borough of Bromley, best known for its RAF base and as an airport for private planes. The aerodrome came into existence during the First World War and brought business to the district. A great deal of nearby land was developed. In the Second World War the airfield achieved great fame; two historic aircraft stand at the entrance as reminders of the Battle of Britain.

Blackheath (177) (TQ 38-76) *1 mi. S Greenwich, and 7 mi. E Central London.* In the small country-style village nestling in a corner of the Heath it is hard to believe Central London is only seven miles away. From the village 267 acres of gently rolling grassland, with playing fields and small ponds, reach out to and beyond the main Dover Road — the Roman Watling Street — which separates Lewisham ★ from Greenwich ★. The rolling fields continue to Greenwich Park and down to the river. Three sides of the Heath are framed by large Georgian and Victorian houses and terraces.

From Ranger's House ★, which is actually in Greenwich, there is a spectacular view over the Thames to St Paul's and beyond. The Paragon, a colonnaded terrace of fine houses in the southeast corner of the Heath, was designed by Michael Searles and built in the first years of the 19th century. They obliquely face St German's Place where Morden College hides in a valley. A beautiful building attributed to Wren, it was put up in 1695 for a London shipping merchant, Sir John Morden, in thanksgiving for the safe return of his fleet from Turkey. Intended as a home for 'decayed Turkey Merchants' who had fallen on hard times, Morden College still maintains homes for the elderly.

From Roman times the Heath has served as a rallying point for troops marching on London. The Danes camped here when they murdered Archbishop Alphege at Greenwich in 1011. During the Peasants' Revolt in 1381 Wat Tyler and his supporters assembled to meet Richard II. When the King came by river to Greenwich the passion of the huge crowd prevented him landing and Tyler marched on to London. Jack Cade also camped here during his rebellion in 1450. In the reign of Henry VII there was a battle when Cornish rebels were defeated by the King's troops. Happier occasions were the scenes of rejoicing that greeted Henry V on his return from Agincourt in 1415, and the pageant staged for Anne of Cleves when she arrived to marry Henry VIII. Great celebrations also greeted Charles II as he rode across the Heath on his way into London at the Restoration in May 1660. In the 18th century large crowds often gathered to hear preachers like John Wesley and George Whitefield.

Blackheath Rugby Club, who still play at Rectory Fields, is the oldest rugby union club in Britain. Royal Blackheath Golf Club, once on the Heath, the oldest golf club in England, is now at Eltham.

Black Park Country Park *See Langley Park* ★

Boston Manor (176) (TQ 16-78) *Boston Manor Road, Brentford, 8 mi. W Central London.* A red-brick and stone Jacobean house with sharply pointed gables in what is now a public park. From 1670 the home of the Clitherow family who acquired the manor built in 1623 for Lady Mary Reade, it was sold to the local Council in 1924. Restored in 1963, the ceiling in the drawing room is a composition of elaborate plasterwork with symbolic cartouches, and there are several remarkable chimneypieces. The main rooms are open once a week in summer. (*Tel: 01-570-7728 ext 4176.*)

Box Hill (187) (TQ 18-51) *near Dorking, 25 mi. SSW Central London.* The soaring chalk hill on the edge of the North Downs has magnificent panoramic views over Surrey and Sussex. The 800 acres of downs and woods, ideal for ramblers and walkers, are named after the tangled groves of box trees. The land is in the care of the National Trust, which has an exhibition room and information centre on the summit where maps outlining nature trails and walks are available. A short distance away the names of faraway landmarks are carved into a stone parapet, a monument to Leopold Salomons who donated part of the woodland to the nation in 1914. A late Victorian fort is being restored by the National Trust with a view to opening it.

Brands Hatch (177) (TQ 57-64) *Fawkham, near Dartford, 25 mi. SE Central London.* This motor-racing circuit is one of the most important in the country, used for Formula 1 British Grand Prix and other major racing and sports car events as well as top motorcycle races. The sloping, curving track with several tricky bends is a favourite with leading drivers. There are meetings at most weekends throughout the year. In 1986 the complex was sold to new owners who plan to improve spectator facilities and to build a hotel. (*Tel: Ash Green (0474) 872331.*)

Brent (176) (TQ 19-85 etc.) *7 mi. NW Central London.* The River Brent in northwest London divides Wembley ★ and Willesden which became part of the new borough of Brent in 1965. A quarter of a million people live in the cluttered maze of roads east of the Edgware Road. Many houses in Kilburn, Neasden and Willesden were built at the end of the 19th century when the Metropolitan Railway was laid down to serve the previously small villages. Before the Second World War large scale development took place in Kingsbury.

Although a very built-up borough, there are several open spaces and Fryent Country Park (176) (TQ 19-88) commands good views over London. Popular leisure activities are provided by a sailing club and nature centre at Brent Reservoir (also known as 'The Welsh Harp') which was formed when the river was dammed in 1835.

Kensal Green Cemetery ★, one of the great Victorian burial grounds, is on the edge of the Grand Union Canal ★ at the southern tip of the borough. Changing exhibitions and permanent displays in the *Grange Museum,* Neasden Lane (176) (TQ 20-86), illustrate the social, commercial and industrial life of the area. (*Tel: 01-452-8311.*)

Brentford (176) (TQ 18-77) *8 mi. W Central London.* Once the county town of Middlesex and since 1965 part of the borough of Hounslow ★. Between Isleworth and Chiswick ★ where a section of the Grand Union Canal ★ enters the Thames, Brentford is rich in historical associations, even though a lack of good buildings in the centre of town does not indicate a glorious past. After years of decline, recent redevelopment, particularly by the river, make it once more a pleasant place to live. *The Waterman's Arts Centre,* at 40 Brentford High Street, has a theatre, cinema, art gallery, bar and restaurant with river terraces. (*Tel: 01-586-3312.*).

Julius Caesar, according to legend, first crossed the Thames near present-day Syon House ★. Long before the Duke of Northumberland's Robert Adam house was built, two famous battles were fought on land that now forms part of the estate. A modern memorial in Ferry Lane commemorates the first, the confrontation between Edmund Ironside and Canute in 1016. The second Battle of Brentford was between Royalists and the Parliamentarians in 1642. It was the nearest Charles I's men got to London. Next day at Turnham Green his followers, seeing the strength of the trained troops awaiting them, turned back to Oxford.

Besides mansions like Syon House ★ and Boston Manor ★, Brentford has two museums — the Musical Museum ★ and the Living Steam Museum at Kew Bridge Pumping Station ★.

Bromley (177) (TQ 40-69 etc.) *10 mi. SE Central London.* Covering 59 square miles, this is the largest of London's boroughs and has a population of 300,000. There are large expanses of countryside on the east and south. The borough is made up of industrial centres at North Cray and residential districts at Beckenham, Chislehurst ★, Hayes, Orpington ★, West Wickham and Penge. With the exception of the latter, these are middle-class areas with sought-after houses. Green fields or woodland surround the more affluent detached residences at Farnborough, Chelsfield, Keston ★ and Cudham.

The narrow mediaeval line of Bromley High Street has been retained from the Market Place to the new Churchill Theatre where it opens into a wide dual carriageway with department stores on either side. Bromley College, in London Road, founded in 1666 to provide housing for 'twenty poor widows of orthodox and loyall clergymen' still fulfils this function although married couples have been admitted since 1976. The original 20 houses, attributed to Wren, are set around a quadrangle with an arcade of pillars. These are reputed to have been salvaged from Gresham's Royal Exchange ★ after the Great Fire.

The southern part of the borough has some small Kentish villages, though a few like Biggin Hill ★ were built up before legislation preserved the Green Belt.

Broxbourne (166) (TL 36-07) *19 mi. N Central London.* Meadows, woods and country parks surround this modern Hertfordshire town through which the River Lee flows. The many leisure activities include a boat centre and lido. At Clayton Hill Country Park (166) (TL 38-05) the lake with a small island attracts wildfowl, and there are good views. This and nearby Broxbourne Meadows are popular play areas for children and for picnics. Hayes Hill ★ and the adjoining Hollyfield Hall farms give town-bred visitors a taste of life on the land.

Burnham Beeches (176) (SU 95-85) *4 mi. NW Slough, and 24 mi. W Central London.* This large woodland was bought for the public in 1879 by the Corporation of the City of London. It is still administered by the City which has cut out pathways and maintains little glades for picnic or play areas. The name 'Burnham' is thought to derive from 'buccan' meaning beech, and great clumps of these trees give the large forest its special attraction, especially in the autumn. Many trees, some hundreds of years old, have twisted into strange shapes, the result of villagers pollarding for fuel in past centuries. The beeches often hide attractive pubs, and there is a hotel.

Bushy Park (176) (TQ 15-69) *11 mi. SW Central London.* The park adjoining Hampton Court Palace ★ was laid out for William III to rival Versailles. The avenue of majestic chestnut trees, flanked by a double row of limes, was intended by Christopher Wren as a grand approach to the palace. The line is broken only by the circular Diana Fountain. The delicate statue, thought to be either Venus or Arethusa, was bought in Italy for the private garden at Hampton Court by Charles I. Near the Teddington Gate is Bushy House, now occupied by the National Physical Laboratory for scientific and industrial research. Early in the 19th

century, the Duke of Clarence (later William IV) and his mistress, the actress Dorothy Jordan, lived here with their ten children.

Camden (176) (TQ 27-84 etc.) *About 2 mi. N Central London.* Bloomsbury, Holborn, King's Cross and St Pancras, in the south of this borough which extends to Barnet, are in the Inner London section of this guide. They were administered by Holborn and St Pancras Councils until the boundaries were redrawn in 1965. Although Camden Town and Kentish Town are tightly packed with Victorian terrace houses, Camden has a population of only about 175,000. This is due to 800 acres of heathland between Hampstead ★ and Highgate ★.

Canons Park (176) (TQ 18-91) *Whitchurch Lane, Stanmore, 10 mi. NW Central London.* This public park with a modest mansion (now a school) has few vestiges of the great house that once stood here. Yet in stately homes, churches and parks all over England there are reminders of Canons, which was built between 1715-25 by James Brydges, Duke of Chandos. He was Marlborough's paymaster-general and amassed a great fortune which he subsequently lost. In 1747 the Duke's son realised a mere £11,000 when he was forced to dismantle the house on which his father had expended over £¼ million. Fragments and contents were sold off and found their way to a great number of other places. Only part of the garden wall survives around well-planted colourful flower beds but one of the

Cassiobury Park

SCALE 1:25 000 or 2½ INCHES to 1 MILE

summer houses may date from Chandos's time. A London builder put up a new house which for a few years before his death in 1788 was the home of Colonel Dennis O'Kelly, owner of the famous racehorse Eclipse.

Next to the park is the small church of St Lawrence which was rebuilt by the Duke of Chandos. The brightly painted ceiling and walls are attributed to Louis Laguerre. The Duke was a patron of Handel who stayed at Canons and, according to tradition, played the church organ.

Cassiobury Park (176) (TQ 09-97) *Near Watford, 16 mi. NW Central London.* 237 acres of public park now occupy a part of the former estate of the earls of Essex. The Grand Union Canal ★ and the River Gade separate it from the West Herts Golf Club and Whippendell Wood. The house was demolished in 1927 and the fine entrance gates removed during a road-widening scheme in 1970. Boat trips on a genuine canal narrowboat start from the iron-bridge lock during the summer months. There are nature trails, a small miniature railway, playing fields, a children's play area and paddling pool. Whippendell Wood has a further 200 acres where hills are used for cycle scrambles, and obstacles have been set up for a survival course.

Chalfont St Giles (176) (SU 98-93) *24 mi. WNW Central London.* On the street just beyond the village pond **Milton's Cottage (1)** ★ survives. The poet came to this rustic home in 1665 to escape the Great Plague in London, and during the year he spent here dictated *Paradise Lost.* A short distance away, among old cottages and quaint little shops, an unusual lych-gate leads to the **Church of St Giles (2)**. Part of the building is 12th century but its

Chalfont St Giles

most valuable assets are 14th-century frescoes: the story of Salome dancing and having John the Baptist's head presented on a platter is vividly captured. The Chiltern Open Air Museum ★ in Newland Park lies between Chalfont St Giles and Rickmansworth.

Charlton House (177) (TQ 41-77) *Charlton Road, Charlton, 2 mi. E Greenwich, and 9 mi. E Central London.* Today used by the London borough of Greenwich as a public library and community centre, this red-brick and stone house is an excellent example of Jacobean architecture. Built in 1607-12 for Adam Newton, Dean of Durham and royal tutor, it is surrounded by pleasant gardens. There is a pavilion attributed to Inigo Jones which is now a public lavatory. Alas poor Inigo! The mulberry tree is said to have been planted in 1612, the year Newton took up residence. Open to the public. (*Tel: 01-856-3951.*)

Chartwell (188) (TQ 45-51) *Near Westerham, 25 mi. SE Central London.* The country home of Sir Winston Churchill from 1924 until his death in 1965. When he was Prime Minister during the Second World War, he only came infrequently to this home which he loved so much. It was felt that the lakes (some created by Churchill by diverting a stream) made the house (and him) easily identifiable targets for enemy aircraft. After his defeat in the General Election of 1945 Churchill felt he could no longer afford its upkeep but a group of close friends came to the rescue, bought Chartwell and presented it to

Chartwell

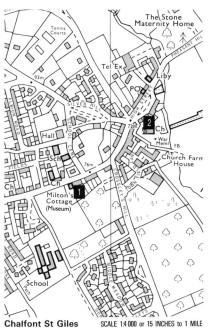

Chalfont St Giles SCALE 1:4 000 or 15 INCHES to 1 MILE

1 Milton's Cottage
2 Church of St Giles

the National Trust on condition that the wartime leader could live out his remaining days here.

Pleasant if architecturally undistinguished, the red-brick house overlooks attractive gardens that roll gently into the Kentish countryside. Inside the house the furniture remains much as it was when Sir Winston and Lady Churchill were here. Gifts he received from many nations are on display and a table at which he wrote standing up. The rose garden — a 50th wedding anniversary present from the four Churchill children — is enclosed by a wall on which a plaque records: 'The greater part of this wall was built between the years 1925 and 1932 by Winston with his own hands.' Open five days a week between March and November. There is a good self-service restaurant for refreshments and lunches. (*Tel: Edenbridge (0732) 866368.*)

Chenies Manor House (176) (TQ 01-98) *Chenies, 3 mi. E Amersham, and 24 mi. NW Central London.* The 16th-century red-brick manor house, next door to an attractive flint church with fine monuments, was an early home of the Russell family, earls of Bedford. The Tudor chimneys with richly ornamented stacks are most distinctive above the deeply pitched roof and stepped gables. Henry VIII and Elizabeth I are both known to have visited the house, which has a sunken garden. There are secret passages, good brickwork and some contemporary furniture and tapestries. Open twice a week between April and October. (*Tel: Little Chalfont (024 04) 2888.*)

Chessington World of Adventures (176) (TQ 16-62) *Leatherhead Road, Chessington, 15 mi. SW Central London.* The Zoological Gardens still form part of what is now a theme park and a monorail gives a bird's-eye view of the animals. At the centre of the 'World' is a picturesque village square and near the remains of a Norman castle, are a watermill, pub and Tudor restaurant. Calamity Canyon is a recreation of a town in the old West during the Californian Goldrush: a runaway mine train goes on a breathtaking trip through tunnels, ravines and over mountain passes. The mysteries of the Orient are another attraction. The thrills of watching sequinned girls on the flying trapeze may be experienced in the big top at Circus World where children are encouraged to join the clowns in the ring. The Zoological Gardens are open daily throughout the year and the World of Adventures daily from Spring to Autumn. (*Tel: Epsom (03727) 27227.*)

Chiltern Open Air Museum (176) (TQ 01-94) *Newland Park, Gorelands Lane, near Chalfont St Giles, 4mi. SE Amersham, and 21 mi. NW Central London.* The buildings set against a backdrop of pretty woodland reflect 500 years of life in the Chiltern Hills. An Iron Age house and very old chalk pits, through which there are several nature trails, are further attractions. There are several places to picnic. Open Easter to end of September. (*Tel: Chalfont St Giles (024 07) 71117.*)

Chislehurst, (177) (TQ 44-70) *6 mi. SE Greenwich, and 12 mi. SE Central London.* A leafy, affluent suburb with modern Tudor-style houses sitting in manicured gardens. The village is bounded by woodland and has a protected common. Despite

Chislehurst

the thousands of detached houses, the area retains some of its individuality and historical associations. The Walsingham family occupied the manor house, and Thomas Walsingham was knighted by Queen Elizabeth I when she visited Scadbury Park in 1597. The Tudor house was demolished and a new house built by Viscount Sydney (after whom the Australian city is named) in the 18th century. This was badly damaged by fire in 1974.

In recent times the Walsingham family tomb in the Church of St Nicholas has been examined by scholars hoping to find evidence explaining the mysterious murder of Walsingham's protégé, Christopher Marlowe, and proof that Shakespeare did not write his plays.

After the Fall of Paris in 1870 the Empress Eugenie moved into Camden Place (today a golf club) where she was joined by Napoleon III and the Prince Imperial. The Emperor's funeral at St Mary's Church was attended by a huge gathering of royalty. His body lay in a specially built side chapel until the ex-Empress went to live in Hampshire taking the body with her. Shortly after the funeral in 1873 Queen Victoria paid her respects at the pretty little church, her only recorded visit to a Roman Catholic church in England. A Celtic cross in the graveyard marks the burial place of the daughter of Mrs Katherine O'Shea and her second husband, the Irish politician Charles Stewart Parnell.

Camden Place was bought by William Willett in 1880 who was riding in Petts Wood (177) (TQ 44-68) when the early morning sunshine gave him the idea of introducing summer time. A pillar in the 77-acre wood, now National Trust property, commemorates his inspiration.

Chislehurst Caves (177) (TQ 43-69) are thought to have been used by the Romans for mining chalk, and during the Second World War they were used as a huge air raid shelter. They are open to the public. (*Tel: 01-467-3264.*)

Chiswick (176) (TQ 20-78) *6 mi. W Central London.* In the loop of the Thames between Hammersmith ★ and Kew ★, there are a number of notable houses near the riverside village although many more by the Great West Road disappeared in Victorian times. Two distinguished survivors are Lord Burlington's Chiswick House★ and Walpole House on the Mall where there are several fine buildings. Walpole House, the family home of the first prime minister in the 18th century, is presumed to be where Charles II's mistress Barbara Castlemaine died in 1709. Later Daniel O'Connell lodged here and early this century it was the home of the actor-manager Sir Herbert Beerbohm-Tree. Barbara Castlemaine was buried at the nearby church of St Nicholas, also the final resting place of William Hogarth who spent every summer at Hogarth House★ from 1749 until his death in 1764. The graves of Colen Campbell and William Kent, both associated with Lord Burlington, and the painter J.M. Whistler are also here.

Chiswick House (176) (TQ 20-77) *Burlington Lane, Chiswick, 6mi. W Central London.* One of the most admired examples of Palladian architecture in the country, this charming house was put up by Richard Boyle, 3rd Earl of Burlington. Designed on strictly classical lines as an antique villa in which to entertain his friends and house his library, its main inspiration was Palladio's Villa Capra at Vicenza. The villa, which Lord Hervey described as 'too small to live in and too big to hang on one's watch', was built more as a gallery for the Earl's pictures than his residence which was a larger house in the grounds (now demolished) as well as Burlington House★ in Piccadilly. After the Second World War the local authority purchased the estate when it was in danger of being redeveloped. In the attractively landscaped gardens there is a gate designed by Inigo Jones. This originally stood in front of Beaufort House, Chelsea★, and was given to Lord Burlington by Sir Hans Sloane in 1736. A verse by Alexander Pope explaining its history is carved on top. Open throughout the year, although not every day in winter. (*Tel: 01-994-3299.*)

Clandon Park (186) (TQ 04-51) *West Clandon, near Guildford, 27 mi. SW Central London.* The former family home of the earls of Onslow was designed in the Palladian style by the Venetian architect Giacomo Leoni c. 1730. The two-storeyed Marble Entrance Hall is particularly fine, and there are some good paintings of the Onslow family, three of whom were Speakers of the House of

Clandon Park

Commons. Besides a famous collection of Chinese porcelain birds, there is a military museum displaying items associated with the Queen's Royal Surrey Regiment. The house, in the care of the National Trust, is open from April to October. (*Tel: Guildford (0483) 222482.*)

Claremont Landscape Garden (176) (TQ 13-63) *Portsmouth Road, near Esher, 16 mi. SW Central London.* Laid out by Sir John Vanbrugh who built himself a house here early in the 18th century, this is the earliest informally landscaped garden in the country still in existence. Later Capability Brown, who owned the estate, tore down Vanbrugh's home, put up one to his own design, and did a little reorganising in the garden — although not as much as Charles Bridgeman, who had earlier added the lake and the turf amphitheatre which the National Trust has recently restored. Amid the 50 acres accessible for walks, there is a lake, remodelled by William Kent who put the island in the centre and also dug out the ha-ha. The house (privately owned

Claremont Landscape Garden

and sometimes open to the public) is a girls' school. For most of the last century it was a royal home, lived in by Louis Phillipe, the exiled Bourbon King, then by Queen Victoria's uncle Leopold (King of the Belgians) and later by her son the Duke of Albany. The grounds are open daily. (*Tel: Esher (0372) 67841.*)

Cliveden (175) (SU 91-85) *Taplow, Maidenhead, 25 mi. W Central London.* Glorious and extensive grounds surround this historic house famous as the home of the Astor family and now a hotel. The original house was first the residence of George Villiers, 2nd Duke of Buckingham and then of Frederick, Prince of Wales, George III's father. Here the Prince received the blow from a cricket ball which subsequently proved fatal. This house burnt down in 1795 and a new one, put up by Sir George Warrender, suffered the same fate. The present mansion was designed by Sir Charles Barry in 1851 for Queen Victoria's close friend the Duchess of Sutherland. From 1893 until 1966 it was the home of the Astors. In the inter-war years, when Nancy, Lady Astor, the first woman to sit in the House of Commons, was châtelaine, influential politicians and statesmen who gathered here became known as the 'Cliveden Set'. Shortly before the Astors left, it was the scene of a political scandal during the Profumo Affair which contributed to the downfall of the Conservative government of the day.

There is a turf amphitheatre where *Rule Britannia*

was first performed in a masque Thomas Arne wrote for George II's son, Frederick, Prince of Wales, in 1740. Plays and entertainments are still given during the summer months. Several temples designed by the Venetian architect Giacomo Leoni are in the beautifully planted gardens which are noted for their herbaceous borders, water and rose gardens. The large shell fountain, a focal point at the end of the main drive which is lined with lime trees, was made for William Waldorf Astor, Ist Viscount Astor, who moved to Hever Castle ★ when his eldest son married Nancy Langhorne. A steep cliff path through hanging woods leads to the River Thames. The house, now a luxury hotel, is shown to visitors on specified days during the summer. The grounds, the property of the National Trust, are open daily from March to December. (*Tel: Burnham (062 86) 5069.*)

Crystal Palace (177) (TQ 34-70) *Sydenham, 7 mi. SSE Central London.* An athletics stadium, an Olympic-size swimming pool, sports hall and playing fields comprise the National Sports Centre which has been built in the park where the Crystal Palace stood from 1854 until it was destroyed by fire in 1936. There is also an open-air concert bowl. The surrounding district took its name from the huge glass pavilion Joseph Paxton built for the Great Exhibition in Hyde Park ★ in 1851. Three years later it was dismantled and re-erected at Sydenham

Crystal Palace Park

where its exhibition halls proved such an enormous attraction that a special railway station was built to cope with the 1¼ million visitors who arrived in 1854. The specially modelled prehistoric monsters on the island in the lake were designed to be frightening. They, and some of the arcades of the terraced garden, are all that remain of what was one of the wonders of London.

Croydon (176,177) (TQ 33-65) *10 mi. S Central London.* Almost 350,000 people live in this heavily populated borough which runs from Upper Norwood to the Surrey border at Coulsdon. Croydon itself is a busy commercial town with large modern tower blocks and two shopping centres, one named after Archbishop Whitgift who built a school and hospital (which still exist) in 1599. The Archbishop, who is buried in the church of St John the Baptist, the largest parish church in Surrey, lived at the Old Palace ★ .

In 1915 Croydon Airport was opened as a military air base. This became London's principal airport and remained so until Heathrow opened in 1946. From here Amy Johnson set out on her flight to Australia in 1930 and Neville Chamberlain arrived with his 'Peace in our time' message from Munich. Imperial Airways, the forerunner of British Airways, operated from here.

There are over 3,000 acres of parks and open spaces in the borough and many private golf clubs. Coulsdon North Station is a good starting point for a walk from Farthing Downs to Coulsdon Common which is reached by skirting Devilsden Wood.

Cutty Sark (177) (TQ 37-77) *King William Walk, Greenwich, 7 mi. E Central London. (See map on page 108)* The prow and towering masts of the famous old tea clipper rise above the landing stage where tourists disembark from river cruisers. Before going into dry dock in 1954, she was one of the fastest ships of her day, sailing in both the China tea and Australian wool trades. Her last passage under the British flag was in 1895, after which she experienced lean times sailing under a different name for the Portuguese, and later as a training ship.

Built in Dumbarton in 1869, she takes her name from the formidable figurehead of a lady said to be the bewitched heroine of Robert Burns's poem *Tam o' Shanter.* She wears a revealing woollen shift or 'cutty sark'.

A remarkable collection of figureheads, marine paintings, and artefacts related to the sea are in the former quarters of the crew. The Cutty Sark is open every day. (*Tel: 01-858-3445.*)

Detillens (187) (TQ 40-52) *Limpsfield, 24 mi. SSE Central London.* The Georgian front, added in 1725, hides a 15th-century half-timbered Wealden house. Fine furniture and china stand against backgrounds of panelling and inglenooks. A very large collection of orders and decorations are on display. Open about twice a week between May and September. (*Tel: Oxted (088 33) 3342.*)

Docklands (177) (TQ 34-80 etc.) *3-7 mi. E Central London.* Multi-billion pound redevelopment schemes are rapidly changing the face of the riverside between Tower Bridge ★ and the Thames Barrier ★ . New industries, expensive town houses, apartment blocks and housing planned by local authorities are replacing the gloomy Victorian warehouses and grimy small homes in mean streets which became derelict following bomb damage during the Second World War and with the closure of the docks.

St Katharine Docks ★ , the landing stage for tea, rubber, sugar and other commodities, closed down in 1968 after 140 years' trading. It has been transformed into an attractive residential and leisure complex. For a century it was closely associated with the older *London Dock* (177) (TQ 34-80) at Wapping, the principal unloading place for tobacco, wine and brandy. Badly bombed in the Second World War, the dock was finally closed in 1969. Recent investment and the arrival of *The Times* and its sister newspapers are transforming a seedy area into a popular place to live and work.

The first and finest docks stretched across the Isle of Dogs, a peninsula in the river facing Greenwich ★ . These were the *West India Docks*

(177) (TQ 37-80), opened in 1802. Ships from all over the world discharged their cargoes, but increasing labour problems forced closure in 1980. New life has come with the move of Billingsgate Fish Market★ to premises in the old dock. The Docklands Light Railway which runs to the City, a new printing plant for the *Daily Telegraph* and other commercial undertakings have ensured the future prosperity of the Isle of Dogs.

The Museum of London★ proposes to open the **Museum of Docklands** in 1989 on the North Quay of West India Docks (177) (TQ 37-80). A storage warehouse with a visitors' centre at the Royal Docks, giving an indication of what the museum will be like, may be seen by appointment *(Tel: 01-600-3699*; ask for Museum of Docklands).

The largest enclosed area of dock water was in the **Royal Docks** at Silvertown. The Royal Victoria Dock (1855), the Royal Albert Dock (1880) and the King George V (1921) were surrounded by industrial and chemical plants in one of which occurred the 'Silvertown Explosion' in 1917. Deterioration to a declining district has been halted by redevelopment in the 1980s. Part of the disused Royal Docks permits such watersports as powerboat racing, and there is **London City Airport** (177) (TQ 42-80), an airstrip for short take-off and landing aircraft. **North Woolwich Railway Museum** (177) (TQ 43-79) in the old station (restored to its 1854 condition) on Pier Road tells the story of the Great Eastern Railway. *(Tel: 01-474-7244.)*

On the south side of the Thames a building and landscaping programme in the **Surrey Docks** (177) (TQ 35-79) is revitalising parts of Rotherhithe and Deptford. These were prosperous residential districts from Tudor times. The whaling industry centred in the Greenland Dock suffered setbacks early this century. This dock, formerly the Howland Great Dock, opened in 1697 not far from the Royal Naval Docks where Henry VII's ships were built. This area was bombed in the Second World War and was virtually derelict when the docks closed in 1970. A new lock into the Greenland Dock is being built and houses will be set around a yacht haven, and the printing works of the *Daily Mail* are in the vicinity.

At least eight museums will be sited in Docklands, among them the Brunel Exhibition Project and a Metropolitan Police Museum at Wapping. The National Maritime Museum hopes to show

about 70 vessels at present in store in a dry dock north of the river. Information about future plans may be obtained from the London Docklands Development Corporation. *(Tel: 01-515-3000.)*

Dorney Court (175) (SU 92-79) *near Windsor, 24 mi. W Central London.* The bright red-brick and timber Tudor manor house has been owned by twelve successive members of the Palmer family since 1600. In the Great Hall a large carved stone pineapple commemorates that the first pineapple in England was grown at Dorney Court. It was presented to Charles II in 1661. In the drawing room there is a portrait of Lady Anne Palmer, stated to be the daughter of Roger Palmer, Earl of Castlemaine, although Charles II claimed to be her father. The original panelling in the bedrooms is exceptionally fine. Open several afternoons a week between Easter and October. *(Tel: Burnham (062 86) 4638.)*

Downe House (177) (TQ 43-61) *Luxted Road, Downe, 15 mi. SE Central London.* A museum run by the Royal College of Surgeons who in 1947 bought the house where Charles Darwin and his wife raised their large family. He lived here for 40 years until his death in 1882, his widow for a further fifteen. When he first saw it Darwin described the exterior as 'ugly', and his alterations did little to improve it. The development of Darwin's theory of evolution is clearly outlined in displays and the old

Dulwich and Dulwich Village (see page 104)

SCALE 1:25 000 or 2½ INCHES to 1 MILE

Dorney Court

study where he worked has been recreated. There are exhibits connected with his voyage on *HMS Beagle* to South America. Open five afternoons a week except in February. (*Tel: Farnborough (0689) 59119.*)

Dulwich (176,177) (TQ 33-73) *6 mi. SSE Central London.* At the southern end of the borough of Southwark ★ the charming village of Dulwich is a happy blend of Georgian, Victorian and Edwardian houses and shops as well as a number of modern buildings. The imposing entrance to Dulwich Park is across the road from Dulwich Picture Gallery ★. Laid out in Victorian days with winding paths and a lake, the park is colourful in May and June when rhododendrons and azaleas are in bloom.

Early in the 17th century land once owned by Bermondsey Abbey was sold to Edward Alleyn, one of the principal actor-managers of Shakespeare's day. The childless Alleyn, who appeared in Marlowe's tragedies and made a fortune as the controller of licences for bear baiting, founded 'The College of God's Gift in Dulwich'. These were almshouses and a school for twelve boys that later became *Dulwich College*. The Old College (entrance under the arch in Gallery Road) outgrew its usefulness and the present massive red-brick school, a few yards south, was opened in 1870. Alleyn is buried in the Chapel (in the original College) which may be seen by appointment. (*Tel: 01-693-3601.*)

Dulwich Picture Gallery, (176,177) (TQ 33-73) *College Road, Dulwich, 5 mi. SSE Central London.* The oldest public art gallery in England is also a mausoleum for three people most concerned with its foundation — Noel and Margaret Desenfans and Sir Francis Bourgeois. The most important paintings in the gallery once belonged to Noel Desenfans, a French-born art dealer, who assembled a

Dulwich Picture Gallery

collection for a national gallery in Warsaw on behalf of King Stanislas of Poland. After the King abdicated in 1795, Desenfans, unable to sell most of them, built up a personal collection which he bequeathed to his wife and to his lifelong friend Francis Bourgeois, landscape painter to George III. Bourgeois left these and his own collection to Dulwich College and Desenfans's widow built the gallery which Sir John Soane designed.

The well-proportioned rooms, furnished with some of Mrs Desenfans's best drawing-room pieces, are hung with masterpieces of the Dutch and Flemish schools. These include three Rembrandts. Poussin, Claude Lorrain, Van Dyck, Rubens, Canaletto and Murillo are also represented. (*Tel: 01-693-5254.*)

Ealing (176) (TQ 17-80) *8 mi. W Central London.* This borough includes the towns of Ealing, Acton, Perivale, Southall, Greenford, Hanwell and Northolt, the last three retaining a little of their original village atmosphere. The opening of the Grand Union Canal ★ which runs along the western boundary, and the nearby Great Western Railway, changed the area from forest and farmland to a dormitory suburb. There are 127 parks and several golf courses providing open spaces for nearly 300,000 people who live within the 20 square miles. Before the rapid 19th-century expansion Ealing had two royal residents — Queen Victoria's father at Castle Hill House and her aunt Princess Amelia at Gunnersbury Park. The Princess's house, pulled down and rebuilt for the Rothschild family, is now a local history museum set in a lovely terraced garden (176) (TQ 19-79). (*Tel: 01-992-1612.*) The film studios, on the Green in Ealing, where the famous comedies were made in the 1950s are now BBC TV studios.

The only building of any interest in Acton was Berrymead Priory, a castellated 18th-century Gothic restoration where the celebrated adventuress Lola Montez spent her honeymoon in 1849 after a bigamous marriage. The Priory was unceremoniously torn down in 1985.

Southall boasts a 16th-century manor house and church, but these are inclined to seem less important today compared to the temples and mosques built to serve the Asian community who have settled here since the 1950s. One trading link with the past remains: the Horse Market in Southall High Street on Wednesdays, the only agricultural market left in London.

Windmill Bridge (176) (TQ 14-80) (also known as Three Bridges) in Hanwell is a unique piece of architecture — a road, rail and canal intersection designed by Isambard Kingdom Brunel. Classified as an ancient monument, the cast iron bridge carries the canal over the railway line.

Edgware (176) (TQ 19-92) *10 mi. NW Central London.* The village of Edgware, now in the borough of Barnet ★, lies west of the Edgware Road at its northern limit. Very few of the old cottages have survived although the smithy where Handel is said to have sheltered from the rain and gained inspiration for his *Harmonious Blacksmith* has been preserved. It is now a gift shop. An obelisk in the grounds of the National Orthopaedic Hospital commemorates occupation by the Romans, who had a pottery at what was then known as Sulloniacae: examples of its wares are in the Museum of London ★.

Eltham Palace, (177) (TQ 42-73) *Court Yard, Eltham, 4 mi. SE Greeenwich, and 10 mi. SE Central London.* A 15th-century stone bridge leads to the Great Hall, the only remains of the mediaeval palace where Edward III is said to have founded the Order of the Garter in 1347. Chaucer was then Clerk of

Eltham Palace

Works. The palace, struck by lightning in 1450, was rebuilt shortly afterwards. Used infrequently by the Tudor monarchs and the early Stuarts, who preferred Greenwich, it fell into disrepair during the Civil War and, except for the Great Hall which has an excellent hammer-beam roof, was pulled down. Excavations in the grounds have revealed details of Henry VII's palace and the chapel where Henry VIII worshipped. Open twice a week. (Tel: 01-859 2112 ext. 267.)

Emmetts Garden, (188) (TQ 48-51) *Ide Hill, near Sevenoaks, 25 mi. SE Central London.* High on a hill, with sweeping views over the Weald, this four-acre garden is most attractive in autumn when the rare shrubs and trees are changing colour. There is a formal garden, and pleasant, winding walks through copses. Opening hours vary. The National Trust will supply details. (*Tel: Lamberhurst (0892) 890651.*)

Enfield (176,177) (TQ 33-96) *12 mi. N Central London.* This most northerly borough with a low population for its size incorporates the towns of Enfield, Edmonton and Southgate. Mentioned in the Domesday Book, its even earlier history has been of immense interest to archaeologists who have discovered Roman and Saxon remains. Digs have also uncovered valuable remnants of the Tudor period and the Industrial Revolution. Huge reservoirs and the River Lee provide a natural boundary between Middlesex and Essex. The Lee Valley Leisure Park★ runs through a large part of Enfield where the Picketts Lock Centre is a notable leisure complex. Adjacent waterways are part of the New River Scheme financed by Sir Hugh Myddelton in 1613 to provide London with clean water. Extensive parks (Trent Park★, White Webbs Park and Forty Hill) cover Enfield Chase — the royal hunting ground from mediaeval to Tudor times. Elizabeth I spent some of her childhood at a manor house demolished to build **Forty Hall** in 1629, which is now an art gallery and museum. (*Tel: 01-363-8196.*)

Capel Manor Garden at Bullsmoor Lane, Waltham Cross, has a good 18th-century house (not open) and 30 acres planted with flowers and herbs of the Stuart period. The walled garden, unusual vegetables, dye plants and greenhouses are of particular interest to horticulturalists. (*Tel: (0992) 763849.*)

Broomfield House, in a pleasant park at Palmers Green, said to have had James I as a visitor, was the local history museum until a recent fire. (*Tel: 01-366 6565 to ascertain future plans.*)

Epping Forest (177) (TQ 41-97 etc.) *12 mi. NE Central London.* The forest, extending north from Wanstead to Epping, was a royal hunting ground. Enveloping a large part of Essex, it was, until Stuart times, even greater than now. During the 18th and 19th centuries parts were enclosed by local farmers and built on. Trees were extensively lopped for firewood before an Act of Parliament in 1878 granted the City the right to protect and maintain the forest for all time. On 6 May 1882 Queen Victoria visited the 6,000 acres of woodland and declared them an open space for 'the enjoyment of her people forever'.

Oak, beech, lime and holly trees grow plentifully and there are more hornbeams in Epping than anywhere else in England. There are picnic areas, lakes, and paths for horse riders. One of the many walks extends 15 miles from Manor Park to Epping. Deer, which once roamed freely, are now contained in an area near Birch Hall, but badgers, weasels, squirrels and foxes are to be found in many parts.

The forest has figured prominently in English history. Queen Boudicca is reputed to have committed suicide near Epping Upland after her final battle against the Romans. Archaeologists have discovered Iron Age earthworks, Roman remains, a Saxon stronghold and evidence of a Viking invasion.

Waltham Forest★, a favourite royal hunting ground from before the Conquest, was especially popular in Tudor times. The three-storey half-timbered pavilion at Chingford known as Queen Elizabeth's Hunting Lodge★ was built in Henry VIII's reign for people to watch the progress of the hunt. In the 17th and 18th centuries the forest was a well-known hideout for highwaymen. William III was nearly kidnapped in 1698 and had to take refuge in Copt Hall (where Mary Tudor had been held prisoner during the reign of Edward VI). The notorious highwayman Dick Turpin knew the forest well and frequently rode out from the 'cave' at Loughton Camp that bears his name. This is where

In Epping Forest

he is supposed to have hidden when the law was on his tail.

A study centre has been set up at **The Epping Forest Conservation Centre** (177) (TQ 41-98), High Beach, Loughton. From here guided walks set out, and maps and books about the forest are available; school parties are encouraged. (*Tel: 01-508-7714.*)

Epsom (176) (TQ 20-60) *15 mi. SSW Central London.* The well-known Epsom salts are named after the mineral spring which brought many visitors to the 18th-century spa town. Now it is more famous for its racecourse, where for over 200 years the rolling Epsom Downs have been associated with the Derby. This, the most prestigious horserace in the world, was first run in 1780 and takes its name from the 12th Earl of Derby who had a house nearby. The race, for 3-year-olds takes place over a mile-and-a-half on the first Wednesday in June. In the same week, an even older classic is run — the Oaks — a race confined to 3-year-old fillies. The countryside to the south — bisected now by the M25 — has some pleasant walks and a number of woods. The town is set amid winding, short roads north of the racecourse.

Eton (176) (SU 96-77) *23 mi. W Central London. (See map on page 131)* Across the Thames from Windsor ★, to which it is linked by a footbridge, the town of Eton is dominated by the ancient brick buildings of Eton College, the most renowned boys' school in the country. In term-time pupils are objects of some curiosity as they walk in stiff wing collars and black frock coats in the streets between classrooms and the houses where they live. The college was founded in 1440 by Henry VII, whose statue stands in School Yard, one of two quadrangles in the main building. The Chapel, begun in 1441, has a series of fine 15th-century murals and contains such recent additions as modern fan

Eton College

vaulting and stained glass. Busts of Old Etonians are displayed in the Upper School, and a frieze commemorates the 1,905 former pupils killed in the two World Wars. Twenty Prime Ministers were educated at Eton, among them Pitt the elder and younger, the Duke of Wellington (hence the saying 'Waterloo was won on the playing fields of Eton'), George Canning, William Gladstone and Harold Macmillan (Lord Stockton). There is a museum, and guided tours of the college may be arranged between April and October. (*Tel: Windsor (075 35) 63593.*)

Eynsford and Eynsford Castle (177) (TQ 54-65) *Eynsford, 6 mi. S Dartford, and 20 mi. SE Central London.* A most attractive village, complete with half-timbered cottages, and a hump-backed bridge over the little River Darent, which is also forded at this point. The castle, built shortly after the Conquest, and once the home of the quarrelsome Norman family of De Eynsford, has been a ruin since 1312 when it was virtually destroyed amid drunken revelries. Seven members of the family lived there. The remnants are on the bank of the river, just off the High Street.

Eynsford

Fenton House, (176) (TQ 26-86) *Hampstead Grove, Hampstead, 5 mi. NW Central London.* This dignified house, built in 1693, contains a remarkable collection of historical musical instruments, including a 1612 harpsichord on which Handel played. Recitals are given at the house from time to time. Fine porcelain and furniture are on show. In the care of the National Trust. Open between February and December. (*Tel: 01-435-3471.*)

Freud Museum (176) (TQ 26-84) *20 Maresfield Gardens, Hampstead, 5 mi. NW Central London.* Opened as a museum in July 1986, this family house in a tree-lined avenue was the great psychoanalyst's last home. He came to England from Vienna in 1938 to escape the impending Nazi invasion and died the following year. His daughter Anna, who lived the rest of her long distinguished life in the house, kept her father's library and study exactly as they were in 1939, and the furnishings have been restored.

The museum contains a large selection of personal ephemera, his library, letters and classical antiquities. The couch on which he pioneered the science of understanding the human mental processes is owned by the charitable trust that runs the museum. Open daily. (*Tel: 01-435-2002.*)

Frogmore Gardens (176) (SU 97-75) *Home Park, Windsor, 23 mi. W Central London. (See map on page 131)* The little estate bought by Henry VIII was added to by Queen Charlotte who took refuge in her 'little paradise' when George III's mad behaviour proved too much. Queen Victoria often came here when her mother, the Duchess of Kent, lived at Frogmore House (due to open to the public in August 1988) and Prince Albert skated on the lake whenever it froze during the royal family's Christmases at Windsor. In accordance with the Prince's 'own inclination' to be interred in a pastoral setting, Queen Victoria built the royal mausoleum near one she put up a short time earlier for her mother. Victoria joined the Prince Consort in 1901. The graves of several members of the royal family, including the Duke and Duchess of Windsor, are in the gardens. The gardens and royal mausoleum are open approximately three days a year — always in May. Information from the National Gardens Scheme (*Tel: 01-730-0359*) or Windsor Tourist Centre (*Tel: Windsor (0753) 852010*).

Fulham (176) (TQ 24-76) *6 mi. SW Central London.* The district to the west of Chelsea ★, a borough in its own right until 1965 when it was reunited with Hammersmith ★, is tightly packed with terraces of Victorian houses that have become most desirable properties. Close by the river's edge is Hurlingham Park, where there is a well-known sports club, and Bishop's Park in which Fulham Palace (176) (TQ 24-76) stands. Until 1973 this had been the Bishop of London's residence for over 1,000 years. All the surrounding land was granted to Waldhere, Bishop of London, in the 8th century, and the present palace, now owned by the local council, was built early in the 16th-century. The Great Hall was the scene of Thomas Tomkins's torture by Bishop Bonner during the Marian persecutions. Bishop's Park is open daily and the palace is occasionally open. (*Tel: 01-736-7181.*)

Sandford Manor House (176) (TQ 26-76), set in the middle of a new housing estate off the King's Road at the bottom of Cambria Street, has a history dating back to the reign of Edward I, although the present house — in a sorry state of dereliction in 1987 — is mid-17th-century. Nell Gwyn is reputed to have lived in it. New owners have made several promises to restore and open the house to the public: at the time of writing these as yet remain unfulfilled.

Geffrye Museum (177) (TQ 33-83) *Kingsland Road, 3 mi. NE Central London.* Each room in these former almshouses is devoted to a different period of English furniture from Elizabethan to present times and gives an indication of the lifestyle of ordinary families.

The residents of the 14 almshouses, established in 1715 under the terms of the will of Sir Robert Geffrye, a Lord Mayor of London, were moved to new premises in Mottingham before the First World War. The Ironmongers' Company, who ran the houses, handed them over to the London County Council who set up this charming museum. There are a number of exhibitions during the year, usually devoted to decorative art or ceramics, and a programme of activities for children. (*Tel: 01-739-8368.*)

Gipsy Moth IV (177) (TQ 37-77) *Cutty Sark Gardens, Greenwich, 7 mi. E Central London. (See map on page 108)* The 53-ft ketch in which Sir Francis Chichester sailed single-handed round the world is in dry dock a few yards from the Cutty Sark ★. He left Plymouth in August 1966, landed in Sydney in December and arrived back at Plymouth Sound the following May. Sixteen days later at the watergate of the Royal Naval College, for this unparalleled feat of bravery by a man of 65, he was knighted by Queen Elizabeth II who used the sword with which Elizabeth I had dubbed Sir Francis Drake. Gipsy Moth IV is named after the light aircraft owned 40 years earlier by Sir Francis when he became the first man to fly the Tasman Sea. Open daily. (*Tel: 01-858-3445.*)

Grand Union Canal (176) (TQ 16-84 etc.) Navigable between London and Birmingham, the canal meanders into outer London taking a semi-circular course in the north-west before dividing at Southall. One section flows into the Thames at Brentford Dock, the other winds north before joining the Regent's Canal ★ to form an arc around Central London and enters the river at Limehouse ★. There are many towpaths along the canal: behind King's Cross Station is a nature reserve, and sections around Uxbridge and Rickmansworth, where there is an aquadrome, are especially attractive. Since 1963 it has been in the care of the British Waterways Board which has an information centre at Camden Town. (*Tel: 01-482-0523.*)

Great Wood Country Park (166) (TL 28-04) *near Cuffley, N Enfield, and 15 mi. N Central London.* This large wood of 540 acres, sometimes called Northaw Great Wood, has imposing trees set in undulating countryside. Several walks of varying length take ramblers through glades and woodland where ponds and clearings provide pleasant contrast to the dark holly and tall silver birches.

Greenwich (177) (TQ 39-77) *7 mi. E Central London.* The historic and noble architecture of the riverside suburb is a most popular daytrip for tourists from Central London. Yet with all its magnificent buildings, this borough with a population of 215,000 is immensely varied and has a number of large estates with low-cost housing.

Virtually every British architect of note is represented at Greenwich: Inigo Jones and John Webb at the **Queen's House (1)** ★, the most finely proportioned building in the land: Webb, Christopher Wren, John Vanbrugh and Nicholas

Café Scene by Muriel Minter, an exhibit at the Geffrye Museum

Greenwich

SCALE 1:10 000 or 6 INCHES to 1 MILE

1 The Queen's House
2 The Royal Naval College
3 Trinity Hospital
4 Greenwich Park

5 National Maritime Museum
6 Blackheath Gate
7 Old Royal Observatory
8 Macartney House

9 The Ranger's House
10 Church of St Alphege
11 *Gipsy Moth IV*
12 *Cutty Sark*

Hawksmoor at the **Royal Naval College (2)** ★, which has a painted ceiling by James Thornhill and a Chapel designed by James 'Athenian' Stuart. Overlooking the river too is **Trinity Hospital (3)**, an almshouse founded in 1613 for 21 local poor men. It is still maintained by the Mercers' Company.

On the lower edge of **Greenwich Park (4)** the twin buildings of the **National Maritime Museum (5)** ★ flank the Queen's House. This royal park was first enclosed in 1433 and landscaped to a plan devised by Le Nôtre in the reign of Charles II, but only the chestnut avenue leading to the **Blackheath Gate (6)** from the statue of General Wolfe survives. By the statue, at the top of the steep hill, is the **Old Royal Observatory (7)** ★ with the distinctive red time ball on the top of Flamsteed House. Wolfe died at the historic battle of Quebec which established British supremacy in Canada. He spent his youth at **Macartney House (8)** which backs onto the Park. A few yards away is **Ranger's House (9)** ★, once home of Lord Chesterfield, famous for his admonitory letters to his son. Next to it, until demolished by the Prince Regent, was Montague House where his estranged wife Princess Caroline set tongues wagging when she adopted two children. A sunken bath in the park is the only evidence left of her home.

An archaeological site on the east side of the Park, not far from Vanbrugh Castle, provided evidence of Roman occupation. The Romans came across Blackheath ★ and through Greenwich on their way to London. So did the Danes centuries later. They murdered Archbishop Alphege in 1012 at the spot where Nicholas Hawksmoor's **Church of St Alphege (10)** stands today. General Wolfe and Thomas Tallis, the father of church music, are among those buried here.

Greenwich's principal legacies come from the Tudor and Stuart monarchs who had more than one residence in the area. The Great Hall of Eltham Palace ★, a home of the mediaeval kings, survives but nothing remains above ground of the great Palace of Placentia where Henry VIII and his daughters Mary and Elizabeth were born. Edward VI, the sickly boy king, died here. James I instructed Inigo Jones to build the Queen's House for Anne of Denmark, but the main palace buildings fell into disrepair during the Civil War and were demolished at the Restoration to be replaced by the present Royal Naval College. During an archaeological dig on the lawn remnants of Placentia were uncovered in 1970.

Gipsy Moth IV (11) ★, the yacht Sir Francis Chichester sailed round the world, is in dry dock beside the great tea clipper, the **Cutty Sark (12)** ★. There are river trips from the pier to the Thames Flood Barrier ★ at Woolwich. About two miles to the east there is a local history museum in Charlton House ★, a Jacobean mansion.

Hackney (176,177) (TQ 34-84) *4 mi. NE Central London.* Almost 200,000 people live in this densely populated East End borough where there were marshes and farmland until building development in the 19th century. Once a well-to-do neighbourhood with villages and thriving market gardens, Hackney became a sanctuary for refugees from Eastern Europe a hundred years ago.

In Shoreditch, just outside the City boundary, James Burbage established a playhouse (simply called The Theatre) in 1576, marked today by a plaque on the corner of Curtain Road and New Inn Yard. When the lease expired his sons, Richard and

The Royal Naval College, Greenwich, with the Queen's House in the background

Hainault Forest Country Park

SCALE 1:25 000 or 2½ INCHES to 1 MILE

Cuthbert, demolished the building, removed the materials to Bankside ★ and with a partner, William Shakespeare, put up the Globe ★. The church of St Leonard in Shoreditch High Street has strong connections with Shakespearean actors. The Burbages and a number of the Globe players were buried in the churchyard.

Former almshouses in Kingsland Road were converted early this century and are now the Geffrye Museum ★.

Hainault Forest Park (177) (TQ 47-93) *Hainault, 15 mi. NE Central London.* Only 1,108 acres remain of the great forest whose primeval trees were cut down and sold for timber. Valence House ★ has a whole room devoted to the history of the forest which was five times larger in the 18th century. Today it is open land with occasional groves of trees planted early this century in an attempt to re-afforestate. There are two golf courses, playing fields and bridle paths. The small island in the centre of the lake is a haven for birds. Fishing is permitted. There are picnic sites and a Pets' Corner.

Hall Place (177) (TQ 50-74) *Bourne Road, Bexley, 6 mi. E Greenwich, and 13 mi. E Central London.* Sir John Champneis, a former Lord Mayor of London, built his late mediaeval-style hall house in 1537 with materials assumed to have come from a dissolved monastery. A century later, another owner, Robert

Austen, added the large red-brick extension to Champneis's chequerboard home and adorned a room on the first floor (not always open) with a fine plasterwork ceiling. Although it has had many owners this Tudor-Jacobean house has survived more or less intact and is now an arts centre. Open throughout the year. (*Tel: (0322) 526574.*)

Ham House (176) (TQ 17-73) *Ham Street, Petersham, Richmond, 10 mi. SW Central London.* The lifestyle of a 17th-century English aristocrat is to be seen in this Stuart mansion which was built in 1610 and became the home of William Murray whose descendants lived here until 1947.

Many of the rich 17th-century textiles, tapestries and valuable sculptures are still in the house. The drawing room with its plaster ceiling, Mortlake tapestries and Persian carpet is exceptionally fine.

The gardens have been replanted in modern times to match the formal 17th-century pattern.

Ham House, administered by the Victoria and Albert Museum for the National Trust, is open throughout the year. (*Tel: 01-940-1950.*) During the summer there is a ferry to carry visitors across the Thames to two fine mansions, Orleans House ★ and Marble Hill House ★.

Hammersmith and Fulham (176) (TQ 22-79 etc.) *6 mi. W Central London.* Until 1834 Hammersmith was an outlying part of land owned by the Bishop of

London whose palace was at Fulham. It was united with Fulham ★ in 1965. About 150,000 people live in the crowded small streets which include the former villages of Parsons Green, Shepherd's Bush, and Wormwood Scrubs. The riverside walk from Hammersmith Bridge to Chiswick ★ has been described as 'the most civilised two miles in England'.

Television Centre at Shepherd's Bush became the headquarters of BBC TV when they moved from Alexandra Palace ★. Wormwood Scrubs, the big prison, is bounded by several acres of heathland. The Lyric Theatre in King Street is noted for the high standard of its productions.

Hampstead Heath

Hampstead (176) (TQ 26-85) *5 mi. NW Central London.* Alleys and courtyards, often connected by flights of steps, lie off narrow streets in this hilly attractive village. The approach roads, in contrast, are mostly wide tree-lined streets with large private houses. Hampstead Heath, 800 acres of wood and open spaces, spreads out on the northeast side. Well Walk is a reminder that Hampstead was a spa in the 18th century and the period houses in Flask Walk and Perrins Lane recall those days. Four houses open to the public — Keats House ★, Kenwood ★, Fenton House ★ and the Freud Museum ★ — give an indication of the lifestyles of very different eminent men and are examples of 17th-century to Edwardian architecture.

The Earl of Mansfield, whose family lived at Kenwood, and local residents fought plans for building on the Heath for 40 years until in 1871 the

land was preserved in perpetuity for public use. More acres have been added: Parliament Fields in 1889, and a further section of Kenwood in 1922. The house and remaining estate were later willed to the nation.

The Spaniards, an 18th-century inn with fine panelling is one of several renowned hostelries in the area. Next to it is a restored toll-gate. At the other end of Spaniards Road is Jack Straw's Castle, a modern reconstruction of the coaching inn named after one of the leaders of the Peasants' Revolt.

Hampton Court (176) (TQ 15-68) *12 mi. SW Central London.* This great rambling red-brick palace with turrets, towers and intricately moulded

Hampstead and Hampstead Heath

SCALE 1:25 000 or 2½ INCHES to 1 MILE

Hampton Court

SCALE 1:25 000 or 2½ INCHES to 1 MILE

chimneys was Henry VIII's favourite home. Its riverside location enabled the King to travel by royal barge between his residences — Hampton, Greenwich, Richmond, Windsor, Nonsuch, Westminster, Whitehall and St James's.

The bridge over the moat by the early-16th-century Great Gatehouse leads to Base Court, the largest and oldest of the palace's courtyards, where another gateway, named after Anne Boleyn, is at the entrance to Clock Court. At the end of the graceful colonnade built by Sir Christopher Wren a door goes into the State Apartments where the walls and ceilings on the King's Staircase were painted by Verrio. Paintings by Titian and other masters hang in the various chambers and Mortlake tapestries are on the Prince of Wales Staircase. The Great Hall, its construction supervised by Henry VIII, has a fine hammer-beam roof. Sunday services in the Royal Chapel are open to visitors.

The gardens owe their present formal style to William III and the famous Maze was laid out in the reign of Queen Anne. The vine planted in 1768 still produces black grapes.

Hampton Court was built in 1514 by Cardinal Wolsey; he was forced to hand over his magnificent house to Henry VIII when he fell out of favour in 1529. The King made extensive alterations. He was so impatient for the Great Hall to be completed that he ordered the plasterers and decorators to work

round the clock — by candlelight once daylight had faded. Two of his marriages — to Catherine Howard and Catherine Parr — took place at the palace, and Jane Seymour died here in 1537, after the birth of Henry's only son Edward VI.

James I came regularly to hunt, and William Shakespeare performed for him in the Great Hall. Charles I was responsible for diverting a tributary of the River Colne to provide a ready supply of running water, and this prevented more serious damage when a fire broke out on Easter Monday 1986.

After the Restoration Charles II came to Hampton Court and was responsible for buying many of the superb art treasures.

When William and Mary came to the throne Wren was invited to submit plans for restoration. He wanted to knock down the Tudor building but William decided against demolition. This is the reason for the two very distinct styles today: a Tudor palace adjoining Wren's classical red-brick addition. The last sovereigns to live here were George I and George II.

No immediate member of the royal family has lived at Hampton Court for over 200 years. The private apartments are 'grace and favour' flats for men and woman who have served the Crown. Since the reign of Victoria the State Apartments have been open to the public, and are very occasionally used for royal functions. Although the

Hampton Court and the River Thames

rooms do not contain much furniture, the paintings and tapestries are priceless. The damage caused by the 1986 fire, when several valuable paintings were burnt, is being restored and the palace is open daily. (*Tel: 01-977-8441.*)

Haringey (176,177) (TQ 31-89) *6 mi. N Central London.* Highgate ★, Hornsey, Muswell Hill, Tottenham and Wood Green are the principal centres of this built-up borough with a population of 230,000. Bruce Castle (177) (TQ 33-90) in Lordship Lane stands on land once owned by the Scottish royal family. Today the local history collection and the Middlesex Regimental Museum are here. (*Tel: 01-808-8772.*)

Tottenham Hotspur Football Club in White Hart Lane and the New River Sports Centre where the Haringey Athletics Club is based, are popular sporting attractions in the locality.

Harrow (176) (TQ 14-88) *12 mi. NW Central London.* This pleasant residential borough, the only one to retain its Domesday boundaries, is dominated by a steep hill. Just under 200,000 people live in well-planned roads where in Harrow itself, and in Pinner and Stanmore, a few of the 15th- and 16th-century village houses survive.

On *Harrow on the Hill* (176) (TQ 15-68) the spire of *St Mary's Church (1)* is a local landmark. There are a number of fine memorials in the church but nothing marks the place in the church porch where Allegra, Byron's daughter, was buried in 1822.

The most important brass commemorates Sir John Lyon and his wife who founded a 'free

Harrow School

Harrow on the Hill   SCALE 1:10 000 or 6 INCHES to 1 MILE

1 Church of St Mary
2 Harrow School

grammar school in the parish to have continuance for ever'. *Harrow School (2)* is next to the church. A school probably existed before Lyon obtained a charter from Elizabeth I in 1572. The red-brick schoolhouse, erected in 1615 soon after the deaths of Sir John and Lady Lyon, crowns the hill, and later buildings were added by a number of distinguished architects. Lord Byron, who played in the first annual cricket match between Eton ★ and Harrow, was an Old Harrovian. Others include the philanthropic 7th Earl of Shaftesbury, Richard Brinsley Sheridan, Anthony Trollope, the orator Charles James Fox and seven Prime Ministers, among them Sir Robert Peel and Lord Palmerston. Sir Winston Churchill regularly returned to his old school for the concert given by the boys each winter. Guided tours of the school (15 London Road, Harrow on the Hill) may be arranged during term-time. (*Tel: 01-422-2303.*)

The Grims Dyke Hotel (176) (TQ 14-92) in Harrow Weald was the home of W.S. Gilbert.

Hatchlands (187) (TQ 06-52) *East Clandon, Guildford, 30 mi. SW Central London.* 'A house he had just finished at the expense of the enemies of his country' was the epitaph attached to Admiral Boscawen's home, a fine brick house he had built in 1758. Boscawen, known as Pitt's 'Great Admiral', had been the victor at Lagos Bay and naval commander at the Battle of Louisburg during the campaigns against the French. Robert Adam designed the splendid interiors. An exhibition room is devoted to the Admiral's life. Pleasant garden. Owned by the National Trust, it is open about three afternoons a week between April and mid-October. (*Tel: Guildford (0483) 222787.*)

Hatfield House (166) (TL 23-08) *Hatfield, 20 mi. N Central London.* Sitting under an oak tree, which is still in the grounds, Princess Elizabeth heard the news that she was Queen and here in one of her principal childhood homes she held her first Council of State in November 1558. The surviving wing of the Old Palace, restored during this century, is now a Banqueting Hall. The great Jacobean house was built in 1607-11 by Robert Cecil, 1st Earl of Salisbury, who acquired Hatfield from James I. Cecil died in 1612 and his successors played no major role in history until the 1st Marquess was appointed Lord Chamberlain in the reign of George III. The 2nd Marchioness was a friend of the Duke of Wellington, of whom there are many mementoes in the house. The 3rd Marquess, leader of the Conservative Party, was Prime Minister three times between 1885 and 1902.

The Jacobean Marble Hall with panelling, a carved screen and a fine ceiling of elaborately decorated wood, paintings and plasterwork, remains much as it was built. The many portraits include several of Elizabeth I.

Hatfield House, today the home of the 6th Marquess, is open six days a week between March and October. (*Tel: Hatfield (07072) 62823.*)

Hatfield House

Havering (177) (TQ 51-93) *17 mi. NE Central London.* Most of this large northeastern borough was in Essex until the boundaries were redrawn in 1965. A large percentage of the population of about ¼ million are concentrated in the towns of Upminster, Hornchurch and Romford, leaving a semicircle of open land around the built-up areas. The 165-acre Havering Country Park, off Pinewood Road, Havering-atte-Bowe, has much to delight naturalists, and a bridle path runs to Hainault Forest ★.

Hayes Hill Farm (166) (TQ 38-03) *Off Stubbins Hall Lane, Crooked Mile, Waltham Abbey, 14 mi. N Central London.* One of the many attractions of the Lee Valley Leisure Park ★ is this farm with authentic-looking buildings and paddocks where many different farm animals are kept. In the 16th-century timber barn craft demonstrations take place most Sundays during the Summer, and a shop sells souvenirs and light refreshments. (*Tel: Nazeing (099 289) 2291.*) At nearby Holyfieldhall Farm visitors may watch the Friesian cows being milked in the modern milking parlour every day at 3 pm.

Hever Castle (188) (TQ 47-45) *Edenbridge, 27 mi. SE Central London.* The small, romantic Tudor house, childhood home of Anne Boleyn, was bought and restored early this century by William Waldorf Astor, who added a Tudor-style 'village' on the other side of the moat for guests and servants. The grounds were landscaped and the River Eden diverted to flow through a man-made lake. A large Italian loggia and piazza were built at one end. Trees that now rise to great heights on the lake shoreline were dug up in Ashdown Forest and transported by special railway line. Behind the colonnaded piazza the formal Italian garden is filled with ancient Greek and Roman statuary.

After the death of Anne Boleyn, Hever was the home of Henry VIII's fourth wife, Anne of Cleves, but then passed into private hands and was forgotten for over 300 years. Lord Astor furnished the castle with mementoes of the Boleyn family. Beneath the richly panelled and plastered ceilings hang portraits of Henry VIII (by Holbein), Mary I and Anne's daughter Elizabeth I. One interesting item on display is the layette made by Elizabeth for Mary Tudor's expected baby which turned out to be a 'phantom pregnancy'.

The Astor family's connection ceased in 1983 when they sold Hever to a property company. Most of the historical contents (apart from the armour) were bought by the new owners, who intend to keep the Castle and gardens much as they have been throughout this century. Open daily from April to October. (*Tel: Edenbridge (0732) 865224.*)

Highgate (176) (TQ 28-87) *4 mi. N Central London.* Heavy traffic invariably clutters the steep hills on the approach to the charming village which somehow retains its rural atmosphere. At the bottom of Highgate Hill the Whittington Stone, with a cat on top, marks the spot where, according to legend, Dick Whittington heard Bow Bells bidding him to 'turn again'. He became Lord Mayor of London three times and when he died left a legacy to St Bartholomew's Hospital ★. With Hampstead Heath on the west, Waterlow Park in the centre and Highgate Wood to the north, the district attracted influential residents in the 16th century.

Lauderdale House in Waterlow Park, built in Elizabeth I's reign by Richard Martin, master of the Royal Mint, was later remodelled by the Earl of Lauderdale. Charles II is reputed to have borrowed it and installed Nell Gwyn. Here she is said to have threatened to drop their son out of the window unless the King did something for him: Charles's resourceful and effective reply was 'Save the Earl of Burford!' The house is used for exhibitions and concerts and is open to the public. (*Tel: 01-348-8716.*) The 27-acre park has an aviary and three ponds. (*Tel: 01-272-2825.*)

Interposed between roads with large Georgian and Victorian mansions or streets full of terrace houses are modern blocks of luxury flats with fine views across to South London.

Highgate Cemetery (176) (TQ 28-87) *4 mi. N Central London.* Divided by Swains Lane, this is one of the great cemeteries of the world. The western section, a Victorian Valhalla, is a maze of winding paths, rising terraces, rich funeral monuments, catacombs and mausoleums. Amid the tangled undergrowth the most elaborate and celebrated tombstones are examples of eccentric funeral architecture. The great mausoleum on the Circle of Lebanon, modelled on the burial chamber at Halicarnassus, commemorates the Beer family who once owned the *Observer* newspaper.

A famous and romantic exhumation took place in 1869 when the coffin of Lizzie Siddal, the wife of Dante Gabriel Rossetti, was opened in order to recover a book of poems he had buried with her. It was said that after seven years her beauty was unimpaired.

After years of neglect, the western section is now run by the Friends of Highgate Cemetery, who are preserving the romantic charm and Victorian melancholy but clearing away the ivy and sycamore trees which were destroying the graves. Conducted tours take place every day. (*Tel: 01-340-1834.*)

In the eastern section the enormous head of Karl Marx surmounts his tomb, which also contains the ashes of his favourite daughter, Eleanor. The writer George Eliot, the Edwardian theatre architect Frank Matcham, and the actor Sir Ralph Richardson are also in this part of the cemetery, which is formal and prim compared to the wilderness across the road.

Hillingdon (176) (TQ 08-83) *16 mi. W Central London.* **Heathrow Airport** (TQ 07-75 etc.) comes within this northwest borough. Experimental flying took place on an airfield in the 1930s and during the Second World War it was an RAF Station. This developed into the capital's principal airport in 1946. Before the main runway was laid, an Iron Age temple and village were excavated. The airport, one of the busiest in the world, has several public viewing areas.

The important centres of the borough are Hillingdon itself, Uxbridge where Brunel University, renowned for its engineering studies, is sited, Harlington, Northwood, Ruislip, West Drayton and Hayes.

Apart from the City no other district can claim so many interesting churches. St John the Baptist at **Hillingdon** (176) (TQ 07-83) still has a 13th-century chancel arch and a later-mediaeval nave and aisle. The magnificent monuments include one to John Mist, 'Paviour to the Royal Palaces...[who] finished the great drain in Pall Mall and since the new road in Hyde Park.' John Rich, who built the Theatre Royal Covent Garden ★, is buried in the churchyard.

The church of St Mary at **Harmondsworth** (176) (TQ 05-77) and St Peter and Paul at **Harlington** (176) (TQ 08-78) both have Norman doors with delicate carving. St Mary's at **Harefield** (176) (TQ 05-89), a village church of exceptional interest, has examples of workmanship from the 12th century to Georgian times. The finest of its many monuments is the effigy of Alice, Countess of Derby, who entertained Elizabeth I at the nearby manor house. One hundred and ten Australian soldiers, brought to a makeshift hospital in Harefield Park after the Gallipoli landings in 1915, later died and were buried here.

Ickenham (176) (TQ 07-85) is one of several villages in the borough which retains period charm. Among the golf courses, woods and parks are Bayhurst Wood ★ and Copse Wood. Park Wood, adjoining Ruislip Lido, has a two-mile nature trail.

Hogarth's House (176) (TQ 21-76) *Hogarth Lane, Chiswick, 7 mi. W Central London.* With his wife, mother-in-law and sister, the artist William Hogarth whose studio was in Leicester Square ★ spent every summer from 1749 until his death in 1764 in his 'little country box beside the Thames'. The 18th-century house, with a wooden oriel window over the front door, was rescued early this century and restored. A collection of engravings reflecting London life as seen by Hogarth's satirical eye hang in rooms which contain a small quantity of 18th-century furniture. The healthy mulberry tree in the garden was planted by Hogarth. Open daily in summer and every day except Tuesday in winter.(*Tel: 01-994-6757.*)

Horniman Museum (177) (TQ 34-73) *London Road, Forest Hill, 6 mi. SSE Central London.* Frederick J. Horniman, tea importer and a great traveller, assembled remarkable ethnographical and natural-history collections on his many forays to foreign lands. These he kept in his house at Forest Hill and in 1890 opened it to the public. The house was later demolished in favour of the present Art

At the Horniman Museum — a wooden sculpture of Queen Victoria from Sierra Leone

Nouveau museum. Besides the aquariums, and fascinating items on animal evolution, there is detailed information about people of all nations. The Indian and African sculptures are especially fine, and some of the magic and ritual objects very beautiful. There is an exceptional collection of musical instruments (over 5,000 from all over the world), a reference library and education centre. Open daily. (*Tel: 01-699-1872.*)

Hounslow (176) (TQ 14-75 etc.) *12 mi. W Central London.* Brentford★, Chiswick★, Heston, Isleworth and Feltham make up the Thames-side borough which has been bisected by London's main route to the West of England since Roman times. The local history museum is in the Rothschild family's former mansion in **Gunnersbury Park** (176) (TQ 18-79), one of the many famous houses in the borough. (*Tel: 01-992-1612.*) These include Boston Manor House★, Hogarth's House★, Syon House★ and Osterley Park House★.

Like neighbouring Hillingdon, the borough has some interesting churches. All Saints, *Isleworth* (176) (TQ 16-76)), a remarkable modern building, incorporates a 15th-century tower with a fine peal of ten bells. Among the graves is that of John Busch, who retired to Isleworth from his position as gardener to the Tsarina of Russia. In St Mary's, **East Bedfont** (176) (TQ 08-73), the 13th-century wall paintings have been restored.

Hounslow Heath (176) (TQ 12-74) is today considerably smaller than when it was a favourite haunt of highwaymen and footpads and used for military manoeuvres.

Ightham Mote (188) (TQ 58-73) *Ivy Hatch, Sevenoaks, 26 mi. SE Central London.* Winding country lanes lead to this mediaeval manor house built in 1340 with Tudor and Jacobean additions. In an exceptionally beautiful setting, lichen-covered mellow brickwork rises out of a moat to meet the pale half-timbered first storey. The interior has some interesting decoration and the great hall has its

Ightham Mote

original oak ceiling and Tudor panelling. Until recently it was the home of an eccentric American who saw it on a bicycling tour of Kent in the 1930s, bought and restored it, and who generously bequeathed it to the National Trust. Open four days a week between April and October. (*Tel: Plaxtol (0732) 810378.*)

Islington (176,177) (TQ 31-85) *2 mi. N Central London.* Because of the proximity of the southern part of this borough to the City, Clerkenwell★ is included in the Inner London section of this gazetteer. The other densely populated and historic districts are Barnsbury, Canonbury, Finsbury, Highbury, Holloway and part of Highgate★. Around 170,000 people live on 4,000 acres covered with terrace houses. As a result of widespread and careful renovation of 18th-century squares and terraces, Islington's immediate post-war deterioration has been halted and the area is now fashionable with artists, writers and City businessmen.

Islington has a long history and some examples of its old buildings survive. Queen Elizabeth I often came to see her friend Sir John Spencer at **Canonbury House** (176,177) (TQ 32-84) (the tower still stands) and Sir Walter Raleigh had a residence (not extant) near Horton Street. Tom Paine wrote the first section of *The Rights of Man* at a house on the site of either the Old Red Lion (a pub theatre today) in St John Street or at the now vanished Angel Inn which was on the corner of Islington High Street.

Islington's nine theatres include Sadler's Wells★, the Almeida and the King's Head in Upper Street, a pub theatre which has transferred shows to Broadway and whose American landlord insists on giving change in pre-decimal figures!

Wesley's House and Chapel at 47 City Road (176,177) (TQ 32-82) was where the founder of Methodism lived and died. His tomb is in the garden. The museum in the crypt of the chapel illustrates the development of the Methodist Church. (*Tel: 01-253-2262.*)

Keats House (176) (TQ 27-85) *Keats Grove, Hampstead, 5 mi. NW Central London.* The poet John Keats settled in one of a pair of semi-detached Regency houses with his friend Charles Armitage Brown in 1818. The adjoining house was let to the Brawnes, to whose elder daughter Fanny he became secretly engaged, a romance which ended when the onset of consumption forced him to leave Hampstead in 1820 for Italy where he died.

The poet's bedroom and sitting room (largely unaltered) are furnished in the style of the time. French windows lead to the garden where he wrote *Ode to a Nightingale* under a plum tree (the present tree is a replacement). Personal ephemera, including Fanny's engagement ring and a lock of her hair, are on show and letters and manuscripts are in the Chester Room. This was added when the houses were converted into one in 1839 by Eliza Chester, an actress who had been reader to George IV. The Keats Memorial Library is open by appointment. Open daily. (*Tel: 01-435-2062.*)

Kensal Green Cemetery (176) (TQ 23-82) *Harrow Road, 5 mi. W Central London.* One of seven large burial grounds established by Act of Parliament between 1837 and 1841 to counteract a health hazard when churchyards became overcrowded. It is still in use, maintained by the original company. Unlike Highgate★ and Nunhead in South London, All Souls, Kensal Green has not been overrun by trees and undergrowth and G.K. Chesterton's lines — 'For there is good news yet to hear and fine things to be seen, Before we go to Paradise by way of Kensal Green' — still seem pertinent.

The burial of two of George III's children, the Duke of Sussex and Princess Sophie, gave the cemetery a certain social cachet and also attracted their nephew, Queen Victoria's cousin, Prince George, Duke of Cambridge, who chose to lie with his morganatic wife, the actress Louisa Fairbrother, rather than at Windsor. The writers Leigh Hunt, Anthony Trollope and Wilkie Collins as well as Sir Mark Isambard Brunel, his wife and their son Isambard Kingdom are among the famous buried here. The cemetery is open daily.

Kenwood House (176) (TQ 27-87) *Hampstead Lane, 5 mi. NW Central London.* Valuable paintings (the Iveagh Bequest) hang in the well-proportioned

Kenwood House

rooms of this 'noble seat' by Hampstead Heath. They were the gift of Edward Guinness, Ist Earl of Iveagh, who bought the attractive Robert Adam mansion in 1925 to house his superb collection. The finest works are those by Vermeer, Rembrandt, Van Dyck and Gainsborough. These paintings, together with the house, furnishings and land were given to the nation on his death in 1927. Before this Kenwood had been the residence of the Mansfield family. William Murray, 1st Earl Mansfield and Lord Chief Justice, bought a Jacobean house and surrounding estate in 1754 and ten years later invited Robert Adam to rebuild it. The ceiling in the entrance hall was painted by Angelica Kauffmann, and the one in the magnificent library by the Venetian she later married, Antonio Zucchi. The side wings were added in 1793.

The unspoiled woods, with pretty glades and a lake, bring a rural atmosphere to an area only three miles from the City. During the summer open-air concerts are given by the lake or in the Orangery. Art exhibitions are held in the house which, now in the care of English Heritage, is open daily. (*Tel:01-348-1286.*)

Keston (177) (TQ 42-63) *15 mi. SE Central London.* This open common land, with spindly birches and conifers, has a series of ponds formed by damming the River Ravensbourne which rises nearby at Caesar's Well. There is a hill-fort, remains of a 1716 post-mill and a little Norman church. One of several walks through Holwood Park goes past the entrance to the home of William Pitt the Younger, though the present house (owned by a private company and not open) was built by Decimus Burton in 1827.

Kew (176) (TQ 18-77) *9 mi. W Central London.* Henry VIII's sister Mary lived at the riverside village, but the Hanoverians were responsible for Kew's greatest royal associations, and for the world-famous gardens. George II's wife Queen Caroline

Kew and the Royal Botanic Gardens
(See page 125)   SCALE 1:25 000 or 2½ INCHES to 1 MILE

owned the estate and leased a Jacobean house known as the Dutch House. Her son Frederick, Prince of Wales acquired the nearby White House and in the grounds he and his wife Augusta cultivated exotic plants. After Frederick's death Augusta laid out the nine acres which became the foundation of the Royal Botanic Gardens ★, known as Kew Gardens. The house was demolished by George III who abandoned plans to build a new palace and moved into the Dutch House. This old red-brick house, known as **Kew Palace** is where the Prince Regent and his many siblings grew up. It charmingly illustrates the simple life of George III and Queen Charlotte, and a formal garden, planted with herbs popular in the 17th century, has been created. The palace, in the grounds of the Royal Botanic Gardens, is open daily in the summer. (*Tel: 01-940-3321.*)

Kew Bridge Steam Museum (176) (TQ 18-78) *Green Dragon Lane, Brentford, 9 mi. W Central London.* Five giant beam engines, built between 1820 and 1871, are in the Pumping Station, from which water was pumped to London homes. After electricity was introduced in 1944 it was decided to preserve the old steam engines and to add others to explain the history of the capital's water supply. The engines operate on Saturdays and Sundays, although the museum is open daily. (*Tel: 01-568-4757.*)

Kingston upon Thames (176) (TQ 18-70) *11 mi. SW Central London.* This royal borough (one of only two in London: Kensington and Chelsea is the

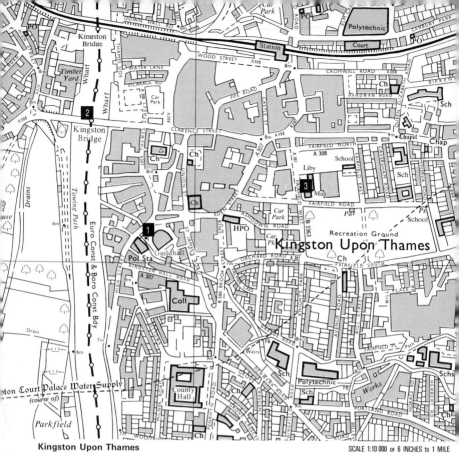

Kingston Upon Thames

SCALE 1:10 000 or 6 INCHES to 1 MILE

1 The Coronation Stone   2 Kingston Bridge   3 Museum & Heritage Centre

other), claims longer royal associations than anywhere else in the metropolis. Between AD 900-975 seven Anglo-Saxon kings are traditionally assumed to have been crowned on **The Coronation Stone (1)**, a slab of grey sandstone, now in the forecourt of the Guildhall in the High Street. The royal palaces of Nonsuch, Oatlands and Hampton Court★ were close by. Kingston's position on the Thames and the advantage of a bridge from pre-Conquest times ensured its importance as a trading centre. Until

Kingston upon Thames

Putney Bridge went up in 1729, **Kingston Bridge (2)** was the first crossing upstream from London Bridge★. The Ancient Market, which continues to present times, was established in the mid-13th century. Just over 130,000 people live in this borough of 9,000 acres which now takes in the pre-1965 boroughs of Surbiton, Coombe and Malden. The local history **Museum and Heritage Centre (3)** in Fairfield West has a rare collection of items associated with Eadweard Muybridge, the pioneer cinematographer. (*Tel: 01-546-5386.*)

Knole (188) (TQ 54-54) *Sevenoaks, 25 mi. SE Central London.* The long, winding drive over parkland lying behind Sevenoaks High Street curves round to reveal the largest private house in England on the crest of a hill. The arched gateway in the somewhat austere west front leads to the first of Knole's seven courtyards. With the exception of the clock tower, which is 18th century, time stood still here hundreds of years earlier.

A mediaeval palace of the Archbishops of Canterbury until Henry VIII persuaded Archbishop Cranmer to move out in 1538, Knole was granted to Thomas Sackville in 1566 by his cousin Elizabeth I. He did not take possession until 1603. Since then the same family, not always in direct line of succession, have lived at Knole.

Thomas Sackville, created Earl of Dorset, Lord High Treasurer and Lord High Steward of England,

118

turned the 15th-century house into a Jacobean mansion, adding the great staircase, the musicians' gallery, installing oak panelling and decorating the ceilings with intricate plasterwork.

In the 19th century the great estate passed to the 3rd Duke's daughter, Elizabeth, Countess De La Warr who assumed her maiden name and added that of her husband — West. From her descend the Sackville-Wests who live at Knole today. Her great granddaughter Vita Sackville-West wrote the history of the house and the family in *Knole and the Sackvilles*.

Edmund Burke, a lover of antiquities, considered Knole 'the most interesting thing in England'. Over the centuries the family added antiques to the 365 rooms. The early English furniture is the best collection in the country. The paintings range from 15th-century portraits to several of eminent Georgians by Reynolds and his contemporaries. The most precious treasure is the silver furniture: the pier glass and table were made in the reign of Charles II. The house, maintained by the National Trust, is open about five afternoons a week between April and October. The extensive park, where a herd of deer roam freely, is popular for picnics and for walks. (*Tel: Sevenoaks (0732) 450608.*)

Lambeth (176,177) (TQ 30-78 etc.) *1 mi. S Central London.* The riverside village from which this borough takes its name comes in the Inner London section of the gazetteer. The other main centres — Brixton, Streatham and Clapham — lie several miles further south. The nearest district to the former Lambeth village is Kennington, famous for the *Oval Cricket Ground* (176,177) (TQ 31-77) where test matches and county games are played. It is the headquarters of Surrey Cricket Club. (*Tel: 01-735-4911.*)

Brixton used to be a country district which attracted affluent residents in the early 19th century. A reminder of its rural past is the windmill in Blenheim Gardens (176,177) (TQ 30-74). This was built in 1816 and restored in the 1950s. Today Brixton has a Caribbean atmosphere. Many West Indians have settled in the area and 40 per cent of the population is black.

Streatham will always be associated with the comfortable ménage Dr Johnson found for himself with Henry and Hester Thrale. The house on the edge of Tooting Bec Common no longer exists, and most of the streets leading off the High Road were developed early this century. Clapham, noted for its common and its sprawling railway junction, was a mostly shabby Victorian region some years ago, but has been regenerated recently.

Langley Park and Black Park (176) (TQ 01-83 etc.) *3 mi. NE Slough, and 18 mi. W central London.* The Uxbridge to Slough road divides these two country parks, both happy mixtures of woodland, lakes and gardens with formal and informal paths. Fishing and boats (without motors) are permitted on the lake in Black Park. An arboretum, an avenue of trees planted by Rotary International and vantage points for views across the Home Counties are added attractions. Good parking facilities and picnic areas.

Lee Valley Leisure Park (177) (TQ 37-96 etc.) *Between Ware in Hertfordshire and Hackney in the*

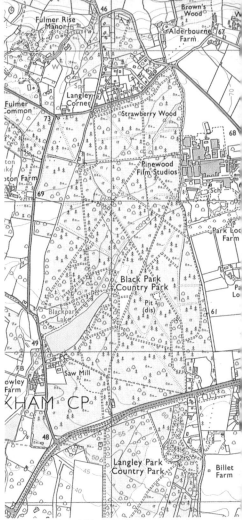

Langley Park and Black Park Country Parks
SCALE 1:25 000 or 2½ INCHES to 1 MILE

East End. Twenty-three miles of sport and leisure facilities on the banks of the River Lee are being imaginatively created. The Lee Valley Regional Park Authority aim at maintaining a semi-rural atmosphere. This body was established by Act of Parliament in 1967 when the river, once an important commercial waterway, had outlived its use and the surrounding land deteriorated.

Much of the Lee Valley Park is attractive countryside with meadow land, country walks, nature trails, and excellent places for birdwatching at the Rye House Marsh Nature Reserve, Hoddesdon (166) (TL 38-10) and at the north end of Hackney Marsh (177) (TQ 35-87). At the marina in Stanstead Abbots, near Ware, cabin cruisers may be hired and there are tracks for horse riding. King George V and Banbury Reservoirs have been opened for sailing. The Lido at Broxbourne ★ has an artificial wave machine and solarium. Hayes Hill Farm ★ allows city dwellers to experience the flavour of country life. A cycle circuit on a 40-acre site is only one of the many strenuous sports for the dedicated at the Eastway Sports Centre (177) (TQ 37-85) in Leyton (*tel: 01-519-0017*) where a health suite provides relaxation after volleyball or squash. The multi-purpose sports centre at Picketts Lock in Edmonton (177) (TQ 36-94) (*tel: 01-803-4756*) caters for outdoor and indoor sports and has a nine-hole golfcourse, floodlit all-weather playing fields, swimming pool, cafeteria and bars. An ice rink for skating and ice hockey is at the Lea Bridge Centre (177) (TQ 35-87) in Leyton. (*Tel: 01-533-3151.*)

Information about the many facilities, including caravan parks, may be obtained from the Lee Valley Park offices, P.O. Box 80, Enfield, Middlesex. (*Tel: Lee Valley (0992) 717711.*)

Lewisham (177) (TQ 38-75) *6 mi. SE Central London.* When James I admired the long main street, declaring that he 'would be king of Lewisham' it was a fashionable village with large houses and farms. Now almost 275,000 people live in this workaday borough which incorporates Deptford, and acre after acre is filled with terrace houses. Blackheath ★ to the east retains much of its 17th- and 18th-century character.

Among the welter of council houses in Deptford only street names remind the inhabitants that this was once a prosperous riverside town, the site of the Royal Naval Dockyards which prospered in the reign of Henry VIII and Elizabeth I. One exception is the church of St Nicholas (177) (TQ 37-77) which still has its 15th-century tower. The playwright Christopher Marlowe, mysteriously stabbed to death in a brawl in a local tavern, was buried here. So were several members of John Evelyn's family. The diarist lived at nearby Sayes Court (remembered in the name of a council estate off Evelyn Street) which he rented to Peter the Great who regularly got drunk, fell in the holly bushes and broke Evelyn's furniture. St Paul's (177) (TQ 37-77) in Deptford High Street, designed by Thomas Archer and completed in 1730, is an ingenious if eccentric example of baroque architecture.

Lewisham has two museums of interest: the Mander and Mitchenson Theatre Collection ★ in Beckenham Place Park and the Horniman Museum ★ at Forest Hill.

Limehouse (177) (TQ 36-81) *4 mi. E Central London.* Nicholas Hawksmoor's impressive church of St Anne, Limehouse was built 1714-24 to minister to a community of over 7,000 families who earned their living either at sea, on the river or in one of the shipyards. The church, its tower a conspicuous landmark in the East End, is now one of the few reminders of a once-thriving district which declined as new roads and housing estates were built. When the river became less important and the shipbuilding industry moved elsewhere Limehouse lost its character, although the gambling activities and opium-smoking habits of the colourful immigrant Chinese community attracted press attention at the end of the 19th century. Oscar Wilde's Dorian Gray went to Limehouse for opium. During the Second World War the Victorian slums were badly damaged. These have been replaced by council houses, and the present redevelopment of the Docklands ★ can only prove beneficial to a neighbourhood which once boasted the Regent's Canal Dock and West India Docks.

Lullingstone Castle (177) (TQ 52-64) *Eynsford, 6 mi. S Dartford, and 20 mi. SE Central London.* The

Gateway, Lullingstone Castle

Tudor house with Queen Anne additions has been the home of the Hart family since c. 1500. Silk for Queen Elizabeth II's wedding dress came from a silk farm established here in 1932 by Lady Hart Dyke, but this has now moved to Compton House in Dorset. The house contains family portraits and some armour. Open at weekends April to October. Other times by appointment. (*Tel: Farningham (0322) 862114.*)

Lullingstone Roman Villa (177) (TQ 52-65) *Eynsford, 6 mi. S Dartford, and 20 mi. SE Central London.* A farm track beyond the ford over the River Darenth leads to the remains of a country villa built about AD 100, possibly by a farmer. When excavations began in 1949 they revealed that at the end of the 2nd century it was enlarged for a wealthy Roman official, and burned down about AD 400. The fine mosaic floor, remnants of sunken baths and an underfloor heating system are imaginatively covered by an airy museum with a walkway which enables visitors to examine the archaeological discoveries. One room was converted into a chapel before the fire and the fragments of wall paintings prove this was one of the earliest places of Christian worship in England. Showcases on the walls contain artefacts recovered from the site. Open daily.

Mander and Mitchenson Theatre Collection (177) (TQ 38-70) *Beckenham Place Park, Beckenham, 9 mi. SE Central London.* The foundations of this rich source of theatrical memorabilia were laid before the Second World War by two actors, the late Raymond Mander and Joe Mitchenson, who acquired all manner of items associated with entertainment. A changing selection of paintings, photographs, costumes, engravings, manuscripts, letters and recordings will eventually be on public display. (*Opening plans not finalised at time of publication.*) The archive of programmes and playbills relating to the performing arts are added to daily. The collection of porcelain and pottery, showing scenes from famous plays or decorated with portraits of well-loved performers, is exceptional.

The Collection was given a permanent home in the 18th-century mansion in Beckenham Place Park by Lewisham Borough Council, which is restoring the period rooms. The library is open for research purposes. (*Tel: 01-658-7725.*)

Marble Hill House (176) (TQ 17-73) *Richmond Road, Twickenham, 10 mi. SW Central London.*

This delightful Palladian villa set in a riverside park was built in 1724-29 for Henrietta Howard, Countess of Suffolk, George II's sensible mistress. The design is assumed to have come from the pen of Colen Campbell and was supervised by the amateur architect Henry Herbert, Earl of Pembroke. A magnificent mahogany staircase leads to the Great Room which was modelled on the single cube room Inigo Jones designed for the Earl of Pembroke at Wilton. The fine carved decorations are attributed to James Richards, Grinling Gibbons's assistant. There is a good collection of early Georgian paintings, excellent furniture and prints. After Lady Suffolk's death in 1767, the house had many owners. In 1902 it was bought by the London County Council and is today in the care of English Heritage. Open throughout the year. (*Tel: 01-892-5115.*)

Merton (176) (TQ 25-69 etc.) *8 mi. S Central London.*

This south-west borough was formerly entirely in Surrey. Its principal centres are Mitcham, Merton, Morden and Wimbledon ★, each of which retains its individual characteristics. Apart from Mitcham and Wimbledon, which both have commons, the borough is built-up. Merton holds an important place in English history. In the chapter house of the Augustinian priory the Great Council, forerunner of Parliament, met in 1236. The Statute of Merton, by which the barons stated they did not wish to change the laws of the country, was the first recorded enactment in the statute book until repealed in 1948. The priory was demolished at the Dissolution, but traces of the wall are in Merton Abbey Station Road. Admiral Lord Nelson's pew is preserved in the church of St Mary (176) (TQ 25-69). His house and estate lay between modern Merton's, Quicks and Haydons Roads. He lived here from 1801 with Emma Hamilton and her elderly husband Sir William until he left for Trafalgar. In the church, next to the tablets with the armorial bearings of Nelson and Sir William Hamilton, is one to Sir Isaac Smith, the first man ashore when Captain Cook reached Australia.

The borough council offices at Mitcham are in The Canons, the fine mid-17th-century manor house which has attractively laid out walled gardens with a dovecote. Cricket has been played on Cricket Green at Mitcham since 1707.

Each street on the St Helier Estate in Morden, a large 1930s London County Council development, is named after a British abbey.

Milton's Cottage (176) (SU 98-93) *Chalfont St Giles, 24 mi. WNW Central London.*

When the 'pretty box' where John Milton wrote *Paradise Lost* was bought in 1887 Queen Victoria headed the list of subscribers with a donation of £20. Milton, already blind, came to the early 16th-century cottage to escape the Great Plague raging in London in 1665. The cottage, where he spent about a year, is preserved as a museum. First and early editions of his works are displayed along with statues, prints, paintings, a lock of his hair and a copy of Keats's *Lines on Seeing a Lock of Milton's Hair.*

The kitchen reflects village life through the ages. The exhibits include cannonballs left by Cromwellian soldiers billeted in the neighbourhood. The cottage has a charming garden. Open six days a week between February and October. (*Tel: Chalfont St Giles (02407) 2313.*)

Moor Park Mansion (176) (TQ 07-93) *Near Rickmansworth, 18 mi. WNW Central London.*

The park around this large mansion with an imposing portico is today a well-known golf course whose club rooms are in the house. It was built in 1678 for Charles II's natural son, James Duke of Monmouth, and 'palladianised' by Sir James Thornhill and Giacomo Leoni in 1720. The decorations by Verrio are exceptionally fine. The mansion is open daily,

Moor Park Mansion, near Rickmansworth

though viewing is sometimes restricted. (*Tel: Rickmansworth (0923) 776611.*)

William Morris Gallery (177) (TQ 37-89) *Water House, Lloyd Park, Forest Road, Walthamstow, 7 mi. NE Central London.*

The boyhood home of William Morris, the artist, craftsman and poet. Now a museum, it has many rooms furnished in William Morris style and contains examples of wallpaper and books printed at Morris's Kelmscott Press. Furniture, textiles, prints, paintings and drawings all illustrate his highly individual taste. A large number of items on show were the gift of the artist Frank Brangwyn, who as a young man met and worked with Morris in the early 1870s. The gallery is open five days a week and on certain Sundays. (*Tel: 01-527-5544 ext. 4390.*)

Museum of Artillery in the Rotunda (177) (TQ 42-78) *Repository Road, Woolwich, 10 mi. E Central London.*

The shell of the circular building on the west side of Woolwich Common was designed by John Nash for the Napoleonic victory celebrations in St James's Park in 1814. Five years later it was brought to Woolwich to house the 'military curiosities' of the Royal Artillery and the original canvas was carefully covered with brick and copper. The development of cannons and guns from the 14th century to the present day is illustrated; one exhibit is a bombard used at the Battle of Crecy in 1346. Open every afternoon throughout the year. (*Tel: 01-854 2242 ext. 3127.*)

Musical Museum (176) (TQ 18-77) *368 High Street, Brentford, 8 mi. W Central London.* The former church of St George contains a collection of automatic musical instruments, among them a giant Wurlitzer, ten reproducing piano systems and pipe organs. There are also approximately 30,000 music rolls, musical boxes, street organs and phonographs. Open weekend afternoons between April and October. Plans to move to a new location have not been finalised. (*Tel: 01-560-8108.*)

National Maritime Museum (177) (TQ 38-77) *Romney Road, Greenwich, 7 mi. E Central London. (See map on page 108)* On the lower slopes of Greenwich Park two buildings, linked by colonnades on either side of the Queen's House ★, contain an unrivalled national collection of material depicting 'Man's Encounter with the Sea'. The archaeology of water transport encompasses marine art from the 17th century, the social background of sailors in the past, as well as the history of the

The National Maritime Museum, Greenwich

Royal Navy and of all who go down to the sea in ships. Particularly popular are the vessels. The State barges with elaborate gilt carving and sedan-chair cabins are dazzling. Two galleries are devoted to Nelson, whose victories are recalled in personal mementoes and silver, and in Turner's turbulent vision of the Battle of Trafalgar. The most poignant exhibit is his Vice-Admiral's undress uniform coat in which the hole made by the bullet that went into his left shoulder on 21 October 1805 can be seen. The voyages of discovery by Captain Cook and explorers who went to America, and later to the Arctic and Antarctica, are charted. The transition from sail to steam is explained, and the history of yachting as a sport shows 17th-century royal yachts and modern glass-fibre craft. The manuscript archives and a maritime library are available to researchers, and the museum hopes to acquire additional space where the large reserve collections in store may be displayed. There is an education centre, and a programme of lectures and films. Open daily. (*Tel: 01-858-4422.*)

National Museum of Labour History (177) (TQ 36-80) *Old Limehouse Town Hall, Commercial Road, 4 mi. E Central London.* Pictures and documents depicting the development of the Labour and Trade Union movement in Britain are on show in this listed building. There are plans to move the museum to a new site in the Docklands ★. (*Tel: 01-515-3229.*)

Newham (177) (TQ 41-82) *7 mi. E Central London.* West Ham, East Ham and Stratford are in this rundown borough which developed from an affluent 17th-century district to an industrial area with the coming of the railway and the creation of the **Royal Docks** (177) (TQ 41-80 etc.). The docks, the largest enclosed area of dock water in the country, are comprised of the Royal Victoria Dock (opened 1855), Royal Albert Dock (1880) and the King George V (1921): always referred to as KG5. The great ships of the world once berthed here. Their closure in the 1960s resulted in the rapid waning of a district already in decline. However, recent development throughout the Docklands ★ has brought new life to the area. The great walls of the Royal Docks have been removed, sporting facilities and museums are springing up and London City Airport — for short-landing-and-take-off aircraft — is open.

The Passmore Edwards Museum (177) (TQ 39-84) in Romford Road, Stratford was the only purpose-built museum in Essex when it opened in 1900. It has an impressive natural history gallery and displays about the area's past, as well as a collection of rare and valuable porcelain produced locally at the Bow factory. Open daily. (*Tel: 01-519-4296.*)

The Theatre Royal Stratford East, built in 1886, and now squeezed in a corner of modern commercial development, achieved fame in the 50s and 60s under the fanatical, sometimes brilliant direction of Joan Littlewood.

Abbey Mills Pumping Station in Abbey Road (*Tel: 01-534-6717.*) and the mills in the Three Mills Conservation Area (177) (TQ 38-83) are important waterside buildings. The former, an ornate, cathedral-like Victorian pumping station with eight beam engines, is open to visitors by arrangement. One of the two mills off Three Mills Lane retains its 1753 clock tower, mill wheels and drying kilns. Plans are afoot to develop it into a working museum.

Abbey Mills Pumping Station

Old Palace (176,177) (TQ 32-65) *Old Palace Road, Croydon, 10 mi. S Central London.* The mediaeval palace of the Archbishops of Canterbury is today a girls' school. Put up as a resthouse for the prelate on the journey between Lambeth ★ and Canterbury, it became a favourite residence. The undercroft is 12th century and the Great Hall, built in

1390, was rebuilt and given a Spanish-chestnut roof 60 years later. Elizabeth I's bed-chamber is preserved on the first floor. She stayed at Croydon several times and in the Long Gallery made Sir Christopher Hatton the Lord Chancellor when she conferred the Great Seal of England on him. There are a number of fine sculptures and carvings in the palace. Open during school holidays. (*Tel: 01-688-2027.*)

Old Royal Observatory, (177) (TQ 38-77) *Greenwich Park, 7 mi. E Central London. (See map on page 108)* In 1675 Charles II decreed that an Observatory should be built 'within our park at Greenwich upon the highest ground'. The original function of the oldest scientific institution in the country was to discover the longitude of places through astronomy. John Flamsteed, the first Astronomer Royal, laid the foundation stone. The Octagon Room, from where he could observe eclipses, is one of Wren's most delightful creations. It has changed little and in it are some of Flamsteed's telescopes. His information about the position of fixed stars led to Greenwich being accepted as 'the prime meridian'. From 1884 countries throughout the world adopted Greenwich Mean Time (recently supplanted by the atomic clock). The meridian line runs across the courtyard and out into the park.

The buildings around the courtyard and the domes to the south of the old Observatory belong to different astronomical buildings put up later. The Victorian terracotta building has a Planetarium in the dome. Fog and smog forced the Observatory to move from here in 1948. Open daily. (*Tel: 01-858-1167.*)

Orleans House (176) (TQ 16-73) *Lebanon Park, Riverside, Twickenham, 10 mi. SW Central London.* An art gallery with an important collection of historical paintings of local interest. Nothing remains of the 1710 house but the Octagon added ten years later by James Gibbs, an impressive example of baroque architecture, survives. The Octagon and its adjoining wing escaped demolition in 1927 thanks to the Hon. Mrs Ionides, who bequeathed it with her collection of 18th- and 19th-century topographical paintings. Changing exhibitions take place throughout the year. The woodland gardens overlooking the Thames are delightful. Open daily except Monday. (*Tel: 01-892-0221.*)

Orleans House, Twickenham

Orpington (177) (TQ 45-65) *15 mi. SE Central London.* This busy town has developed from a small village surrounded by agricultural land in the early 19th century to a middle-class residential district. In the local history museum evidence of Stone Age settlements are displayed as well as archaeological discoveries indicating Roman and Saxon inhabitation. The collection, which contains material from other parts of the borough of Bromley★, is in the Priory on Church Hill (177) (TQ 44-66). (*Tel: 0689 31551 X 9.*) Despite its name, this building, still in use after 700 years, was not a monastic establishment but a hostelry for the priors of Christ Church, Canterbury. Orpington Hospital was originally built for Canadian servicemen during the First World War.

Osterley Park House (176) (TQ 14-78) *Osterley, 11 mi. W Central London.* The imposing red-brick

Osterley Park House

house with a double screen of columns is the work of Robert Adam, who transformed the Tudor house where Sir Thomas Gresham had entertained Elizabeth I. The decoration typifies Adam's development from a simple designer to a man with an exuberant love of ornamentation. Horace Walpole declared Osterley 'a palace of palaces'. Two years after Adam completed his 19 years' work, the house passed from Robert Child, the 18th-century owner,

Osterley Park   SCALE 1:25 000 or 2½ INCHES to 1 MILE

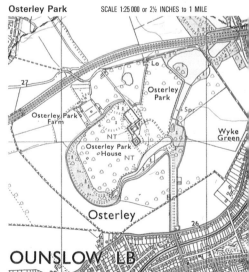

to his granddaughter. Her husband was George Villiers, 5th Earl of Jersey, and in 1949 the Villiers family gave the house, magnificent Adam furniture and the park to the nation but the paintings were removed. Those on show today come from the Victoria and Albert Museum which administers the house for the National Trust. Open daily except Monday. (*Tel: 01-560-3918.*)

Owletts (177) (TQ 66-68) *near Cobham, 25 mi. ESE Central London.* This small red-brick house built in the reign of Charles II retains its original staircase and has fine plasterwork ceilings. There is a small garden. Open on two weekday afternoons between April and September. The National Trust will supply details. (*Tel: Lamberhurst (0892) 890651.*)

Polesden Lacey (187) (TQ 13-52) *Near Dorking, 25 mi. SW Central London.* The Regency villa set around a courtyard was built in 1821 on the site of the country house where Richard Brinsley Sheridan lived for the last 20 years of his life. The present two-storey yellow-washed building was extensively remodelled in 1906 by the Hon. Mrs Ronald Greville, a society hostess. She entertained three generations of the royal family at her Surrey home and lent it to the Duke and Duchess of York (later King George VI and Queen Elizabeth) for their honeymoon in 1923. The billiard room and smoking room

Polesden Lacey

reflect Edwardian taste. The furniture, paintings, silver and porcelain of various periods are especially fine. The house and extensive grounds were given to the National Trust by Mrs Greville in 1942. It is open on certain days from March to November; the grounds all year. (*Tel: Bookham (0372) 58203.*)

Quebec House (187) (TQ 44-54) *Westerham, 23 mi. SE Central London.* The red-brick and ragstone house was the childhood home of James Wolfe, the British general who led the attack against the French at the Heights of Abraham above Quebec in 1759 in which the British were victorious, but Wolfe was killed. The house, then called Spiers, was over 200 years old when the Wolfes moved to Westerham. James was born at the Vicarage, a short distance away. The family lived here until the move to Greenwich ★ in 1738. After many owners, it was presented to the National Trust. A collection of memorabilia associated with Wolfe's victory is on display including several versions of Benjamin West's famous picture of his death. An exhibition in the stables gives details about the Battle of Quebec and further information about General Wolfe. Open

on specified days March to October. (*Tel: Westerham (0959) 62206.*)

Queen Elizabeth's Hunting Lodge (177) (TQ 39-94) *Ranger's Road, Chingford, 12 mi. NE Central London.* The upper floors of the three-storey half-timbered house formerly opened onto platforms to give spectators unimpeded views of deer hunts in Epping Forest. It was built in the reign of Henry VIII, but despite the name there is no evidence his daughter used it. Today it is a museum, the exhibits depicting the history of the forest and its natural history. Open Wednesday to Sunday. (*Tel: 01-529-6681.*)

Queen's House (177) (TQ 38-77) *Greenwich, 7 mi. E Central London. (See map on page 108)* The first classical domestic building in England, an architectural masterpiece, was built in 1616 for James I's wife, Anne of Denmark. James I and his architect Inigo Jones had the unusual idea of building the white house to straddle the main Deptford to Woolwich Road so that the Queen would have unimpeded access to both Greenwich Park and to the old royal palace (where the Royal Naval College ★ is now). Anne died in 1619 and work was halted but resumed ten years later when Charles I gave it to his French wife, Henrietta Maria, whose dower house it became. Jones's successor John Webb increased the number of bridges across the road from one to three and transformed the H-shaped building into today's square one.

In the hall is a carved wooden gallery at first-floor level where musicians could play. The gallery gives access to a series of perfectly proportioned salons (now hung with paintings). The Queen's Bedroom provides an idea of furnishings in Henrietta Maria's time. Open daily. (*Tel: 01-858-4422.*)

Ranger's House (177) (TQ 38-76) *Chesterfield Walk, Greenwich, 7 mi. E Central London. (See map on page 108)* On the edge of Blackheath ★, with a panoramic vista across London, the large red-brick house which became the sinecure residence of the Rangers of Greenwich Park in 1814 was built in 1608. More than a century later it was the home of the 4th Earl of Chesterfield who here wrote the famous *Letters* full of moral aphorisms to his natural son.

The rooms are hung with an important series of 17th-century portraits. The Grand Salon is often used for music recitals. The pretty rose garden at the back opens onto Greenwich Park. In the care of English Heritage. Open daily. (*Tel: 01-853-0035.*)

Redbridge (177) (TQ 42-89) *9 mi. NE Central London.* The modern name of this northeast borough, formerly in Essex, is coined from John Rocque's 1746 map which shows a Red Bridge over the River Roding. The population of ¼ million live mainly around the towns of Ilford, Woodford and Wanstead. About a third of the borough is farmland, and there is a 140-acre park in the grounds of the long-demolished Wanstead House (177) (TQ 41-87), of which part of the stables survive as a golf club. In the park are lakes, a grotto and a temple.

Richmond upon Thames (176) (TQ 16-72) *9 mi. SW Central London.* With the river flowing past attractive villages like Ham and Petersham, Richmond is a borough of special interest. The Royal Botanic Gardens★ at Kew and Hampton Court Palace★ are the two most important places in the area and there are other historic houses like Strawberry Hill at Twickenham, Ham House★, Orleans House Gallery★, and Marble Hill House★. The three royal parks at Bushy★, Hampton Court★ and Richmond cover two fifths of the borough.

Richmond's royal connections go back to the reign of Henry I. Until the Stuart monarchs, Richmond was a favourite palace. During the Commonwealth the palace fell into disrepair but fragments of the old Tudor building still stand beyond the Maids of Honour Row. The Green, the largest in London, is lined with a fascinating mixture of houses from the 17th to the 19th centuries. The Theatre Royal of 1899 appears a little ornate in such dignified company.

Twickenham (176) (TQ 14-73) is synonymous with Rugby Union Football. Guided tours are given of the pitch, the changing rooms with the famous double baths, and committee rooms where the trophies are displayed, and a museum traces the history of the RFU and the grounds in Rugby Road (176) (TQ 15-74). *(Tel: 01-892-8161.)* West of the grounds is the early-18th-century *Kneller Hall* (176) (TQ 14-74), named after the Restoration portrait painter Sir Geoffrey Kneller who had a house here. It is the headquarters of the Royal Military School of Music. The most exotic building in the district is *Strawberry Hill* (176) (TQ 15-72), the Gothick castle Horace Walpole spent 30 years decorating. His inspiration for the ceiling in the gallery was the roof in the Henry VII chapel in Westminster Abbey★. Now a training college, the house may be visited by writing in advance to St Mary's College, Strawberry Hill, Waldegrave Road, Twickenham. *(Tel: 01-892-0051.)*

Ham and Petersham have fine period houses and are worth exploring on foot.

Richmond Park (176) (TQ 20-73 etc.) *10 mi. SW Central London.* The largest of the royal parks was enclosed by Charles I when he enlarged the grounds of Richmond Palace. During the Commonwealth the park was given to the City of London but at the Restoration was returned to the Crown. About 600 deer roam the 2,670 acres in which there are ancient oak trees, two ponds for anglers and another for sailing model boats. The Isabella Plantation is noted for the colourful displays of rhododendrons in May and June. White Lodge is the home of the Royal Ballet School and Thatched Lodge is the residence of Princess Alexandra.

Sports facilities include 24 football pitches, cricket grounds and two golf clubs.

Royal Air Force Museum (176) (TQ 21-90) *Grahame Park Way, Hendon, 8 mi. NW Central London.* The national museum devoted to the history of the airborne fighting force was opened in 1972, and is appropriately sited on Hendon Aerodrome, where pioneer work in aviation was carried out from 1910 until the Second World War. Over 40 planes on view in a former hangar show the progress of flying. A monoplane similar to Bleriot's (the first to fly the Channel in 1909), fighter planes used in the First and Second World Wars are on display and personalities as well as machines are recalled.

At the Royal Air Force Museum, Hendon

The Battle of Britain Museum, on an adjacent site, recalls the exploits of the pilots who defended the country in 1940 and there is a reconstruction of the Uxbridge operations room. **The Bomber Command Museum,** opened in 1983, illustrates the history of Bomber Command. The only surviving De Havilland 9a is one of the prized aircraft on show. The three museums are open daily. *(Tel: 01-205-2266.)*

Royal Artillery Regimental Museum (177) (TQ 42-77) *Royal Military Academy, Academy Road, Woolwich, 10 mi. E Central London.* Since 1945 part of James Wyatt's early 19th-century building has been a museum outlining the history of the Royal Regiment of Artillery from its formation in 1716 to the present, with emphasis on the personal bravery of its soldiers. *(Tel: 01-856 5533 X 2523.)*

Royal Botanic Gardens, Kew (176) (TQ 18-76) *9 mi. W Central London (See map on page 117).* The gardens, which also serve as a research institute, are planted with trees, shrubs, flowers and vegetables. Some are indigenous but a great many are exotic species cultivated in the greenhouses. Tropical plants are grown in the oldest, which was

Royal Botanic Gardens, better known as Kew Gardens

designed by John Nash and moved from Buckingham Palace in 1836. The great curving glass Palm House was built to Decimus Burton's design in 1848. This is undergoing extensive restoration. The new technically advanced Princess of Wales Conservatory is able to grow the greatest variety of plants at varying temperatures. Nearby is the Water Lily House. A museum displays rubber and medicinal plants and information on the work at Kew. In the huge Temperate House, another Burton design and reminiscent of the Crystal Palace, over 3,000 species are grown.

The Orangery, built in 1761 by William Chambers in the style of Wren, exhibits the history of the gardens which owe their foundation to Augusta, Princess of Wales who lived on the royal estate at Kew★. She also invited Chambers to design the Great Pagoda which provoked Horace Walpole to say: 'A solecism may be committed even in architecture'. Princess Augusta's nine-acre garden was extended by her son George III who lived at Kew Palace. His wife, Queen Charlotte, had the thatched Queen's Cottage put up in 1772 as a summerhouse.

Plants collected in the South Pacific by Sir Joseph Banks, who accompanied Captain Cook, were brought to Kew and formed the nucleus of the scientific institute that has introduced vital plants to foreign countries. Quinine was sent to India in 1860 and when disease destroyed European vines in the 19th century Kew imported roots from America.

The 300-acre gardens, a pleasant mixture of architectural delights, sculpture and colourful seasonal plants, are open throughout the year. (*Tel: 01-940-1171.*)

Royal Naval College (177) (TQ 38-77) *Greenwich, 7 mi. E Central London. (See map on page 108)* Twin celestial and terrestrial globes flank the entrance gates of the College which, until it became a college for Naval officers in 1873, was Greenwich Hospital for seamen. The finest building on the river was begun in 1664 as a palace on the site of the sprawling Palace of Placentia, the favourite home of the Tudor kings. It fell into disrepair during the Civil War. In 1694 a charter was signed for the relief and support of disabled sailors. Christopher Wren decided to outdo Chelsea Hospital ★ with a building of baroque splendour and added the two domed buildings. Building took 50 years and several architects, including Sir John Vanbrugh and Nicholas Hawksmoor (probably responsible for the Queen Anne block) were employed.

James Thornhill spent 20 years on the Painted Hall, one of London's few examples in the grand baroque manner. After a fire in 1779, the Chapel was reconstructed by James 'Athenian' Stuart, who decorated it in Robert Adam and Wedgwood colours.

The old sailors enjoyed the river view until the hospital was closed in 1869. Four years later it was taken over by the Admiralty and renamed the college for the instruction of officers 'in all branches of theoretical and scientific study'. The Hall and Chapel are open several afternoons a week. (*Tel: 01-858-2154.*)

Royalty and Empire (176) (SU 96-76) *Windsor and Eton Central Railway Station, Thames Street, Windsor, 23 mi. W Central London. (See map on page 131)* Advanced computer technology and the skills of Madame Tussaud's ★ bring to life the famous people who attended Queen Victoria's Diamond Jubilee celebrations in June 1897. The Queen-Empress greets her extensive family 'who have arrived by train from Paddington' to be met by the Coldstream Guards. A theatre-style presentation traces the 60 glorious years of Victoria's reign. Eminent Victorians like Charles Dickens and Florence Nightingale 'come to life' in audiovisual presentations which describe historic events. Open daily. (*Tel: Windsor (0753) 857837.*)

Runnymede (176) (TQ 00-72 etc.) *20 mi. WSW Central London.* The unfenced riverside meadow on the side of the Staines to Windsor Road is almost certainly where King John sealed Magna Carta in 1215, and not as is often thought on Magna Carta Island in the nearby Thames. The two kiosks and memorial buildings were designed by Sir Edwin Lutyens in 1929, while the Magna Carta Memorial was the gift of the American Bar Association.

The Thames at Runnymede

Nearby is the John F. Kennedy Memorial. The Air Force Memorial to the airmen who died in the Second World War and have no graves is on Cooper's Hill with a lovely view over the Thames.

St Albans (166) (TL 14-07) *20 mi. NW Central London.* Modern shops and houses have fortunately failed to bury the older parts of a city which was one of the most important in the western world about 2,000 years ago. In AD 43 the Roman armies occupied a small Belgic settlement, naming it Verulamium ★ and granting it the distinction of a municipium, or free town, a privilege not bestowed on any other town in Britain. Early in the third century Alban, a Romano-British citizen beheaded for his faith on the hill outside Verulamium, became Britain's first Christian martyr. The Saxon abbey, on the site of his shrine, was rebuilt by the Normans and later enlarged into the great cathedral that still dominates the city. Formerly part of the most important Benedictine Abbey in England, it was built with bricks from the Roman site, and at 550 ft it has the longest nave in Europe.

Several streets retain their period character and three coaching inns survive. The Fighting Cocks, beside the River Ver, is reputed to be the oldest licensed house in England.

The Gardens of the Rose, at Chiswell Green (166) (TL 12-04), 12 acres maintained by the Royal National Rose Society, have a collection of over 30,000 roses, spectacularly colourful at the beginning of July when an annual show is held. Open. (*Tel: St Albans (0727) 50461.*)

St John's Jerusalem Garden (177) (TQ 56-70) *Sutton at Hone, 19 mi. ESE Central London.* A winding drive leads to this informal, rather unexpected garden around which the River Darenth forms a moat. The house, formerly occupied by the Knights Hospitallers, was rebuilt and is a private residence but the 13th-century chapel and gardens are open one afternoon a week. National Trust property. (*Tel: Dartford (0322) 20468.*)

Savill Garden (176) (SU 97-70) *Windsor Great Park, 22 mi. WSW Central London.* At the eastern end of Windsor Great Park★, rhododendrons, camellias, magnolias and a wide range of trees and shrubs, intermingled with herbaceous borders, have been planted to provide colour throughout the year. With encouragement from George V and Queen Mary, the gardens were begun in 1932 in 35 acres of woodland by the royal gardener Sir Eric Savill, and were named after him. Open all year. The self-service restaurant is closed in winter. (*Tel: Windsor (0753) 860222.*)

Southwark (176,177) (TQ 33-76) *1 mi. SE Central London.* The more interesting parts of this borough (housing ¼ million people) lie on the riverside in the ancient suburb of Southwark, which is included in the Inner London 'Places of Interest' section. In the Bermondsey area there was a prominent abbey from the 11th to the 16th century. Rotherhithe, still with the 1715 church in which Captain Jones of the *Mayflower* is buried, was formerly a fashionable village where wealthy City merchants lived. These areas have declined but their old prosperity looks like being restored thanks to the Docklands★ redevelopment.

The Dulwich Picture Gallery★, the oldest public art gallery in the country, is in the far south of the borough and the **Passmore Edwards South London Art Gallery**, at 63 Peckham Road (176,177) (TQ 33-76), is the oldest municipally owned gallery in London. It has a permanent collection of paintings by Lord Leighton, Ford Madox Brown and their contemporaries, as well as modern British works by John Piper, Graham Sutherland and others. (*Tel: 01-703-6120.*) **The Cuming Museum** at 155-157 Walworth Road (176,177) (TQ 32-78) has interesting archaeological discoveries, items associated with Charles Dickens and Michael Faraday, and objects relating to superstitions. (*Tel: 01-703-3324.*)

Squerryes Court (187) (TQ 44-53) *Westerham, 23 mi. SE Central London.* The red-brick William and Mary manor is set in front of a shimmering lake and expansive lawn. Since 1731 it has been the home of the Warde family who were friendly with James Wolfe who lived at nearby Quebec House★. Several were Lord Mayors of London and a Georgian John Warde, 'the Father of Foxhunting', was the first man to keep hounds exclusively for hunting foxes. In the well-furnished rooms there are very rare Soho tapestries made between 1720-30. The Wolfe Room has various pictures connected with the General. Open March to September. (*Tel: Westerham (0959) 62345.*)

Sutton (176) (TQ 25-64 etc.) *11 mi. S Central London.* Beddington, Carshalton, Cheam, Sutton and Wallington are the main centres in this 20th-century residential borough of about 170,000 inhabitants. Although archaeological discoveries indicate a rich historical past, little of note has survived. A whole village was levelled by Henry VIII to build Nonsuch Palace at Cheam and Charles II gave the royal home to his mistress Barbara Castlemaine who sold it for demolition. Today the only reminders of Nonsuch are three pillars marking the site in the 250-acre wooded park (176) (TQ 23-63).

Sutton Place (186) (TQ 01-53) *near Guildford, 30 mi. SW Central London.* The house, an example of Early English Renaissance architecture with a Tudor great hall, was built c. 1525 by Sir Richard Weston, whose son Francis was beheaded because of his alleged adultery with Anne Boleyn. Its many owners have included the Duke of Sutherland, Lord Northcliffe and the American oil tycoon Paul Getty, who installed a pay phone for his guests to use. Recently the home of Stanley J. Seeger, an American art collector, it was sold in 1986 to another American art collector. At the time of writing re-opening plans have not been announced. (*Tel: Guildford (0483) 504455.*)

Syon House (176) (TQ 17-76) *Park Road, Brentford, 10 mi. W Central London.* The Percy lion, once on the gateway to Northumberland House in Trafalgar Square★, was brought here in 1873 when the Duke of Northumberland's principal London house was demolished. It now stands on an arch at the entrance to his descendant's riverside home. The house where Lady Jane Grey accepted the crown in 1554 was re-modelled by Robert Adam. Opulently decorated with richly patterned ceilings, red silk hangings and painted pilasters, Syon contains many examples of Adam's furniture, fine oak carved panels and copies of Roman sculptures.

Syon Park, laid out by Capability Brown, has an artificial lake, and a mulberry tree planted when the house was first built in the 16th century for Protector Somerset. The park, in which there are two restaurants and a garden centre, is open all year, and the house from Easter to October. (*Tel: 01-560-0881.*)

The British Heritage Motor Museum, with a large collection of historic British cars from 1895 to

Syon House

the present, is in the grounds. Open all year. (*Tel: 01-560-1378.*) **The Butterfly House**, also in the park, has a great variety of species flying in a simulated natural environment. Open daily. (*Tel: 01-560-7272.*)

Thames Barrier (177) (TQ 41-79) *Unity Way, Woolwich, 9 mi. E Central London.* An engineering feat unparalleled anywhere in the world, the movable barrier was built across the Thames to prevent serious flooding in London. Discussions had taken place well over a hundred years ago and various plans were put forward before a start was finally made in 1972. Dubbed the Eighth Wonder of

The Thames Barrier

the World even before the Queen officially opened it in 1984, the flood barrier has a series of shimmering stainless steel piers, which rise from the river and which resemble mediaeval knights' helmets. Between the piers are ten steel-plated gates, the four massive central ones each weighing over 3,700 tonnes. These lie on the river bed and are swung up through 90 degrees to form a continuous steel wall against a rising river. An exhibition and audio-visual show in the Visitors' Centre explain the engineering intricacies. Open daily. (*Tel: 01-854-1373.*)

Thorndon Country Park (177) (TQ 61-91) *near Ingrave, Brentwood, 22 mi. ENE Central London.* The former estate of a leading Roman Catholic family was split up when the 16th Lord Petre died in the First World War. The North Park, where the ruin of Thorndon Hall stands, is separated from the South Park by a narrow path. Birches, ancient hornbeams and oaks proliferate. Hidden deep in the wood is a little mausoleum and a chapel designed by Pugin. The southern park has a lake for fishing, and the ruins of a Tudor hall.

Thorpe Park (176) (TQ 03-68) *Staines Road, Chertsey, 19 mi. WSW Central London.* Former gravel pits have been transformed into water gardens and lakes with facilities for sailing, swimming, water-skiing and sailboarding. These form the central feature in the 500-acre leisure park which has models of over 40 world famous structures reduced to $\frac{1}{36}$th scale models, including the Statue of Liberty. A heritage area is devoted to items that have shaped British history from the Stone Age to Magna Carta. A 1930s farm has been recreated, and as well as animals and machinery there is a craft centre. There are carnival rides, a rollercoaster,

Fun for all at Thorpe Park

a waterbus, nature trails, and picnic areas. Open daily from end of March to beginning of September. (*Tel: Chertsey (0932) 562633.*)

Tower Hamlets (177) (TQ 36-82) *4 mi. E Central London.* The heart of London's East End lies in this modern borough created in 1965. It takes its name from its most famous building, the Tower of London ★, which is included in the Inner London 'Places of Interest' section. Long before the docks at Wapping and on the Isle of Dogs were formed, Whitechapel, Stepney and Limehouse ★ were enclaves in which foreigners settled, and the expansion of overseas trading brought seamen of many nationalities to the neighbourhood. Industry was introduced by such immigrants as the Huguenots, who established silkweaving in Spitalfields ★. The street markets in the borough include Petticoat Lane ★, Columbia Road in Shoreditch and Roman Road, Bethnal Green. The Bell Foundry at 32-34 Whitechapel Road is over 400 years old and has supplied the bells of Westminster Abbey since 1583.

The Bethnal Green Museum of Childhood ★ has a celebrated collection of dolls, and ***The Whitechapel Art Gallery***, 80 Whitechapel High Street mounts large and important exhibitions of modern art (*Tel: 01-377-0107*).

Trent Park Country Park (176) (TQ 28-97) *near Enfield, 12 mi. N Central London.* South of the former royal hunting ground at Enfield Chase, 680 acres of wood and park, partly landscaped by Humphry Repton, surround a teacher-training college. The house, built in the 18th century for George III's physician, later became the home of Sir Philip Sassoon who had it refaced in 1926 with bricks from the demolished Devonshire House, Piccadilly ★. He also erected the obelisk to Queen Victoria's father. Nature trails and bridlepaths have been cut through the woodland. Open daily.

Valley Gardens (176) (SU 97-69) *Windsor Great Park, 22 mi. WSW Central London. (See map on opposite page)* Stretching back from the edge of the lake at Virginia Water ★ to the polo ground at Smith's Lawn, over 400 acres have been developed to form exceptional woodland gardens. These were laid out after the Second World War by Sir Edward Savill after he completed the nearby Savill Garden ★. The rhododendrons, azaleas and shrubs create spectacular colour in the Spring when expanses of grass are smothered in daffodils. A ten-acre heather garden is in flower all year. Open daily. (*Tel: Windsor (0753) 860222.*)

Verulamium (166) (TL 13-06) *Verulamium Park, St Albans, 20 mi. NW Central London.* The Roman Verulamium, one of the great cities of Western Europe, lay beside the River Ver to the southwest of the present St Albans ★. The Roman city is now largely covered by a park, the forum lost under a vicarage garden, and is bisected by a busy ring road. But still visible is a short section of the Roman wall and a hypocaust, a short walk across the park from the museum in St Michael's Street. The museum houses antiquities, mosaics and a charming little 2nd-century figurine of Venus recovered from different parts of the large site. Foundations of Roman town houses and shops have been excavated but little is visible. The most spectacula

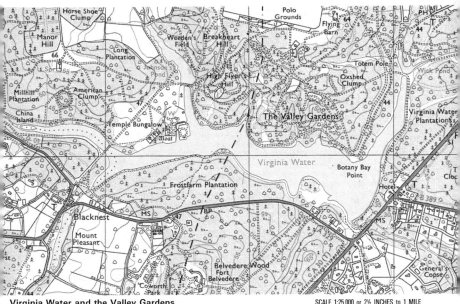

Virginia Water and the Valley Gardens

SCALE 1:25 000 or 2½ INCHES to 1 MILE

Roman remains are of the 2nd-century theatre which was almost circular, had a segmented stage and seated about 5,000 people; it is the only one in England completely exposed and not an amphitheatre. The museum and theatre are open all year. (*Tel: St Albans (0727) 54659.*)

Virginia Water (176) (SU 96-68) *22 mi. WSW Central London.* The artificial lake to the south of Windsor Great Park ★ is surrounded by woods. Designed by Thomas Sandby, it was constructed in the 1750s for William, Duke of Cumberland, the 'Butcher of Culloden', who was also Governor of Virginia, hence the name. After the Second World War the undergrowth in Valley Gardens ★ on the north bank was grubbed out and ancient and decayed trees were removed. Roughly a mile along a walk on the north of the lake there is a good view across the water to the Roman ruins removed from Leptis Magna in Libya and re-erected on the south side by Sir Jeffry Wyattville, George IV's architect at Windsor Castle ★. Boulders on the waterfall are intended to give a Scottish air. The 100-ft totem pole in the woods behind the north side was the gift

Virginia Water

of the Indians of Vancouver Island to celebrate the centenary of British Columbia.

Waltham Abbey (166) (TL 38-00) *Waltham, 14 mi. N Central London.* Remains of the great pre-Conquest monastic establishment founded in the 11th century by King Canute's standard bearer can still be seen in the abbey garden. After the Battle of Hastings, King Harold II's body was buried beneath the high altar. His statue is near the west front. Henry II raised the church to the status of an abbey in 1177 as part of his penance after the murder of Thomas à Becket. The peal of bells in the 16th century tower inspired Tennyson to write 'Ring out, wild bells' in his *In Memoriam*. The abbey is surrounded by ten acres of enclosed landscaped garden and a moat.

Waltham Forest (177) (TQ 37-90 ETC.) *7 mi. NE Central London.* The principal districts in this long narrow borough are Chingford, Walthamstow and Leyton, once all in Essex. The 15½ square miles have on their boundaries Epping Forest ★ in the east, chains of reservoirs in the west and Wanstead Flats, near the Thames, to the south. The reservoirs form a section of the Lee Valley Leisure Park ★. Prehistoric, Iron Age and Roman finds have been discovered and a Bronze Age canoe from Lockwood Reservoir is in the British Museum. The William Morris Gallery ★ and Queen Elizabeth's Hunting Lodge ★ are the most important places of interest, although the church of St Mary the Virgin in Leyton (177) (TQ 37-86) deserves a visit. This was established late in the 11th century, has surviving 17th-century work and possesses most unusual brasses and funeral monuments.

Wandsworth (176) (TQ 25-73) *5 mi. SW Central London.* On the south bank of the Thames between Vauxhall and Putney, with Roehampton in the west and extending south to Wimbledon Common, this heavily populated borough has almost 300,000 residents. Battersea★ has a large park which provides a pleasant walk along the river facing Chelsea★. Putney is a popular residential area which has had a river crossing since 1729. Several houses at Roehampton, now converted into institutions, were built for noblemen in the 17th century. The finest of these is now St Mary's Hospital.

Weald Country Park (177) (TQ 57-94) *near Brentwood, 22 mi. ENE Central London.* Wide open parkland leads down to a good-sized lake, one of three in the estate that belonged to one of Henry VIII's courtiers after the Dissolution of the Monasteries. The house has disappeared but a cottage, where Mary Tudor is said to have taken refuge when anti-Papist feelings were running high, survives. There is a fine avenue of horse chestnuts, pleasant glades and modern copses. Fishing is permitted on the lakes. Open daily.

Wembley (176) (TQ 19-85) *8 mi. WNW Central London.* The best-known place in this residential suburb is Wembley Stadium, a huge sports complex which can accommodate 100,000 spectators for such important football matches as the Cup Final every May. Originally built for the 1924 British Empire Exhibition, the centre includes the Wembley Arena where major show-jumping competitions and concerts are held. Formerly known as the Empire Pool, this can still be filled with water and is frozen for an annual ice show. Tours of the stadium include visits to areas normally seen only by the players and performers. (*Tel: 01-902-1234, 01-902-4864.*)

Wembley Stadium

Westerham (187) (TQ 44-54) *23 mi. SE Central London.* The old and the new merge in this busy commuter town which you approach through modern housing estates and factories to reach the former homes of two great British heroes — General Wolfe and Sir Winston Churchill. Wolfe was born at the Vicarage, a few yards from Quebec House★ where his parents lived until he was eleven. Churchill bought his country home of Chartwell★ in 1924 and, except during the war years, spent a great deal of time here, working in the garden, painting and writing. Westerham has a third stately house, Squerryes Court★, home of the Warde family from 1731 to the present day. By choosing the right day and planning carefully visitors can comfortably see all three houses and wander in the pleasant country town during the course of a day.

Quebec House, Westerham

Wimbledon (176) (TQ 23-70) *8 mi. SW Central London.* The name of this hilly South London suburb is known across the world for the famous tennis championships. *The All England Lawn Tennis Club* was founded more than a century ago in Worple Road, and in 1922, was moved to its present headquarters near the centre of Wimbledon's 'village'. At the end of June the important tennis championships are played on grass courts. *The Wimbledon Lawn Tennis Museum*, within the grounds, tells the story of the game and its best-known personalities. Open six days a week. (*Tel: 01-946-6131.*)

Few of the tennis fans probably have any idea that the village was inhabited during the Iron Age. A fortification, called Caesar's Camp (though certainly pre-Roman), can be seen on the Royal Wimbledon Golf Course. This borders on Wimbledon Common, 1100 acres of unenclosed rough grass and bracken with a restored windmill (open at weekends in Summer) at its centre. The modern village centred on The High Street is a pleasing blend of period and modern buildings; the most interesting, Eagle House, still has its 1613 façade. In Ridgeway, on the line of a Roman road, the John Evelyn Museum is open on Saturday afternoons. (*Tel: 01-946-9529.*) The diarist had little connection with Wimbledon but it is named after him because of his interest in preserving the past. Along with archaeological finds, paintings and a natural-history collection, there are the title deeds to Admiral Lord Nelson's house at Merton★.

Windsor (176) (SU 96-76) *23 mi. W Central London.* The royal borough is dominated by the

Windsor and Eton   SCALE 1:10 000 or 6 INCHES to 1 MILE
1 Windsor Castle
2 State Apartments
3 St George's Chapel
4 Queen Mary's Dolls' House
5 The Home Park
6 Frogmore Gardens (off map to SE)
7 Windsor Great Park (part only)
8 The Long Walk (part only)
9 The Guildhall
10 The Royal Mews
11 Burford House
12 Household Cavalry Museum (off map to SW)
13 Royalty and Empire
14 Eton College
15 The Playing Fields of Eton

fortress William the Conqueror built on a hill overlooking the Thames more than 900 years ago. Until the arrival of the railway in the 1840s, Windsor was primarily the home of Court officials and a garrison town. Expansion followed, and today the town has more tourists than anywhere else in Britain except London.

Windsor Castle (1)★, where the **State Apartments (2)** are open when the Court is not in residence, is the main attraction and is described separately along with the historic **St George's Chapel (3)** and **Queen Mary's Dolls' House (4)**. The terrace above the Orangery (now a royal swimming pool) overlooks **Home Park (5)**, by the river to the east, where the annual Royal Windsor Horse Show is held. When heads of other countries pay State Visits to Windsor they are met by the Queen in a specially erected pavilion in Home Park. **Frogmore Gardens (6)★**, the royal mausoleum and the royal farms are in the south of the park which is linked to **Windsor Great Park (7)★** by the **Long Walk (8)**. Frogmore House is due to open to the public in August 1988.

In the town, Christopher Wren is said to have been in a playful mood when he put up a structurally superfluous colonnade of Tuscan pillars on the **Guildhall (9)** in 1689. This was in defiance of critics who said more support was needed. Fine portraits of 19th- and 20th-century members of the royal family hang on the walls, but unfortunately the Guildhall is one of the few historic buildings in Windsor not open to the public.

Part of the **Royal Mews (10)** is in a red-brick building in St Albans Street, **Burford House (11)**, which was built for Nell Gwyn and named after the Earl of Burford (later Duke of St Albans), her son by Charles II. The Mews, built by Queen Victoria in 1842, are her greatest contribution to the reconstructions started by her uncle George IV 20 years earlier. Pictures of the present Queen riding her horse Burmese and of the Duke of Edinburgh driving his carriages are on display. The Scottish State Coach is one of many ceremonial carriages and horses shown to visitors. There is also a display of gifts given to the Queen on the occasion of her Silver Jubilee in 1977, and at other times since. Open all year, except on certain dates specified in advance. (*Tel: Windsor (0753) 868286.*)

A collection of saddlery is to be seen in the **Household Cavalry Museum (12)** at Combermere

Barracks, St Leonard's Road. The Standards are displayed as well as arms, uniforms, swords and guns, many donated by sovereigns from Charles II to Elizabeth II. Second World War armoured vehicles stand sentinel outside.

The Royalty and Empire (13)★ exhibition is in Central Station. The Station was built in 1897 by the Great Western Railway Company to celebrate Queen Victoria's Diamond Jubilee. Windsor Tourist Information Centre is also in the Central Station. (*Tel: Windsor (07535) 51046.*)

Windsor Bridge, built over the Thames in 1821, links the town to Eton★, famous for its great public school, **Eton College (14)**, while to the college's north lie the **Playing Fields of Eton (15)**, made famous by the Duke of Wellington's much-quoted saying, that 'the Battle of Waterloo was won on the playing fields of Eton'.

Windsor Castle, (176) (SU 97-76) *Windsor, 23 mi. W Central London. (See map on page 131)* The weekend home of the Queen and the Duke of Edinburgh has been owned by the sovereign for just over 900 years, making it the oldest royal residence in continuous use. The outer walls with battlemented towers today occupy an almost identical area to the fortress put up in 1080.

Down the centuries fires and time have caused damage but many monarchs have repaired, altered and added to the Castle since William the Conqueror built it to protect the passage of the Thames into London. His younger son Henry I held his first Court at Windsor; Henry II enlarged it and was responsible for the first use of stone. Although heavily restored, his perimeter wall with rectangular towers still stands.

After the Restoration Charles II demolished sections of the mediaeval building and employed Hugh May to design new chambers. King Charles was the first monarch to move his treasures from London to Windsor. Three baroque rooms of this period have decorative panelling by Grinling Gibbons and ceilings painted by Verrio.

The Castle owes most of its present splendour to George IV. When he inherited the throne he had already established a reputation for architectural improvements in London, and at Windsor he employed Sir Jeffry Wyatville. Massive reconstruction in the 1820s cost over £1 million. An extra

Windsor Castle — a distant view from the Thames

storey was added to the main building and Henry II's Round Tower was raised some 30 ft and topped with battlements. The private apartments were moved to the east and south of the Quadrangle where they still are. Most of the remaining rooms were converted into guest suites, several of which form part of the State Apartments.

The Waterloo Chamber, used by the Queen for large dinner parties, is hung with Sir Thomas Lawrence's portraits of the statesmen and soldiers who played major roles in Wellington's victory over Napoleon. The seamless carpet, said to be the largest in the world, was specially made in India for Queen Victoria. In the Garter Throne Room (once part of Charles II's Presence and Audience Chambers) the Queen invests new Knights of the Garter. The richly gilded ceilings and furnishings in the reception rooms and bedrooms reflect the taste of George IV, who acquired priceless paintings and antiques from the Continent after the French Revolution and the Napoleonic Wars. Glittering Georgian chandeliers hang from the ceilings, and superb sculpture, sparkling silver, fine furniture and Gobelins tapestries enhance all the rooms.

Conservation is the main concern of the present Queen, her keen interest attested by the restoration carried out over the last 35 years.

Queen Mary's Dolls' House (separate entrance), designed by Sir Edwin Lutyens, was first put on public display at the British Empire Exhibition at Wembley in 1924. Famous authors of the day contributed stories, many in their own hands, for the miniature library books. Distinguished artists painted pictures to hang on the walls. The tiny guns can fire real bullets, and the wine in the bottles is vintage by now.

An **Exhibition of Drawings** from the royal collection, in an adjacent room, always includes a selection from the 600 drawings by Leonardo da Vinci believed to have been acquired by Charles II.

St George's Chapel, a superb example of late perpendicular architecture rivalled only by the Henry VII Chapel in Westminster Abbey ★, was begun in 1477 by Henry Janyns for Edward IV, and completed 51 years later by William Vertue for his successors. Ten monarchs, including Henry VIII and George VI, lie buried here, many in the vault Henry VII built. Of the numerous funeral monuments the most elaborate is the dramatic tomb of Princess Charlotte, the Prince Regent's daughter. The effigies of Edward VII and Queen Alexandra, with his dog Caesar at his feet, are on their tomb near the high altar. When George V died in 1936 Queen Mary had her effigy sculpted by Sir William Reid Dick so that on her death she and the King would appear the same age on their tomb. The banners of the Knights of the Garter hang above their stalls in the choir, and the gilt stall plates of former knights are fixed to the back of their stalls. Dating from the 14th century, these are a remarkable collection of heraldic work. New knights are installed before the annual Garter Service held each June. The adjoining ornate Albert Memorial Chapel was designed by George Gilbert Scott for Queen Victoria after the death of the Prince Consort. The heads of their nine children are sculpted on plaques above the illustrated panels of multi-coloured marble.

The precincts of the Castle are open every day during the year, with the exception of Garter Day. The State Apartments are not open when the Court is in residence (normally Christmas and Easter and for three weeks in June). (*Tel: Windsor (075 35) 68286.*)

Windsor Great Park (176) (SU 95-71 etc.) *To immediate S Windsor, and 23 mi. W Central London.* The three-mile Long Walk runs from the King George IV Gateway of Windsor Castle to the equestrian statue of George III known as the Copper Horse. Put up in 1831, this is so large that the workmen who built it are said to have had lunch inside to celebrate its completion. From the hill there are splendid views over the 400-acre park, once royal hunting grounds, and now open fields, woodland and farms. Savill Garden ★ and Valley Gardens ★ by Virginia Water ★ were laid out this century, the latter bordering Smith's Lawn, a polo field where the Prince of Wales plays regularly. Although the park is owned by the Crown, the public are admitted to most areas.

Windsor Safari Park (175) (SU 94-74) *Winkfield Road, Windsor, 25 mi. W Central London.* Hundreds of wild animals roam the reserves in the drive-through section of the park. Elsewhere visitors can walk in the forest where deer and wallabies live, admire the dolphins and sealions performing for their trainers, and watch the lions being fed. A butterfly house, a bear reserve and, in summer, birds of prey are other attractions. A boating lake, picnic areas and children's amusements cater for family outings. Open daily. (*Tel: Windsor (0753) 869841.*)

Wisley (187) (TQ 05-58) *20 mi. SW Central London.* The main road to Portsmouth (A3) separates Wisley Common from Ockham Common and now cutting across both is the M25 motorway. By the edge of the A3 a charming lake surrounded by pine trees makes a good picnic stop. Wisley Common is less wooded than Ockham and the natural environment is a contrast to **Wisley Gardens**, the beautifully laid-out grounds of the Royal Horticultural Society. Formal flower beds, lily ponds, lawns lined with herbaceous borders and a wild garden intermingle with the shrubberies and trees. There is a plant shop and information centre. Scientific research is centred in the laboratory and young gardeners are given horticultural training. Open all year.

Wisley Gardens

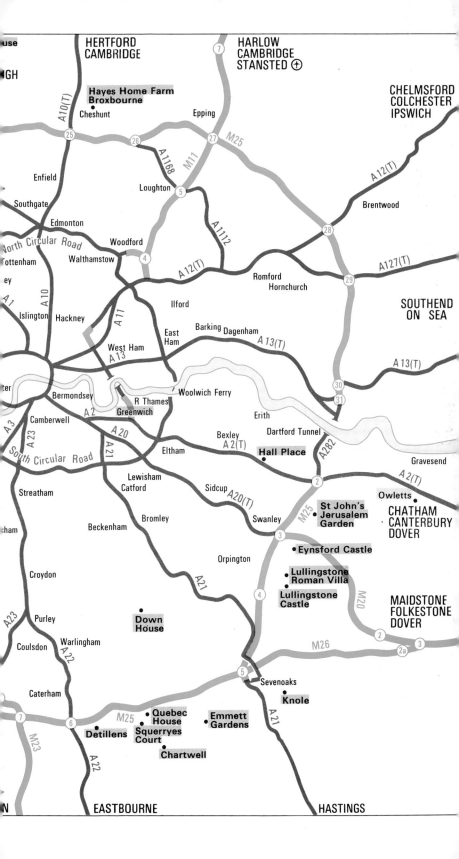

Inner London Walks

Walk 1
Prince Albert's Legacy

Allow 2½ hours

This walk takes you to South Kensington, an area of museums and colleges of further education. Almost every building you pass is in some way connected with the Prince Consort, Queen Victoria's husband, who died in 1861. They are all built on land bought from the profits of the 1851 Great Exhibition which Prince Albert organised.

The arcade from **Kensington High Street Underground Station (1)** *(off map to west)* leads to Kensington's busy main shopping thoroughfare where you immediately turn right, passing Barkers department store before crossing the road at the second set of traffic lights. *(Now on map)*. On the left, just beyond the Royal Garden Hotel **(2)**, by an entrance marked 'Private Road', there is a brick wall and beside it a gate into **Kensington Gardens (3)**. Either of the two paths takes you to **Kensington Palace (4)** where the statue of William III stands in front of the private apartments, today the home of the Prince and Princess of Wales and other members of the royal family. Queen Victoria was born in the palace in 1819. With the palace on your left walk up the slight incline where the statue of Queen Victoria stands. This was sculpted by Princess Louise, Duchess of Argyll, the 4th daughter of Victoria and Albert. The entrance to the

State Apartments is a few yards ahead. These you should visit, but you will need several hours. Walk beneath the arbour of trees surrounding the rectangular lily pond and enjoy the glorious colouring in the formal terraced garden.

Cross the grass to the Round Pond **(5)**, for which we must thank Queen Caroline, wife of George II. Over-friendly ducks assume everyone has brought them something to eat and go for your shoes if you haven't! The path beyond the bandstand goes down to the railed Flower Walk where you are discouraged from feeding wildfowl or squirrels: they tend to eat the lovely displays of flowers if tempted to this area.

Now take the path leading to the **Albert Memorial (6)**, chosen from a number of designs submitted to Queen Victoria after the Prince Consort's death in 1861, and part of the national memorial to him. It is worth examining in some detail, although the names underneath the figures on the frieze are not very legible. A few yards south is the main road with pedestrian traffic signals directly opposite the **Royal Albert Hall (7)**, another memorial. This was opened in 1871 by Albert's eldest son, the Prince of Wales, when the Queen, overcome with distress, felt unable to perform the ceremony. The modern building to the immediate west is the **Royal College of Art (8)** and next to it the ornate Royal College of Organists. The great red-brick edifice of the **Royal College of Music (9)** faces you as you descend the wide steps at the rear of the hall where there is another statue of the Prince. This commemorates the large role he played in organising the 1851 Great Exhibition. It was sculpted three years before his death and moved here in 1899.

Springtime in Kensington Gardens

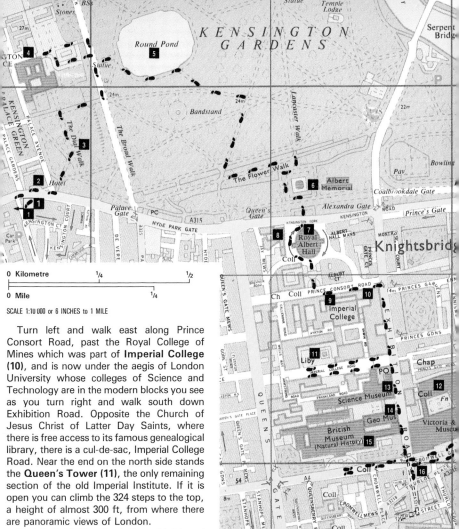

Turn left and walk east along Prince Consort Road, past the Royal College of Mines which was part of **Imperial College (10)**, and is now under the aegis of London University whose colleges of Science and Technology are in the modern blocks you see as you turn right and walk south down Exhibition Road. Opposite the Church of Jesus Christ of Latter Day Saints, where there is free access to its famous genealogical library, there is a cul-de-sac, Imperial College Road. Near the end on the north side stands the **Queen's Tower (11)**, the only remaining section of the old Imperial Institute. If it is open you can climb the 324 steps to the top, a height of almost 300 ft, from where there are panoramic views of London.

Back in Exhibition Road, the red-brick and terracotta building on the left is the Henry Cole Wing of the **Victoria and Albert Museum (12)**, but before you reach its front entrance there is the **Science Museum (13)**, a place where you can spend days. Immediately inside, an exhibition area, named the Synopsis, skilfully whets the appetite by giving a brief outline of what each gallery holds. You can spend a good hour merely admiring the exhibits here, and there is a display devoted to Albert and the Great Exhibition. Next door is the **Geological Museum (14)** with precious stones liable to make you think you've wandered into an expensive jeweller's. The modern wing of the **Natural History Museum (15)** is on the corner of Exhibition Road, and you have to turn right into the Cromwell Road to appreciate the front entrance of Alfred Waterhouse's Romanesque building. This is another museum where you can lose yourself for a while, and it's always packed with excited children. Retrace your steps back to the front of the **Victoria and Albert Museum (12)**, a large treasure house of fine and decorative arts. On what proved to be her last important public engagement, Queen Victoria laid the foundation stone in 1899. A number of visits are required before you can drink in the enormous variety of objets d'art on show in rooms along its nine miles of corridors.

The **Ismaili Cultural Centre (16)**, facing the V & A, has an art gallery where fascinating exhibitions dealing with aspects of Islamic history and life are mounted. At its side — on the corner of Thurloe Place and Exhibition Road — an entrance to **South Kensington Underground Station (17)** saves you crossing several busy roads, and heralds the end of **Walk 1**.

Walk 2
Chelsea People and Chelsea's Buildings

Allow 2½ hours

This walk beginning and ending in Sloane Square will provide many reminders of Chelsea's royal past, of its artists and writers. You will see fine mansions and quaint streets with desirable houses. With its river aspect and tree-lined squares, Chelsea is a favoured residential district of London.

From **Sloane Square Underground Station (1)** walk down Lower Sloane Street to the traffic lights at the junction with Pimlico Road. A little detour straight ahead into Chelsea Bridge Road will allow you to see **Chelsea Barracks (2)**, the modern army barracks where the Household Division are often stationed. **Ranelagh Gardens (3)**, facing the barracks, were famous pleasure gardens in the 18th century. Nowadays the Chelsea Flower Show is held here every May. Return to the crossroads and go into Royal Hospital Road. The Old Burial Ground on the left, a cemetery for Chelsea Pensioners and others associated with the hospital, has been closed since 1854 but through the railings you can see several monumental tombs.

Go through the gates into the grounds of

the **Royal Hospital (4)**, which Charles II founded for old and disabled soldiers. It has continued that role without a break since 1692. Visit the Chapel and Great Hall (normally open 10 am − noon; 2 pm − 4 pm) and do not miss Grinling Gibbons's statue of the founder on the square. The old soldiers who live here do not always wear their scarlet coats at home, but you will still recognise them in their navy uniforms. They need no encouragement to regale visitors with historical military stories. Walk through to the Chelsea Gate, turn left and immediately you will see the tanks and guns outside the **National Army Museum (5)**, a modern building which tells the story of the British Army from the 16th century to the present day.

Beyond the museum take the left turn into Tite Street where you will pass the home of Oscar Wilde at No. 34 and, unmarked by any plaque, the studio of John Singer Sargent at

SCALE 1:10 000 or 6 INCHES to 1 MILE

| 0 Kilometre | ¼ | ½ |

| 0 Mile | ¼ |

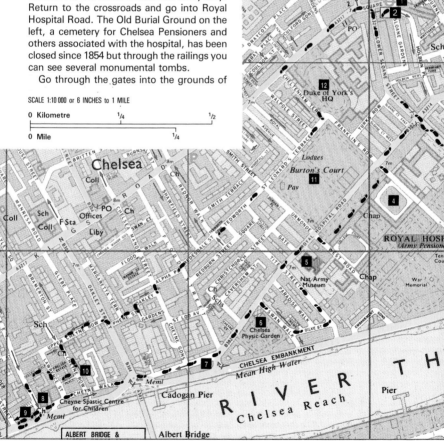

The Royal Hospital, Chelsea

No. 31. This faces more studios; No. 50, as you can see, is still used as one. Turn right into Dilke Street going past attractive mews to Swan Walk, where you go right and walk along the east wall of the **Chelsea Physic Garden (6)**, after Oxford the second oldest botanic garden in England. If you look through the gate you will see in the centre the statue of Sir Hans Sloane by Rysbrach. It is surrounded by rare and unusual plants and herbs, water and rock gardens. The gardens, not open every day, are worth a separate visit. Follow the wall round to the left and before you come to Chelsea Embankment, cross the road. With the little park on your left go along **Cheyne Walk (7)**. No. 4 has a plaque commemorating George Eliot's short residence, though there is none next door to tell you that this was the home of James Camden Neild, a miser who left Queen Victoria £500,000 which she spent on Balmoral. Several of these splendid old houses have fine period gates. Trailing creeper often hides the plaque on No.16 which Rossetti shared with Swinburne and George Meredith. The peacocks and menagerie he kept here caused considerable annoyance to his neighbours. Take note of Cheyne Mews, between Nos. 23 and 24. A notice on the wall identifies the exact site of Henry VIII's manor house and if you walk into the mews you may just catch sight of one of the mulberry trees said to have been planted by Elizabeth I.

Further westwards along the Embankment a statue of Sir Thomas More stands outside **Chelsea Old Church (8)**, and a short distance west, on the corner of Danvers Street (and just off map), is **Crosby Hall (9)**, the house owned by More in Bishopgate and

re-erected here in 1908. Return to Old Church Street, passing through the sunken Roper's Garden, named after More's daughter Margaret Roper. The winding route (first turning right into Justice Walk, then right into Lawrence Street and left into Lordship Place) shows you a mixture of old houses, all worth looking at for their variety of architectural styles, and takes you into a narrow street built in the reign of Queen Anne — **Cheyne Row (10)**, where Thomas Carlyle lived at No. 24.

At the Catholic church on the north-east corner, turn right into pretty Upper Cheyne Row where Leigh Hunt lived — there's an old LCC brown plaque on No. 22. The pedestrian crossing in Oakley Street leads almost directly across into Phene Street. The novelist George Gissing, author of *New Grub Street*, lived in the corner house — No. 33. In tree-lined Oakley Gardens a jarring design note is struck by the ugly wall of the electricity power house in Alpha Place, but the next three roads (turn left at end of Oakley Gardens) — almost a straight line through Redesdale Street, Tedworth Gardens and St Leonard's Terrace — have at least three centuries of different types of housing, the creeper-covered homes overlooking **Burton's Court (11)**, where the Brigade of Guards plays cricket, being the oldest by far. The imposing portico of the Duke of York's Headquarters **(12)**, where the Royal Corps of Signals is quartered, faces you as you turn left into Cheltenham Terrace, and finally right at the top into the **King's Road** where **Sloane Square** and the **Sloane Square Underground Station (1)** are then straight ahead, thus completing **Walk 2**.

141

Walk 3
Royalty and State, Part 1

Allow 1½ hours

On this circular walk, starting and ending at Piccadilly Circus Underground Station, you will pass a number of houses with royal associations. The theme of the walk — royalty and state — may be continued by joining the beginning of Walk 4, before the return to Piccadilly.

Leave **Piccadilly Circus Underground Station (1)** by the 'Piccadilly North' exit. Along Piccadilly you pass on the left Wren's **St James's Church (2)**, next to the Midland Bank designed by Sir Edwin Lutyens. Beyond Sackville Street, set back in a courtyard up to the right, is **Albany (3)**, the home of George III's second son, Frederick, 'the Grand Old Duke of York', in 1800. Further on, on the left is the distinctive green-and-cream façade of **Fortnum and Mason (4)**, the affluent department store. It faces an even more impressive building, **Burlington House (5)**, home of the **Royal Academy of Arts** and several learned societies.

A short detour through **Burlington Arcade (6)** and back down Old **Bond Street** takes you past exclusive shops and art galleries, many with royal warrants. Continue along Piccadilly, and beyond Half Moon Street is the **Naval and Military Club (7)**, known because of the directions on the gateposts as the 'In and Out'. The Blue Plaque commemorates Queen Victoria's Prime Minister Lord Palmerston. Before him her uncle, the Duke of Cambridge, lived here.

Cross to the **Green Park** side of the street where the railings are hung with paintings every Sunday morning. You may follow the railings round the edge of **Hyde Park Corner (8)** or cut across the Park to Constitution Hill. The spiked wall on the right as you walk down the Hill encloses the 40-acre garden of **Buckingham Palace (9)**. The gilded figure of Victory above the fountain on the roundabout opposite the London home of the Queen and the Duke of Edinburgh is the **Queen Victoria Memorial (10)**. Keeping the Palace on the right, turn into Buckingham Gate where you will find the entrance to the **Queen's Gallery (11)**. This is usually open, and so — on certain days — is the **Royal Mews (12)** further along.

Now double back and up Buckingham Gate into Birdcage Walk where **Wellington Barracks (13)** and the **Guards Chapel (14)** (worth a visit and often open) are on the right. Cross the road into **St James's Park** and walk along the attractive lakeside which is full of birds and wildfowl. Go over the bridge and continue north to **The Mall (15)**. At the traffic lights cross over and walk west (left). The large cream stucco building behind the wall is **Clarence House (16)**. The right turn into Stable Yard, a private road which is open to pedestrians only, leads to the main entrance of Clarence House, the home of

Carlton House Terrace, overlooking the Mall

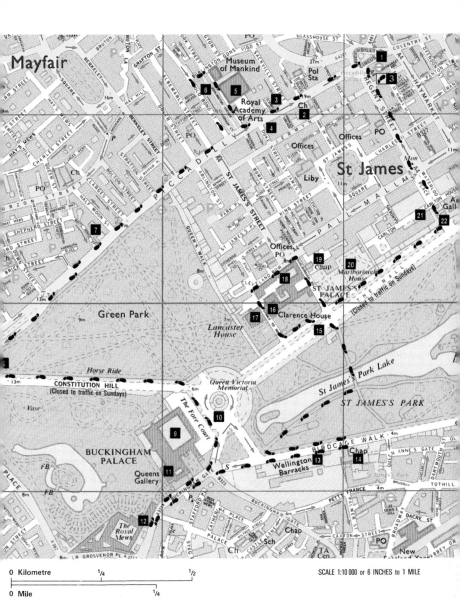

Queen Elizabeth the Queen Mother, and takes you on to **Lancaster House (17)**, another of the houses lived in by 'the Grand Old Duke of York'. **St James's Palace (18)**, opposite, has been a royal residence since the reign of Henry VIII. Today the Duke and Duchess of Kent have apartments in it.

On the way back to the Mall, you pass the **Chapel Royal** and Inigo Jones's beautiful **Queen's Chapel (19)** (details of its Sunday services are listed in *The Times* on Saturdays). Carry on eastwards, past **Marlborough House (20)**, the home of Edward VII when he was Prince of Wales. Queen Alexandra moved back here when she was widowed and it was also the home of Queen Mary,

widow of George V, and earlier of William IV's widow, Queen Adelaide. There are memorials on the walls to Queen Mary and Queen Alexandra, and to George VI on the steps going up to the cream buildings above the wall as you go towards **Admiralty Arch**. These grand mansions form part of **Carlton House Terrace (21)**. The large flight of steps **(22)** to the **Duke of York's Column** is on the site of the Prince Regent's exotic Carlton House. You may either go up the steps and walk via Lower Regent Street to return to **Piccadilly Circus Underground Station (1)**, thus completing **Walk 3**, or join **Walk 4** at the top of the approach road to **Horse Guards (6 on Walk 4)**.

143

Walk 4
Royalty and State, Part 2

Allow 1½ hours

This walk from Charing Cross Station to St James's Park Underground can, if you wish, be a continuation of Walk 3. Its theme is still royalty and state, although the palaces have either disappeared or become government buildings.

Make sure you use all the traffic crossings when you leave **Charing Cross Station (1)**. With eight roads leading in and out of **Trafalgar Square (2)** it is quite a trick to get to **Admiralty Arch (3)** unscathed and through into **The Mall**. The statue of Captain Cook is on the pavement ahead, the Captain's back to the warm red brick of the **Admiralty (4)** which was built in the reign of George III. Take the path along the side of the solid concrete fortress agreeably camouflaged in Virginia creeper. This is the Citadel, put up as a government communications centre during the Second World War. In Horse Guards Approach *(we are joined here from Walk 3)*, with **St James's Park (5)** on the right, walk along the edge of the parade ground to the sentry box in line with the clock above the **Horse Guards (6)** building. In front of the central archway the Queen takes the salute at Trooping the Colour every June. Look at the buildings surrounding the parade. These are all government offices, and the trees near the statue of Lord Mountbatten shield No. 10 Downing Street from prying eyes. Walk under the central arch into **Whitehall (7)** where the Life Guards will be looking stoically eyes front despite endless

0 Kilometre   ¼   ½

0 Mile   ¼

SCALE 1:10 000 or 6 INCHES to 1 MILE

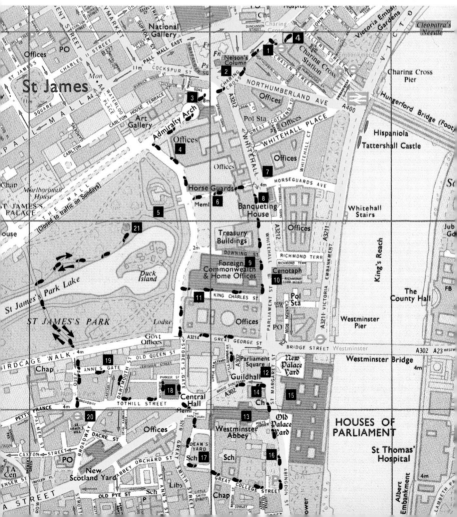

The Cenotaph

photography by tourists.

You are now standing in what once was part of the Palace of Whitehall, a royal home from the reign of Henry VIII until it was destroyed by a fire in 1698. Various government offices are on either side of the wide road today known as Whitehall and a number of statues on the side or in the centre of the road commemorate men with military associations. Facing you on the south corner of Horse Guards Avenue there is a surviving part of the Palace of Whitehall, a Stuart addition. This is the **Banqueting House (8)**, Inigo Jones's masterpiece and architecturally one of the most important buildings in the country. Jones began work on it in 1619 and it was completed 15 years later. It is well worth a visit, especially to see the wonderful ceilings Rubens painted for Charles I. On 29 January 1649 the King stepped from a window on the first floor to his execution.

The Scottish Office, on the right, is best appreciated from the parade ground. Formerly Melbourne House, it was the scene of the assignations between Lord Byron and Lady Caroline Lamb during their tempestuous affair. On the opposite side of Whitehall the sombre front of Gwydyr House, the Welsh Office, comes a few yards before the modern block housing the Ministry of Defence. Underneath this building, preserved intact, is another part of the Palace, Henry VIII's Wine Cellar, which is rarely open to the public nowadays. The statue on the grass outside is of Field Marshal Lord Montgomery who looks across to **Downing Street (9)**. Access is restricted to those who have official business with the Prime Minister, or at one of the other important government offices in the street.

The Cenotaph (10), the country's most important war memorial honouring the men and women who died in two World Wars, is in the centre of Whitehall, just before the Treasury building which is on the corner of King Charles Street. Here you turn right, paying no attention to the cul-de-sac sign: this applies only to vehicles. The entrance to the **Cabinet War Rooms (11)** is by the steps leading back down into Horse Guards Approach where two left turns bring you by way of Great George Street to **Parliament Square (12)**. This is another place where traffic is a hazard: best cross at the first set of lights and walk towards **Westminster Abbey (13)**, with statues of George Canning and Abraham Lincoln, and **Middlesex Guildhall** on your right. At the side of the Abbey turn left and pass **St Margaret's Westminster (14)**, the parish church of the House of Commons, which was consecrated in 1523 and is a fashionable place for society weddings.

Immediately ahead are the **Houses of Parliament (15)**. Unless you wish to examine the outside in detail keep to the right-hand footpath of this busy road as you walk around the back of the church and the Abbey to the statue of George V in Old Palace Yard. The path across the small Abingdon Gardens, where the **Jewel Tower (16)** stands in a little moat, takes you past a modern bronze sculpture by Henry Moore. Over the road in the Victoria Tower Gardens you can glimpse a replica of Rodin's statue of *The Burghers of Calais*. A sharp right turn at the entrance to the underground garage brings you down Great College Street. Straight ahead is a building with three shields high on the wall. A gateway on its corner leads into **Dean's Yard (17)**. Stroll around, mingling with the pupils of **Westminster School** if it's term time. In the north-east corner is the entrance to the cloisters of **Westminster Abbey**, which you should see. The way out is through an archway where the Great West Door of the Abbey is to the right.

Cross the road at the traffic signals. Walk in front of **Central Hall Westminster (18)**. The new building on the right is the Queen Elizabeth II Conference Centre. Matthew Parker Street takes you around the back of Central Hall. Go to the right into Tothill Street until you reach Dartmouth Street. It leads to **Queen Anne's Gate (19)**, a charming street of delightful early 18th-century houses with unusual keystones on Nos. 15-25 and 26-34. At the end of the street **St James's Park Underground Station (20)** is on the left, and this is the end of **Walk 4**.

However if you have time to sit and rest, **St James's Park** is only 100 yards in the other direction. A restaurant **(21)** (open in summer months) is on the far side of the lake, on the path to the right after you walk over the bridge.

Walk 5
London's Entertainment

Allow 2 hours

Beginning at Piccadilly Circus Underground Station, this walk goes past many of London's principal places of entertainment, a few historic, others more associated with the 20th century. Some interesting architecture and a couple of secret little hideaways that most Londoners do not know exist are on the way as well as a number of places — some quieter than others — to sit and rest and watch the world pass by.

From **Piccadilly Circus Underground Station (1)** go up **Shaftesbury Avenue (2)**, a street laid out a century ago and now an important part of theatreland. On your way you pass the Apollo, Lyric, Globe and Queen's Theatres. Opposite the Curzon West End Cinema, just before the Palace Theatre, take the short right turn by the Fire Station through Newport Place and turn right again into **Gerrard Street (3)**. As you walk along you see this is London's Chinatown. A left turn at the end takes you down Wardour Street to the Swiss Centre and then left into **Leicester Square (4)**, with its cinemas, restaurants and dance halls, and often in the evening buskers to entertain passers-by.

Leave diagonally opposite your entry to the square by Irving Street, named after the famous Victorian actor whose statue is under the plane trees at the side of the **National Portrait Gallery (5)**. Sir Henry looks across

to the Garrick Theatre, named after another famous actor, David Garrick.

Go a few yards north and turn right into Cecil Court, a fascinating passageway with shops selling rare books, prints and memorabilia. As you turn right into St Martin's Lane, facing you are Nos. 55-56 where a few steps lead into a narrow alley. Do not miss this opportunity to go in to see the enchanting Georgian bow-fronted windows on the houses of Goodwin's Court.

The Lumiere Cinema, the Duke of York's Theatre and the **London Coliseum (6)**, home of English National Opera, and the statue of Nurse Edith Cavell, are on the way to **St Martin-in-the-Fields (7)**, where Nell Gwyn was buried. The parish church for Buckingham Palace — the Queen has a pew — is worth a visit. The thoroughfare running along the railings at the side of St Martin's, the only one in London without a name, faces the side of Coutt's Bank which you follow around until **Zimbabwe House (8)**, with its mutilated Epstein sculptures, confronts you.

Go up Agar Street and turn right into Chandos Place and Maiden Lane where there are several tiny alleys with reminders of times past. Five yards beyond the entrance to the first and most interesting of these, **Exchange Court (9)**, is the royal entrance to the Adelphi Theatre where the actor William Terriss was murdered by a jealous, mad rival in 1897. Rules restaurant, a quiet haunt of Edward VII, and the stage door of the Vaudeville Theatre come before the Catholic Church of Corpus Christi which has connections with the stage. At the end of Maiden Lane turn left into Southampton Street, pass the Jubilee Hall and, for a few

Goodwin's Court

minutes, ignore the Piazza so that you may visit **St Paul's Covent Garden (10)**. Inigo Jones's church is approached either through a gateway (not always open) in the wall just before St Peter's Hospital in Henrietta Street or by the main entrance in Bedford Street. The church, known as the actors' church, has memorials to many famous players, and flowers and trees in the garden are planted in their memory.

King Street takes you back to **Covent Garden (11)**, one of the liveliest spots in London. Here you may stroll and explore the market and shops, and refresh yourself. If you're lucky you may catch some street theatre in front of Inigo Jones's porch where Shaw's Eliza Doolittle sold her flowers. The **London Transport Museum (12)** is on the south-east side of the Piazza.

Leave the Market by walking around the back and side of the **Royal Opera House (13)**. Facing the home of the Royal Opera and Royal Ballet is Bow Street Police Station, where the police force originated, and there is a Magistrates' Court. Turn right down Bow Street and a few yards south, at the cross-roads, look east and you'll see London's most historic theatre, the **Theatre Royal, Drury Lane (14)**. The new **Theatre Museum (15)** is also on the corner of Russell Street: at its rear a house with a Blue Plaque reminds one it was here that Boswell first met Dr Johnson.

Going down Wellington Street you pass the Lyceum Theatre, scene of Sir Henry Irving's triumphs. At the traffic lights on the Strand, **Somerset House (16)** is on the approach to Waterloo Bridge, and you may catch a glimpse of the **National Theatre** over the river. A turn sharp right into the Strand and then immediately left takes you down Savoy Street to the **Savoy Chapel (17)** on Savoy Hill and on to the river entrance of the Savoy Hotel.

Go right into **Victoria Embankment Gardens (18)**, where Robert Raikes, the founder of Sunday schools, has a bird's-eye view of the entertainment complex on the **South Bank** from his statue. There are several memorials and statues in these colourful gardens, the most inspired being the sculpture of a First World War soldier on a camel, commemorating the Imperial Camel Corps. Steps go down to the watergate — dating from 1626 and once the entrance to a great house — and up to Buckingham Street, where Pepys lived, and bring you to John Adam Street, part of the area known as **Adelphi (19)**. Sir James Barrie is one of several famous men who lived in Robert Street where, at the bottom, you will find remnants of the famous terrace. Turn left into Adam Street and left again into the **Strand**, with its two theatres, the Vaudeville and Adelphi, both only yards from the Players' Theatre, underneath the arches in Villiers Street, and **Charing Cross Underground Station (20)**, the end of **Walk 5**.

0 Kilometre   ¼   ½

0 Mile   ¼   SCALE 1:10 000 or 6 INCHES to 1 MILE

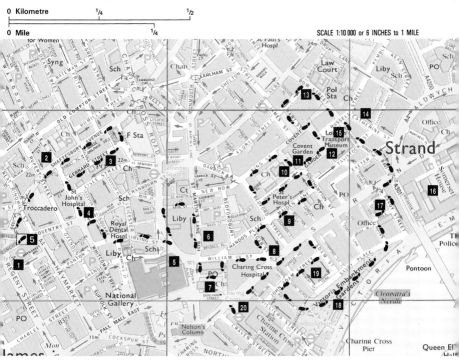

Walk 6
Legal London

Allow 2 hours

This walk from Temple Underground Station to Chancery Lane goes past buildings associated with the legal profession. The Inns of Court, where lawyers have their chambers, are private property. Visitors are welcome so long as they respect their surroundings.

From **Temple Underground Station (1)** walk eastwards along the Embankment, and after a hundred yards you pass two plinths topped by dragons. These mark the boundary between the City of London and Westminster. One is by Temple Gardens, just before entrance gates where you should turn left into the two Inns of Court — Middle Temple and Inner Temple — jointly known as the **Temple (2)**. Lawyers have practised here since the 15th century. Explore the alleys and courtyards off Middle Temple Lane, and as you stroll around you will see that each doorway has the nameplates of lawyers who occupy the various chambers. The top floors are mostly the private flats of barristers.

Do not miss **Temple Church (3)**, the round church with fascinating memorials to mediaeval knights. Admire the elegant Wren houses in King's Bench Walk and return to Middle Temple Lane. At the top of a short flight of steps is the door to Middle Temple Hall. It has a fine hammer-beam roof. Elizabeth I is believed to have come here to watch Shakespeare perform in *Twelfth Night*. The

Lincoln's Inn Fields

gate at the top of the Lane may be closed (usually at weekends) but you can reach Fleet Street through Brick Court.

Across the road are the **Royal Courts of Justice (4)**, the chief civil and appeal courts in the country, but before you cross, turn left to glance at No. 217 **Strand**. This narrow shop with the sign of the golden lion is Twinings, the tea merchants, one of the oldest businesses in London. Dr Samuel Johnson, whose statue is on the grass at the rear of the church in the middle of the road, was a regular worshipper at **St Clement Danes (5)**. It is now maintained by the Royal Air Force. Dr Johnson looks towards the Gothic-style Law Courts, designed between 1866-82 by George Street, who died exhausted before completing the massive undertaking.

Bear right into Clements Inn (at the west end of the long court building) which was one of nine, less important Inns of Chancery. Continue past the site of the headquarters of the Suffragettes to steps leading to Grange Court and Carey Street. Because the Bankruptcy Courts are here, 'in Carey Street' has come to mean 'in financial difficulties'. Turn left into Serle Street by a red-brick building on the corner which has a Victorian statue of Henry VIII's Lord Chancellor, Sir Thomas More, a member of Lincoln's Inn. This is at the top of the street.

First, however, walk around **Lincoln's Inn Fields (6)**, preferably in the gardens where there are fine old plane trees. The buildings on the square include the Royal College of Surgeons, with an impressive Ionic portico. No. 13, on the north side, is the **Sir John Soane Museum (7)**, the home of the late-Georgian architect who left his valuable paintings and famous collection of architectural drawings to the nation.

Inside **Lincoln's Inn (8)**, an Inn of Court founded in the 14th century, there are fine gates at the top of New Square which is surrounded by gracious 17th-century houses. At the open undercroft, a staircase goes up to the early 17th-century Chapel, which some attribute to Inigo Jones. Old Square leads to Stone Buildings, put up 1774-80, and a small gate leads to the Library and Hall. (Ask the porter at 11a New Square for permission to see the Chapel and Hall.)

When you emerge in **Chancery Lane (9)** through a fine Tudor gateway near Old Buildings, turn right and walk towards Fleet Street, peeping into the alleys, reminders of the mediaeval City, and passing the elaborate **Public Record Office (10)**, the state archive.

Clifford's Inn, the oldest of the former Inns of Chancery, is immediately to your left in **Fleet Street (11)**, for centuries the street of newspapers. Since most national news-

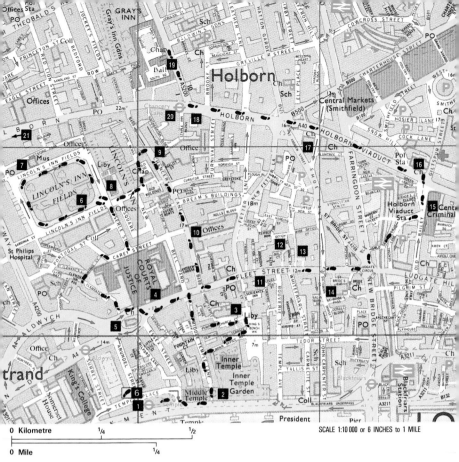

papers are moving, the fate of the *Daily Express* 'paper palace' and the *Daily Telegraph* building is uncertain. Many centuries-old alleys have survived. Two of them on the left — Johnson's Court or Bolt Court — take you to **Dr Johnson's House (12)** in Gough Square. The doctor is said to have frequented **Ye Olde Cheshire Cheese** in Wine Office Court **(13)**, a tavern which proudly proclaims that it was 'rebuilt' in 1667 after the Great Fire. **St Bride's (14)**, the parish church with close newspaper and printing associations', is behind the Reuters-Press Association building on the corner of Salisbury Court.

At Ludgate Circus cross into Farringdon Street and weave to the right up under the dark, dank railway arches. This is Old Seacoal Lane, its wine cellars and cobblestones evocative of a Dickensian London. In *Pickwick Papers* Dickens described the notorious Fleet Prison by Fleet Lane where debtors were sent until 1824.

Straight ahead is the **Central Criminal Court (15)**, or the **Old Bailey** where important murder cases are heard. The older part of the building, surmounted by the statue holding the scales of justice, is on the site of old Newgate Prison demolished in 1902.

The Church of **St Sepulchre-without-Newgate (16)** is on the other side of the road as you go left towards Holborn Viaduct, passing the City Temple and Wren's **St Andrew's Holborn (17)** where Disraeli became a Christian at the age of 12. Along Holborn, Thavies Inn and Barnards Inn, once Inns of Chancery, have been replaced by modern buildings bearing the old names. By Chancery Lane Underground Station a fine half-timbered Tudor building slightly overhangs the street. This is the front of **Staple Inn (18)**, another of the minor inns. The hall, reconstructed after bomb damage, is in a corner of the courtyard through the archway.

Gray's Inn (19), with fine gardens and a famous hall, is the last of the four great Inns of Court. It is behind the shops on the north side of the street. A gateway just by No. 23 Holborn, the quaint Cittie of Yorke pub, will take you to the Inn where Sir Francis Bacon had chambers and Lord Burghley, Elizabeth I's greatest statesman, studied.

To complete **Walk 6** return to **Chancery Lane Underground Station (20)**, but if this is closed (on Sundays) **Holborn Underground Station (21)** *(off map to west)* is only a short walk westwards along High Holborn.

Walk 7
Shakespeare's London

Allow 3 hours

In search of Shakespeare and his contemporaries this walk from St Paul's to London Bridge almost certainly follows paths the playwright trod on his way from the City to Southwark. On the way you also pass City institutions that have played an important role in the development of London.

From **St Paul's Underground Station (1)** go up St Martin's le Grand to the **Museum of London (2)**, reached by going onto the podium by a stairway at Little Britain. Beyond the Museum the remains of the Roman wall are in a garden below. Pass between the shops to see the tower of St Giles Cripplegate where Ben Jonson worshipped and Shakespeare probably attended his nephew's christening. To the right of the church is the **Barbican Centre (3)**, *(just off map to north)*, home of the Royal Shakespeare Company. You are looking down on Monkswell Square but the corner of Silver Street and Monkswell Street where Shakespeare lodged was on the other side of **London Wall (4)**. He is thought to have written *Othello* in Christopher Mountjoy's house in 1603. The location can be pinpointed. The 'No Entry' sign to the car park between Noble Street and Wood Street is where the gabled house stood.

| 0 Kilometre | ¼ | | ½ |
| 0 Mile | | ¼ | |

SCALE 1:10 000 or 6 INCHES to 1 MILE

Cross the walkway over London Wall to Wood Street. Wren's tower, built in 1685 (now flats), is all that remains of the pre-Conquest church of St Alban which Shakespeare would have passed. Once beyond Gresham Street, keep a careful lookout for the tiny entrance on the left to **Mitre Court (5)**. There is no evidence Shakespeare drank at the Mitre Tavern but his contemporary Ben Jonson knew it well enough to put it in *Bartholomew Fair* and *Every Man in his Humour*. There is still a pub on the site. The railed stairs in the courtyard lead down to the Wood Street Comptor, a debtors' prison from 1555 until 1791. St Peter's Church, which Shakespeare knew, on the corner of Wood Street, was not rebuilt after the Fire. Clauses in the church lease forbid the destruction of the plane tree (immortalised in *The Reverie of Poor Susan* by Wordsworth), in the little garden and prevent two shops on Cheapside — the smallest in the City — rising above one storey.

Turn left into Cheapside but before you turn left again into Milk Street, observe the church of **St Mary le Bow (6)**. Although rebuilt, the Norman undercroft is still intact. **Guildhall Library (7)** is at the top of Milk Street, and before you go into Guildhall Yard, visit the gardens of St Mary's Church in Aldermanbury. Stones mark the foundations of the church where Shakespeare almost certainly worshipped. You can see his likeness on the Victorian memorial to two parishioners, John Hemminge and Henry Condell, actors who were his friends. After his death they preserved his works by editing the First Folio. The bombed church was dismantled in 1965 and re-erected at Fulton, Missouri to commemorate Sir Winston Churchill's 'Iron Curtain' speech there in 1946.

Guildhall (8) has been the civic headquarters of London for over 800 years. **St Lawrence Jewry (9)** is a reminder that this was the old Jewish quarter of the City and to the east along Gresham Street you find **Old Jewry (10)**. On one side of Lothbury is the wall that encloses the **Bank of England (11)**. The **Stock Exchange (12)**, taking up most of Throgmorton Street, may be visited. The entrance is in Old Broad Street which runs into **Threadneedle Street** where the **Royal Exchange (13)** is on the left. This faces the **Mansion House (14)**, the office and home of the Lord Mayor of London.

Remains of **The Temple of Mithras (15)**, a 1st-century Roman temple, are on a raised platform outside No. 11 Queen Victoria Street. You are following the old Roman road in Watling Street on your way to **St Paul's Cathedral (16)**.

When you finish looking around Wren's great building, cross the road by the statue of Queen Anne and go down Dean's Court. Explore the little alleys along Carter Lane and look at the **Apothecaries' Hall (17)**, on the corner of Blackfriars Lane and Playhouse Yard. This is where James Burbage built the Blackfriars Playhouse in 1590 on part of the mediaeval monastery of **Blackfriars**. Shakespeare performed in it with his company, the King's Players. He also bought the gatehouse of the Priory in Ireland Lane. This was certainly within yards of the Cockpit public house on the corner of St Andrew's Hill. A passage at the back of Wren's **St Andrew-by-the-Wardrobe (18)** leads by steps to Queen Victoria Street, and the Bard's 'Seven Ages of Man' are carved on a statue over the road. Further east is the **College of Arms (19)** where the heralds once refused to grant arms to Shakespeare's father.

Across the road from the college recent demolition has made possible a river walk and a monumental stairway. Be sure to look back up Peter's Hill for a superb uninterrupted view of St Paul's. You also have the best general view of **Bankside** across the river — in Shakespeare's day the City's playground.

Shakespeare would probably have taken a ferry from Queenhithe Stairs to reach **Bankside** but you must walk along Upper Thames Street, past the Samuel Pepys riverside pub and the **Vintners' Hall (20)** and over **Southwark Bridge (21)**. Stairs take you to the water's edge. Walk west as far as **Cardinal Cap Alley (22)** to see the narrow house where Wren is said to have lodged while building St Paul's. A few yards away a reconstruction of Shakespeare's **Globe** is being built. The actual Globe was in Park Street, east of the existing commemorative plaque, and you reach it passing Bear Gardens and Rose Alley, sites of bear-baiting pits and the Rose Theatre.

On the site of an Elizabethan tavern, the 18th-century **Anchor Inn (23)** overlooking the river contains mementoes of the area and a model of the Globe. It was once owned by Henry Thrale, Dr Johnson's friend. Great Victorian warehouses in Clink Street cover the **Clink (24)** prison. Some have been converted recently and by the side of one, vestiges of Winchester Palace have been picked out on the ground, and at night the remaining 14th-century wall and rose window are floodlit. *The Kathleen & May*, a schooner is in wet dock. In **Southwark Cathedral (25)** an early 20th-century monument depicts a reclining Shakespeare with the buildings of Southwark in low relief behind him. His fellow dramatists, Philip Massinger and John Fletcher, and his brother Edmund were buried in the church. **London Bridge Station and Underground Station (26)** are ahead; the latter marks the end of **Walk 7**.

Walk 8
Fire, Torture and Trade

Allow 3 hours

Between Monument Underground Station and Liverpool Street Station you will see 2,000 years of London history. As well as remains of the Roman city, there are buildings which tell us about the Great Fire, and gruesome reminders of torture and execution. The development of trade and industry is evident in a former dock, in factories, street markets and vast international business centres.

Leave the **Monument Underground Station (1)** passing **The Monument (2)**, Wren's column commemorating the Great Fire of 1666, a few yards from Pudding Lane where the fire started in Thomas Farrinor's bakery. A plaque on the bank on the corner is close to the site. Until 1982 **Billingsgate (3)** had been London's main fish market for over 1,000 years, centred latterly in the Victorian building with the elaborate portico facing you on Lower Thames Street. Further along is the austere **Custom House (4)**. At the top of the hill a subway goes to **All Hallows by the Tower (5)**. Pepys, who lived across the road and worked at the Admiralty in Seething Lane, watched the Great Fire from the tower. Model ships, illustrating the church's maritime connections, hang between the arches. Two fine modern bronze effigies on tombs are examples of how the dead are still remembered in a building which has been a place of worship since Saxon times.

Another subway, beyond the church, takes you across to **Trinity Square (6)**. The gardens are on the site of Tower Hill, once a grim place of execution. More than 125 men were put to death on the ancient scaffold, among them Sir Thomas More and Thomas Wentworth, Earl of Strafford. Plaques on the ground bear the names of some. Men of the Merchant Navy and Fishing Fleet lost in both World Wars are remembered on two memorials. Looming over the gardens is the former headquarters of the Port of London Authority. Beside it is Trinity House, an elegant Georgian building owned by the fraternity responsible for maintaining lighthouses around the coast.

The City Wall is ahead in Wakefield Gardens. Halfway down the steps to the subway go into the small enclosure to examine this large fragment of Roman London and read the explanatory display panels. A replica of London's earliest inscribed monument (1st century) is also here and a statue of Trajan, the Roman Emperor in whose reign London

took shape. At the Tower side of the subway remnants of the 13th-century postern gate have been preserved. Follow the signs to St Katharine Docks, walking above the site of the moat and ditch on the north side of the **Tower of London (7)**. By the side of the World Trade Centre old cellars have been transformed into garden grottoes. Before the river's edge, go through the gate under **Tower Bridge (8)**, and along the cobblestone wharf to see the Bloody Tower which is above **Traitors' Gate (9)**. These are the grimmest places in this famous fortress which has been a notorious prison, a royal palace and the scene of terrible tortures. The White Tower, now over 900 years old, is behind the Middle Drawbridge.

Go back under the bridge, round the front of the Tower Hotel, and cross the drawbridge over the lock to **St Katharine Docks (10)**. Explore this most attractive part of the **Docklands** redevelopment. Beside the expensive boats and the timber-galleried but modern Dickens Inn, there are restaurants and shops. At the back of the Ivory House, a converted warehouse, sign-posts to Tower Hill take you up a staircase to East Smithfield.

The subway by the traffic lights will take you back to the Roman Wall and you can see another section of this beyond the modern arches of the City of London Polytechnic. First you have to cross the Crescent with its Georgian houses, and the wall is through the gate immediately below the railway bridge in Vine Street. Continue north, going into the Minories at **Crosswall (11)**. At the Church of St Botolph without Aldgate, turn right, and then cross the busy intersection by taking the subway to Exit 15. This is now Whitechapel High Street. Tubby Isaacs, a famous East End character, often has his jellied-eel stall on the corner of Goulston Street, a few yards from Blooms, the well-known kosher restaurant. Most of the shop and factory signs have the exotic, foreign-sounding names of immigrants who have settled for centuries in the East End.

Turn left into **Osborn Street (12)** *(just off map to east)* which leads to Brick Lane, so called because bricks were manufactured here in the 16th century. Turn left again by the London **Jamme Masjid (13)**, a mosque on the corner of Fournier Street. This has previously been a synagogue, a Methodist church and, in 1743 when it opened, was a chapel for French Protestants. Although Fournier Street is shabby now, the elaborate doorways on the 18th-century houses suggest a far grander past. In the high attics the silkweavers of **Spitalfields** worked 200 years ago, hoping to catch extra hours of daylight. The fortunes of Nicholas Hawksmoor's impressive **Christ Church, Spitalfields (14)**, undergoing extensive restoration, declined when machinery replaced the Huguenot handweavers. Turn left here into Commercial Street. The pub on the corner is named after Jack the Ripper who was familiar with this area. He committed one of his murders in nearby Hanbury Street and another across the road near where there is a car park today.

Turn right into White's Row, left into Bell Lane and right into Wentworth Street where the overspill stalls from **Petticoat Lane (15)** are set up every Saturday afternoon in readiness for the early start of London's famous Sunday street market. The heart of the market is in Middlesex Street and once you've passed the quaintly named Frying Pan Alley, ahead lie Bishopsgate and tower blocks housing international banks: **Liverpool Street Station (16)**, just across the road, marks the end of **Walk 8**.

SCALE 1:10 000 or 6 INCHES to 1 MILE

Walk 9
Mediaeval Martyrs, Meat and Marx

Allow 2 hours

Between Barbican Underground Station at the start of the walk and Farringdon Underground Station at the end, you will see traces of the mediaeval City that escaped the Great Fire of 1666, and the even older remains of Roman London. Although new buildings are encroaching, many centuries-old institutions and commercial enterprises have survived.

Start the walk from the **Barbican Underground Station (1).** *(But when this station is closed (on Sundays), start from* **St Paul's Underground Station (1A)**, *walk north up St Martins le Grand and Aldersgate (see start of Walk 7.)*

Starting from the **Barbican Underground Station (1)** cross to Beech Street, a tunnel rather than a road. To the right of the City of London coat of arms is an opening with directions to the **Barbican Centre (2).** The difficulties of finding your way through the largest arts centre in Europe and the massive complex of flats are notorious. But by following the yellow lines on the pavement you will get fine upper-floor views of the gardens, lake and other striking features of the building. More yellow lines on the podium above the lake direct you to the Museum of London. On the way look down at the church of **St Giles Cripplegate (3)** where Milton is buried and which Shakespeare knew. Near the museum, fragments of the Roman City Wall and a mediaeval tower are in the

gardens of the 1969 neo-Georgian Barber-Surgeons' Hall.

The **Museum of London (4)** is the best place to learn about this historic city, but there is so much to see it should be left to another day. To reach the little church of **St Botolph-without-Aldersgate (5)** over the road walk around the railings above the patio garden and down the steps. The ornate Georgian church has a superb ceiling. Rather than go down narrow Little Britain, a diversion through Postman's Park (entrance on left of church) is more pleasant. Plaques on a wall record acts by forgotten heroes.

The large building ahead is the rear of **St Bartholomew's Hospital (6).** To get to the entrance turn right but first, at the top of Little Britain, look for the Tudor gateway (on the right as you enter Smithfield) that goes into the Church of **St Bartholomew-the-Great (7).** Founded in 1123, this is the second oldest church in London after St John's in the Tower of London. Over the gateway to the hospital is the only statue of Henry VIII in the capital. Inside, St Bartholomew the Less and the Great Hall are worth seeing if open. Cross Giltspur Street and turn right into Cock Lane, on the corner of which is the statue of the Golden Boy which marks the spot where the Great Fire ended in 1666. The neo-Georgian house at No. 20 is on the site of the house that Dr Johnson and others visited in 1762 to witness a 12-year-old girl make contact with a dead woman. The Cock Lane Ghost proved a hoax and the girl's father was gaoled.

At the end of the street double back up Smithfield Street to **Smithfield (8),** a meat market for over 800 years. It was also the scene of the Bartholomew Fair and a place of public executions. Beyond West Smithfield go up Cloth Fair, a street where two houses

Ely Place

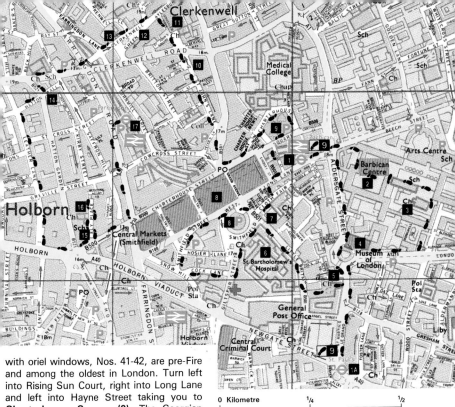

with oriel windows, Nos. 41-42, are pre-Fire and among the oldest in London. Turn left into Rising Sun Court, right into Long Lane and left into Hayne Street taking you to **Charterhouse Square (9)**. The Georgian houses are on the site of the 14th-century Carthusian monastery, of which traces remain. This became Charterhouse School and almshouses. The school is now at Godalming, Surrey, but the pensioners remain. Charterhouse is private property (although open one afternoon a week in early summer) but you can peep though the railings and gates to get an impression of life long ago.

Having looped around the square, go briefly into Charterhouse Street before turning right into St John Street and St John's Lane which is straddled by **St John's Gate**, a Tudor replacement for the entrance to the 12th-century priory of the Order of St John of Jerusalem. This now houses the **Museum of the Order of St John (10)**. A modern red-brick building has been built over the extant Norman crypt of the 12th-century round church, but its site is outlined in a circle of cobblestones in St John's Square.

Narrow **Jerusalem Passage (11)** leads to Aylesbury Street and **Clerkenwell Green (12)** where the most imposing building is the Georgian Middlesex Sessions House. This is the heart of **Clerkenwell**, a village surrounded by religious establishments in mediaeval times. The yellow building on the Green is the **Marx Memorial Library (13)**, dedicated to Karl Marx (open weekday afternoons). At No. 14 Farringdon Lane, just beyond the courthouse, the Tudor replace-

ment for the original Clerk's Wells (that gives the village its name) can be seen through a window.

Cross Farringdon Road and walk to St Peter's Roman Catholic Church which has an impressive porch and serves London's Italian community. In **Hatton Garden (14)**, where gold and diamond merchants trade, the first right turn goes into Hatton Wall and after this the first left turn goes into Leather Lane, a typical London street market filled with stalls. At the end go left along Holborn, cross the end of Hatton Garden, named after Elizabeth I's Chancellor whose yearly 'rent' included the payment of a red rose. Now bear left into Charterhouse Street where entrance gates on the left guard **Ely Place (15)**, a road of Georgian buildings. A narrow alley between Nos. 9 and 10 goes to Ye Olde Mitre Tavern, an 18th-century building on the site of a 16th-century inn. At the end of Ely Place is the church of **St Etheldreda's (16)**, parts of which date from the 13th century when it was the chapel attached to Ely House, John of Gaunt's home. Retrace your steps to Charterhouse Street and, turning left, continue down the hill to the traffic lights where you turn left into Farringdon Road to walk to **Farringdon Underground Station (17)** ahead on the right, thus completing **Walk 9**.

Walk 10
Bloomsbury —
Intellectual London

Allow 2 hours

Bloomsbury has attracted many men and women of letters and learning, and on this walk which goes from Holborn Underground to Euston Station and Underground you will see some of their houses, and also a number of internationally famous museums, libraries, universities, hospitals and centres of learning.

A few yards east of **Holborn Underground Station (1)** is Procter Street, which you quickly leave as you turn right into **Red Lion Square (2)** where Dante Gabriel Rossetti's landlord once requested he kept the models who visited him at No. 17 'under some gentlemanly restraint'. William Morris and Sir Edward Burne-Jones lived

in the same house a few years later. Take Lamb's Conduit Passage, the narrow exit by Conway Hall, and continue east along Theobald's Road until you cross to go left down **Great James Street (3)**, where almost every one of the houses built c. 1720 still stands. A winding route into Northington Street, along John's Mews and Roger Street, brings you to Doughty Street.

A discreet plaque by the front door of No. 48, the terrace house on the right (east) side with green shutters, announces you have reached the **Dickens Museum (4)**. This was the great novelist's home for over two years, and the only London house he lived in that still exists. On the way to the north side of Mecklenburgh Square there are some good late Georgian houses. A gravel path — the entrance by the Wolfson Centre — goes along one side of **Coram's Fields (5)**, and here, as you emerge in the corner of Brunswick Square, is the **The Thomas Coram Foundation (6)**, a splendid, little-known London gallery. Cut across the gardens to Lansdowne Terrace, where on the left are the

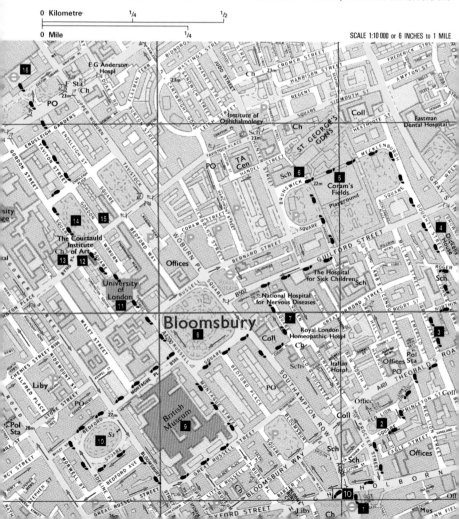

Dickens Museum

colonnades of Coram's Foundling Hospital. Turn right along Guilford Street and turn left taking the passage at the back of the President Hotel to **Queen Square (7)** where Dr Charles Burney and his daughter Fanny lived in 1771-72. The Square, which has a number of hospitals, is named after Queen Anne although the statue in the gardens is thought to be of Queen Charlotte. Read some of the history of the Church of St George the Martyr on the notice board as you turn right into Cosmo Place.

A right and left turn takes you to **Russell Square (8)** where the statue of Francis Russell, the 5th Duke of Bedford, who laid out the square, is on the edge of the gardens. A great agriculturalist, he stands with a sheep beside him and his hand on a plough. Turn left down Montague Street and then right into Great Russell Street where the combined wonders and pleasures of the **British Museum (9)** and the **British Library (9)** await you. These two institutions are among the best in the world. If you ever emerge from admiring the treasures, turn right along the side of the museum and take a turn around **Bedford Square (10)**, one of the best Georgian squares in London. Almost every house in the Square is the office of a publisher. You pass the less impressive north entrance to the British Museum in Montague Place as you return to Russell Square.

Leave the square by paved Thornhaugh Street — with its mixed architecture — and go into Woburn Square, but as you pass the School of Oriental Studies look over your left shoulder and you'll see a tall white sky-scraper. This is the Senate House of the **University of London (11)** whose various schools and colleges you will have seen dotted all over the area. In Woburn Square the delightful **Courtauld Institute Galleries (12)** are on the west side.

The University Church of Christ the King (13) is beside the Victorian Gothic Dr Williams's Library at the start of **Gordon Square (14)**, the place associated more than any other with the Bloomsbury Group. Lytton Strachey's house was No. 51 and a plaque next door commemorates Virginia Woolf and Clive Bell. The Stephen family were at No. 46, where John Maynard Keynes later lived. Bertrand Russell resided at No. 57 at the end of the First World War. **The Percival David Foundation of Chinese Art (15)** is at No. 53. The brick building at the end of Taviton Street — which takes you out of the square — is the Friends House, the head-office of the Society of Friends — the Quakers. Turn left and walk through its small garden where the War Memorial at the entrance to **Euston Underground Station (16)** is straight ahead. This marks the end of **Walk 10**.

Walk 11
Regency London

Allow 3 hours

This walk, beginning and ending at Baker Street Underground Station, takes you to a district which retains vestiges of its village atmosphere and on to the elegance of Georgian times. Then you come to a wide street created by the Adam brothers and preserved by John Nash, whose magnificent terraces and villas are an integral part of Regent's Park, one of the capital's loveliest royal bequests.

Leave the **Baker Street Underground Station (1)** by the Marylebone Road exit and turn left towards the **London Planetarium (2)** where you cross the main road to the Polytechnic of Central London. From here you get a better view of the long façade of **Madame Tussaud's (3)**. No time to visit the waxworks now but you may meet one or two of the famous people displayed there as you continue eastwards along Marylebone Road past the Methodist Missionary Society headquarters to **St Marylebone Parish Church (4)**. Here Robert Browning and Elizabeth Barrett were married, Lord Byron was christened and Charles Dickens worshipped. The red-brick and stone building on the other side of the road is the **Royal Academy of Music (5)**, founded at the instigation of George IV in 1822. Ferguson House, the modern building on the corner, is on the site of one of Dickens' homes. A large sculpture on the wall shows characters from the six novels he worked on whilst living here.

Turn right into Marylebone High Street. The **obelisk (6)** in the small garden commemorates Charles Wesley, the brother of John who founded Methodism, and there are several interesting tombstones laid against the wall. A few provision merchants in the street still serve the residents of nearby streets, and help retain the neighbourhood's village atmosphere.

Turn right opposite the Angel public house into George Street where you will find the **Roman Catholic Church of St James's**, Spanish Place **(7)**. This has some fine mosaics and lovely stained glass in the sanctuary. Further on turn left into Spanish Place and walk along the side of Hertford House to Manchester Square. This is the home of the **Wallace Collection (8)**, well worth a visit. A quick look around the entrance hall is a good appetizer for the treat that awaits visitors interested in fine paintings, furniture and ceramics. Walking around Manchester Square you may glimpse through the windows of the tall, elegant

houses with their richly ornamented ceilings.

A few yards into Hinde Street turn right to Marylebone Lane which leads to Wigmore Street, then left where you pass Welbeck Street, the **Wigmore Hall (9)**, and Wedgwood's, the china firm, who have had a London showroom for well over 200 years. Wimpole Street — which was the home of Robert Browning's wife Elizabeth Barrett — is the next street you cross. Like Harley Street and so many other roads in the area, it is filled with doctors' consulting rooms. Above **Dean's Mews (10)** — an opening on the north of Cavendish Square — is a concrete bridge and on it Epstein's bronze of the Madonna and Child. Turn left beyond Cavendish Square into Chandos Street and then right, into Portland Place where John Nash's **All Soul's, Langham Place (11)**, faces you. The church is just by the entrance to **Broadcasting House (12)**, from which the BBC transmits most of the national network radio programmes.

On the way up **Portland Place (14)** you pass the **statue (13)** (in the middle of the road) of a man reading in a chair with a boy either side, one with a football. He is Quintin Hogg, who developed the idea of his Youths' Christian Institute when he founded the Polytechnic. His son and grandson (also Quintin) became Lord Hailsham and distinguished Lord Chancellors. In this wide street laid out by the Adam brothers for the Duke of Portland, Nos. 46-48 have recently been restored and show what the rest of the street must have been like 200 years ago. Opposite No. 60 is the equestrian statue of Field Marshall Sir George Stuart White, a soldier who distinguished himself by winning two Victoria Crosses. On the corner of Weymouth Street the modern building with three sculptures on the façade is the **Royal Institute of British Architects (15)**, and in the centre of the road, the bust on a stone base is of Joseph Lister, the pioneer of antiseptics. Looking down Portland Place from his pedestal in the little park is a small statue of Queen Victoria's father, the Duke of Kent. Park Crescent, Nash's gracious curved terrace of stucco houses, runs on both sides but take the left arc to the Marylebone Road and cross to Regent's Park.

The **Outer Circle (16)** is ringed with elegant terrace houses, also built by Nash, and villas hidden behind trees were also his idea. These you see in the distance from the long pathway which leads from the Outer Circle to Chester Road. To the left are the gilded gates on the **Inner Circle (17)**. Go through these gates and sharp left into **Queen Mary's Gardens (18)**. Each rose-bed is labelled, so you are able to identify the individual species. Wildfowl wander around the lake where, just before the little bridge, a large bronze Japanese sculpture of an eagle looks more fearsome than any of the birds in the water. Continue in the direction of the **tea rooms (19)** with the copper-coloured roof. Here you cross the Inner Circle again. The red-brick building on the left is **Regent's College (20)** — the London branch of an American university — and the stucco villa to the right is The Holme, one of the Park's best known villas, built by Decimus Burton for his father. Take the path down past the bandstand and around to the iron bridge where a short right and left leads to more of Nash's terraces; and then to traffic signals where you cross the Outer Circle, turn right and follow the road around to Clarence Gate.

Ahead is Baker Street and the **Baker Street Underground Station (1)**, which marks the end of **Walk 11**. Opposite the entrance is Abbey House (the tall building with the clock), the headquarters of a building society at No. 221b — where Sherlock Holmes 'lived', now marked with a plaque. His existence is still so real to readers that dozens of letters addressed to him arrive weekly from all over the world, and the building society employs a secretary to answer them. On your way to the train if you look carefully you may see Sir Arthur Conan Doyle's detective silhouetted on the walls of the station.

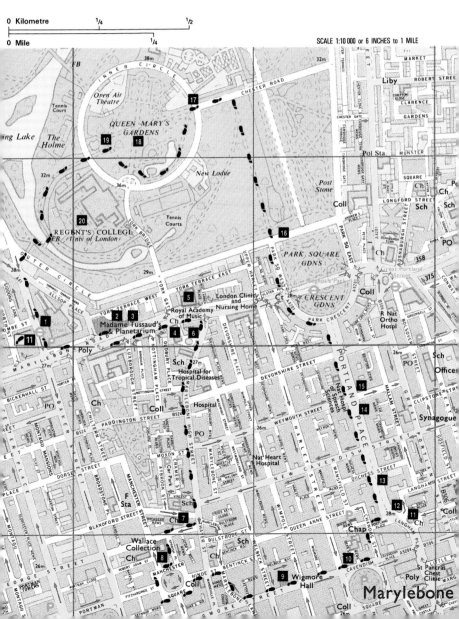

Walk 12
Mayfair

Allow 2 hours

This almost circular walk from Bond Street Underground Station to Marble Arch goes to the heart of Mayfair, leaving busy Oxford Street for more exclusive shopping streets with boutiques, and near Bond Street, expensive jewellers and antique shops. The elegance of this district can best be appreciated in two of London's best-known squares, in the quiet side streets and quaint backwaters, and in the charming 'village' you pass before you reach Hyde Park. For maximum enjoyment you are recommended to reserve this walk for early on a summer evening or a Sunday.

Start from **Bond Street Underground Station (1)** which opens onto **Oxford Street** but do not delay in this busy shopping area. Immediately to the right is Davies Street, but go diagonally across the entrance to South Molton Street, a pedestrian area with old-fashioned street lamps and benches. Above the boutiques there are a number of pleasing Georgian buildings. As you turn left to Brook Street, glance over your shoulder to see the red-brick building with flags flying. This is **Claridge's (2)**, a famous and luxurious hotel patronised by foreign royalty. Beyond **Fenwick's (3)**, the department store on the corner of New Bond Street, and immediately opposite the quaintly named Haunch of Venison Yard is No. 25 Brook Street, Handel's home for over 30 years. The composer died here in 1759.

You pass the statue of William Pitt the younger, Prime Minister at the age of 24, as you finish your circle of **Hanover Square (4)**. One or two houses illustrate days when this was a fashionable place to live and St George Street has several pleasant Georgian residences. **St George's, Hanover Square (5)** (actually not in the square) has the distinction of the first portico on a church in London. Here Handel worshipped and James Boswell was diverted in his prayers by the Duchess of Grafton who 'attracted his eyes too much'.

At the end of St George Street go right into Conduit Street, cross at the lights and walk down New Bond Street until you come to **Asprey (6)**, goldsmiths and jewellers, and one of the most luxurious shops in London. In Grafton Street there are more jewellers; **Wartski (7)**, whose private collection contains several of the wonderful eggs given as Easter gifts by the Imperial Russian family, is known the world over as the great expert on the work of Carl Fabergé. Follow the street around to the top of Hay Hill which leads

down to the south-east corner of **Berkeley Square (8)**. Walk up the west side of the square or look at the gracious houses from the central garden. Prime Minister George Canning lived at No. 50, today occupied by Maggs, a renowned dealer in rare books. This house and those next to it with wrought-iron entrances are especially fine; the best, No. 44, is now the Clermont Club built by William Kent in 1742. The Prince Regent used to dine here regularly when it was the home of Lord and Lady Clermont.

At the end of **Berkeley Square (8)** bear left into Mount Street, passing a couple of notable antique shops before you reach the large red-brick building on the corner of Carlos Place. This is the **Connaught Hotel (9)**, one of the most exclusive hotels in the country.

Carlos Place runs into **Grosvenor Square (10)** where the first building you pass is the Canadian High Commission. Although the square has been rebuilt, uniformity has been preserved except on the west side which is dominated by the **Embassy of the United States of America (11)** topped by a large gold eagle. The statue of President Franklin Roosevelt in the Square's garden was paid

Shepherd Market

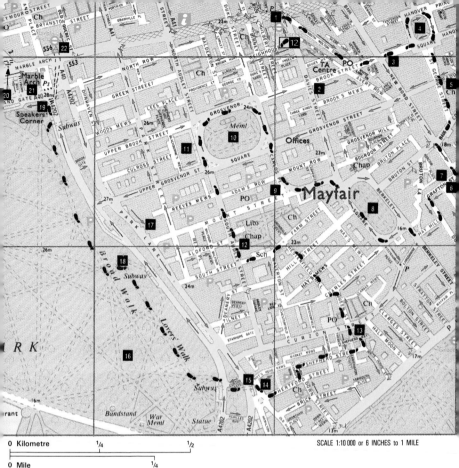

for by the people of Britain with a fixed limit of five shillings per person. Nearby, the eagle on the plinth commemorates the Eagle Squadron, in which 244 American and 16 British fighter pilots served in the Royal Air Force before America's entry into the Second World War. The memorial was put up by William Randolph Hearst, the publisher.

After the US Embassy continue southwards, straight down South Audley Street, past the **Grosvenor Chapel (12)**, where the Duke of Wellington's parents and John Wilkes, the radical 18th-century politician, are buried. Turn left by the side of T. Goode & Co., the long-established china and glass store into South Street. Turn right into Chesterfield Hill, and then cross Hill Street and Hay's Mews, a backwater where you will feel time has stood still. There are some lovely Georgian houses on the east of the hill and more when you get to Charles Street and cross to Queen Street. Here Nos. 11-13 are especially charming. Facing you at the end is Curzon Street, where an archway between Nos. 42-43 leads to **Shepherd Market (13)**, an attractive area with a village-like atmosphere. The little shops, restaurants and narrow streets should be explored before you

go west up Shepherd Street to Hertford Street. As you walk towards the **Hilton Hotel (14)** (the skyscraper in front of you) note the two blue plaques on No. 10, the home of General John Burgoyne, who surrendered at Saratoga, and the dramatist Richard Brinsley Sheridan.

A subway in **Park Lane (15)**, opposite the front door of the Hilton, takes you under this busy six-lane highway to **Hyde Park (16)**. With the Dorchester Hotel on your right and later the **Grosvenor House Hotel (17)**, whose four towers figure prominently above the trees, walk towards the star-shaped **fountain** with dancing figures **(18)**. Further north, beyond a kiosk, is **Speakers' Corner (19)**, always thronged on a Sunday. It is better to leave by the subway through the gate near the kiosk and here you can decide if you wish to take exits 3 and 10 for some final exploring. The first goes to the traffic island where the executions on the hanging tree of **Tyburn (20)** are commemorated; the second enables you to examine the **Marble Arch (21)** more closely, and you re-enter the subway to reach the **Marble Arch Underground Station (22)**, thus completing **Walk 12**.

Outer London Walks

Walk 13
Latimer, Chenies and the Chess Valley

Allow 3 hours

This walk explores the delightful Chess Valley, the wooded country to its north and the two attractive villages of Latimer and Chenies, both of which are remarkably unspoilt considering their proximity to London's busy northwestern suburbs. On no account miss the church at Chenies nor, if it is open, the lovely 15th- and 16th-century Chenies Manor with its fortified tower and its distant memories of the dukes of Bedford.

The River Chess, near Latimer

Motorists should take the A404, Rickmansworth to Amersham road, to Stoney Lane, which is second on the right after Chenies. Take this right turn at entry to Little Chalfont, following sign to Latimer, and the starting point car park (TQ 005-983) is on the left at a bend in the lane. Travellers by **train** *can join the route by walking from Chalfont and Latimer Station (on the Metropolitan Line from Baker Street). Walk up Amersham Road to Chelsfield Park which is second on the left. Go through an alley following a footpath sign and along the edge of a recreation ground. Turn right to join the walk coming from the car park as it goes into the woods.*

(A) Start the walk north-westwards from the car park between Little Chalfont and Latimer (176) (TQ 005-983), staying on the same side of the road as the car park, soon

taking a bridlepath on the left. Go westwards along the edge of the woods until you come to a bridlepath just before the recreation ground on the left (where those who come by train join the walk from the south). Bear right and go downhill into the woods, following the path over a stile into a field.

(B) Cross the B485 road, continue into another field (possibly with Christmas trees planted) and over a bridge crossing the River Chess with the Neptune Falls on the left. Now up the lane and turn left onto a minor road. Turn right off the road opposite the church onto a path leading to **Latimer** village green, which is overlooked by pretty timber-framed houses and is complete with village pump and, most unusually, the grave of a horse. Latimer House and the church are Victorian but of some interest. Turn left at the green and go northwards up Flaunden road out of the village.

(C) After 400 yards (beyond **Latimer**) fork right off the road onto a bridlepath which goes steeply uphill. On entering the woods take the bridlepath on your right, following it out of the woods as it turns left at a horse barrier. Bear right along the edge of the wood after passing through a felled area. Turn left along a well-marked path at the side of Martin Top Farm. Follow the waymarked path around to the left of the farm buildings, and then -

(D) Turn right beyond Martin Top Farm, cross a farm road and continue down the footpath running along the side of Baldwin's Wood. There are spectacular views south-

wards from here over the Chess Valley and **Chenies** village. Now continue directly down to Mill Farm. From the farm first turn down right to look at the millhouse and River Chess, and then back up the road re-passing Mill Farm, and turn right onto the path. This is on higher ground a short distance from the river, but it eventually joins the river (the Chess) before turning right across the ford.

(E) Over the ford and go up the lane a short way before turning left into the woods. Go right, uphill along the edge of Mount Wood, at first parallel with the lane. At the top of the hill go over a stile leading out of the woods keeping Mountwood Farm on your right. Turn right onto the lane by the farm and walk down this to **Chenies**. This is a very attractive village with a fine 15th-century manor house built by the dukes of Bedford (sometimes open to the public). The church's Bedford Chapel, which is visible through a glass screen, contains one of the finest collections of monuments in any English parish church. The inn has a varied menu with full meals and bar snacks.

(F) Go up the gravel road to the manor house. Turn right down a path between the churchyard and the manor-house garden wall. Turn left at the woods, then left again at the back of the manor house to Greathouse Farm. Now turn right (westwards) down a track with excellent views of the valley and Latimer village. Continue into the woods before coming out at Stoney Lane opposite the starting car park **(A)**, thus completing **Walk 13**.

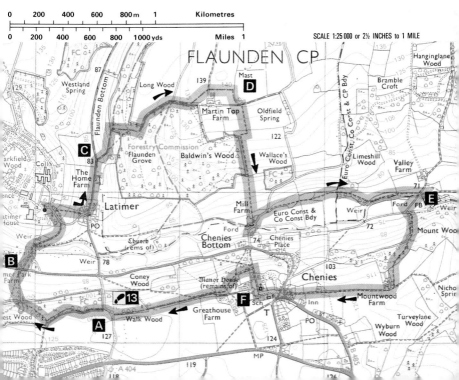

Walk 14
Burnham Beeches

Allow 3½ hours for long walk, 3 hours for shorter walk

This walk explores Burnham Beeches, the large and beautiful area of natural woodland which was purchased by the Corporation of London as long ago as 1879.

Motorists should turn off the M4 at Junction 6 or off the M40 at Junction 2, onto the A355, Beaconsfield to Slough road, turning west at Beeches Road and down Lord Mayor's Drive to its end, then turn left into a car park (SU 94-84). There is an inn, refreshment booth, and toilets. There is an hourly **bus service** from Slough (but not on Sundays). Get off at the stop beyond Royal Oak, take the footpath to Egypt (SU 95-85) and start the walk there. Travellers by **train** can join the route by walking from Gerrards Cross Railway Station to Pennlands Farm (SU 95-87) (allow an extra 1½ hours).

Note: *If starting from Gerrards Cross Station, walk down Bulstrode Way to cross the A40 to the Bull Hotel and down the main drive at the side of the hotel. At the car park take the left-hand path going south to gatehouse. Turn right onto the road, taking the path on the left under the M40, then follow the low-voltage line to Hedgerley, and down Kiln Lane by the Brickmould Inn to link onto the walk at Pennlands Farm (beyond Point E).*

(A) Start the walk from the west end of Lord Mayor's Drive (175) (SU 94-84). Turn left in front of a large wooden shelter and soon you will come to earthworks looking like old quarries (but actually an early settlement). Move to the unpaved Juniper Drive, and cross it, taking one of the many paths on the other side. Our path is clearly marked by a tree with the initials JA carved about 3 ft up the trunk. Bear right and you will soon come to a bank about a foot high. Now turn left and follow the bank around to the left, until you reach a clear gap in the bank. Take the path on the right uphill, which soon ends. Now turn right, still going uphill, noting a number of shallow pits up to 5 ft wide. Turn left onto a wide path with the ground rising on each side, still going uphill until you reach two wooden gate posts, the unpaved Dimsdale Drive, and then the paved Halse Drive.

(B) Turn right then sharp left down a narrow, paved, rhododendron-lined path to Abbey Park Lane.(**Note:** There are numerous paths through the woods and wayfinding is difficult, but if you keep going uphill bearing right, but not too far-right, you will come to the western end of Halse Drive.) Cross Abbey Park Lane and follow the footpath through the woods to a swing-gate and a grass field. Go over the stile keeping the woods on left, to Common Lane. Turn right past Blackwood Arms Inn.

(C) Turn right on Boveney Wood Lane to the footpath at Abbey Wood Cottage. This starts as an unpaved green lane and continues just inside the woods. Soon you will come to a wide but overgrown track going deep into the woods and immediately afterwards **(D)** the path forks.

(D) For the 'shorter walk' fork right here, going into the woods, along a path that eventually becomes a track coming out on Egypt Lane at **(F)**, see below. To continue the main walk take the left-hand fork along the path with a barbed-wire fence on the left, soon going into wood to emerge finally onto the A355.

Autumn in Burnham Beeches

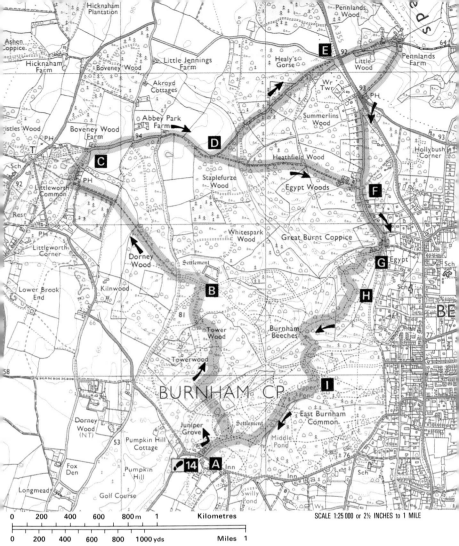

0 200 400 600 800m 1   **Kilometres**

0 200 400 600 800 1000 yds   **Miles** 1

SCALE 1:25 000 or 2½ INCHES to 1 MILE

(E) Cross the A355 road and go down the track to Pennlands Farm. (**Note:** At this point you can continue straight on through the farmyard and down Kiln Lane for about ¾ mile to Hedgerley, an attractive village with two pubs.) Turn right at Pennlands Farm (do not enter the farmyard) and up a rise to the start of a row of trees. Keep on the right side of the hedge and cross the A355 at the Yew Tree Inn and down Egypt Lane.

(F) Go past the footpath at Portman Burtley Estate which is used in the 'short walk'. There is a sign indicating the start of Burnham Beeches. Turn right at a letterbox in the wall and go straight to the map and large sign indicating 'Burnham Beeches'. (**Note:** Wayfinding on the next part of the walk can be difficult.) Keep near Stewart's Drive to your left for most of the way, then bear right. You will come out on Halse Drive just above Lord Mayor's Drive. Even if you bear right early on you won't be too far out.

Take the path behind the sign, bearing right.

(G) Turn left just after a depression on the right. Keep Stewart's Drive on your left and you will soon see a ridge about a foot high (earthworks). Follow the path, keeping the ridge on your left. When the path ends turn left and cross the ridge. Turn right onto a wide path recrossing the ridge and going downhill.

(H) Keep to the main path bearing left, crossing another ridge. Walk down the hill keeping a stream on your left. As the stream turns away from the path turn left following the stream. Climb to higher ground as soon as possible and turn right on the first path, then left at a road crossing Lord Mayor's Drive.

(I) Take the first path on the right and bear left away from Lord Mayor's Drive, following the path alongside ponds and a connecting stream, keeping them on your left. At the last pond the path ends; turn right to Lord Mayor's Drive (**A**), thus completing **Walk 14**.

Walk 15

Bayhurst Wood, the Colne Valley and the Grand Union Canal

Allow 3 ½ hours

This walk explores the Bayhurst Wood Country Park and drops down into the Colne Valley, which has been much used for sand and gravel supply — hence the number of extensive 'lakes', which are in fact flooded gravel pits. It then follows the course of the famous Grand Union Canal, one of the main arteries of England's once vital canal system, and now busy again, but with leisure traffic. Before returning to Bayhurst Wood the walk passes Harefield Church, which has a most interesting interior.

Motorists should take the A4180 north from Ruislip and turn left at Breakspear Road. Then bear left at the fork with Fine Bush Lane, just past the Crematorium. Turn right at the end of Fine Bush Lane into North Breakspear Road, then left into Bayhurst Wood Country Park. The starting car park is now on the right. To arrive by **train** and **bus**, take the Metropolitan Line from Baker Street to Harrow-on-the-Hill or Ruislip stations, and the No. 114 Bus to the stop before Ruislip Lido. Walk northwards up to the Six Bells Inn

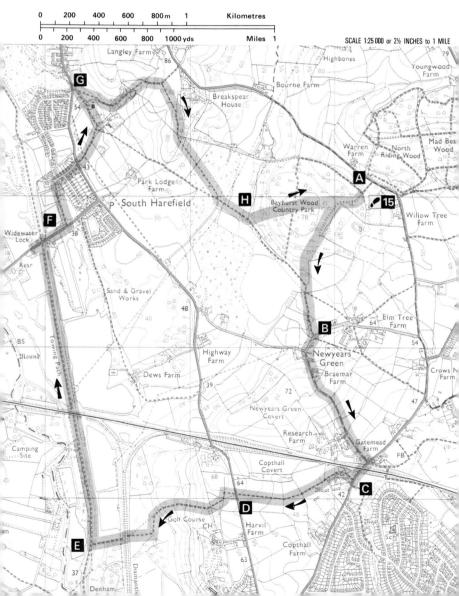

The Grand Union Canal at South Harefield

and take the path to the left at the side of the inn. Keep on the edge of Mad Bess Wood until you come to a footpath sign, then turn right into the woods. Turn left onto a bridleway at the next sign (possibly a pole with no sign). You should soon come to a war memorial (a stone cross laying flat on a lawn surrounded by bushes). Continue around the edge of the woods bearing right as you come near North Breakspear Road. When you come to a barrier to stop horses, turn left, cross North Breakspear Road into Bayhurst Wood Country Park. The car park from which the walk starts (A) is now on the right.

(A) From the **Bayhurst Wood Country Park** car park (176) (TQ 07-89), walk down the road that you came in on, which soon becomes unpaved. Turn left off the bridleway at a path marker and go down a slight bank. Continue on the path going left and under a horse barrier onto a bridleway enclosed by a wire fence. The bridleway with white markers goes along the edge of the woods, and then along the edge of the field to Green Lane.

(B) Turn right onto Green Lane, past a pond and then left uphill on a lane marked as a bridleway. At the highest point of the lane there are good views of the suburban landscape, its harshness being muted by gently wooded hills. Turn right at the end of the lane onto Breakspear Road South, keeping on the same side of the road and going under the railway bridge.

(C) Turn right beyond the railway bridge onto a footpath at a farm. The path goes left around the back of the buildings and over a stile, keeping the hedge on the right in the next field. The line of the path goes straight across the field keeping a roughly equal distance from the woods on the right and the hedge on the left.

(D) Cross Harvil Road onto a path and a golf course. Take the hard path going across the golf course until it ends, then go straight on, disregarding the path on the left. Go through a gap in the bushes and across a clearing where there is a stile and gateposts but no gate. Follow the path passing between two lakes, and cross the dismantled railway line which is now a track. The path continues between another two lakes and across another track. Go up a bank over a canal bridge and turn right.

(E) Now follow the towpath northwards, going under a railway viaduct to a road bridge. Turn left just before the road bridge to an inn with access to the towpath. Cross the road and go over the bridge on Moorhall Road.

(F) Go past a factory and then turn left onto a path beside a recreation ground. Turn right onto Priory Avenue and cross Harvil Road. Go up a track, turning left at the top past a First World War Australian Cemetery and into the churchyard by way of the main gate. (There is a water tap on the right.)

(G) Turn right at the side of Harefield Church (interesting interior — see page 115), through a small wood turning right alongside Breakspear House, joining a path coming in from the right with red waymarks indicating the route as far as Bayhurst Wood.

(H) Go over a stile into Bayhurst Wood, not walking alongside it. Continue uphill into the wood until you come to a post with '11' marked in red. Turn right into a picnic area with three barbecues in the centre. Now turn left onto a paved track to the starting car park **(A)**, thus completing **Walk 15**.

Walk 16

The Best of Windsor Great Park

Allow about 4½ hours

This walk takes in three fine memorials from which there are impressive views out over the Thames — the RAF, the Kennedy and the Magna Carta. It also passes the splendid Savill Gardens, Smith's Lawn, two delightful lakes, and the massive equestrian statue of George III. This stands at the far end of the great avenue known as the Long Walk, which stretches southwards to this point from Windsor Castle itself. In the course of its journey the walk also passes through great stretches of open parkland, and many plea- *santly wooded areas, all of which offer a host of tempting diversions.*

Motorists *should leave the M25 at Exit 13, take the A30 Egham bypass and the turn right onto the B338 to the junction with the A328. Take the first right and then right again, down to Cooper's Hill Lane, where the starting car park is on the right (SU 99-71). Travellers by* **train** *can join the route by taking one of the regular services from Waterloo or Richmond to Egham Station. There is also a limited service to Egham from Woking. From Egham Station walk up Station Road, cross High Street and turn left. When you reach Egham bypass, turn right onto it for about 100 yards. Then cross the bypass and walk up Cooper's Hill Lane and the starting car park is on the left.*

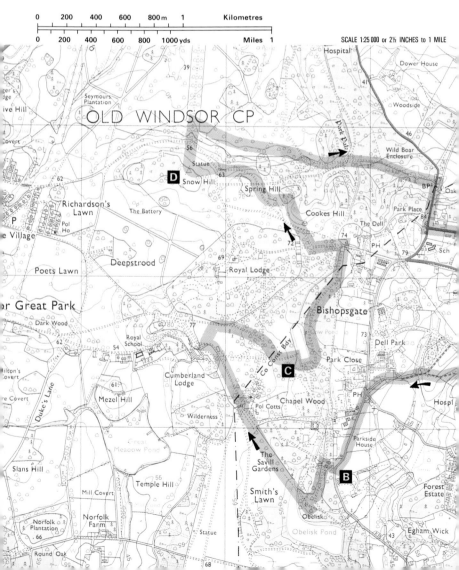

Motorists wishing to start the walk from the Savill Gardens Car Park (**B**) should leave the M25 at Exit 13, and take the A30 to Wick Road which is on the right just past the A328 turn. Turn right onto Wick Lane and the car park is well beyond on the left.

(**A**) Cross the road from the starting car park (176) (SU 99-71) to the RAF Memorial which is worth a visit both for its own sake and for the superb views eastwards across the Thames. On coming out of the memorial turn left, immediately cross the road and walk down the footpath on the right, past playing fields and then alongside Kingswood Drive to Tithe Hill. The footpath continues across the road to Middle Hill, the B388. Cross the road and go down Barley Mow Road just on the right. Cross the A328 to the Barley Mow pub on Englefield Green (well worth a stop). Go down Northcroft Road by the side of the Barley Mow. Take the footpath on the right (it is well marked) and bear left, turning into a

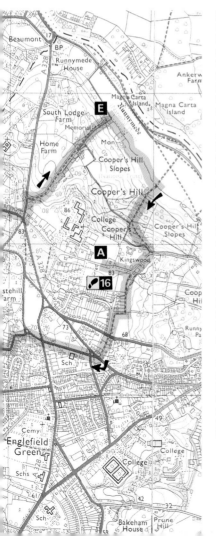

track called Prospect Lane. Turn left onto Wick Lane, passing the Sun Inn, to the car park at the **Savill Gardens**.

(**B**)Cross the **Savill Gardens** car park (visit the gardens if time allows), turn right beyond the car-park gate, passing the Obelisk and keeping to the right of the Obelisk Pond . Cross a bridge at the head of the pond, and keeping Smith's Lawn Polo Grounds on your left, keep staight ahead for a red-brick gatehouse (Cumberland Gate). Head for this gatehouse, continue straight on past it, then bear slightly left, keeping as near as possible to the fence on the left, to a large house (Cumberland Lodge) and a worthwhile view. Turn right, crossing the grass, and then turn right onto the road. Carry on until you arrive at the King George V Coronation Grove at the road junction. There are trees planted here by every country in what was then the British Empire. Turn left on the path at the right-hand end of the grove and continue on to Cow Pond.

(**C**) At Cow Pond turn right (southward), left around its lower end, then left up Rhododendron Ride and through a gate to Bishopsgate. Follow the road on the right of a large pink house and main gate lodge to the Royal Lodge. Turn right, cross the road, and take the path on the right that bears away from and then back towards the road, giving the first views of **Windsor Castle**. Cross the road, keeping to the high ground but within view of the road, and continue to Snow Hill and the equestrian statue of George III, known as the Copper Horse. Now arrive at the Copper Horse, from which there are more fine views down the Long Walk to **Windsor Castle**.

(**D**) From the Copper Horse drop down to the Long Walk and lower ground, soon turning right (eastwards) and, keeping close to the trees and high ground on the left, cross open ground. Now enter the woods, bearing right, then left onto a track, taking the right fork to the gate at Wild Boar Enclosure. Turn right onto the road at Crimp Hill, then left down Ridgemead Road and at the end bear left across the green. Cross the A328, down Oak Lane and continue straight on down the hill to the Kennedy Memorial and then down to **Runnymede** Meadows.

(**E**) If refreshments are required turn left at the cafe, but the walk continues by turning right and walking past the Magna Carta Memorial to a path on the right going into the woods. Go uphill to Cooper's Hill Lane, then turn right and right again to return to the starting car park (**A**), thus completing **Walk 16**.

Walk 17
Richmond Park and Richmond Hill

Allow 4 − 5 hours

This walk passes through much of Richmond Park, with its woods and grassy rides, its herds of deer and great expanses of open parkland. It also passes close to the National Trust's Ham House before following the Thames and finally climbing up to Richmond Hill, with its splendid views out over the great river.

Motorists can enter Richmond Park from the A3/A308, Wandsworth to Kingston Road;

the A205/A305, Putney to Richmond Road; or the A307, Kingston to Petersham Road. The starting car park **(A)** is near Pembroke Lodge, south of Richmond Gate (176) (TQ 18-73). Travellers by **train** can use British Rail from Waterloo, British Rail's North London Link, or London Regional Transport's District Line. Turn left from Richmond Station to George Street past Richmond Bridge, up Richmond Hill, joining the walk at Richmond Terrace before point **K**.

Note: The walk is a long one and can be split in two at Ham Gate. There are roads in the park connecting the main gates and a car park near Isabella Plantation.

(A) Start walk from the Pembroke Lodge car park (176) (TQ 18-72), and go through the gate to Pembroke Lodge (food available).

0	200	400	600	800 m	1	Kilometres

0	200	400	600	800	1000 yds	Miles 1

SCALE 1:25 000 or 2½ INCHES to 1 MILE

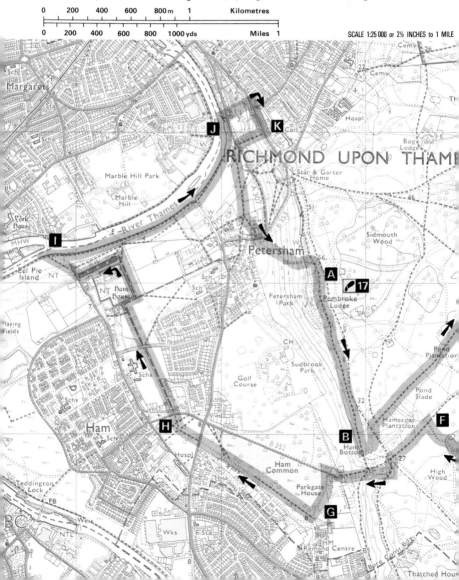

Turn left (southwards) onto the path at the back of the house, going out of the enclosure and walking on the second path just below the road, keeping to high ground from where there are some good views across the Thames. Continue until you reach the trunk of what was a large tree and Ham Gate below on the right.

(B) Now turn sharp left and cross the road. A signpost should be on your right. Turn left, keeping the road on the left and the ride on your right, then turn right at the first track, just past a bench on the right and where the ride bears slightly away from the road. As you come near Pond Plantation bear left, continuing past both Pen Ponds until you come to the grassy Queen's Ride.

(C) Turn right onto the Queen's Ride, and White Lodge, the Royal Ballet School, is now visible ahead. At White Lodge turn right onto the road, then left along the side of the house taking a path going between two horse-

hestnut trees. Head south towards Spankers Hill Wood, keeping a small pond in the woods on your left and coming out of the woods with some small gorse enclosures on the right.

(D) At the right-hand end of the enclosures go across open ground towards the road as it curves up Broomfield Hill in the distance. Cross a road at a small pond and a ride at the right-hand end of the pond on the way. Now take the path making for high ground and trees of Broomfield Hill and once past the trees there is a car park on right.

(E) Turn right at the car park onto a gravel track, then left at the first path, with more views of high-rise flats behind you. Follow path to Isabella Plantation (a riot of colour at azalea time — the late spring and early summer). Enter the enclosure and turn left, following the path along the stream to the other gate at Peg Pond.

(F) Turn left and take the path almost straight ahead to the signpost at Ham Cross and out of Ham Gate. Follow the path just inside the woods alongside Church Road.

(G) Turn right staying just inside the woods and eventually pass St Andrew's Church on the left. Beyond here the path soon bears right to Ham Gate Avenue. Now cross Ham Road and Ham Common following the horse ride to the pond.

(H) Now cross Sandy Lane to a long, straight bridleway. Turn right, then left and left again, to the front of **Ham House** (the gardens are free and there is a café) and onto Ham Street.

(I) Turn right and right again along the Thames towpath. Walk along the towpath until you come to **(J)**, a point beyond Petersham Meadows where the Petersham Road comes near the towpath. Cross the road by an ivy-covered flintstone tunnel entrance and up Terrace Gardens (there is a café in the gardens). Go past the hothouse, then left to a thatched shelter and on to Richmond Hill, turning right along Richmond Terrace with good views of the Thames.

(K) Go down to Petersham Meadows by turning right onto a paved path just after the viewpoint area. Cross the main road and turn sharp left, going back across Petersham Meadows to St Peter's Church. Dating from the 13th century, this has Georgian pews and also has several notable monuments. Go back to the path leading up beside the church and cross the road into Petersham Park. Turn left following the signposted path uphill through a gate and turn right to Pembroke Lodge and the starting car park **(A)**, thus completing **Walk 17**.

Walk 18
Chobham

Allow 3 hours

This walk covers an interesting and unusual area for southeast England, comprising a mixture of grass, gorse and heather, as well as woods and scrubland. Stout footwear is recommended as it can be fairly wet underfoot. However, the only real problem is the noise from the M3.

Motorists *should leave the M3 at Exit 3, drive to Bagshot and then go east on the A30 to the B383 at Broomhall (which can also be reached from Exit 13 on the M25, going west on the A30, Egham bypass, to the B383). From Broomhall take the B383, Chobham road for 1 mile and then turn left onto the B386 at a roundabout. Continue on the B386 over the M3 and the starting car park is just before Longcross on the B386 (176) (SU 97-65). Travellers by **train** can leave Waterloo for Longcross (not Sundays, when they should alight at Sunningdale, which is the next station). Turn right outside Longcross Station and follow the road southwards to the roundabout and over the M3 to the starting car park just before Longcross.*

(A) Start walk from the car park on the south side of the B386 (176) (SU 97-65), follow the bridleway southwards, past the trees and then turn left on a narrow path just before the bridleway drops into a hollow. Follow the path to high ground and when you reach a bridleway, turn left onto it and almost immediately right. Take the right-hand path, which soon goes steeply downhill and becomes indistinct and slightly overgrown. Follow the path a short way to another bridleway and then follow the path on the other side of the bridleway with rhododendrons on each side and cross over a stile into a field, with Longcross House now on your left. Follow the path to the road just in front of the church.

(B) Turn right onto the road and walk a short way before turning right onto a track just before Lily Pond Farm. Continue on this track to a point just before the last house. Go into the woods and through the gate on the right of the house, following the track a short distance to the edge of the woods, then taking the track on the right. When coming out into open ground, go left for a short distance, crossing the bridleways going into fir plantations. Continue in the same direction and take the footpath that can be identified by the horse-barriers across it, at the point where it goes into the woods, and where it becomes much wider. Now you will arrive at more horse barriers where the path joins a bridleway. Turn right on the bridleway and soon you will come to Gracious Pond Road where it makes a right-angle turn.

(C) Turn left onto the road and walk for a short distance until you reach the woods on the right. Take the path to the right, along the edge of the woods, and when coming near to Stonehill Road (traffic noise should be apparent) watch for a footpath sign on right. Take this footpath to Blackberry House and the path then becomes a track. (If you wish you can carry on down the track to Chobham where there are inns, restaurants and shops.)

(D) The main route continues by following the footpath on the right across fields, which ends at a road near a T-junction. Take the

Chobham Common near Albury Bottom

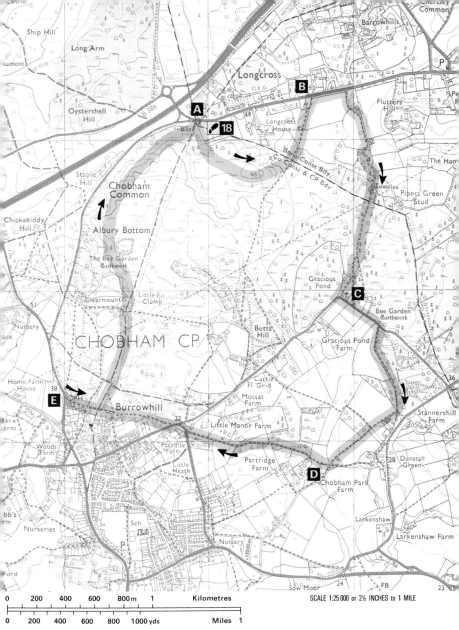

footpath on the right off Red Lion Road, which is the continuation of Gracious Pond Road. Follow the path until you arrive at a large electricity substation, then turn left here and continue to Killy Hill, where there is a short road at the end of which you turn right onto the B383 and a welcoming inn.

(E) You are now at Burrowhill, which is a good place for a rest, pub visit or picnic. Now return to the substation and take the path northwards that continues straight ahead. Continue on this path, not taking the paths turning off on the left or going too far to the right when coming to higher ground. Continue on the path — it is not marked in detail on our map but can be followed by keeping to the high ground. Pass close to an earthwork known as 'The Bee Garden'. Local tradition speaks of this as the site of one of two bee gardens (the other being near our Point **C**), enclosures against cattle and the wind, and planted with early- and late-blossoming plants so beloved by bees. However, archaeologists now suspect that both earthworks date from prehistoric times. Soon you will come to a car park and the path continues near the road to another car park. Now head back north-eastwards towards our starting car park at Longcross **(A)**, thus completing **Walk 18**.

173

Walk 19
Epping Forest

Allow 4 hours

This walk explores some of the best of Epping Forest, with its great open spaces, its grassy rides, and its fine areas of woodland. There are also several ponds and ancient earthworks, together with an interesting Conservation Centre, to be encountered along the way.

Motorists *should take the A1069, Ranger's Road, from the A104, to arrive at car-parking space at the first turning on the right, which is the start of our walk (177) (TQ 40-95). Those coming by* **train** *or* **bus** *should leave Chingford Rail and Bus Station, turning right and walking across The Plain. Keep to the high ground to arrive at Queen Elizabeth's Hunting Lodge (177) (TQ 39-94). Continue on until you come to Green Ride, where there is a tea place and the starting car park (TQ 40-95) near the end of Ranger's Road.*

(A) Start the walk from car park on Ranger's Road (177) (TQ 40-95) by keeping Connaught Water (lake) on the right. Just after crossing a culvert take a path on the left, until arriving at Green Ride. (Rides are easily recognised by their sand and gravel surface.) Turn right up Green Ride going slightly uphill, crossing another ride in a more open area called Almshouse Plain. You soon come to another open area called Whitehouse Plain. The Green Ride turns twice right, then left and you will see a metal sign saying 'No vehicles beyond this point'. Turn right across the open ground until you come to a car park.

(B) Turn left uphill (not crossing the paved lane) and keep to the high ground, bearing slightly left until you are back on Green Ride where it turns and then goes uphill. At this point turn left, crossing the ride onto higher ground and continue uphill over the brow and down to a swampy stream. Turn right onto a path just beyond the stream, going up another hill at the brow. You should see some houses on the left. Continue until you come to a road T-junction.

(C) Cross over the road and walk up it, passing High Beach Church on right. Bear right at Y-junction in High Beach. At High Beach there is a large inn and a little further on, a green refreshment hut on the left of the road. (From High Beach the walk follows the Three Forests Way, a 60-mile circular walk devised by the West Essex Group of the Ramblers' Association to celebrate the Queen's Silver Jubilee.) Take the path at the

back of the hut, and continue up it, keeping on the high ground of the ridge until you come to a golf course. Bear right, walking around the right-hand perimeter of the course as far as Pynest Green Lane.

(D) Turn right on to Pynest Green Lane, and passing Forest Close on the left you will see some fine views across the M25 to Upshire. At Tile Hill Farm turn right into woods and follow the path until it crosses a wider path. Turn left onto this path and continue on to a car park.

(E) Now back at High Beech, fork left onto the road to the Conservation Centre (do not miss a visit) and continue on the path alongside the Centre's fence. Turn right, still alongside the fence, until you come to an overgrown area. Turn left until you come to a ride and cross it to arrive at New Road.

(F) Cross New Road to the car park and take the path on the right. Follow the path to Loughton Camp (possibly Iron Age) and, keeping on the same contour, go around its northern and eastern earthworks. Then walk on southwards until you arrive back at Green Ride.

(G) Bear right onto Green Ride, crossing Earl's Path, keeping Strawberry Hill Ponds on the right, and still following the course of the Three Forests Way. Continue on the drive but do not turn right. At Warren Hill take the signposted path and when you come to a solitary oak, bear left going down the hill. (Continuing on would take you to the start of Ranger's Road.)

(H) Cross Manor Road, and at the cricket ground turn right, then right again, soon crossing New Road, the A104, near an inn (excellent views of the Forest). Keep to the extreme right, crossing Ranger's Road to the car park **(A)**, thus completing **Walk 19**.

Quiet waters in Epping Forest

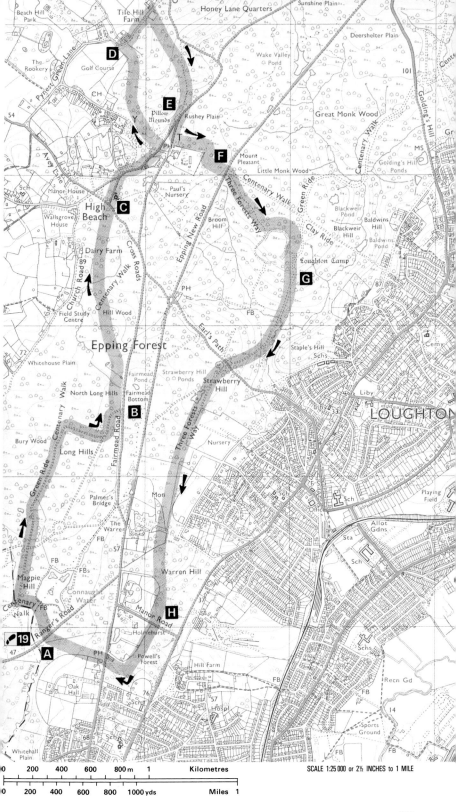

SCALE 1:25 000 or 2½ INCHES to 1 MILE

0   200   400   600   800 m   1   Kilometres

0   200   400   600   800   1000 yds   Miles   1

Walk 20

Lullingstone Country — a Mediaeval Castle and a Roman Villa

Allow 3½ hours

This walk follows the course of the little River Darent, and heads over quiet fields and through woodlands and a golf course before passing Lullingstone Castle and Lullingstone Roman Villa, both of which are of considerable interest. The M25 is not far away to the west, but should not disturb walkers unduly.

Motorists should leave the M25 at Exit 3, go east on the A20, and then bear right onto the A225 and through Eynsford village, passing the station and continuing beyond the railway bridge for a short distance to a layby on the left side of the A225. This layby (TQ 53-64) is part of the old road and is separated by

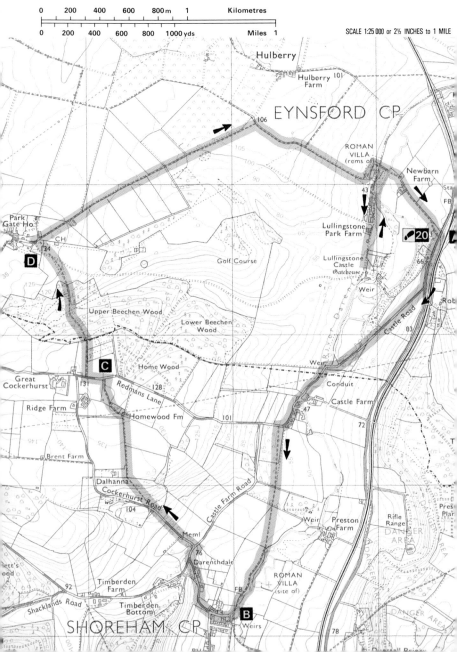

Mosaic at Lullingstone Roman Villa depicting 'The Rape of Europa'

a verge from the main road. Travellers by **train** *may leave from Holborn Viaduct Black-friars (weekdays), from Victoria (weekends) to Eynsford Station. All services hourly.*

Note: *It is possible to walk on the verges by the A225 and other roads used are generally quiet.*

(A) Walk from the starting layby on the east side of the A225, to the south of **Eynsford**, past the entrance to **Lullingstone Castle** on the right. Turn right down Castle road and past Castle Farm to the last house (both on the left). Before the road turns right, take the track straight ahead alongside the house and cross a stile at a line of trees. The track now becomes a footpath and continues across a concrete track. At this point there is a field boundary on the right marked by a hedgerow which goes diagonally away from the footpath. The footpath continues straight on but some care is needed because the path may have been ploughed (although the farmer does restore it). Cross the field to trees on the left, beyond which is the River Darent. Continue until the path is crossed by a road.

(B) At this point, if you require refreshments turn left, cross a bridge and walk alongside the river to Shoreham. But to continue the walk, turn right past Queen Anne House and then right again uphill to a road junction. Take the road on the left signposted to Well Hill; this is lined by trees and is rather reminiscent of France. At the end of the line Coombe Hollow Cottage is on the left and a footpath on the right. Take this footpath and continue uphill over open ground (there are excellent views) and watch out for a stile on the right. Go over the stile, walking alongside the woods on the left to a small house. Turn left onto an enclosed footpath (not across the field) and then turn right onto a concrete farm track and arrive at Redmans Lane.

(C) Turn left onto Redmans Lane and after a few yards turn right onto a path with a fence on the right. Go across iron railings by high iron steps and enter woodlands. This part of the walk is well signposted, so follow the footpath across the golf course to a car park, with the Club House on the right, and go out of Lullingstone Park.

(D) Once on the road out of Lullingstone Park turn right immediately down a track to the riding stables. Continue on past the riding stables and the track goes into a path alongside a row of poplars. As they continue on the left, turn right (at height 106 on map) onto a small path through a gap in the trees following waymarks. Continue on this path to a road. Although Lullingstone Castle may be closed and the road is private, access is allowed to the nearby parish church, so if time allows it is worth turning right to visit this. Now continue the walk by turning left to a building enclosing the very interesting Lullingstone Roman Villa (English Heritage). At the villa turn right across the River Darent and down a farm track to the A225. Cross this with great care to the starting layby **(A)**, thus completing **Walk 20**.

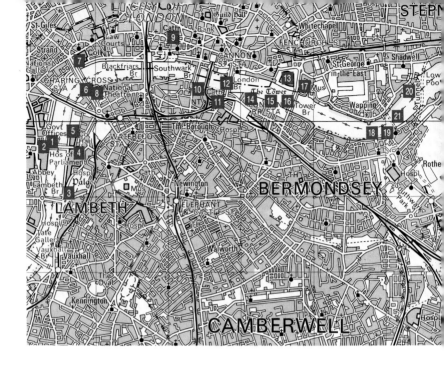

London's River — A Journey Down the Thames

By Felix Barker

An excursion of just under ten miles from Westminster Pier to the Thames Barrier at Woolwich is a unique London experience. It takes you from the very heart of the city, past the once-bustling docks to the glories of Greenwich and on to the flood barrier which has been called the Eighth Wonder of the World.

For many years after the last war this voyage was a drab progress past bombed factories. Derelict warehouses presented a dispiriting face to the waterfront. But the river is making a startling recovery. Already there are dramatic changes, and before the end of the century a vast transformation will have been achieved. (For further details of river trips, see page 13.)

Interest starts the moment you go aboard a launch at **Westminster (1)**. To provide a view of the Victorian Parliament buildings that so cunningly give the illusion of mediaeval architecture, the launch goes briefly upstream and in summer you may well glimpse Members of Parliament entertaining their guests on the terrace. If you are on the hour **Big Ben (2)** will boom out sonorously.

There are a few moments to glance at **Lambeth Palace (3)**, the Archbishop of Canterbury's London home, and **St Thomas's Hospital (4)**, where Florence Nightingale nursed. Then it is back under **Westminster Bridge** to see, on your right, **County Hall (5)** formerly headquarters of the GLC, London's governing body until 1986.

After a railway bridge, and immediately after **Waterloo Bridge (6)**, note the architectural contrast between the classical splendour of **Somerset House (7)**, once the repository of the nation's wills, and the concrete fortress of the facing **National Theatre (8)**. On the City skyline above the trees of Temple Gardens where lawyers stroll is **St Paul's Cathedral (9)** and the spire of Wren's lesser masterpiece, **St Bride's**, Fleet Street. Both stand out in pleasing contrast to the modern monoliths that surround them.

The guide points out the site of Shakespeare's **Globe Theatre (10)**; there is a momentary squint at **Southwark Cathedral (11)** sandwiched between office buildings; and a view up newly created monumental steps to the south side of St Paul's. Then comes the low, functional **London Bridge (12)** which does little to remind you of the romantic outline of its mediaeval shop-lined forerunner. Do not spend all your time contemplating William the Conqueror's **Tower of London (13)** or the Traitor's Gate through which the doomed Anne Boleyn made her last journey. The Pool of London, the reach below London Bridge, has other new attractions to offer. For a quarter of a

SCALE 1:50 000 or 1¼ INCHES to 1 MILE

1 Westminster Pier
2 Big Ben
3 Lambeth Palace
4 St Thomas's Hospital
5 County Hall
6 Waterloo Bridge
7 Somerset House
8 National Theatre
9 St Paul's Cathedral
10 The Globe Theatre (site of)
11 Southwark Cathedral
12 London Bridge
13 Tower of London
14 London Bridge City
15 HMS *Belfast*
16 Tower Bridge
17 St Katharine Docks
18 The Angel, Rotherhithe
19 The Mayflower Tavern
20 The Prospect of Whitby
21 Thames Tunnel
22 Cuckold's Point
23 Docklands
24 Royal Naval Victualling
   Yard (site of)
25 Napier's Wharf
26 *The Cutty Sark*
27 Royal Naval College
28 Queen's House
29 Old Royal Observatory
30 Execution Dock
31 Thames Barrier

mile on the right before Tower Bridge are old warehouses recycled and transformed into offices, a private hospital and glass-covered galleries. Complete with the *art nouveau* façade of Hay's Wharf this is **London Bridge City (14)** which, combining old and new, has defied the pundits of ultra-modern architecture.

Moored here in the Pool of London is the cruiser **HMS *Belfast* (15)**. She seems a little incongruous; somehow you don't expect to find a formidable grey battleship in these peaceful waters. Launched in 1937, this veteran of the Normandy landings and Korea has been a floating museum since 1971.

If, as you pass under it, **Tower Bridge (16)** raises its twin girder Gothic bascules, that is a bonus, for fewer and fewer tall ships now sail in and out of the Pool. Although the double drawbridge weighing over 1,000 tons has outlived its original 1894 purpose of relieving river congestion, the bridge remains an engineering marvel; its Gothic design was intended to blend in with the Tower.

Once past the well-placed but architectur-ally 'brutal' Tower Hotel, you will see how Londoners are winning back the great commercial river for their own use. On the left is **St Katharine Docks (17)**, a yacht haven where modern craft lie berthed amid historic warehouses, and old terraces along Wapping High Street have been converted into luxury apartments and startling modern offices. No palazzos here, but this transformation has brought a hint of Venice to the East End waterfront.

All along the river are waterside taverns. Although more frequented by tourists than thirsty sailors these days, they retain much of their old charm. **The Angel, Rotherhithe (18)**, on the right, has a wooden balcony over the water with a superb view back to Tower Bridge. Half a mile further on is **The May-flower (19)**, named after the Puritan Fathers' ship whose captain returned from the New World to be buried in the nearby church. On the north shore is the most famous riverside tavern of all, the crowded, rowdy **Prospect of Whitby (20)** which, like many Thames pubs, has a claim to being more than 300 years old.

179

Westminster Pier — the start of our journey

Just before you see the Prospect you will be passing over the first tunnel ever built under a navigable river. Designed by Sir Marc Brunel and opened in 1843, the **Thames Tunnel (21)** links Rotherhithe with Wapping, its double tunnel used by the underground railway.

Now the river curves past **Cuckold's Point (22)** (named from the legend of King John's seduction of a miller's wife). From Limehouse Reach to the great bend of the river at the Isle of Dogs you see the old **Docklands (23)** (once Britain's largest after Southampton) being transformed by the arrival of new industries. These days few vessels are towed by little thrusting tugs; no red sails on old barges; but, instead, occasional container ships carrying materials for modern industries. Mingling with factories are new estates of houses for the generation of residents who have replaced the stevedores and watermen. Not far beyond Cuckold's Point (see above) are Georgian warehouses, converted into flats, remnants of the old **Royal Naval Victualling Yard (24)** which once supplied the Naval ships built and repaired here. You must coax your imagination to transform modern warehouses into the dockyards founded by Henry VIII in 1513. From Petts Wood and the heights of Sydenham, oaks and elms were brought to these yards to create the wooden men-of-war that Queen Elizabeth I ordered 'against all evil haps', a move that was to ensure the defeat of Spain's great Armada. And somewhere along this stretch of the Deptford shore Drake's *Golden Hind* was preserved in dry dock for eighty years to commemorate her voyage around the world.

On the opposite shore is the rapidly developing Isle of Dogs and you should be able to catch a glimpse of a sign at **Napier's Wharf (25)** which recalls that it was here that the steamship *Great Eastern* was built by Isambard Kingdom Brunel, Sir Marc Brunel's son. In 1857 she was one of the largest vessels

afloat, and, being no less than 692 feet long, she had to be launched into the river sideways. Even so 'the great iron ship' was stuck in the mud for a month before she went on to become a legend, if not a commercial success, famous for laying the first Atlantic telegraph cable.

In Greenwich Reach the Thames attains unexpected dignity. You leave modern commercial development to lose yourself in the past. Fully rigged, and with her proud figurehead, the **Cutty Sark (26)**, last of the old tea clippers, takes her rest in dry dock. Here at Greenwich Pier Dickens and Thackeray disembarked for whitebait suppers at the Trafalgar Tavern. The grey baroque splendour of the **Royal Naval College (27)** comes into view. Between Wren's twin-domed building the **Queen's House (28)**, Inigo Jones's masterpiece and prototype of English classical architecture, stands neat as a doll's house. On the summit of green-sloped Greenwich Park is the **Old Royal Observatory (29)** of the first Astronomer Royal, John Flamsteed. Octagonal, perfectly proportioned, it could only be by Wren. If you pass at 1 pm you can set your watch by the red time ball on the observatory roof which has given seamen a visual timecheck since 1833.

You may arrange to disembark at **Greenwich.** The temptation is almost irresistible, but ahead that Eighth Wonder, the Thames Barrier, awaits you as you round the next serpentine curve of the river. Ask the guide to point out the entrance to Blackwall Tunnel and Blackwall Point which was marked **Execution Dock (30)** on the old maps. Here a gibbet, previously at Wapping, was put up towards the end of the 18th century. The bodies of convicted pirates hung there in iron cages until three tides had washed over them: a salutary warning to all passing sailors.

For centuries the low-lying land you see on either side of the river was threatened with flooding at exceptionally high tides. This danger grew to disaster proportions until the building of the **Thames Barrier (31)**. You see it ahead of you in Woolwich Reach spanning 600 yards from the Kent to the Essex shore. Ten separate steel gates between giant concrete piers can be raised to defeat the rising water or lowered beneath the surface to allow ships to pass. Engineers keep watch by day and night. Londoners sleep safe.

Look back as the launch turns upstream for the return to Westminster. If it's a good day the sun catches the shining metal hoods that protect the machinery. They are pointed with narrow openings like the helmets of mediaeval knights. Reminders of the old saying that the Thames is 'liquid history' are rarely absent on this river journey.

LEGEND TO CENTRAL LONDON ATLAS MAPS

TOURIST INFORMATION

Royal Academy of Arts

Selected places of interest

Horse Guards

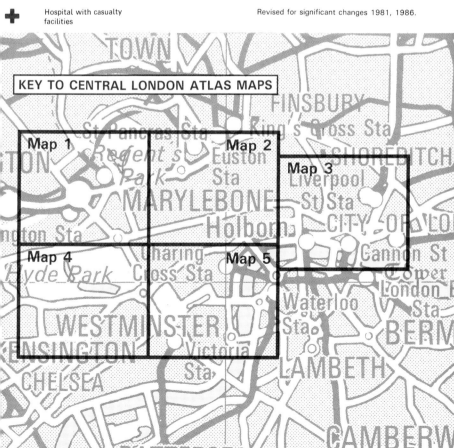

i Information Centre

Railway Station

Underground Station

Bus/Coach Station

P Parking

+ Hospital with casualty facilities

ABBREVIATIONS

Ch	Church
Chap	Chapel
Coll	College
FB	Foot Bridge
F Sta	Fire Station
Liby	Library
Mus	Museum
Pol Sta	Police Station
PO	Post Office
Sch	School
TH	Town Hall

ROAD INFORMATION

Main Roads and Bus Routes

One way traffic routes

No access in direction shown

OXFORD STREET
-open to buses and taxis only between 7am-7pm, Monday to Saturday

(restrictions where shown may not apply at all times or to all vehicles)

The representation on this map of a road, track or path is no evidence of the existence of a right of way.

Revised for significant changes 1981, 1986.

KEY TO CENTRAL LONDON ATLAS MAPS

Map 1

Map 2

Map 3

Map 4

Map 5

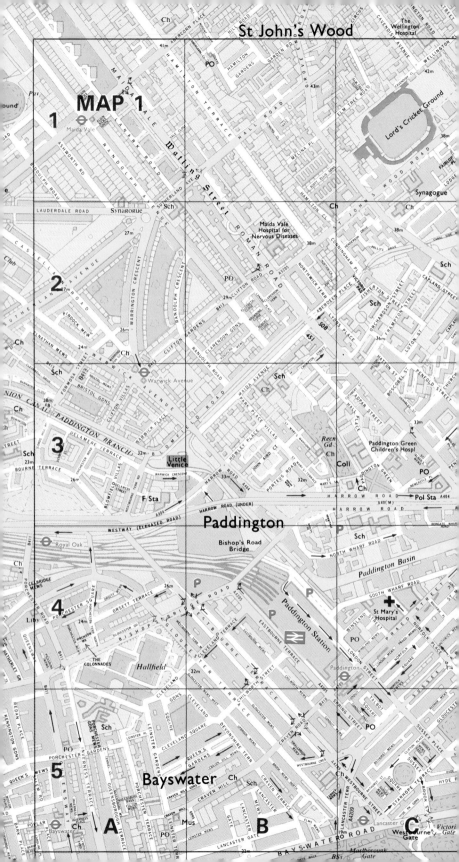

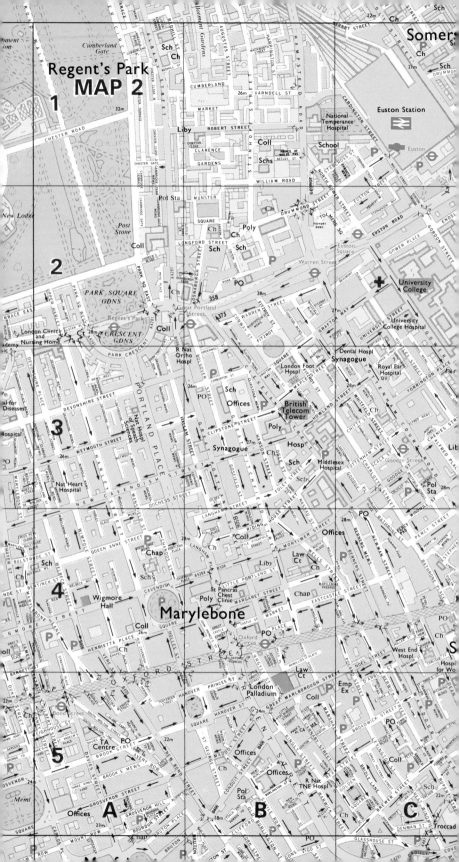

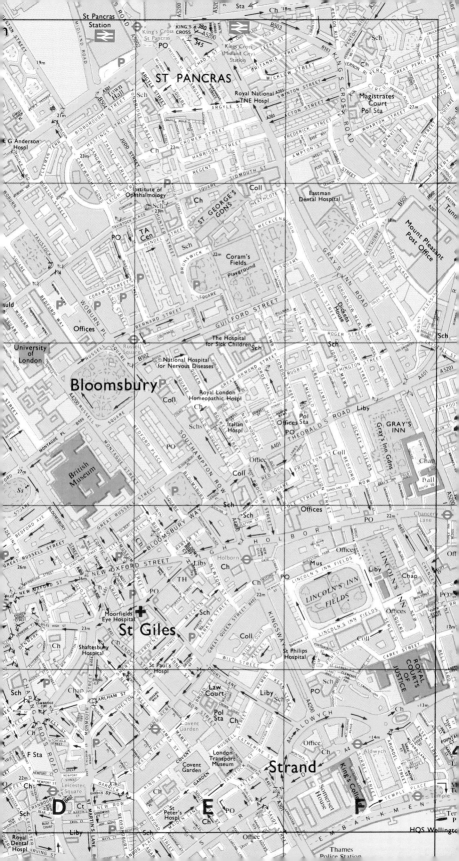

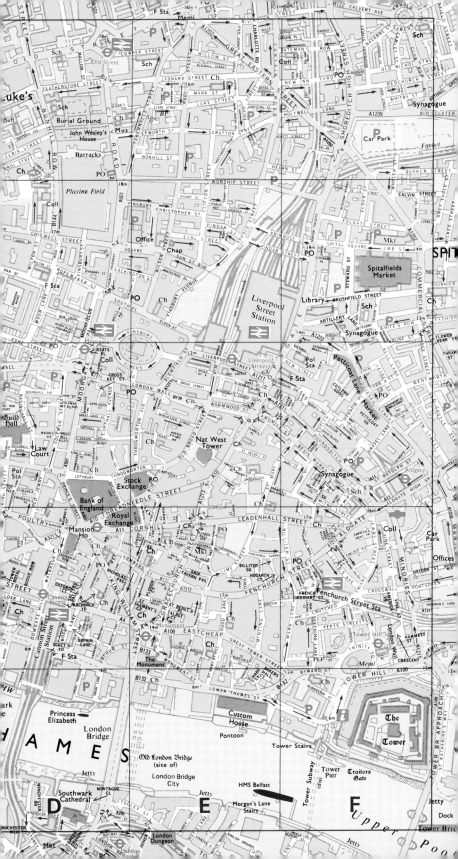

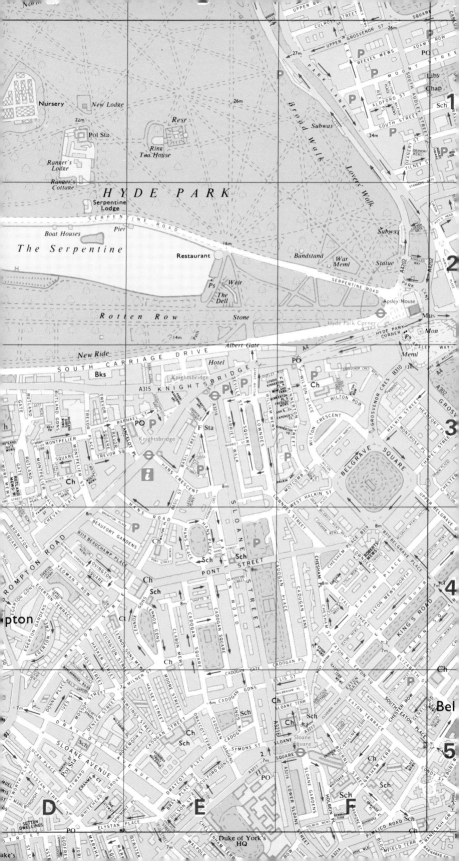

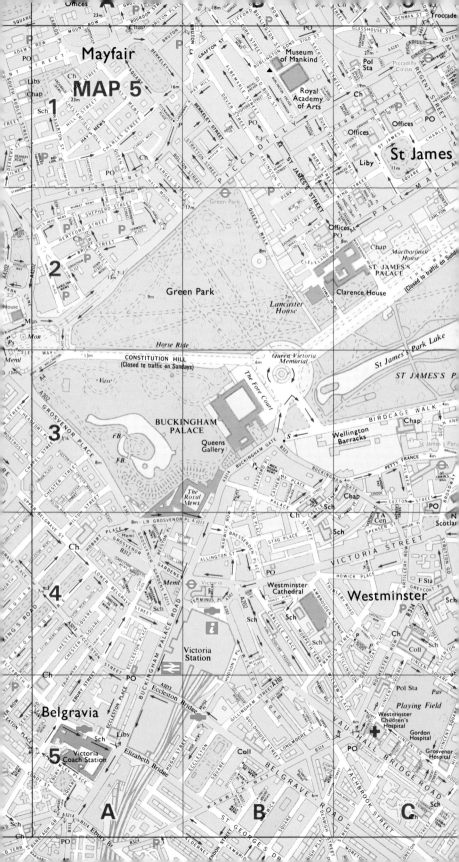

Index of People

Index of Places

199

201

	Page	Map Ref
TAVITON ST	157	2 C2
TELEGRAPH ST	–	3 D3
TELEVISION CENTRE	111	
TEMPLE	83, 148	3 A4
TEMPLE AVE	–	3 A4
TEMPLE BAR	35, 84	3 A4
TEMPLE CHURCH	84, 148	3 A4
TEMPLE GARDENS	148	3 A4
TEMPLE LA	–	3 A4
TEMPLE OF MITHRAS	84, 151	3 D4
TEMPLE PL	–	2 F5
TENISON CT	–	2 B5
TENISON WAY	–	5 F2
TENNIEL CL	–	1 A5
TENTER GROUND	–	3 F2
TENTERDEN ST	–	2 A5
TERMINUS PL	–	5 B4
TERRACE THE	–	3 A4
TEXAS	73	
THACKERAY ST	–	4 A3
THAMES BARRIER	127–128, 180	
THAMES EMBANKMENT	31	5 E1
THAMES, RIVER	178–180	
THAMES TUNNEL	180	
THANET ST	–	2 D1
THATCHED LODGE	125	
THAVIE'S INN	–	3 A3
THAYER ST	–	1 F4
THEATRE MUSEUM	33, 84, 147	2 E5
THEATRE ROYAL DRURY LANE	33, 84, 147	2 E5
THEATRE ROYAL HAYMARKET	40, 84	5 D1
THEATRE ROYAL, RICHMOND	125	
THEATRE ROYAL, STRATFORD EAST	122	
THEOBALD'S RD	156	2 F3
THIRLEBY RD	–	5 C4
THOMAS CORAM FOUNDATION	32	2 E2
THORNDIKE ST	–	5 C5
THORNDON COUNTRY PARK	128	
THORNEY ST	–	5 E5
THORNHAUGH MEWS	–	2 D2
THORNHAUGH ST	157	2 D3
THORNTON PL	–	1 E3
THORPE PARK	9, 128	
THREADNEEDLE STREET	20, 68, 84–85, 151	3 D4
THREE BRIDGES	104	
THREE FORESTS WAY	174	
THREE KINGS YD	–	2 A5
THREE MILLS CONSERVATION AREA	122	
THREE NUN CT	–	3 D3
THROGMORTON AVE	–	3 E3
THROGMORTON ST	34, 151	3 E3
THURLOE PL	–	4 D4
THURLOE PL	–	4 D4
THURLOE PLACE MEWS	–	4 C4
THURLOE SQ	–	4 C4
THURLOE ST	–	4 C5
TILNEY CT	–	3 D1
TILNEY ST	–	4 F1
TIMBER ST	–	3 C1
TISBURY CT	–	2 C5
TITCHBORNE ROW	–	1 D5
TOKENHOUSE YD	–	3 D3
TOLMERS SQ	–	2 B2
TONBRIDGE ST	–	2 E1
TOOLEY ST	50	3 E5
TOOTING BEC COMMON	119	
TOPAZ ST	–	5 F5
TOPHAM ST	–	3 A1
TORRINGTON PL	–	2 C3
TORRINGTON SQ	–	2 D3
TOTHILL ST	145	5 D3
TOTTENHAM	113	
TOTTENHAM CT RD	–	2 C3
TOTTENHAM HOTSPUR GROUND	113	
TOTTENHAM MEWS	–	2 C3
TOTTENHAM ST	–	2 C3

	Page	Map Ref
TOURIST INFORMATION CENTRES	12	
TOWER BRIDGE	85, 152, 179	3 F5
TOWER BRIDGE WALKWAY	85	3 F5
TOWER CT	–	2 D5
TOWER GREEN	77, 86	3 F5
TOWER HAMLETS	128	
TOWER HILL	86, 152	3 F5
TOWER OF LONDON	52, 85–87, 152, 178	3 F5
TOWER ROYAL	–	3 D4
TOWER ST	–	2 D5
TOYNBEE ST	–	3 F3
TRAFALGAR SQUARE	28, 59, 87, 144	5 D1
TRAITOR'S GATE	152, 178	3 F5
TRANSEPT ST	–	1 D3
TRANSPORT MUSEUM	33, 51	2 E5
TRAVELLERS' CLUB	61	5 C2
TREBECK ST	–	5 A2
TRENT PARK COUNTRY PARK	105, 128	
TRESHAM CRES	–	1 D2
TREVOR PL	–	4 D3
TREVOR SQ	–	4 D3
TREVOR ST	–	4 D3
TRINITY HOSPITAL	109	
TRINITY HOUSE	152	3 F4
TRINITY PL	–	3 F4
TRINITY SQ	152	3 F4
TRITON SQ	–	2 B2
TROCADERO	87–88	2 C5
TROOPING THE COLOUR	40–144	
TRUMP ST	–	3 D3
TRYON ST	–	4 E5
TUCK'S CT	–	3 A3
TUDOR ST	–	3 A4
TUFTON ST	–	5 D4
TURF CLUB	26	5 C2
TURNAGAIN LA	–	3 B3
TURNMILL ST	–	3 B2
TWEEZER'S ALLEY	–	2 F5
TWICKENHAM	125	
TWICKENHAM RUGBY GROUND	125	
TWINING'S	82–83, 148	2 F5
TWYFORD PL	–	2 E4
TYBURN	27, 40, 60, 161	1 E5
TYBURN WAY	–	1 E5
TYERS ST	–	5 F5
TYSOE ST	–	3 A1

	Page	Map Ref
UPPER TACHBROOK ST	–	5 B5
UPPER THAMES ST	34, 151	3 C4
UPPER WIMPOLE ST	–	2 A3
UPPER WOBURN PL	–	2 D2
UXBRIDGE	115	

V

	Page	Map Ref
VALE CL	–	1 A1
VALENCE HOUSE	94, 110	
VALLEY GARDENS	128, 129, 133	
VANBRUGH CASTLE	109	
VANDON PAS	–	5 C3
VANDON ST	–	5 C3
VANDY ST	–	3 E2
VANE ST	–	5 C5
VARNDELL ST	–	2 B1
VAUXHALL	129	
VAUXHALL BRIDGE	62	
VAUXHALL BRIDGE RD	–	5 C5
VAUXHALL ST	–	5 F5
VAUXHALL WLK	–	5 F5
VENABLES ST	–	1 C3
VERE ST	–	2 A4
VERNON PL	–	2 E3
VERNON RISE	–	2 F1
VERNON SQ	–	2 F1
VERULAM ST	–	3 A2
VERULAMIUM	126, 128–129	
VIADUCT BLDGS	–	3 A2
VICTORIA	88, 139	5 B4
VICTORIA & ALBERT MUSEUM	88	4 C4
VICTORIA ARC	–	5 B4
VICTORIA AVE	–	3 F3
VICTORIA EMBANKMENT	35	5 E1
VICTORIA EMBANKMENT GARDENS	88, 147	5 E1
VICTORIA GR	–	4 A4
VICTORIA PAS	–	1 C2
VICTORIA RD	–	4 A3
VICTORIA SQ	–	5 B4
VICTORIA ST	–	5 C4
VICTORIA STATION	88	5 B4
VICTORIA TOWER	41	5 E3
VIGO ST	66	5 B1
VILLIERS ST	147	5 E1
VINCENT SQ	–	5 C5
VINCENT ST	–	5 D5
VINE HILL	–	3 A2
VINE ST	152	3 F4
VINE ST	–	5 C1
VINERY VILLAS	–	1 D1
VINEYARD WLK	–	3 A1
VINTNERS' HALL	34, 88, 151	3 D4
VINTNERS PL	–	3 C4
VIRGIL PL	–	1 E3
VIRGIL ST	–	5 F4
VIRGINIA WATER	128, 129, 133	
VISCOUNT ST	–	3 C2

W

	Page	Map Ref
WAITHMAN ST	–	3 B4
WAKEFIELD ST	–	2 E2
WALBROOK	–	3 D4
WALKER'S CT	–	2 C5
WALLACE COLLECTION	54, 89, 158	1 F4
WALLINGTON	127	
WALMER PL	–	1 D3
WALMER ST	–	1 D3
WALNUT TREE WLK	–	5 F4
WALPOLE HOUSE	101	
WALTHAM ABBEY	129	
WALTHAM CROSS	105	
WALTHAM FOREST	105, 129	
WALTHAMSTOW	121, 129	
WALTHAMSTOW HERONRY	11	

	Page	Map Ref
WALTON PL	–	4 E4
WALTON ST	–	4 D4
WANDSWORTH	129–130	
WANSTEAD	124	
WANSTEAD PARK	124	
WAPPING	102, 128	
WARDOUR MEWS	–	2 C5
WARDOUR ST	146	2 C5
WARDROBE PL	–	3 B4
WARDROBE TERR	–	3 B4
WARE	119	
WARNER ST	–	3 A1
WARNER YD	–	3 A1
WARREN MEWS	–	2 B2
WARREN ST	–	2 B2
WARRINGTON CRES	–	1 A2
WARRINGTON GDNS	–	1 A2
WARTSKI	160	5 B1
WARWICK AVE	–	1 A3
WARWICK CRES	–	1 A3
WARWICK CT	–	2 F3
WARWICK HOUSE ST	–	5 D1
WARWICK LA	–	3 B3
WARWICK PL	–	1 A3
WARWICK PL N	–	5 B5
WARWICK ROW	–	5 B4
WARWICK SQ	–	3 B3
WARWICK SQ	–	5 B5
WARWICK SQ MEWS	–	5 B5
WARWICK ST	–	2 B5
WARWICK WAY	–	5 B5
WARWICK YD	–	3 C1
WATER GDNS THE	–	1 D4
WATER ST	–	2 F5
WATERGATE	–	3 B4
WATERGATE WLK	–	5 E1
WATERLOO BRIDGE	80, 89, 147, 178	5 F1
WATERLOO CHAMBER	133	
WATERLOO PL	34	5 C1
WATERLOO RD	–	5 F2
WATERLOO STATION	47	5 F2
WATERLOW PARK	114	
WATERMAN'S ART CENTRE	97	
WATLING CT	–	3 C4
WATLING ST	151	3 C4
WATSON'S MEWS	–	1 D4
WAVERTON ST	–	5 A1
WEALD COUNTRY PARK	130	
WEDGEWOOD'S	158	2 A4
WEIGHHOUSE ST	–	2 A5
WEIR'S PAS	–	2 D1
WELBECK ST	158	2 A4
WELBECK WAY	–	2 A4
WELL CT	–	3 D4
WELLCOME INSTITUTE	89	2 C2
WELLESLEY PL	–	2 C1
WELLINGTON ARCH	42	4 F2
WELLINGTON BARRACKS	38, 89, 142	5 C3
WELLINGTON PL	–	1 C1
WELLINGTON RD	–	1 C1
WELLINGTON ST	–	2 E5
WELLS MEWS	–	2 C4
WELLS SQ	–	2 F1
WELLS ST	–	2 B4
WELLS WAY	–	4 B4
WELSH HARP RESERVOIR	97	
WEMBLEY	130	
WEMBLEY STADIUM	130	
WENTWORTH DWELLINGS	–	3 F3
WENTWORTH ST	153	3 F3
WERRINGTON ST	–	2 C1
WESLEY ST	–	1 F3
WESLEY'S HOUSE & CHAPEL	116	
WEST CARRIAGE DRI	–	1 C5
WEST CENTRAL ST	–	2 D4
WEST DRAYTON	115	
WEST EATON PL	–	4 F4
WEST EATON PL MEWS	–	4 F4
WEST HALKIN ST	–	4 F3
WEST HAM	122	
WEST HARDING ST	–	3 A3
WEST INDIA DOCKS	102–103, 120	
WEST MEWS	–	5 B5
WEST POULTRY AVE	–	3 B2
WEST SMITHFIELD	154	3 B2

Further Reading

Books

General

Banks, F.R. *The Penguin Guide to London.* Penguin

Barker, F. & Jackson, P. *London: 2000 Years of a City and its People.* Papermac

Barker, F & Gay, J. *Highgate Cemetery, A Victorian Valhalla.* John Murray

Barker, F. & Hyde, R. *London As It Might Have Been.* John Murray

Barker, F. & Silvester-Carr, D. *The Black Plaque Guide to London.* Constable

Burke, J. *Around the M25.* Hale

French, Y. *Blue Guide — London.* A & C Black

Piper, D. *The Companion Guide to London.* Collins

Weinreb, B. & Hibbert, C. *The London Encyclopaedia.* Macmillan

Art, Architecture & History

Barker, F. *Historic Greenwich.* Jarrold

Blatch, M. *A Guide to London's Churches.* Constable

Byron, A. *London Statues.* Constable

Jackson, P. *George Scharf's London.* John Murray

Pevsner, N. *London Vols 1 & 2. Buildings of England Series.* Penguin

Saunders, A. *The Art and Architecture of London.* Phaidon

Young, E. & W. *London's Churches.* Grafton

The River Thames

Ebel, S. & Impey, D. *A Guide to London's Riverside.* Constable

Prichard, M & Carpenter, H. *A Thames Companion.* Oxford

Walks and Walking

Chesterton, K. *A Guide to the London Countryway.* Constable

Davies, H. *A Walk Round London's Parks.* Zenith

Jebb, M. *The Thames Valley Heritage Walk.* Constable

Turner, C. *London Step by Step — The Walking Guide to London's Streets and Sights.* Pan

Periodically Published Guides

Fortnightly. *Events in London.* London Tourist Board

Quarterly. *Where to Eat in London.* Where Publications

Annually. *Historic Houses, Castles & Gardens.* British Leisure Publications

Annually. *Museums and Galleries in Great Britain & Ireland.* British Leisure Publications

Annually. *The National Trust Handbook.* The National Trust

Maps

This guide is, with few exceptions, largely covered by Ordnance Survey **Landranger** Maps 176 and 177 at 1:50 000 scale (1¼ inches to 1 mile). These maps provide a wealth of information including footpaths, bridleways and many tourist features. The area is shown in still more detail in the Ordnance Survey's **Pathfinder** Maps at 1:25 000 scale (2½ inches to 1 mile), and these are ideal for walkers; 20 **Pathfinder** Maps cover the guide area.

For exploring the countryside beyond the guide area Ordnance Survey **Routemaster** Map 9 (South East England) at 1:250 000 scale (1 inch to 4 miles) will be found useful, as will the **Ordnance Survey Motoring Atlas** at the larger scale of 1 inch to 3 miles. The Ordnance Survey also publishes a special **M25 and London** Map (at 1 inch to 2 miles scale), which covers the whole of the capital and the surrounding towns serviced by the M25 Motorway.

To place the area in an historical context the following Ordnance Survey **Archaeological and Historical Maps** will also be found useful: **Londinium** — descriptive map and guide to Roman London, **Roman Britain**, **Britain before the Norman Conquest**, and **Monastic Britain**.

Ordnance Survey maps are available from officially appointed agents and from most booksellers, stationers and newsagents. The addresses of Ordnance Survey agents in London together with stockists in Windsor are shown on page 13.

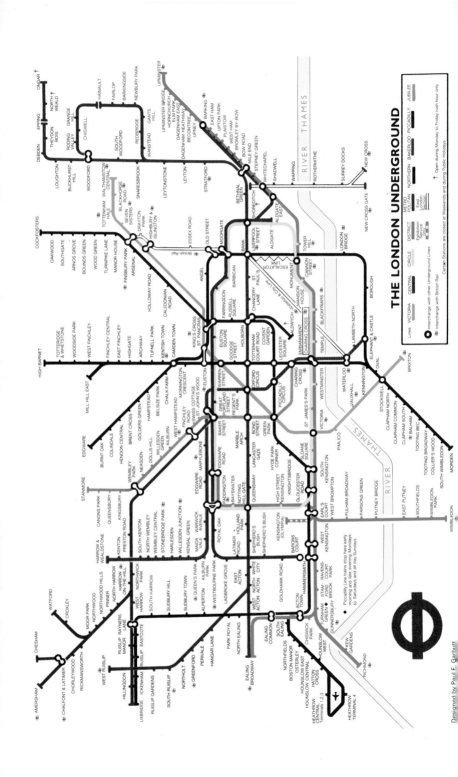

THE LONDON UNDERGROUND

Designed by Paul E. Garbutt

| Lines | VICTORIA | CENTRAL | CIRCLE | DISTRICT | METRO- POLITAN | NORTHERN | BAKERLOO | PICCADILLY | JUBILEE |

| | | | | | East London Section | | | |

Exhibition Service

○ Interchange with other Underground Lines

⇌ Interchange with British Rail

† Open during Monday to Friday rush hour only

⇌ Open during Weekends and during Public Holidays

⬩ Certain stations are closed at Weekends and during Public Holidays

♦ Piccadilly Line trains stop here early morning and late evening Mondays to Saturdays and all day Sundays

RIVER THAMES